The Prentice-Hall Series in Personality
Richard S. Lazarus, editor

This volume is one of a series of short textbooks
being developed for undergraduate instruction
in the fields of personality. There will be separate volumes
on personality theory, personality assessment,
abnormal personality, and special issues of
contemporary research.

LOUIS BREGER

From
Instinct
to
Identity

The Development of Personality

Prentice-Hall, Inc., Englewood Cliffs, New Jersey

Library of Congress Cataloging in Publication Data

BREGER, LOUIS
   From instinct to identity.

   (The Prentice-Hall series in personality)
   Bibliography: p.
   1. Personality. 2. Child study. I. Title.
[DNLM: 1. Personality development. BF 698 B496f
1973]
BF698.B668   155.4   73–5766
ISBN 0–13–331637–8

Printed in the United States of America

15 14 13 12

PRENTICE-HALL INTERNATIONAL, INC., LONDON

PRENTICE-HALL OF AUSTRALIA, PTY. LTD., SYDNEY

PRENTICE-HALL OF CANADA, LTD., TORONTO

PRENTICE-HALL OF INDIA PRIVATE LIMITED, NEW DELHI

PRENTICE-HALL OF JAPAN, INC., TOKYO

For Lisa, Sam, and Josie and, of course, for Gail.
You are each a part of this book.

Contents

Acknowledgments

The ideas presented in this book grew to their present form during some 15 years of experience as student, professor, researcher and psychotherapist. During this time I was influenced by teachers, colleagues, and students too numerous to mention. I would like, here, to give special thanks to those whose comments were directly helpful in the preparation of the book. First and foremost, my thanks to Richard S. Lazarus who has given both encouragement and needed criticism from the beginning. Jane Lancaster made comments and supplied valuable references for chapter 2, as did Thayer Scudder for chapter 3. Jane Loevinger gave a critical reading to chapter 8 which was helpful in reworking that material. Robert R. Holt offered valuable comments on chapter 7. Other colleagues and former students whose general comments and encouragement were useful include Phil Cowan, John Dyckman, Richard Hertz, and Abby Wolfson. Thanks to all of you.

LOUIS BREGER

chapter one

The Developmental Perspective

The development of human personality is one of those grand topics—the concern of philosophers, novelists, psychologists, and theologians (not to mention parents) for centuries. All cultures and societies contain beliefs or theories about the psychological development of their people. Such beliefs or theories, which are usually not stated in any formal sense, are embodied in child-rearing practices; social institutions such as schools; beliefs about human nature, man's "instincts" and how they can be legitimately expressed or how they must be controlled; the sorts of expectations held for children; and a host of other ideas, laws, values, and social practices. Such views enable parents to raise their children, and institutions to influence them, so that they become functioning members of their societies.

There are, thus, a great number of theories and ideas about personality development, ranging from the most abstract philosophical views to the "theory" implicit in the way a peasant mother tends her child. There is no way in which all of these could be covered in a single book and I will make no attempt to do so. Rather, I will trace the development of personality as seen from a particular perspective. The overriding focus will be on the growth of self, from the sense- and action-dominated self of infancy to the formation of identity in adolescence and early adulthood. Attention will be directed at the evolutionary heritage of man, the centrality of emotion in human relationships, the role of fantasy, play, and dreams, unconscious processes, repression, and moral development. In dealing with these topics I will bring together observations and theory from Freud, Erikson, Sullivan, and others of the Neo-Freudian group, with the ideas and observations of Jean Piaget and his followers.[1] To these views will be added evidence from the broader field of child development, and from ethology, primate studies, anthropology, and such other areas as are relevant. The point of view will not be "psychoanalytic" in what has come to be the accepted usage of that term, nor will I survey various theories of personality or attempt to summarize the views of individual theorists or schools. Rather, I will attempt to synthesize the ideas of selected observers and theorists around key topics. If the book has an original contribution to make, it is not in reporting new discoveries, but in coordinating and synthesizing elements from the fields and theories mentioned above.

The thread that ties these various theories and fields of study together is what I am calling "the developmental perspective." The concept of development is one of those seminal ideas that has influenced fields as diverse as philosophy, history, economics, biology, and psychology. Although early versions can no doubt be traced to Greek philosophers such as Heraclitus— who likened life to a moving stream, always changing, never the same—the greatest impact of developmental thinking was felt in the nineteenth century. Developmental ideas appeared in the philosophy of Hegel and, from there, shaped the social and economic theories of Karl Marx. More central to our present concern, however, is the developmental model found in biology and epitomized by Charles Darwin's (1859) theory of evolution. This developmental-evolutionary theory has had a profound influence—directly on biologists and workers in related fields such as ethology and primate studies, and also on psychologists such as Freud, Erikson, and Piaget. Let us now examine the general development model, and then trace its course through biology and psychology.

THE DEVELOPMENTAL MODEL

Persons in even the most primitive of cultures were exposed to development—the growth of human beings, other animals, plants, and trees. Their observations of growth prompted explanations, but these tended not to be

---

[1] A number of references to the work of these psychologists will be cited in later chapters. The reader who wishes to sample further some of their work at this time is referred to the following introductions and summaries: Erikson, *Childhood and Society* (1950); Freud, *Introductory Lectures on Psychoanalysis* (1963); Piaget and Inhelder, *The Psychology of the Child* (1969); Sullivan, *The Interpersonal Theory of Psychiatry* (1953).

"developmental" in the sense that I will define the term. Primitive ideas—
and these have lasted until quite recently in many areas—viewed growth
as a one-stage process in which something smaller gets bigger. The seedling
is a miniature tree, the infant a miniature adult, and both will, over time
and with the addition of food and water, reach their mature forms. This is
a linear model of growth and it is also seen in primitive explanations for
the origins of the human species. All cultures have myths, religions, or theories to explain the origins of their people. And most of these are essentially
the same as the Book of Genesis: the first man and woman were plunked
down somewhere by God or a great spirit in the same physical forms as the
men and women familiar to contemporary members of the culture. Development, in such early "theories," is simply a matter of getting from the first man
to the present state by the addition of more people. Such single-stage or linear
models of growth contrast with the more complex developmental model that
grew out of biology and embryology, and which is seen in sophisticated form
in Darwin's theory of evolution.

As the early biologists looked more closely at the structure of plants and
animals, it was gradually recognized that the process of growth was a more
complex affair than was first imagined. As we now know, growth is not
always a linear process in which something smaller becomes bigger. Rather
growth, or what can now rightly be called *development,* involves progression
through successive stages. *What exists at one stage becomes transformed into
something related to, but also different than, what existed earlier.* Thus, an
animal begins its life as a single cell (this is an arbitrary starting point, of
course, since the cell itself develops from simpler elements) ; cells divide and
group themselves into clusters with new forms and functions. Such clusters—
for example, muscles, skin, bones, and other organ systems cf the body—are
related to the common cells from which they all originated, but are also different in ways suitable to their new groupings. The segregation of cells by
function and grouping is called *differentiation* and it is one of the basic
processes of all development. The various differentiated systems—nervous,
skeletal, muscular, circulatory, digestive, reproductive—are interrelated at
ever more complex levels of organization. These new arrangements illustrate
integration, the other basic process of development.

The growth of an organism proceeds through stages during which there
is differentiation and integration at successively more complex levels of organization. This model of development describes the growth of animals from
single cell to mature adult form and, as we will see, is useful in understanding the development of species and the psychological development of persons. The model differs from a single-stage or linear growth model: the first
cell does not simply get bigger or multiply; rather, development progresses
through stages in which cells become both differentiated and integrated at
more complex levels of organization.

It took biologists some time to arrive at this model of development. Early models of the sperm cell, for example, pictured a complete, miniature person inside, showing the persistence of the one-stage or linear growth model (see Figure 1.1). Gradually, the developmental model supplanted the earlier one-stage model. The general features of the developmental model may be summarized as follows, using embryological development as an example.

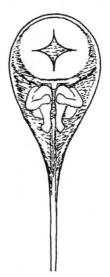

FIGURE 1.1

The stage-wise development in which cells become differentiated from each other and integrated into more complex organizations has already been noted.

Development proceeds in one direction only; what happens at any point in the process is dependent on what has occurred up to that point.

The process always goes from simple to complex and there is a fixed order to the development of the different body systems, the nervous system developing first, the heart and circulatory system later, and other systems still later.

Finally, *events have significance depending on when they occur during development.* The different body systems are specially sensitive during those embryological stages during which their development is rapid, and relatively insensitive before and after. An example of this would be the way in which German measles in the mother can lead to blindness of the fetus during the first three months of pregnancy. This is the time during which the nervous system, including those parts serving the visual apparatus, are undergoing rapid development, and, for this reason, the system is particularly vulnerable at this time.

The Theory of Evolution

The general model of development is also illustrated by Darwin's theory of the evolution of species. Early views pictured man as "created" in essentially his present form. Darwin showed, by contrast, that the existing form of any species is the result of a long process of evolutionary development. The life of a species, just as the life of the individual organism, begins in a simpler form and then undergoes *transformations* over the many generations of species evolution. This evolution shows the same characteristics of integration and differentiation, as the different species of animals adapt to different environments, as well as the same increase in complexity, that one sees on the level of the individual organism. One can construct a developmental ladder of evolution with one-celled organisms at the bottom and complex animals such as mammals, at the top. Such a ladder is analogous to the development of the individual embryo: both illustrate the general model of development. We will look at the theory of evolution in more detail in the next chapter; it is mentioned here to show how the developmental model has been used to explain both individual growth and the evolution of species.

The Developmental Model in Psychology

The general model of development, as well as Darwin's theory of evolution, are now well established in biology and related areas. Developmental thinking came later to psychology and has been incompletely absorbed in this field. Let us consider a few brief examples of essentially nondevelopmental models in psychology, and then look at psychoanalytic theory which can be interpreted with both a developmental and a nondevelopmental emphasis. This will lead us to the more clearly developmental-psychoanalytic theories of Erikson and Sullivan and, finally, to Piaget, whose work is explicitly within the developmental-evolutionary framework.

Many psychological theories—like the one-stage or linear model of growth outlined above—are nondevelopmental in character. Explanations of personality in terms of "traits" and "types" are examples of such static models. The ancient Greeks explained differences in personality in terms of four basic personality types. You simply *were* one of these types or, perhaps, some mixture of them. Later type theories have focused on body-build or psychological predispositions such as introversion-extroversion. While such theories may become quite complicated, they imply the same model as that illustrated by the picture of the little person inside the sperm cell; the assumption is that a person's type resides within and is stimulated to unfold with experience.

Probably the most widespread type theory still influential today is that embodied in the psychiatric classification system which categorizes disturbed persons as neurotic, schizophrenic, manic-depressive, and so on. While the categorization of persons in all of these type theories describes certain important ways in which individuals differ from each other, the type model distracts attention from the evolving, developmental nature of personality. Although usually not explicitly stated, type models assume that one's basic introversion or schizophrenia has existed from the beginning, like the miniature person inside the sperm cell. In a developmental theory, by contrast, an introvert or schizophrenic is not something that a person *is* but something that he may *become* as he develops.

Theories of learning that rely on models of conditioning are not static in the way the type and psychiatric diagnostic models are; indeed psychologists within this tradition have stressed the openness of persons to change. Some of them seem to assume that anyone can learn anything at any point in the life span. Most stimulus-response or conditioning models of learning, however, are based on a linear or one-stage model of growth. There is typically no conception of stages, of special sensitivity to certain kinds of experience during specific stages of development, nor of a nonreversible, hierarchical, developmental sequence. The assumption seems to be that infants, children, and adults learn by the same principles (reinforcement, rewards, and punishments) and that if there is any sequence to learning it is simply a process of starting with "little" (associations, stimulus-response connections, learned responses) and acquiring "more" as one gets older. Now let us consider some psychological theories which are developmental in nature.

Psychoanalytic ideas will be examined in a variety of ways in later chapters, so it will not be necessary to discuss them fully or critically at this time. Let us note very briefly some ways in which Freud's ideas fit a developmental model. Freud was trained as a physician, worked at developmental-neurological research before turning to psychology, and was, in a general way, committed to biological-evolutionary thinking. His model of *psychosexual* development clearly stems from this biological background. Before Freud, human sexuality was thought of as something that simply appeared at puberty. With his theory of psychosexual development, Freud attempted to show how sexuality began in infancy as something related to, but also different from, adult sexuality and how it developed through a sequence of stages. Each stage is defined in terms of an area of the body which is presumed to be specially sensitive at the time of its predominance. Thus, during the first or *oral* stage, the mouth, lips and general oral zone are particularly sensitive, and the most influential experiences are those such as feeding and sucking—of oral pleasure and its frustration—which involve this zone. Stimulation or experiences involving other body zones are of less importance during this stage. Development then progresses to the *anal* zone during which experiences involving elimination and toilet training become central. Following this comes an initial *genital* stage, then a period of *latency,* and finally, after puberty, the emergence of *adult genitality.* The order of stages is always the same and each stage involves a transformation of the experience from the preceding stage. The impact of experience or learning is dependent on when it occurs during the sequence of development. It can be seen from these examples that Freud's psychosexual model is a developmental one.

The psychosexual model is perhaps the clearest instance of developmental thinking within psychoanalysis, though there are other ways in which developmental considerations appear. Freud presents what is essentially a two-stage theory of thinking: he assumes that the thought of the infant is different in form from that of the adult. Infantile thought, which he termed the *primary process,* is visual or "hallucinatory," and is dominated by the search for immediate gratification. It is also undifferentiated, tending to blur distinctions between the self and the outside world or between inner bodily experiences and outer reality. Such thought gives way to the *secondary process* which is more logical and differentiated. Other examples of a developmental model could be cited but these should suffice to show that such a model is consistent with major aspects of psychoanalytic theory.

From Psychosexual to Psychosocial

A point that should be stressed is the lag which typically occurs when a model developed in one field is applied to another. I mentioned earlier that the developmental model appeared in philosophical thinking and was initially used in biology to explain the growth of cells and animals. It remained for Darwin to *reshape* the model into a theory that explained the origin and evolution of species. Certain principles of the earlier model remain but the rest is analogy; a species of animals evolving over millions of years is not the same as embryonic development. The use of the developmental model in psychology requires a similar reshaping. The theorist must retain those general ideas that apply to both biological and psychological development but also recognize what are purely analogies and feel free to abandon them where necessary. Freud's use of the developmental model is a sort of transition between biology and psychology and it remained for later psychoanalytic theorists such as Erikson and Sullivan to reshape the model to psychological development. For example, in Sullivan's theory it is clear that developmental stages are to be defined in terms of crucial *interpersonal* experiences. Each stage of development—infancy, early childhood, and adolescence—contains its particular sensitivities, and the way in which each is affected by interpersonal experiences prepares the way for what happens in the next stage.

Similarly, Erikson reshapes Freud's psychosexual stages into *psychosocial* stages. His work represents an important reformulation of psychoanalytic ideas which retains what is important—the developmental model, the role of different body areas—but which brings more clearly into focus the psychological, social, and interpersonal aspects of the different stages. Let me cite just two examples. The central issue in the oral stage, as Erikson describes it, is not the pleasure derived from sucking. Oral pleasure is important, but only as a part of the broader interaction between mother and infant. What *is* central is the overall quality of care provided by the mother. This includes nourishment and sucking, but also other aspects of handling, playing, paying attention to, consistency, and so forth. Erikson calls this stage *infancy and the mutuality recognition*. Similarly, what is central in the anal stage is not anal "pleasure" and its frustration, but the clash of wills between the very young child, attempting to express his newly sensed freedom in such crude ways as not going to the toilet, and the imposition of parental authority. The essence of this stage of development is a particular kind of psychological interaction between the young child and his caretakers. Erikson calls this stage *early childhood and the will to be oneself*. Both Sullivan and Erikson apply the developmental model within a more strictly psychological framework. Their ideas will be elaborated in later chapters; here let me conclude with a brief introduction to Piaget.

Piaget

Of all the theories discussed so far, Piaget's is most explicitly based on a developmental model applied within the psychological sphere. Piaget began his work as a biologist and then turned his attention to human intelligence. Although he uses the general developmental model from biology, he has also been able to completely transform it into a psychological theory.

The thrust of Piaget's work is to show that adult thought, even in its most intellectual or logical forms, can only be understood within a developmental context. Each stage of thinking evolves from a preceding stage; each stage represents a transformation—a more complex, differentiated, and integrated version of the mode of thought that preceded it. In this sense, the development of the individual mind, as Piaget describes it, is analogous to the development of an embryo or the evolution of animal species—the thought of the infant is as different from that of an adult as the germ cell is from the developed fetus, or as a human being is from a monkey. Piaget has taken the developmental model, described earlier in terms of embryological and psychosexual development, and applied it to purely psychological experiences. For example, in the development of the embryo, physical structure becomes more complex and differentiated as cells multiply and new organ systems develop. In Piaget's work it is psychological structures—ways of viewing the world, modes of thought or strategies for processing information—which become more complex and differentiated with development.

The main features of the general developmental model, implicit in the work of Freud, Sullivan, and Erikson, and most clearly enunciated by Piaget, may be summarized as follows: (1) There is an invariable order of the stages of development; (2) no stage can be skipped; (3) each stage is more complex than the preceding one; it represents a transformation of what existed before in a new form; and (4) each stage is based on the preceding one and prepares for the succeeding one (after Loevinger, 1966). The developmental model assumes an inner logic, a built-in plan that gives direction to the sequence of development.

The principal stages of cognitive development according to Piaget are: the *sensorimotor,* from birth to age one and a half (ages are approximate); the stage of *intuitive* or *preoperational thinking,* from one and a half to six; *concrete operations,* from six or seven to puberty; and *formal operations,* from early adolescence to adulthood. The order of the stages is invariable; none can be skipped; they flow, developmentally, one from the other; and each represents a more complex way of viewing oneself, the world and one's place in it. Roughly, we may say that the person goes from an undifferentiated state of sensations and reflexes; to a physical (sensorimotor) apprehension of self and the world; to crude symbolic (intuitive) categories; to a more differentiated—but still literal or concrete—mode of thought to, finally, the ability to manipulate abstractions. This highly condensed presentation of cognitive stages will be expanded in later chapters. Here, let us turn our attention to the concept of egocentrism, a key idea in Piaget's theory of development. Consideration of this concept will enable us to move from individual development to the larger issue of psychological development in a cultural-historical context.

EGOCENTRISM AND THE
EXPANSION OF PERSPECTIVES

Egocentrism is central to Piaget's theory though its meaning is often misunderstood. The concept refers to a state in which thought is "centered" on the self and, while it bears some relation to the common ideas of "selfishness" or being "self-centered" it more precisely refers to intellectual or cognitive limitations. An individual is egocentric when his perspective—his mode of viewing the world and his own relation to it—is limited to, or trapped within, a particular stage of development. The egocentric person sees the world only from his self-centered point of view and, what is more, is *unaware* of other points of view and of his own limitations in perspective.

Egocentrism appears in different forms at successive developmental stages. In the sensorimotor stage the infant is centered on his immediate sensations and actions; initially he does not differentiate his actions from the things acted upon. In Piaget's terms the infant *assimilates* the world to his egocentric perspective. Over the first year and a half of life, the infant, from repeated experiences with the physical world, discovers that it does not comply so easily: interaction with reality forces *accommodation*. Eventually, a balance is reached—an equilibrium between assimilation and accommodation—ending the period of sensorimotor egocentrism. The infant's perspective has broadened, at the level of interaction with the physical world, so that he comprehends the difference between his own actions and the world beyond himself; he has acquired the means of coordinating action with reality. His perspective has been broadened beyond his sensorimotor ego or self.

Once an equilibrium has been reached, the young child is ready to move to the next stage. By age two he begins, increasingly, to manipulate symbols. This is the period of the rapid growth of language, play, and fantasy and the child discovers a whole new mode of interacting with the world. Egocentrism reappears as the child attempts to assimilate the world to his newly acquired intuitive or *preoperational* schemes. The child pushes his new fantasy skills to their limits. His sense of self is inflated and only out of repeated interaction with the world does the egocentrism of the intuitive stage become balanced by accommodation.

With the onset of the final cognitive stage, formal operational thinking, the adolescent "discovers" ideals, abstractions, and introspection. An *egocentrism of ideas* is common in which the adolescent believes he has discovered idealism for the first time and attempts to assimilate the world to his new, and typically overdone, perspective.

The basic cycle is: egocentrism and assimilation → contact with reality → accommodation → equilibrium. The initial tendency at each stage of development is to overdo the new perspective, and, at each level, the person must work through to an equilibrium that balances his tendency to view the world from his own perspective with the wishes and views of others.

The psychological development of the individual may be thought of as a cyclical process in which each new egocentric perspective becomes tempered as the person extends his range of experience. As development is traced through the life span in succeeding chapters, we will note that this process not only describes the development of intelligence but is a valuable model in understanding the development of self and morality. But this is getting ahead of the story; let me conclude this introduction to egocentrism by pointing out some ways in which cultural and historical development parallel the growth and changes observed on the individual level.

The members of primitive societies typically think of themselves as being at the center of the world. Their own experiences, the customs and practices that they are familiar with, and what history is available to them in oral legends and folklore, comprise the standards by which they judge the world. In our eyes, the customs of neighboring tribes may seem nearly identical. Yet each tribe usually views the other as hopelessly barbaric and totally unlike itself. Most primitive people are extremely *ethnocentric;* their view of the world is centered on their own, immediate, cultural experience.

Modern civilization began to move beyond primitive ethnocentrism more than two thousand years ago, and today we are aware—if still largely intolerant—of the ways of life and points of view of other social groups and nations. Still, as recently as five hundred years ago it was believed that the earth was the center of the universe. This *geocentric* view, a more abstract form of the earlier, primitive ethnocentrism, was challenged and eventually gave way before the findings of Copernicus, Kepler, and the other astronomers of the fifteenth and sixteenth centuries. We now know that the earth is but one planet, rotating around one small star, in one of many galaxies that make up what may be an infinite universe. The special place of man's world has again been put in perspective.

Man's unique status as an animal—as celebrated in that well-known primitive legend *The Book of Genesis,* for example—represents another way in which we viewed ourselves at the center of things: in this case at the apex of creation. This form of *homocentrism* (for want of a better term) was not seriously challenged until the last century. Darwin, by demonstrating man's place as one species among many and, perhaps even more important, by showing that we have evolved from animal origins and are still evolving and changing, did much to challenge the view of man's God-given place on earth. The human species is certainly special in that it possesses uniquely evolved biological characteristics, but so are birds, insects, and sharks; and so were dinosaurs. According to the theory of evolution, man's "specialness" has a very different meaning.

The impact of Darwin's ideas was to change our perspective regarding our place among the various species of animal life. Initially this meant recognizing and accepting the fact that man is an animal—a talking, upright, latter-day ape—and therefore shares animal characteristics even if these seem brutish, sensuous or nasty. This was the early and popularly appreciated impact of the theory of evolution and those nineteenth-century men (some of whom are still with us) who reacted violently against Darwin's ideas were reacting against the challenge of the theory to homocentrism. As Darwin himself put it:

> It is notorious that man is constructed on the same general type or model as other mammals. All the bones in his skeleton can be compared with corresponding bones in a monkey, bat, or seal. So it is with muscles, nerves, blood-vessels, and internal viscera....
> ...Man and the higher animals, especially the primates, have some few instincts in common. All have the same senses, intuitions, and sensations, similar passions, affections, and emotions, even the more complex ones, such as jealousy, suspicion, emulation, gratitude, and magnanimity; they practice deceit and are revengeful; they are sometimes susceptible to ridicule, and even have a sense of humour; they feel wonder and curiosity; they possess the same faculties of imitation, attention, deliberation, choice, memory, imagination, the association of ideas, and reason though in very different degrees. (1871, pp. 5, 87)

The "very different degrees" is important for, once the older homocentric view is deposed, man, as a biological animal, can be examined in a new way. Attention can be paid to the very important differences between man and the other animals, as well as to similarities.

Through the course of history the narrow viewpoints of ethno-, geo-, and homocentrism have all been superceded. These manifestations of egocentrism at the social level have given way to broader, more complex perspectives. Interestingly enough, man's understanding of himself and his own development has one of the last areas to change; we have been slow to move beyond the unquestioned perspective of adult consciousness. This change in view began with Freud and those who have followed him; it is supported, in a slightly different way, by the work of Piaget. The perspective that stems from these psychological theories is still changing; it has yet to be integrated into the wider cultural perspective in the way that Darwin's theory has been.

Freud has shown that adult consciousness, as we think of it, is but one part of the mind. His work emphasizes the importance of unconscious processes, of dreams and fantasies, of the meaning hidden in "accidents" and commonplace mistakes or in the very pattern of a person's life, and of the lingering importance of childhood. An awareness of these aspects of life makes it increasingly difficult for a person to remain centered on his adult consciousness. Just as the primitive who has been exposed to the world beyond his tribal borders can never return to his simple ethnocentric views, so modern man, once aware of the greater range of his own mind, can never quite return to the simple perspective of adult consciousness.

Freud also awakened interest in the childhood origins of adult experience. His observations and theories cause us to question the adult perspective that we take for granted. In this sense, the trend begun in his work poses a challenge to "adultocentrism," the tendency to assume that our adult perspective is the only way to see things; the only mode of psychological experience. Piaget's description of the early forms of childhood thought shows, even more strikingly, the differences between child and adult perspectives. The ability to see things from the child's perspective has important ramifications, as we will see later. Let me illustrate the point here with some brief examples.

Ariès, in his historical study *Centuries of Childhood,* points out that until the eighteenth century, children in western societies were viewed as miniature adults. Childhood as a separate state with its own ways of thought, special feelings, and sensitivities was not yet "invented." This failure to recognize the child's perspective led to many damaging practices. For example, apprenticing of young children was a near universal custom in Europe during the Middle Ages. Although this may have seemed a desirable practice to adults, it meant a painful separation from home and family to the child who was apprenticed; in many instances it amounted to abandonment. Abandonment and separation, for example to public institutions, have continued until quite recently. Only when the child's reactions to separations were understood did such practices cease. The enlightened treatment of children requires moving beyond adultocentric perspectives—moving to a broader vision that includes the child's experience of the world as well as the adult's.

Some versions of adultocentric thought saw young children as asexual —a belief that Freud's theory of psychosexual development did much to change. The immediate and most forceful reaction to Freud's theory of infantile sexuality was one of unbelieving revulsion. Everyone "knew" that infants and young children were innocent; sex was something that appeared after puberty—this reaction being based on "sex" as seen from the adult perspective. But from the point of view of a one-year-old, sucking can be the high point of sensual pleasure. Thus, the theory of psychosexual development broadened our conception of human sexuality, challenged the adultocentric view of the innocence of young children, and, in the process, greatly expanded the meaning of sex.

These examples show how Freud, Piaget, and others have broadened our view of individual psychological experience. Both individual psychological development and the broader cultural-historical development of man's view of his relation to the world progress along the same lines. Cultures move from a primitive ethnocentrism to an appreciation of the views and values of social groups other than themselves. We recognize that the earth is not the center of the universe. As human animals, we have come to a more balanced view of our place in the evolution of species. All of these developments involve moving from a simpler perspective in which everything is centered on immediate experience—of self, of tribe, of species—to more complex perspectives. Development on the individual and cultural levels involves a challenge to egocentrism and a broadening of perspectives.[2]

The more complex perspectives of new levels of development are transformations of what existed earlier. They encompass the older views in new forms. So, for example, the older geocentric view is not shown to be exactly wrong by our modern conception of the universe. The sun *does* seem to revolve around the earth when viewed from a particular perspective; the earth even seems flat, for that matter. Modern astronomy takes a larger view; it asks us to view the solar system, or the milky way galaxy, as if we were an observer outside, looking at the whole. Similarly, a nonethnocentric view of societies is obtained when we "step outside" all individual cultures and view them as equally valid ways that different groups have come to terms with each other and their environments at particular points in history. At the individual level, we gain a new perspective when we are able to see ourselves from nonegocentric points of view. Going through the cycles of development involves a series of progressive changes in viewpoint. At each new stage, a new and more complex perspective is available until finally, with the attainment of the most abstract level, a person is capable of viewing all of his previous experiences—his previous "selves"—as well as the views and selves of others, from a broadened perspective.

A SYNTHESIS
OF PERSONALITY THEORIES

The developmental perspective will provide an overall framework within which to place the ideas, hypotheses, observations, and theories of a number of psychologists. Beginning with the next chapter I will trace the development of personality from the evolutionary origins of the human species to the psychology of the human adult. Before taking on that somewhat grandiose task, I should describe the way other writers have dealt with these same topics and point out some ways in which this book departs from what has almost come to be standard form in the field.

There is a tendency in psychology for workers to cluster around the ideas of great men (such as Freud) or around single ideas (such as reinforcement). This tendency produces "schools" of orthodox psychoanalysts, orthodox behaviorists, and even orthodox existentialists. Psychoanalysis became such an orthodoxy, in fact, that persons who did not adhere to par-

---

[2] The parallel between individual cognitive development and the development of cultural or social views is a central concern of Piaget. My attention was drawn to this parallel—and indeed much of the preceding discussion draws on—Philip Cowan's forthcoming book on Piaget which he has been good enough to let me see in draft form.

ticular ideas were expelled from membership in its official organizations—whereupon they set up their own competing groups.

The tendency for psychologists to form orthodox groups has been reinforced by a number of recent textbooks organized around "theories of personality." The implication of such books is that Freud's theory, or that of Carl Rogers, or stimulus-response learning theory are coherent entities—even though some of these writers may never have thought so themselves—and that the student should choose between the different theories or theorists. What probably began as a convenient strategy for writing textbooks ended by structuring the field more firmly into "schools." It is my belief that this trend toward schools and orthodoxies has been unfortunate in several ways.

When the field is structured into competing theories or schools one feels compelled to take sides—to choose one or the other. When Freudians assert that sexuality is the primary motivation of human behavior and Adlerians stress the role of aggression and competitiveness, one feels compelled—since the issue is typically presented as an argument between Freud and Adler or their supporters—to agree with one and not the other. When environmentalists stress the importance of external events such as rewards and punishments or social and cultural factors, and others point to innate human drives, instincts, and the rigidity of adult behavior based on infantile learning, we again feel compelled to take sides; to agree with one and not the other. But both sexuality *and* aggression are important human motives, and behavior is determined by *both* environmental influences and intrinsic factors. So the tendency to identify with schools has led many to structure their views around a few main observations or hypotheses and to neglect other equally important ideas.

The theories of many psychologists are valid and noncontradictory; they point to phenomena that are important in understanding human development. To illustrate, let us review some of the principal ways human motivation has been conceptualized. The most orthodox psychoanalysts emphasize the role of sexual pleasure, its satisfaction and frustration, and the importance of infantile experiences. Adler and his followers stress aggression and competitiveness, sibling rivalry, and social relationships within the family. Sullivan, more clearly than Freud in some ways, describes the development of self via personal encounters, emphasizing the role of anxiety. Robert White (1963) summarizes evidence on the role of competence motivation—the intrinsic striving to master the environment. Piaget stresses the "need to function," the drive to interact with the environment simply to exercise one's mind. Are these different models contradictory or do they, rather, call our attention to the major sources of human motivation and require an overall framework within which they can all find expression? I think the latter.

I do not mean to imply that *all* theories of motivation are equally valid. In fact, there are real differences and contradictions and, where these exist, one must take sides. For example, there is a view of motivation—found in the work of the psychologist Clark Hull and his followers (Dollard and Miller, 1950), as well as in certain interpretations of Freud—which attempts to explain all of human behavior as resulting from a few "primary drives" such as hunger, thirst, or sexual pleasure. This view is invalid, and it stands in contradiction to a number of the models cited above. When sides must be taken, choices should be based on a careful weighing of evidence and argument. This is different than adhering to one view and deemphasizing others because that view is associated with one's "school" or was emphasized by Freud or some other great thinker with whom one wishes to associate oneself.

Related to the issue of schools of thought is the problem of special or technical terms. Many theorists have developed elaborate languages that are only fully understood by members of the in-group. When the same or closely related ideas are being discussed by different writers, it is desirable to use the same terms. Insofar as technical jargon maintains the special status of schools and obscures communication I will try and dispense with it. It is my own belief that many of the important topics in the field can be discussed effectively in everyday terms. Love, anger, pleasure, anxiety, aggression, sensuality, guilt, action, passivity—these are the things that all the great theorists have been interested in. By using common terms, it is easier to synthesize different approaches.

Adherents to a particular school may object to a synthesis of ideas around common terms, feeling that *their* theory is being tampered with and that specific meanings are being lost. Such objections would be valid if the terms used by theorists had clear and unambiguous definitions or were used in consistent ways. Although many writers aspire to such a goal, particularly if they desire to identify their work with science, even a casual examination of actual practice reveals a good deal of looseness in the use of terms. If a psychologist wishes to have something to say about human thought and action, his terminology almost always includes, or moves back toward, the use of concepts from the common domain. In my view this is a necessity. Attempts to develop special jargon are often pseudoscientific. If we are explicit about theoretical terms and their relation to observations on the one hand, and knowledge from the common domain on the other, and if we avoid the use of scientific-sounding technical jargon, the field may move toward an integration of common cultural wisdom with the special insights gained by psychologists.

As we trace psychological development through the life span, the meaning of such concepts as love, aggression, or dependency will be sharpened and enriched by a synthesis of ideas drawn from Freud, Sullivan, Erikson, Piaget, and others.[3] The overall framework for this synthesis will be

---

[3] My own ideas concerning a synthetic approach were shaped in working on an earlier book (Breger, 1969a). Several other psychologists have been concerned

the developmental perspective presented in the earlier portion of this chapter. In accord with that perspective let me begin not with infancy but with man's evolution as a species. In the next two chapters we will examine the human heritage—where we have come as a result of our unique evolution—drawing on studies of our close animal relatives, the monkeys and apes. This will provide an overall picture of human instincts—those innate tendencies that characterize us as a species. From there we will move to a consideration of the earliest forms of social organization. With this background we can then undertake our journey proper, beginning with human infancy.

---

with these same issues in one way or another, including Robert White (1963) and Robert Holt (1967—see particularly the chapters by Klein, Holt, and Wolff). I have drawn heavily on the work of George Klein (1969, in press) and Jane Loevinger (1969, 1970) who have both been concerned with an approach that abstracts the best in Freud, Erikson, and Sullivan and integrates these with developmental theory, including that of Piaget. Klein's influence is seen especially in chapter 7 (of this volume), and Loevinger's in chapter 8.

chapter two

The
Primate
Heritage

The human species is the product of a long evolution. Many simple forms of life—single-celled organisms, insects, reptiles—evolved long before mammals, and many simple mammals long before primates. Within the primate group, the simpler monkeys evolved before the great apes, with human beings the last to evolve. The developmental perspective outlined in the previous chapter suggests that we examine primate evolution as a way of understanding the biological heritage of the human species.

According to the theory of evolution, different animals have attained their present forms because of their contributions to species survival. By genetic mutation, species aquire properties that make them either more suited—*adapted*—to their environments, or less suited to their environments. Those animals that *adapt* themselves to their surroundings are the ones that survive to pass on their genes to the next generation. In this manner a species evolves over many generations in the direction of increasing adaptation. Consider a few examples:

Let us assume an environment filled with meat-eating predators and small, slow-moving, tasty animals (the precursors to the modern turtle). Let us further assume that among these turtle ancestors there occurs, by random genetic mutation, some whose shells are harder and more resistant to the predator's teeth. During any one generation fewer of these hard-shelled fellows will be eaten, more of them will be around to reproduce and, gradually over a number of generations, they will evolve as the dominant form of the species. This is the way the theory of evolution explains the selection, over time, of the characteristics of any species. Giraffes evolved long necks because it fitted them to survive in an environment where edible leaves could be found high up in trees. Deer evolved as swift runners with keen senses of smell and hearing because these characteristics enabled them to avoid predators. Different species of birds have evolved beaks of different shapes which allow them to get at available food supplies.

What general characteristics have evolved in primates? Many features are shared with other mammals and need not be elaborated here. Several distinctive features include: (1) an omnivorous digestive capacity from teeth to intestines, which permits survival on a variety of diets; (2) specially dexterous hands-fingers-thumb, useful in obtaining food, locomoting through trees, and using tools; (3) teeth and jaws fitted for protection against predators as well as predation. In addition, each species has evolved its own unique features that aid in adaptation to specific environments. This is known as *species specificity,* the principle that each species has evolved to fit a particular ecological niche and that its characteristics must be understood within the context of both its evolutionary history and its current environment. As we shall see, all primates are curious and aggressive but some much more so than others. Many are intelligent, but only two—chimpanzees and humans—regularly use tools. And only one species—human beings—has language and culture. Humans share the general primate heritage as intensely social, aggressive, sensual, curious, and intelligent creatures. In addition, we possess our own uniquely evolved linguistic and cultural characteristics.

THE EVOLUTION OF BEHAVIOR

Evolved characteristics such as the shells of turtles, the necks of giraffes, or the fingers and thumbs of primates are all physical or bodily structures, while aggression, curiosity, and language are complex *patterns of behavior.* Although the general principles of evolution can be used to explain both physical characteristics and behavioral patterns, their application to the latter is more complex. Because of this, I will take some time to develop the concept of evolved behavior patterns or *instincts.*

Birds sit on their eggs, mammals nurse their babies, and sea lions engage in courtship rituals. These behavior patterns promote the reproduction of the species or the survival of the young so that they, in turn, can reproduce their kind. As we move up the scale of evolution from simple to complex organisms, the evolution of such patterns of behavior becomes increasingly important. For example, very simple organisms reproduce by division of cells and are mature at "birth." Reptiles emerge from their eggs in a small and weak state but are still capable of living an existence independent from their mothers. Mammals are not only dependent on their mothers for milk but are sufficiently immature at birth to require maternal care for their survival. Within the mammalian group, the primates, and within primates, man, are the most immature at birth, take the longest time to reach maturity and, hence, require the most maternal care. As we will see, evolution has structured or "built-in" the components of mother-infant relations because these behavior patterns are so important for the survival of the young and the species.

Maternal care is one area that illustrates the evolution of behavioral patterns. Others include various rituals involved in courtship and reproductive mating; patterns of fighting to protect territory or to insure that species members are spaced over a territory that can support them; and patterns that inhibit fighting, such as appeasement gestures. We will examine those patterns of greatest importance to primates shortly, but let us first look in more detail at the evolution of instincts.

Ethology

Ethologists, of whom Konrad Lorenz is the most popularly known, study the evolved characteristics of animals in dynamic interaction with their environments. The ethological studies provide a framework that will be useful in conceptualizing the human heritage; those instinctual potentialities that we possess by virtue of our evolution as a special subspecies of primate. Presented below is some of the work done by ethologists on the way baby birds become attached to their mothers. Several general principles emerge from this work that will prove helpful in understanding the evolution of adaptive behavioral patterns.

Attachment and Imprinting: An Example of Instinctual Behavior. The process of attachment—the creation of bonds between mother and infant—is of obvious importance for the survival of any species in which the young need care at birth. How does it come about that birds, who may coexist in an environment with many similar species, care only for their own young? The investigation of this problem began as early as 1910 when Heinroth reared birds in isolation in order to determine the relative importance of innate and learned factors in attachment. This early work was later expanded by Lorenz who developed the concept of *imprinting*.

Various species of birds (prominent among them the graylag goose which we will use for discussion here) have been studied by Heinroth, Lorenz, and subsequent investigators and their findings may be summarized as follows: When one of these birds is raised from the egg by humans, in isolation from other geese, it attaches to humans in the way geese ordinarily do to each other. The goslings follow humans in preference to adult geese and, when they reach maturity, direct sexual approaches to people. They are *imprinted* on humans rather than on other geese. The *following response* is the most prominent feature of the gosling's attachment to its mother. It appears to be an innate, fixed-action pattern—that is, it is a complex behavioral sequence which has become built in over the course of evolution because of its value for the survival of the species. It is easy to imagine those goslings who, because they were weak or deficient in this behavioral pattern, became separated from their mother shortly after birth and either perished or never reproduced, while those good followers had a better chance for survival and, upon reaching sexual maturity, were prepared to produce more geese with the same characteristic.

The ethological experiments have also shown that the pattern of stimulation that releases the response of following allows for some variability during a specific period of time—a *critical period*—after which it becomes fixed or imprinted. Thus the baby graylag will initially follow any large moving object which, under natural conditions, would be its mother. It becomes imprinted rather quickly and irreversibly to this first object, however, with only a relatively brief exposure during the critical period. Thus, those goslings who became imprinted on Lorenz's large moving body during a brief exposure continued to follow him about for years, even though they were given the opportunity to join a normal brood. They would call in distress when separated from him and, upon reaching maturity, directed their sexual behavior toward him and other human beings.

Subsequent work by Lorenz and other ethologists has demonstrated similar patterns in other birds, as well as variability between species in the patterns of stimuli that are acceptable as releasers of different behavioral patterns. Thus, while the graylag will imprint on any large moving object, certain other birds will attach only to patterns of stimuli identical, or very close in appearance, to their own species. For still others, attachment is accomplished in ways that do not include imprinting at all.

Let us look at the concept of critical periods in a bit more detail. Hess (1962) has found that imprinting in certain ducks occurs during the period after they are mature enough to walk but before they show fear to strange objects. The young duck cannot walk until it is about 13 hours old and shows no fear of strange objects until 16 hours. It will follow and become imprinted on that moving object which appears in its immediate environment during the period between 13 and 16 hours after its birth. Once imprinted during this brief, critical period, its pattern of attachment behavior is determined for life.

The ethological work with imprinting in birds, and work with many other patterns of behavior in other species, may be summarized around three concepts: (1) action patterns, (2) releasing stimuli, and (3) critical periods. Adaptive behavior patterns become built in to a species over the course of its evolution. The patterns consist of actions, such as the following behavior of young birds, that may be more or less fixed or narrow in scope. Action patterns are released by certain classes of stimuli—again, in the case of geese or ducks, following behavior is released by the sight of an object of a certain size, moving at a certain speed. And, finally, the process whereby action pattern and releasing stimuli are linked occurs during a specific period of time—a critical period—which may vary in onset and duration. Some examples from other species will illustrate some of the variations in action pattern, releasers, and time period.

A good deal of ethological work has been done with fish who fight with members of their own species to defend a specific territory (Lorenz, 1966). Since fish of the same species eat the same food it is adaptive for them to spread out over a wide food-supplying territory. If they bunch up they will quickly exhaust the available food supply and cause their mutual starvation. Such "species spacing" is important enough in terms of survival that a number of species of fish have evolved with brightly colored, distinctive markings which make them easily recognizable. These markings are releasers for built-in patterns of fighting which serve to drive fellow species members off one's territory. When one observes an area around a coral reef, one finds these species of fish living and feeding within their own territory and attacking any member of their own species who ventures into this territory. The attack and fighting behavior is the instinctual or fixed-action pattern, the distinctive coloring serves as the releaser, and the adaptive purpose of the entire sequence is the spacing of species members over a wide territory to insure an adequate food supply. A critical period does not seem to be a part of this particular pattern. The distinctive songs of many birds also serve the function of species-spacing.

A more familiar example is the pattern of attachment in infant monkeys. Monkeys, like people, are relatively weak and helpless at birth and for some period of time thereafter. Obviously, it is essential for their survival that they have mechanisms which strongly promote and maintain attachment to the mother. These actions are familiar to anyone who has seen monkey or ape families in a zoo: infants cling to their mothers' bodies and are held, in turn, by their mothers. During early infancy they are almost inseparable from each other. The initial action pattern is clinging and, subsequently, looking at the mother, crying for her attention, and so on.

The releasing stimuli are the soft, warm, and furry parts of the mother's body, and certain features of her appearance and actions. Unlike simpler species such as geese or ducks who can imprint in less than a day, the process of attachment in infant monkeys develops over several months. It is a more complex pattern of behavior and, since it takes longer to become established, is more varied as a result of the different experiences that occur during the longer time period.

THE CONCEPT OF INSTINCT

The concept of instinct is so important to an understanding of human psychological development that I have placed it in the title of this book. At the same time, instinct has been surrounded with so much misunderstanding that I use it with some hesitation. In what follows, I will try to show why it seems the best term to use, and to sort out some of the misunderstandings that occur when the concept is applied to complex animals like human beings.

The ethological work provides us with a general model of instinct. Instincts are behavior patterns that have become centrally built into a particular species because of their importance for survival. They consist of action patterns, classes of stimuli which release or trigger these actions, and variable periods of time during which the patterns become firmly established.

In a sense one can say that *each species member is so constructed that it "wants" or is "urged" to do those things that must be done for its survival.* Of course geese or fish don't "want" in the same sense that we do, but stating it this way calls attention to the imperative, strongly motivated, "want" or "must do" quality of instincts. Instinctual patterns make it more likely that an animal will do—and with human beings, that we will want or feel we must do—those things most essential for species survival. The common usage of instinct reflects this same quality. We speak of instincts getting "out of control," of individuals who are "a prey to their instincts," "blinded by passion," or "driven by rage." All of these uses suggest behavior that is strongly motivated, that the person feels he must do, or, in extreme instances, that seems to take over and direct action to the neglect of all else.

The *imperative* quality of instincts is common across a number of species, but it is important to specify the differences with which instincts manifest themselves in different species. One of the typical misunderstandings with the concept stems from a neglect of these differences. For example, one can agree that the fighting behavior of fish or the following behavior of goslings are instinctive and then argue (precisely because one cannot observe anything that is so fixed in humans) that human behavior is *not* governed by instincts. But should we expect instincts to manifest themselves the same way in different species? The evolutionary viewpoint leads us to expect species specificity; instinctual behavior patterns are as variable as the different physical forms of animals. Instincts exist in primates in forms peculiar to the evolution of these species. One common characteristic of these forms is that instinctual patterns are less fixed, take longer to develop, and are more variable in final outcome than those of other animals. They are, nonetheless, there. Apes and humans are animals and our evolution has left us with instinctual predispositions to act and react in those areas centrally related to survival.

In simpler organisms, instinctual patterns are "wired in" to the nervous system in a preset fashion. When a fighting fish sees the colors of a territorial invader it automatically attacks. Birds "know" what the songs of another species member mean—"watch out, this is my territory!" At the appropriate time, a gosling will follow and imprint on whatever large moving "mother" is available. When we look at more complex animals such as primates, we find that instinctual action patterns are not nearly as fixed as in fish or geese. Instincts set boundaries or limits within which a good deal of variation may occur. Attachment behavior in the infant monkey consists of a variety of actions to a variety of stimuli and develops over a fairly long period of time as compared with the imprinting observed in birds. The attachment instinct in monkeys is mediated by an *emotional reaction*. The infant monkey "wants" to cling in a way that is much closer to our understanding of "want." He does it because it makes him feel good, because not to cling feels bad, and he may relate to other objects in his environment because they too are associated with *pleasurable or unpleasurable emotional experiences*. As we will now see, emotions play a crucial role in primate instincts.

Instinctual Boundaries and Emotion

The more complex the animal the less mature it is at birth and the longer it takes to reach maturity. More complex organisms have larger and more complex brains and nervous systems and these, too, take longer to mature. In terms of instinctual behavior patterns, there is a wider array of actions and a wider array of releasing stimuli interacting with each other over longer periods of time. Because of these factors we should think of *instinctual boundaries* rather than instincts when referring to primates, both ape and human. Boundaries refer to the limits circumscribed by the instinctual evolution of a species—limits which may be narrow or wide. As species become more complex, the boundaries become wider and, therefore, primates have wide instinctual boundaries. In other words, apes and humans are relatively open to learning; our actions are less fixed at birth and we can profit from experience in ways that simpler animals cannot.

Another way of looking at the problem of instincts in complex, slow-maturing species, is to note how easy it would be for things to go wrong, in terms of individual and species survival, given the more variable outcome made possible by wide instinctual boundaries. Many authors have pointed to the adaptive value of the lack of fixed instincts. Humans are perhaps the least fixed in this sense and are certainly the most able to adjust and readjust their way of life as environmental circumstances change. At the same time, there is the danger that species members will lose sight of what is necessary for survival. If *nothing* were built in—if the species were completely open to learning—then individuals might develop who failed to care for their young, or weren't interested in sexual reproduction or in fighting off predators. What is needed—and, in fact, what seems to have evolved in primates—is a system which confers value on the crucial, survival-related areas while at the same time leaving the way open for a good deal of learning. This building-in of value is accomplished by the system of *emotions*. Emotions are what "tell" primates "this feels good, do more of it," or "this is frightening: run!" or "this animal is threatening you, threaten him back." *Emotions serve the survival-related purpose of sensitizing the animal to certain classes of events and of calling forth, or making more likely, certain classes of action.*

Since emotions are built in, rather than fixed action patterns to specific releasers, a good deal more flexibility is possible. For example, as development proceeds new events may acquire the capacity to serve as releasers and new actions may develop out of earlier ones, all still given instinctual force by the same emotion. The infant monkey becomes attached to his mother with the strong emotions of sensual pleasure and anxiety upon separation. Later in development, he may play with peers, maintain a general closeness with the social group, and experience anxiety upon separation from this group—a somewhat different set of actions than the earlier clinging, but one which is mediated by the same emotions of attachment pleasure and separation anxiety. In human infancy and early childhood the emotion of anger is released by specific threats and frustrations and brings forth simple fighting behavior—hitting, biting, kicking. In adults, anger may be aroused by threatening ideas or communications, as when one gets angry at the government or another nation when reading the newspaper. The action patterns released by these events may be quite different from simple fighting; they may consist of verbal expressions of anger or politely phrased sarcasm. These examples demonstrate the great flexibility of instinctual systems that are mediated by emotions.

The idea that emotions are the manifestations of instincts in more complex animals is clearly stated in Darwin's classic, *The Expression of the Emotions in Man and Animals* (first published in 1872), and may be found in the work of William James, William McDougall, Lloyd Morgan, and other classic sources. Fletcher (1957) reviews the work of these authors and shows how their ideas (with some minor modifications) may be integrated with the ethological model of instinct as well as with psychoanalytic theory. *Emotion* is the central idea in all these models of instinct. McDougall, Lorenz, and Freud would all agree that human instincts are manifest whenever one observes emotions. "Instinctual force," "driven by instinct," "blind propulsion" and so on refer to states in which the amplifying power of emotion is intense. Similarly, psychoanalytic conceptions of "drive" or of "id instincts" refer to states in which strong emotions are aroused. It will be worth a brief detour to examine the issue or instinct and emotion in Freud's theory.

Drive and Emotion in Psychoanalytic Theory

The theory of drive in psychoanalysis is a very tangled one and it will not be possible to consider it in detail here. Clarifying discussions may be found in Holt (1965), Breger (1968), and Klein (in press). Very briefly, in his early writings Freud put forth a theory that had one instinct at the base of all human behavior: a striving for tension reduction that he termed the *pleasure principle*. Satisfaction of this "drive" was presumably experienced by the person as pleasure, with tension buildup experienced as pain. The attempt was then made to derive all motivated behavior from this one source. This attempt was never very successful and it ran into particular difficulty when Freud tried to explain aggression. His solution, the postulation of a "death instinct," has been questioned even by some of his more faithful followers.

The theory of drive became increasingly encumbered with such ideas as psychic energy or "libido," "cathexis," "fixations," and "regressions" of energy and other complications, until only the psychoanalytic house theoreticians could follow it. Meanwhile, the theory of emotion occupied a curious status in psychoanalysis. Anger, anxiety, guilt, the pleasure of sexuality—these are the ideas with which the day-to-day work of psychoanalysis is carried out. But, because of the single-instinct or tension-reduction view, these emotions could only be accorded a secondary status as "signals" in the drive or energy version of psychoanalytic theory. Presumably, they signaled information about some underlying state of tension or libidinal energy.

The view of instinctual boundaries and emotions previously outlined is more in keeping with the clinical observations of Freud and a number of other psychoanalysts. In this model there are a number of instinctually bounded areas rather than the one tension-reduction or pleasure-pain principle. One would expect more than a single instinct in a species that is the product of such a lengthy and complex evolution. Each of these instinctual areas is characterized by an emotional system which gives value to a class of perceptions and makes a class of actions more likely. Emotions convey information about the desirability of some activities and the need to avoid others; about what to be afraid of and what to fight with; about what feels good and what feels bad. One need not assume, as Freud's single instinct theory suggests, that there is one primary emotional state—pleasure–pain—and that all others are later modifications of it, nor that emotions are somehow secondary in importance to a primary tension reduction. Instead, the present model postulates a group of primary instinctual areas, each with its characteristic emotion. These are the building blocks of motivation; they provide the "instinctual force" behind a variety of later perceptions and actions.

One additional advantage of the present model of instincts should be mentioned since it lays the basis for much of what comes later. Primates have evolved as social species and the instinctually bounded areas that I will discuss are *social instincts*—they have to do with the regulation of relationships between species members. Freud's theory of the pleasure principle, as well as a number of other motivational theories in psychology, assumes that people are born with drives such as hunger, thirst, or pleasure seeking which have no specific social focus. These theorists then assume that social motives develop fortuitously, presumably because other species members are around while the "primary drives" are being satisfied or frustrated. The present view does not deny the significance of hunger, thirst, the need to avoid pain, or other such drives, nor does it deny that these may play a role in the development of social relationships. But it goes beyond the typical drive theory in calling attention to specific social instincts, apart from these other drive systems, which are uniquely evolved in primates.

Emotion

What, then, are emotions? The preceding discussion has stressed their central role in primate instinctual areas, and various references to sensual pleasure, anger, and anxiety suggest states that we are all familiar with from everyday experience. It is common to distinguish three components that make up an emotional reaction: (1) internal physiological processes, (2) subjective, conscious or semiconscious states of experience, and (3) an expressive, action, or behavioral component. The physiological component may involve many body systems, though the autonomic nervous and endocrine systems are prominent. An example of physiological arousal is the flooding of the body with adrenaline in a general state of threat or fear, leading to changes in heart and respiratory rates, dilation of certain blood vessels, and other changes. States of experience—fear, anger, happiness—are familiar enough on the subjective level and can be shared via communication with others. The expressive component is specific to the emotional state being described and consists of *vocalization* (cries of distress or screams of rage);

actions (running in fear or clinging in pleasure); and, of great importance, *facial expressions* specific to the different emotional states. The expressive component points to the intrinsically social nature of emotion. Other species members recognize and react to facial and bodily expressions of anger or appeasement, of sexual excitement, or of fear. It is important to add that although it is convenient to discuss emotion in terms of one or the other of the three components, in life all three occur together in *integrated patterns*.

Physiological arousal, facial expression, and body movements are general across primates and at different age levels within man. A monkey's state of anger, a young child's intense curiosity, or a baby's cry of despair are easily recognizable. The subjective or experiential component is more variable since it involves cognitive or intellectual capacities that sharply differentiate humans from apes and, within humans, that differentiate individuals at different ages. What it *means* to feel angry or loving, afraid or happy depends on the ability to deal with increasingly complex meanings. Humans, with their much larger brains, experience emotional states in very different ways than apes do. Cognitive abilities undergo a long and complex development within each human individual and the subjective component of emotion will be different at progressive stages—the sensorimotor infant will differ from the concrete operational child and each will differ from the adult capable of formal operational thought.

In summary, the instinctually bounded areas are characterized by specific emotional patterns. The general arousal and expressive (facial expression and body movement) components of emotion are fairly general across primates while the subjective or experiential component is variable, depending on the cognitive ability of the ape or person. Since instinctual-emotional reactions occur in integrated patterns, one can say that we humans share certain of the basic instincts with our fellow primates but also differ from them in the way these are experienced.

SOCIAL INSTINCTS
OF MONKEYS AND APES[1]

The evolutionary viewpoint teaches us that a number of survival-related functions will be built in to any adapted species. Primates, like other animals, are strongly motivated to breathe, to obtain nourishment, and to avoid pain. Hunger, thirst and pain avoidance are important systems and, since I will not be paying much attention to them in what follows, I just

---

[1] The discussion of primate social instincts draws on ethological work, laboratory studies of monkeys and, most heavily, field observations of monkeys and apes. The field observations are an extremely important source of evidence which have only recently come to light. The work of investigators from the United States, Europe and Japan is represented in four edited volumes: Altmann (1967); De Vore (1965); Jay (1968); and Morris (1967).

wish to make clear that they play their part as sources of primate motivation. They will be relatively neglected because I don't think they shed much light on the more interesting motivational problems of human beings. They are not specific to primates and as motive systems they are evolutionarily "old," well-ingrained, and smoothly functioning. Under states of extreme starvation, hunger can become the dominant motive in life. When this happens, strong emotions become involved. But in the normal course of affairs we are not starving or suffocating, and these motives are of less interest than the more recently evolved social instincts.

All primates live in groups; group living evolved because of its adaptive advantage, and the instincts that regulate it are strongly felt by all species members. Hamburg (1963), in an excellent discussion of this issue, says:

> ... primates are group-living forms; the primate group is a powerful adaptive mechanism; emotional processes that facilitate interindividual bonds (participation in group living) have selective advantage; the formation of such bonds is pleasurable for primates; they are easy to learn and hard to forget; their disruption is unpleasant and precipitates profound psychophysiological changes that tend to restore close relations with others of the same species. (p. 305)

There are many reasons for the evolution of group living among primates. For example, it is common to point to the intelligence and the manual dexterity of monkeys and apes as adaptive mechanisms. These features necessitate a long period of maturation after birth which means that infants will be relatively helpless for a long period of time. This, in its turn, means that the mother will have to care for them—itself a social skill—incapacitating her to a certain extent. Living in a group provides protection and support for mother-infant pairs. The group can specialize with the stronger, more aggressive members assuming protective functions, and the mothers performing maternal roles. This is one example of the adaptive advantage of group living; others will become apparent as we examine the social instincts in greater detail. Many other animals are social—bees live together in hives, ungulates in herds, some fish in schools—but primate social life is dependent on emotional reactions and communication systems that are unique; they are the precursors to man's social life.

Attachment and Love[2]

Observations of monkeys and apes, both in captivity and in their natural environment, make clear that the bonds of attachment between infant and mother are among the strongest of instincts. Attachment is a two-

---

2 An excellent discussion and review of the evidence relating to attachment may be found in Bowlby (1969) who also presents a discussion of instincts and emotions that closely parallels the present model.

way process. The infant is strongly motivated to cling, to seek for mother if she is missing, and to cry and "punish" her with anger when she returns from a separation. The mother is strongly motivated to care for her infant, to hold and cuddle it, and to respond to its cries and demands. Indeed, the maternal instinct is so strong that field observers report baby-snatching among wild baboons and chimpanzees in which females will take infants away from their natural mothers in order to care for them. The emotions involved in these examples include the pleasures of attachment—the sensual gratification that both mother and infant receive from physical contact, nursing, rubbing, and rhythmic movements; the anxiety and grief of separation; and the anger that appears in certain instances of reunion. Love, anxiety, and anger—certainly a varied and powerfully motivating set of emotions.

Field Observations of Attachment. Field observations of several species of monkeys and apes demonstrate variations in patterns of attachment behavior. For example, baboon infants become independent from their mothers about a year sooner than do rhesus monkeys, and there are variations in timing and style between chimpanzees, gorillas, and other species. Despite these variations, there is a core of attachment behavior common to all the primates observed and, for present purposes, it seems reasonable to speak of a general pattern, overlooking the differences.

Almost immediately after birth, an infant monkey or ape clings to his mother's body, holding on to the hair on the underside and gripping the nipple with its mouth, even when not nursing. The mother supports and holds the infant when this is necessary. This close contact continues for the first few months as the infant matures. With increased skill, the infant can ride on mother's back, and later follow her. By the second year, the young primate is playing with agemates and venturing out more and more on his own; but it is clear that he does so under the watchful eye of his mother and, especially in the early stages, is quick to return to her when trouble arises. As a typical example, let me describe the pattern of attachment among chimpanzees, probably man's closest relative among the living apes. What follows is based on the field observations of Lawick-Goodall (1968a, 1971).

The baby chimpanzee spends the first four months of life close to mother, clinging to her underside, or sitting beside her. If he ventures more than a few feet away, mother pulls him back. From six months to a year and a half the infant progresses from clinging to backriding to playing with peers but is never out of mother's sight. Whenever mother moves off, the infant is quick to climb aboard. From a year and a half to age three the young chimp spends increasing amounts of time with agemates, being away from mother for as much as 75 to 90 percent of the day, as compared with 25 percent during the earlier period. He is still carried by her when she moves, however, and continues to sleep with her at night. As childhood progresses from age three to seven, independence grows in the areas of feeding, transport, and sleeping. The young chimp spends more and more time with peers, younger animals, or adolescents. Puberty occurs around age seven and, from this point on, chimps of both sexes increasingly associate with the dominant, mature males. Even in late adolescence, however, when the chimp has achieved adult size, it is not uncommon for both males and females to return and spend time with mother. This persistence of "family" ties is unusual; baboons, for example, have broken the tie with mother by age three.

Although the bond of attachment in all the monkeys and apes is most prominent between mother and infant, it can be observed between other members of the group as well. Baby-snatching has already been mentioned; it illustrates the inherent attraction that young infants have for other females. Sharing of infants among more than one mother is reported in some species. "Paternal" behavior (in quotes because all mating is promiscuous and the real father is never known) occurs in some species; two-year-old baboons, rejected by their mothers who are usually busy with a new baby, run to adult males when alarmed and are accepted by them. Baby gorillas are attracted to dominant adult males, and may sit near, play on, or even ride on the tolerant old fellows' backs.

One can speculate that the more general bonds of affection within primate groups have their origin in the bond of attachment between mother and infant. What begins as mother–infant love lays the basis for later bonds between peers and, eventually, plays an important role in the adult primate's own sexual, grooming, maternal, and paternal behavior. One way to test this idea would be to disrupt the relationship between mother and infant and observe the effects on these other areas. The following laboratory experiments provide such a test and, at the same time, point up the differences between the present view of instinctual boundaries and those theories that attempt to explain attachment behavior as a derivative of some other drive such as hunger or tension-reduction.

Harlow's Experiments. Harlow and his coworkers (1958, summarized in Harlow, 1971) have carried out a number of experiments in which rhesus monkeys were raised from infancy under different conditions. Because these studies have been carried on for a number of years, it has been possible to assess the effects of the different forms of early experience on adult social behavior. The work is of great importance because it allows a more precise specification of the instinctual boundaries of attachment, or, as Harlow likes to call it, "love."

In one of his early experiments, Harlow put to a direct test the "primary drive" theory which holds that attachment or love of an infant for its mother arises in a secondary manner because the mother satisfies the infant's "primary" drives such as hunger. Simply put, this theory states that you love your mother because she feeds you. Harlow separated infant monkeys from their natural mothers shortly after birth and raised them on different sorts of dummy or surrogate mothers. Some of the dummies were constructed of wire with a nipple from which the infant monkey could obtain milk, and some were constructed of soft cloth to which the infant could cling. If the primary drive theory was correct, the monkeys should have become attached to that surrogate mother from which food was obtained. This did not prove to be the case. The monkeys showed an overwhelming preference for the cloth mother, even in those instances where hunger was satisfied only on the wire mother. They spent a great deal of time clinging to the cloth mother, would go to her in time of distress, and clearly derived security from her presence. For example, if placed in a room of strange and somewhat frightening objects, a young monkey normally clings to its mother and only gradually moves away from her to explore. Monkeys with cloth mothers were able to use them in this way, and even seemed to gain some comfort from their mere presence under a clear plastic case. With no mother, or a wire mother, the monkeys huddled on the floor and did much less exploring. In this and other ways, Harlow was able to demonstrate that a monkey's love for its mother is not secondary to the satisfaction of hunger but comprises a primary system in itself. The infant monkeys who had access to a cloth mother spent a great deal of time clinging to her, went to her in strange or frightening situations, were upset at her absence, with all of these indices of attachment persisting even in cases where the monkey and its cloth mother were separated for two years. In other words, they behaved as if she were a real monkey mother. This system of attachment is made up of a group of actions, the most prominent of which is clinging to the mother's soft and furry body. Other components include sucking and mouthing, rhythmic rocking, looking at mother's face, and, later in development, following. Harlow uses the phrase *contact comfort* for the primary actions involved in attachment between infant and mother; *contact* refers to the dominant action between infant and mother, and *comfort* to the emotional component of this instinctual pattern.

So far, the discussion of Harlow's work has demonstrated the primary nature of certain actions and emotions involved in attachment but it has not told us much about the relationship of contact-comfort to other aspects of the monkey's life—especially his later social life. Harlow also studied other sorts of early mothering—including none at all—and has followed the effects of these various early experiences into monkey adulthood. This work shows the far-reaching effects and great importance of primary attachment.

In addition to raising monkeys with wire and cloth mother surrogates, Harlow also raised groups of infants in total isolation for varying periods of time, some for as long as two years. Others were allowed to play with peers but had no mothers to become attached to, while still others could look at other monkeys but not make any contact with them. Thus, there was a range of conditions going from complete isolation for long periods of time, through shorter isolations, to visual contact only, to peer contact, to dummy mothers of various kinds, to the normal experience of a real mother. What were the effects, both immediate and long-term, of these varying early experiences?

In general, Harlow's results show that the deprivation of normal social experience or maternal contact has damaging effects in a number of areas of the monkey's life, and that the more deprivation, the more disastrous the effects. Those monkeys who were raised in isolation or whose only social experience was with dummies, failed to relate to other monkeys in later life. They did not play or groom, did not defend themselves when attacked, were uninterested in sex, were less curious, and spent less time exploring and much more time sitting by themselves engaged in repetitive activities such as rocking. The monkeys raised in total isolation for two years showed the most severe effects and, important to note, the damage to social behavior seemed to be permanent. No amount of later experience or opportunities to learn were able to undo the ill effects of prolonged early social isolation. Monkeys raised in isolation for shorter periods of time, or those with surrogate mothers, were less severely disturbed, though in all cases the damage to social behavior was marked compared to those infants who had experience with other monkeys, either peers or mothers. For example, the monkeys raised with cloth mothers showed many of the same social and psychological deficiencies upon reaching maturity as did monkeys raised in isolation. They did not play or groom and were unable to engage in sexual reproduction. Harlow was able to get a few of these aberrant females pregnant by mating them with sophisticated, normal males. Interestingly, they showed no ability to care for their own infants, ignoring them or becoming annoyed by their cries and treating them in a most aggressive and unloving fashion. This finding illustrates the boundaries of instinctual maternal behavior. Normal adult female monkeys and apes are strongly motivated to care for infants, as a variety of field observations have demonstrated. The failure of socially deprived monkeys to engage in maternal behavior shows that if certain early experiences are missing, maternal behavior fails to develop. Monkeys must experience love themselves as infants in order to later love and care for their own babies.

Harlow also found that play with agemates could markedly reduce the negative effects of isolation or an inanimate mother. Monkeys who had the opportunity to play with peers did not show the abnormality in social skills, self-defense, and sexual behavior. In fact, he suggests that peer play may be more important than the mother-infant relationship since the monkeys raised on cloth mothers with peer play experience seemed to fare better than those raised with real mothers but in isolation from peers. Observations of such peer play revealed the young monkeys literally practicing their later social behaviors: attempting to mount each other and enjoying aggressive games related to dominance relations.

The irreversible effects of social deprivation suggest a critical period during which normal attachment will take place and beyond which it will not. This is one of the boundaries of the attachment instinct. On the basis of a number of studies, Harlow believes that the boundary for rhesus monkeys is the first six months of life. Total social isolation during this critical period leads to irreversible damage.

The findings from Harlow's work have been extended in a number of studies by Sackett (1970) and others. In this work more of the details of attachment behavior have been discovered. It has been found, for example, that rhesus infants, raised in isolation or with peers, show a preference for adult rhesus females as compared with females of other, closely related, species. The boundary here is probably fairly wide since there are a number of reports of monkeys and apes raised by humans to whom they attach in a more or less normal manner. Nevertheless, the built in preference for one's own species is an interesting finding related to the attachment instinct.

In an interesting investigation of the role of visual stimuli, Sackett raised monkeys in social isolation where they were exposed to color photographs of monkeys, humans, landscapes, buildings, and geometric patterns projected on the wall of their cages. Pictures of monkeys, especially infants and other monkeys in threat positions, produced greater exploratory and play responses and higher levels of activity than did the other pictures. Of special interest is the finding that none of the visual stimuli produced fear until 80 days of life, while from 80–120 days, pictures of monkeys in threat positions produced fear responses even though the isolation-reared monkeys had had no actual experience with other species members. These findings (natural preference for own species mother and innate fear reaction to pictures of threatening monkeys) indicate the presence of innate recognition mechanisms for certain classes of complex visual stimuli. It also suggests an interaction of these innate or instinctual propensities with maturation, similar in form, though very different in its specific manifestations, to imprinting in birds.

A quote from Sackett summarizes the many laboratory studies which demonstrate the great significance of primary attachment. Field observations confirm and, if anything, lend greater weight to the centrality of attachment in all the monkeys and apes:

> The data suggest that this preference for own species may be based on unlearned visual and/or auditory cues. Such unlearned, prepotent stimuli may play an important causal role in the development of attachments under normal rearing conditions. However, the development of this early preference into permanent own-species attachment appears to depend on the nature of the early rearing conditioning. Many studies have shown that the behavior of partial isolates is grossly abnormal compared with either mother-peer laboratory raised or feral-born animals. . . . In general, partial isolates are deficient sexually and maternally, and show low levels of play, environmental explora-

tion and positive affiliative behaviors, especially those involving physical contact. Maintenance of the initial own-species preference depends on having physical interaction with species members during the early rearing history of the monkey. (1970, p. 136)

It is clear that the actions and emotions which promote social bonds are centrally built in to the nonhuman primates. The discussion so far has focused on the positive emotions—for example, the pleasure that both infant and mother derive from contact comfort or from the mutual stimulation of play. In addition to the pleasures of attachment, social bonds are maintained by a powerful set of negative emotions which make separation a painful or unpleasant experience and which motivate the animal to reunite with his fellows. This negative emotion will be called *separation anxiety*. It plays many important roles in primate social life. As a way of approaching this central motive system, let us first consider the related emotion of *fear*.

Fear

A number of psychologists influenced by behaviorism have attempted to explain complex actions as the result of learning based on a few simple drives. Such theorists are similar to Freud who also attempted to derive all motivation from one or two basic sources. One of the earliest of these social learning theories—that of Dollard and Miller (1950)—even attempted to combine the psychoanalytic and behaviorist learning approaches.

Although later workers in this tradition, such as Bandura and Walters (1963), have stuck closer to behaviorism, the form of their models is the same. Social learning theory assumes that an organism initially has no specific or innate fears. He starts with only the capacity to feel pain when injured or deprived of necessities such as food and drink. Fear then develops secondarily as a result of experiences of pain and deprivation. This can be called the "burned-child-fears-the-fire" model. Anxiety is treated in a similar way; indeed in most social learning thories fear and anxiety are not clearly distinguished from each other. In sum, these theories conceptualize fear and anxiety in the same way as love and attachment; both are thought to arise *secondarily* as a result of their association with so-called primary drives such as hunger or pain.

It would be foolish to argue that such learning does not take place—it certainly does. But it can be argued that this model of fear and anxiety is too limited in scope. Social learning theories overlook the specific motive systems that primates possess by virtue of their unique evolution. In the previous section we have reviewed some of the evidence that establishes attachment-love as a *primary* motive system—one that does not arise secondarily to the satisfaction of hunger or oral pleasure. Sackett's findings suggest that primates possess innate fears of the threat gestures of other species members. Here let me review some additional evidence that points to fear as a primary instinctual system and then consider separation anxiety as a related system with its own distinctive functions.

Fear as we usually think of it—a sense of wariness and hypersensitivity to danger—plays important roles in the survival of any species. It is obviously advantageous for animals to avoid predators or other sources of danger in their environments, and the arousal of an instinctual-emotional pattern can function to make fear as a protective warning longer-lasting. That is, it is not only important that an animal run when he sees a predator but that he keep running even when the predator is out of his visual field. The arousal of an emotional fear reaction heightens the animal's sensitivity; it makes him keep running or causes him to remain wary.

Primates also communicate fear socially and such communcations may have long-lasting effects. Washburn and Hamburg (1965) cite the following case:

> In the Nairobi Park there are many groups of baboons that are accustomed to cars. A parasitologist shot two of these baboons from a car and eight months later it was still impossible to approach the group in a car. It is most unlikely that even a majority of the animals saw what happened and the behavior of the group was based on the fear of a few individuals. *It is highly adaptive for animals to learn what to fear without having to experience events directly themselves. . . .* (p. 619)

What happened in this instance is probably that a few baboons witnessed the actual shooting which aroused a great deal of fear in them. The very sight of a dead species member has the capacity to arouse fear in primates (as Hebb and Thompson [1954] point out), and is probably why we humans go to the elaborate precautions of funerals, mortuaries, and related paraphernalia to protect ourselves from such sights. Primates also possess alarm calls, facial expressions and related actions which clearly communicate fear to other group members. Hence, those baboons who witnessed the shooting from the car communicated their fear to others and continued to do so at the sight of other cars. Once communicated, other group members would then possess the same sensitivity and pass it to still others. As Washburn and Hamburg point out, selection favors the animal who is overly prepared for such dangers as being shot. It takes only one small mistake to be killed, hence, the adaptive advantage of long-lasting and easily communicated fear reactions.

Field observations provide a number of other examples of the sensitive-fearful reactions of monkeys and apes both to known dangers such as predators and to novel objects or events whose potential danger is unknown.

Most wild apes are quite cautious about human observers and take a good deal of time before they accept their benign presence (when it is benign). And, as the example of the shooting in Nairobi Park illustrates, they are quick to become fearful again when the situation warrants. Laboratory experiments also indicate the fearful reaction of monkeys to new situations or objects. Monkeys are curious—another instinctual pattern that we will examine in more detail later—as well as fearful in the presence of novel stimuli. They will either explore or withdraw in fear depending on the stimulus: a monkey will be curious and explore things that are not too different from what he knows well. This can include other females who look like his mother, peers, objects, locations that resemble known feeding places, and so on. Things that are markedly different will illicit fear that will only gradually diminish with familiarity. The primate watchword is "caution is the better part of valor."

Fear is also expressed in reaction to the threat communications that make up many dominance interactions among monkeys and apes. We have seen how monkeys raised in total isolation showed fear reactions to photographs of monkeys in threat positions. This finding indicates that the fear component of dominance-submission interactions is innate. Like the components of the attachment instinct, the fear associated with dominance is also dependent on certain types of social experience. Harlow's monkeys who were raised in continuous isolation eventually lost the capacity to react appropriately to social threats, just as they ceased to show appropriate attachment behavior. Monkeys and apes who grow up in a natural environment show a great deal of dominance-submission behavior. In fact, as we will see in the forthcoming section on aggression, dominance hierarchies, along with the bonds of attachment, are the basic organizing patterns of primate social life. Reactions of fear are communicated by the submissive primate to the dominant member of the pair and these emotional reactions play an important role in ritualized, social relationships. As the animals develop they learn the many nuances of the rituals: they learn who to be afraid of and when, how to show the appropriate appeasement gestures, and how they themselves can display threat and attempt dominance. As with attachment, the boundaries of this instinctual system are wide, and appropriate adult social behavior is dependent on the learning that occurs through interaction with mother, peers, and older group members.

Fear of unknown dangers and predators, fear of the unfamiliar, fear of dead species members, and the fear displayed to threat gestures illustrate several important roles played by the same emotion. Fear of dangers and the unfamiliar are widespread phenomena among many animals. The fear shown to threat gestures is peculiar to those species whose social organization is based on dominance. As an instinctual building block, the emotion of fear is a part of more than one survival pattern.

Separation Anxiety

Although related to fear, anxiety has evolved in primates for different purposes. It appears early as a powerful negative emotion that keeps mother and infant together. Later in life it is seen as grief and, in a general way, is a central force binding primate groups together.

The British psychoanalyst John Bowlby has been a consistent spokesman for the central role played by attachment and separation anxiety. His early papers (Bowlby, 1960, 1961) are important in two ways. First, he reviews a good deal of evidence demonstrating the widespread importance of separation anxiety. Second, he recognizes the inadequacy of the primary drive or tension-reduction model within psychoanalysis and replaces it with a model in which attachment and separation are conceptualized as primary systems; a model that I follow here. Bowlby's recent book, *Attachment and Loss* (1969), greatly expands on his early work and is an important statement. What follows draws on Bowlby's work as well as on an excellent review of grief and mourning by Averill (1968).

Once the primary bond of attachment is established, disruptions and separations occasion reactions of anxiety in both mother and infant. As our previous discussion has shown, attachment begins very soon after birth in the nonhuman primates. In a few weeks the infant monkey or ape is securely attached to its mother and within the first few months it can distinguish her from other members of the group. The infant's attachment becomes more and more specific to its own mother. The pleasures and securities of love, contact comfort, grooming, and play have already been described. With secure attachment established, separation brings forth a special form of anxiety. It is interesting to note the connection between the anxiety of separation from mother and the fear illicited by unfamiliar objects or situations. As we have seen, many animals show a balance between fear and curiosity depending on how discrepant objects or situations are from their previous experience. Somewhat familiar stimuli elicit curious exploration while those that are less familiar provoke fear. With secure attachment, the mother—her body and the many tactile, auditory, and visual cues she provides—becomes the most familiar total situation for the infant. Anything apart from mother is strange and likely to provoke fear. As the infant matures, he gradually expands his experience away from mother, using her as a base of familiar security. Thus, the fear of the strange and separation anxiety are linked together.

Bowlby and many others have noted at least two phases in the separation pattern. The first is a phase of protest and alarm during which the separated infant screams, cries, and clearly makes his anxiety known. Mothers, as well as other members of the group, are extremely responsive to the infant's communications of alarm and, in the large majority of naturally occurring instances, reunion is rapidly effected. This part of the pattern is the instinctual basis for later reactions of anxiety. In general terms, we can say that *anxiety arises from abandonment or from a disruption of vital relationships.*

The second phase occurs when protest fails to bring about reunion. After a period of time, protest gives way to apathy, despair, and withdrawal; the separated animal shows, by his facial expression and in other ways, that he is depressed. Separations of sufficient duration to produce depression are probably rare in the wild since separated infants would not be likely to survive. Nevertheless, depression or grief shows again how an unpleasant emotional state can serve as a powerful motive in promoting closeness to other group members. For example, Washburn and Hamburg (1965) describe the way an injured baboon will attempt to keep up with his troop when it moves, even though his injuries make this a very painful exercise. The pain of separation is a more powerful motive than the pain of physical injury. And, of course, the injured animal, separated from the troop, would be easy prey and not survive for long in the natural environment.

The motives of attachment and the pain of separation operate within the mother as well as the infant. Schaller (1963) describes a female gorilla observed in the wild who carried her dead infant for four days before abandoning it on the trail. Field observations are also supported by controlled laboratory studies. For example, Kaufman and Rosenblum (1967) separated infant rhesus monkeys from their mothers in an experimental situation where they could observe the effects more closely than is possible in the wild. Following the typical protest phase, they observed marked reactions of grief and depression in both infant and mother, attempts to reestablish the severed relationship, and excessive clinging for a long period of time when reunion did take place. As Averill summarizes:

> If there is a "natural" occasion for grief, in the sense of possessing important biological consequences, it should be separation of an infant from its mother. Observations would indicate that dissolution of the mother-infant relationship is in fact, one of the most potent occasions for grief-like reactions in subhuman primates, from the point of view of both the infant...and the mother. (1968)

Although grief is an extremely unpleasant state for the individual, and may even contribute to his physical debilitation, it possesses important advantages for the survival of the group. The pain of this emotion promotes the mother-infant bond and, more generally, group cohesiveness. In the wild, one small mistake by the mother is likely to prove fatal for the infant. Since troops typically move about every day, and since infants are relatively helpless, separation would rapidly lead to death. Situations of danger allow one to observe the attachment and separation instincts at work. The alarm cries of other group members, which signal the approach of a predator, are cues for mother and infant to scramble for each other and to cling all the more closely. Such tight clinging is important, also, if the mother joins the group in rapid flight.

To sum up, separation anxiety has evolved as an instinctual-emotional pattern which promotes the mother-infant bond. Grief is a related instinctual-emotional pattern which occurs when an established bond is disrupted or, in other terms, when one loses an important love object. While both anxiety and grief have their origins in the mother-infant situation, social experience and later learning fill in the area bounded by these instincts. Attachments come to include other members of the social group; separation from the group itself becomes an occasion for anxiety and the loss of other individuals the occasion for grief. In the next chapter, the development of these instinctual patterns in humans will be examined and we will see how, with the greater complexity of our cognitive skills, we become capable of feeling anxious, depressed, and still later, guilty, over a greater number of things than any ape ever conceived of. Let us move on now to a consideration of the other great force in primate social organization—aggression and its control.

Aggression

A discussion of the instinctual basis of aggression at the present time is likely to arouse the same sort of protest and argument that greeted Freud when he introduced his theory of sexual instincts to Victorian society over half a century ago. Few would deny that human aggression poses a tremendous problem—perhaps *the* problem of our age—as nations pursue their traditional warlike ways, with the capacity to destroy all life on earth. Yet, although they recognize the extent of the problem, the very idea that human aggression has an instinctual basis seems overly pessimistic to many persons; they prefer to attribute the vast amount of war and fighting to the imperfections of existing societies. Admitting an instinctual basis of aggression seems tantamount to accepting the inevitability of war and killing; putting the blame on societal imperfections seems more hopeful since societies, presumably, can be changed. In part, this reaction stems from a misconception of instinct (which I will attempt to clarify) and in part from a reluctance to face up to the great aggressive potential that exists within each of us.

Societies have, indeed, undergone many changes but human aggression is still with us. It is my belief that a solution to the problems posed by aggression can best be approached by taking full account of the realities involved, including the reality of our instinctual heritage, the biological basis of primate aggression. If accepting the instinctual basis of aggression seems pessimistic, it is only so in the sense that aggression will always be a problem that humans must struggle with. But this does not mean that war and killing are inevitable, nor does it provide any justification or excuse for their perpetuation.

Those who think there is an instinct of aggression which justifies war as well as those who would deny instincts and place the blame for human aggression on social imperfections have too narrow a view of instinct. They are equating instinct with a fixed action pattern, one that completely determines behavior and is unaffected by learning or social experience. But, as we have seen in the discussion of attachment, primate instincts do not produce fixed behavior; rather, they set boundaries within which learning and social experience operate. To say there is an instinctual basis for primate aggression is to say that various aggressive actions are easy to learn and, under a variety of existing environmental conditions, will be learned. The biological equipment—muscle, teeth, jaws, hormones, parts of the brain and nervous system, and structures of display—is present, as are social customs which reinforce and channel the way this equipment is used. Aggression has evolved in primates for the survival of both individuals and groups. In what follows, I will summarize the forms and functions of aggression in monkeys and apes. This discussion will draw on field studies, particularly of chimpanzees, baboons, and gorillas; on the summaries of Hall (1968) and Washburn and Hamburg (1968); and on the overall perspective provided by Lorenz in his somewhat speculative book *On Aggression*.

The Evolution of Aggression in Primates. Aggression is typically defined as action harming or damaging, attempting to harm, or threatening to inflict harm on another animal. The definition should be broad enough to include redirected or displaced aggression, as when attack is directed against inanimate objects or against oneself. Aggressive actions are accompanied by movements and expressions that are fairly easy to recognize, especially among closely related species. For example, we have no difficulty knowing what it means when a baboon bares his teeth or when a chimp advances with great shouts, throwing rocks, and waving branches in the air (nor when a dog growls menacingly or a cat hisses). There is some question in the literature over whether predation—the killing of other animals for food—should be termed aggression. Some ethologists wish to restrict the definition of aggression to actions within a species, thus ruling out predation. Lorenz, for example, points out that when lions or wolves kill their prey, analysis of their facial expressions indicates that they are not angry, as they are when fighting with others of their species. Wolves and lions are not primates, however, and although it is true that most aggression takes place within species, I agree with Washburn and Hamburg (1968) who suggest a broad enough definition to include predation. They state that. "...if one is concerned with aggressive behavior in men, the degree to which human carnivorous and predatory activity is related to human aggressiveness should be kept open for investigation and not ruled out by definition (p. 463)."

Aggression is an instinctually bounded system involving the arousal of powerfully motivating emotions, most notably anger. As with other instinctual-emotional systems such as attachment and separation, we should think of it as a total, integrated pattern which, for purposes of discussion, may be broken down into its action, physiological, and subjective components. The actions of aggression are its most noticeable aspect. Fighting, biting, clawing, hitting, loud sounds such as shrieks and growls, threat gestures such as the baring of teeth or positioning for attack, as well as subtler actions such as widening of the eyes or the erection of body hair to create an appearance of greater size, are all prominent. Among the apes, aggressive actions tend to be highly *ritualized* into threat displays, the assertion of dominance, and appeasement gestures; actual fighting is infrequent.

The physiological component of aggression involves portions of the brain and nervous system as well as hormonal systems which interact with brain and body. Of special importance is the male sex hormone testosterone. Farmers and breeders have known about the role of testosterone in aggression for centuries, turning potentially aggressive bulls into placid steers with castration. In the nonhuman primates, differences between males and females are more marked than among humans; the males are larger, stronger and more aggressive. Adult male baboons are twice as big as adult females and possess large canine teeth that are lacking in the female. Similar differences in size, strength, body structure, and aggressiveness can be seen in chimpanzees, gorillas, and most other monkeys and apes. A number of experiments (summarized by Washburn and Hamburg) have demonstrated the importance of testosterone in the production of aggressive behavior in monkeys and apes. For example, female monkeys who are given testosterone early in life become more active and aggressive—initiating rough play and displaying threats—as compared with control females who were not given this hormone. These differences persist into later life.

The final component of aggression is its subjective aspect and, of course, we cannot know what a monkey thinks or feels when he is fighting. The subjective component is prominent in humans and we are familiar with our own experiences of anger and know of the subjective experience of others from their reports. Differences in brain structure between humans and other primates indicate that language and other complex cognitive skills that only humans possess serve some of the functions of the more primitive threat and display systems of monkeys and apes.

Several points should be stressed in summarizing this discussion of the components of aggression. The first is that action, physiological arousal, and subjective appraisal all function together as integrated patterns. The instinctual-emotional system of aggression is, like other instinctual areas, a bounded *system,* though it may be picked apart for purposes of discussion. Primates recognize cues in the environment such as the threat gestures of other species members or an attacking predator. Such recognition is a cognitive process, involving an appraisal of input. The specific nature of the appraisal obviously depends on the level of cognitive skill of the animal; it will differ widely, for example, among apes, two-year-old humans, and human adults. Appraisal brings with it physiological arousal and the actions characteristic of aggression. The components of the process occur together and include mutual facilitative effects. For example, once the system is activated, the animal responds to the cues of his own internal arousal as well as to input from the environment. Aggressive patterns tend to be ritualized; the animal goes through certain sequences of action such as the facial expressions and body movements of dominance and submission, until a termination point is reached.

The whole pattern is built in to primates as a potential blueprint of the form; recognition → emotional arousal → action sequence → termination. This blueprint comprises the boundaries of the instinctual area of aggression. How these boundaries are filled in—that is, how the blueprint is transformed into actuality in the adult animal—depends on the learning and social experience that occur over the years of development. The biological structure for aggression exists; primates have the equipment and the propensity to use it. Monkeys raised in a laboratory environment of total isolation, and thus deprived of all social experience, eventually lose the ability to protect themselves or engage in adaptive aggression, but all natural environments provide ample opportunity for the young monkey or ape to exercise his aggressive equipment. In fact, most social play of juvenile primates involves fighting and practice at dominance. Schaller, for example, describes the young gorilla versions of tug-of-war and king-of-the-mountain, as well as the usual rough-and-tumble rolling about and chasing. Similar aggressive play, as well as experiments at aggressive interaction with older males and females, is very frequent among primates of all species. Out of the years of social experience with aggressive play, the instinctually-bounded propensities become shaped into ritualized, well-integrated patterns.

In sum, the reality of primate biology makes aggression easy to learn and hard to unlearn; easy to engage in and hard to inhibit. With this conception in mind, we may now consider the adaptive purposes served by primate aggression and then examine some specific examples of the patterning of aggression in different species.

The Function of Aggression in Primates. Compared to other mammals, primates are a fairly aggressive group. From the perspective of evolution we may ask what purposes are served by aggression. Generally speaking, more aggressive animals control territory and, because of this, access to food. Among mammals, the male tends to be the primary aggressive actor, and the most aggressive males control reproduction by asserting their rights to receptive females. In these two ways—control of food and reproduction—the more aggressive animals gain a tremendous survival advantage since they are less likely to starve and more likely to reproduce. Aggression serves these purposes in many vertebrates where control of territory, male dominance hierarchies, and control of reproduction are primary adaptive mechanisms. These same functions are seen in primates, but they do not provide a complete picture of primate aggression. An organized group of animals can be much more successful at territorial control than a single individual no matter how aggressive he may be. Primates, as we have seen, are group living forms—King Kong, the image of the superaggressive individual ape, does not correspond to anything in primate reality. Aggression of all monkeys and apes functions within the context of social organization. It is patterned and ritualized and, although the aggression of dominant males is central to the very creation of primate social organization, even the aggression of dominant males is controlled and expressed in predictable ways. *The evolutionary advantage of group living interacts with the general advantages of aggression leading to the control, channeling, and ritualization of aggression within primate groups.* The King Kongs were probably eliminated during the course of evolution because their uncontrolled aggression could not be channeled into successful group existence.

There is no reason to expect that a system as widespread as aggression will be restricted to a single purpose—for example, protection against predators; in fact, several functions are served by this general instinctual system. Let us examine primate aggression in three categories, each defined in terms of a general adaptive purpose. These categories are: (1) predation and protection—*aggression between species;* (2) territorial spacing—*aggression between groups* of the same or closely related species; and (3) social order and dominance hierarchies—*aggression within the primary group.* Aggression is most frequent in the last category and rarest in the first.

Aggression Between Species. The popular image of "wild" animals who are either running away or fighting with each other does not fit the facts. Conflict between different species is infrequent; most animals are indifferent to members of other species. The flight of animals in the wild is mainly due to a well-grounded fear of human hunters. But when animals become used to human observers they eventually come to ignore them also. Several water holes in Africa afford opportunities to observe many different species together. Washburn and Hamburg describe the scene as follows:

> ...it is not uncommon to see various combinations of baboons, vervet monkeys, warthogs, impala, gazelle of two species, zebra, wildebeest (gnu), giraffe,

elephant, and rhinoceros around one water hole. Even carnivores, when they are not hunting, attract surprisingly little attention. When elephants walk through a troop of baboons the monkeys move out of the way in a leisurely manner at the last second, and the same indifference was observed when impala males were fighting among baboons or when a rhinoceros ran through the troop. On one occasion two baboons chased a giraffe, but, except where hunting carnivores are concerned, interspecies aggression is rare. Most animals under most conditions do not show interest in animals of other species, even when eating the same food—warthogs and baboons frequently eat side by side.[3] (p. 468)

Although aggression between species is infrequent, some does occur. Primates are potential carnivores and field observers report baboons hunting and eating vervet monkeys, and chimpanzees killing and eating red colobus monkeys, young baboons, and bush pigs. Chimpanzees and baboons have been observed fighting with each other, presumably over control of territory. Many monkeys and apes also fight to protect themselves against predators: baboons, for example, have been observed fighting with leopards and chasing cheetahs. These two forms of *interspecific* aggression—predation and protection against enemies—are dependent on local conditions, such as the available food supply and the presence of other species. Most monkeys and apes can survive quite well on a diet of fruit, vegetables, and insects; meat eating is infrequent. Nevertheless, chimpanzees are predators and there are even reports of their capturing and attempting to eat human infants. In sum, although aggression between species is infrequent, primates have the potential to hunt, kill, and fight furiously when attacked.

Aggression Between Groups. Aggression is much more frequent among animals of the same species. Lorenz presents a clear discussion of why this is so. One's vital interests are most directly related to other species members who eat the same food, live in the same habitat, and mate with the same animals. Survival depends on a sensitive balance between population density and available food supply. Since members of the same species eat the same food it is crucial that they spread out over as wide a food-supplying territory as possible. Thus, *species spacing* is the major adaptive function of aggression between groups of the same species.

Earlier in this chapter I described the behavior of fighting fish who, in response to the colorful markings of members of their own species, attack and drive them off their territory. This was an example of aggression in the service of species spacing in a nonsocial animal. Since primates are social, they obviously cannot spread out as single individuals. The individual is

[3] From Phyllis C. Jay (ed.), *Primates: Studies in Adaptation and Variability.* Copyright © 1968 by Holt, Rinehart and Winston, Inc. This and all other excerpts from this work are reprinted by permission of Holt, Rinehart and Winston, Inc.

replaced by the troop or primary group and it is such primary groups who fight to protect territory. As was true with predation and protection, the amount of *intergroup* aggression is dependent on local conditions, particularly the availability of food, and on differences between species. Gibbons are the most aggressive of the apes in defending territory (Ellefson, 1968), and gorillas the most nonchalant (Schaller, 1963). Since intergroup aggression for species spacing is dependent on local conditions, and since it is interwoven with primate social organization, it is likely to be more variable than is the case with simpler animals. For example, with ample food and a low population density there is less need for intergroup fighting. Studies of many primate species demonstrate this sort of balance. Given these variations, however, intergroup conflict is more the rule than not and most groups of monkeys and apes keep their distance from other groups.

Aggression Within Primate Groups. Aggressive encounters between members of the local or primary group are far more frequent than either intergroup or interspecies aggression. Several important functions are served by this *intragroup* aggression. Conflicts within monkey and ape groups tend to be well structured in accord with dominance hierarchies and rituals of display. These hierarchies and rituals allow aggression to be expressed without serious injury, most of the time. Most encounters consist of threats, counterthreats, and appeasement gestures. Minor fights and chases occur but fighting that might produce serious injury is infrequent. Thus, *the mechanisms that control and channel the expression of aggression provide organization and order to primate social life.* This is one of the central—perhaps one of the most important—functions served by aggression within the local group. Group living, the division of labor, the advantage that the group has in protecting its members against predators, and providing for the care of infants—all survival related functions—necessitate some means of organization. Dominant males are the leaders of most monkey and ape groups; they determine where the group will move, where it will look for food, where it will sleep at night, and what it will do when attacked. Many interchanges in the daily life of the group are determined by dominance. When several animals arrive at a source of food the problem of who eats first is solved by dominance. This prevents a free-for-all which would waste energy, spoil the food, and cause injury. Dominance plays a similar role in determining access to sexually receptive females and in settling potential disputes over local territory—for example, who gets to pass first when two animals meet on a trail.

It may be said that dominance hierarchies are the monkey and ape forerunners of government. I can't stress how important an evolutionary step this creation of social order is. It marks the line between primitive animals, who can only act as individuals or whose group behavior is determined by rigidly fixed patterns, and the emergence of social acts that are relatively flexible and responsive to changing environmental circumstances.

The social-order function of dominance provides an interesting example in the evolution of interacting systems. We have seen that aggression is advantageous in predation, the general control of territory, and species spacing. Primates were evolving in the direction of greater aggression, especially toward own species members. At the same time, the need to care for infants, attachments, and social bonds were evolving, all of which tended to pull group members together. Some means was then required which would allow aggressive individuals to live together in close groups without tearing each other apart—some means of controlling and redirecting aggression. Dominance hierarchies were evolution's solution to this problem. It is important to stress that the structures controlling the expression of aggression are as much a part of the primate heritage as are the propensities to fight. Finally, it is worth noting that aggression within the group varies from species to species and with local conditions. Baboons and macaques are very aggressive, with frequent and intense threats and assertions of dominance; chimpanzees have an open or loose social organization and relatively less fighting; gorillas are quite placid (though there is no question about the dominance of the larger males in these last two species).

Local conditions, particularly changes in what the group is accustomed to, may upset the balance and lead to a breakdown in the social control of dominance. Washburn and Hamburg (1968) describe a group of macaque monkeys who lived in captivity for two years under the dominance of a single male without a serious fight. When this dominant male was removed, the social order continued peacefully for two weeks, whereupon the number two animal asserted his power. Serious fighting broke out, two infants were killed in the melee, and several adults suffered severe canine bites. This example shows how, in the normal course of events, dominance serves to prevent fighting. It also illustrates the instinctual primacy of dominance, since all the animals had ample food, opportunities for grooming, and adequate sexual outlets. As Washburn and Hamburg put it:

> Being dominant appears to be its own reward—to be highly satisfying and to be sought, regardless of whether it is accompanied by advantage in food, sex, or grooming. In the long run, position guarantees reward, but in the short run, position itself is the reward, as this monkey's actions suggest; satisfaction apparently comes from others being unable to challenge effectively, as well as from more tangible rewards. (p. 473)

Other examples illustrate how abnormal living conditions can upset the social order. For instance, Zuckerman (1932) was persuaded that baboons were a particularly vicious species on the basis of the amount of serious fighting he observed in a London zoo. Subsequent observations of baboons in the wild have failed to confirm these early reports and it now appears that the fighting Zuckerman observed was a result of the abnormally restrictive zoo environment. It was as if an anthropologist from Tralframadore were to observe the inmates of a typical prison and conclude that all human beings were surly and uncooperative. The natural environment is not always benign or stable, of course: failures of vegetation, disease, and other factors may upset the ecological balance. But few naturally occurring events are as disruptive as being locked in a small cage and, within a fairly wide range, aggression within the group is expressed in accord with dominance hierarchies and rituals of display.

The expression and control of aggression within the primary group results from an interaction of biological givens and social experience. The male possesses greater size and strength, fighting teeth, especially strong neck and jaw muscles, and hormones such as testosterone which—in interaction with parts of the brain and nervous system—initiate and intensify the emotional state of rage or anger. Aggressive action is then practiced in play during the years of development. In the adult, aggression meets with consistent social rewards. The dominant males get what they want—first call on food and sex and the freedom to push others around. Other animals are attracted to dominant males and will move to be near them, groom them, and in other ways show their respect and admiration. At the same time, the expression of aggression is channeled within limits that all members of the group understand and adhere to. Let us look briefly at the specific form of aggression of three species—baboons, gorillas, and chimpanzees.

Baboon Aggression. More field data is available on baboons than for the other two species (perhaps because they live in the open). The following account draws on Washburn and DeVore (1961) and Hall and DeVore (1965). Baboon society is among the most tightly structured of all the nonhuman primates. Dominance is the basic organizing principle. Males are much bigger, stronger, and more aggressive than females and, among the males, there is a definite, though complex, hierarchy. Rather than a simple linear "pecking order," the hierarchy is constructed around shifting coalitions of the leading males. Even with this complexity, there is still usually one largest male who: (1) has primary access to sexually receptive females, (2) engages in more aggression than any other troop member, (3) leads the group in attacks against predators, (4) has the greatest amount of submissive behavior directed towards him, and (5) is most active in protecting mother-infant pairs. Much of this aggression consists of ritualized threats, chases, and fights that stop short of serious injury. Baboons engage in a great deal of this action; their highly structured social organization seems to require a consistent expression and reassertion of dominance relations. Typical components of threatening behavior include: yawns which display the teeth, pacing about in a tense manner, eyebrow-raising, barks, grunts, roars, teeth-grinding, ear-flattening, raising of the hair around the head, and shaking of rocks and branches. Fighting behavior includes: the charging run, hitting, pushing and rubbing the other animal on the ground, and biting which ranges from mild incisor nips to serious canine wounds. Threatening without actual contact is more frequent than actual fighting and most sequences end with the less dominant animal running away or making his submissive fear known by lying on the ground, giving a "fear grin," and in other ways.

Redirection of aggression is important and takes several forms. When a dominant animal threatens a less dominant one, it is not uncommon for the less dominant one to then threaten an animal below him in the hierarchy. Thus, A threatens B who, since he cannot aggress against A, threatens C, and so on down the line. Such behavior serves to reinforce the dominance hierarchy through the group. Occasionally, aggression will be redirected against inanimate objects as when an aroused animal hits trees or pulls on rocks. Another form of redirected aggression occurs when a dominant male is aroused but prevented from directing his aggression against the source of arousal. Hall and DeVore describe an instance when a tame baboon was introduced into a troop. The dominant male attempted to threaten the intruder who took refuge near the human observers, thus preventing the normal expression of aggression. The dominant male thereupon redirected his aggression at a number of other animals in the troop—as if he were "taking it out on" whoever came near. Redirected aggression is, thus, another way in which threat and fighting are channeled within the social organization.

Gorilla Aggression. The following account is drawn mainly from Schaller's (1963, 1965) description of the mountain gorilla. In contrast to the popular stereotype which pictures the gorilla as a ferocious and terrifying beast, gorillas in their natural habitat are, in Schaller's words, "rather amiable vegetarians." They live in cohesive groups of from five to thirty animals and spend their time leisurely moving from place to place, foraging for food. Their great size exempts them from the predation of other animals (except man) and they themselves do not hunt or kill. Contact with other gorilla groups vary; in some instances there is a tolerance and intermingling, while on other occasions aggressive threats between dominant males drive the groups apart. The ecology of the area seems to provide ample food for all, making group spacing less of a necessity.

Within the primary group there is clear organization based on the dominance of the single, largest male. The movements of the group during the day, how far they will travel, where and when they stop or nest for the night, are all determined by this dominant leader.

The dominance structure in gorilla groups is maintained with much less effort and hoopla than in baboon troops. Placidity and tolerance are the rule among gorillas. Dominance is typically asserted with a brief stare, a single tap with the hand, an incipient charge, or, much more rarely, with biting or wrestling. In the large majority of cases the submissive animal simply moves away in response to a stare or movement from the dominant animal.

Gorillas do engage in a highly ritualized chest-beating display which seems to be a displacement activity to channel the emotions of excitement, fear, and anger. The display, which can be quite complex, consists of a series of hoots, the placing of a leaf or other vegetation between the lips in symbolic feeding, rising on the hind legs, the throwing of vegetation, beating on the chest and kicking the legs, running sideways while swatting trees, shaking branches, and thumping the ground. The complete display is only carried out by full-grown males, usually in response to man, other groups, or the displays of other apes.

Finally, it should be stressed that gorillas are individualistic and that the behavior of any particular group depends on the idiosyncracies of its dominant male as well as on local conditions. The placidity and relative lack of aggression that Schaller saw depends on the ample food supply and lack of danger in the environment where his observations were made, as well as on the particular instinctual boundaries of aggression in this species.

Chimpanzee Aggression. Two recent field studies are available on chimpanzees, one by Reynolds (1965) and the other by Lawick-Goodall (1965, 1968a, 1971). They reveal some interesting differences resulting from life in differing environments, as well as the commonalities which I will concentrate on here.

In contrast to the relatively structured group life of baboons and gorillas, chimpanzee social organization is loose and informal. There is no clear primary group, but rather, a shifting array of small groups or bands which mingle, come together into larger clusters, break up, and reform. Social organization seems more dependent on affectionate family ties, primarily between a mother and her children, than on the male dominance of baboons and gorillas. It is interesting to note that chimpanzees engage in a great deal of mutual grooming and touching in contrast to gorillas who display very little. These affectionate interactions may serve some of the purposes of group bonding served by dominance in the baboon and gorilla.

Aggression does play an important part in chimpanzee life, however. The animals that Lawick-Goodall observed were predators—they hunted and killed monkeys, bush pigs, and other animals for food. Aggressive interactions with other groups were difficult to determine because of the lack of fixed group structure. Some dominance and aggression was observed within the central group, following the typical form in which larger males asserted their right to food or local space. Some fighting was observed but, again, aggression was the exception rather than the rule. Threat gestures include glaring, waving the arms, running toward the victim, ground slapping, branch shaking, and loud calling. The threatened or attacked animal usually runs off, sometimes screaming. Appeasement gestures are common and consist of an appeasement grin; touching the dominant animal on the arms, lips, or scrotum; or presenting (assuming a posture suitable for sexual intercourse) if the subordinate is female. Displacement activities seem more common in chimpanzees than most other species and include redirecting aggression toward other animals, hitting or loud drumming on trees, shaking branches, and throwing vegetation and rocks. Chimpanzee "carnivals," characterized by extremely loud yells, thumping, and running about for as long as several hours, are reported by many observers. They seem to be a displacement activity in which general excitement, fear, and aggression are discharged.

Chimpanzees are clearly the most intelligent of the nonhuman primates. Lawick-Goodall observed them using tools and even making crude tools (modifying twigs or sticks to be used in getting insects out of a nest). Their greater intelligence, communicative ability, and particular environmental conditions account for the greater flexibility of their social structure and the lack of fixed hierarchical behavior.

In summary, we have seen how aggression plays several roles in species who differ in their biological equipment and in the environments in which they live. Although aggression is a central instinct in all monkeys and apes, the boundaries of expression are wide, ranging from the frequent aggressive interchanges of baboons to the peaceful tolerance of gorillas. Aggression may play a role in predation (as it does with chimpanzees), territorial spacing (most prominent in gibbons), or hierarchial organization (of baboons and gorillas). As we look ahead to the role of aggression in man, we can expect it to serve important functions, but we should also be prepared to look for forms specific to the human species. A clear lesson of the field studies is that of *species specificity*: one cannot generalize from one species to another with any degree of certainty. Each species must be studied directly in the environment within which it lives. As we will see in the next chapter, man lacks many of the display structures so prominent in the ritualized aggression of monkeys and apes. We do not flip our eyelids back nor make our body hair stand on end. Human language becomes the primary means of communication introducing greater flexibility and, at the same time, more possibilities for misunderstanding messages. The redirection or displacement activity observed in ape aggression acquires an ever-wider scope in humans.

Sexuality

Sexuality, in the narrow sense of sexual intercourse between male and female animals, plays a relatively minor role in the life of monkeys and apes as compared to its role in the lives of human beings. Some early accounts of monkey and ape societies saw sexuality as the prime force in binding groups together. Chimpanzees, for example, were described as living in "harem groups" composed, supposedly, of a male, his female sexual partners, and their children. The recent field observations have proven this view mistaken, however. Chimpanzee social organization is not structured in harems; promiscuity is the rule. When a female is receptive, many males engage in sexual intercourse with her.

While the particulars differ among species, clear periods of estrous are the rule among all the nonhuman primates. This means that the female is sexually receptive during a relatively brief period during her menstrual cycle. Receptivity is signaled during this estrous period by outward signs such as a swelling of the genital area and presenting behavior in which the female approaches males and assumes a posture suitable for copulation. When the female is not in the receptive phase of her cycle, which is most of the time, neither she nor the males are particularly interested in sex. Here are some representative examples:

The female sexual cycle averages 35 days in chimpanzees, with a period of genital swelling and receptivity of from 6 to 7 days. While there is some tendency for the more dominant males to claim first access, tolerance and promiscuity are the rule. Lawick-Goodall observed one instance in which seven males copulated with a single female. Frequently, the male will engage in a brief courtship display, swinging about from branch to branch with hair erect, prior to copulation.

The cycle is similar for baboons, about 35 days, with swelling and heightened receptivity during a period of 8 days. Dominance and aggression play a central role in mating, as one would expect from baboons. During the early days of a female's sexual swelling the less dominant males copulate with her, but as she approaches the maximum point—which is also the time at which fertilization is most likely to occur—the dominant male claims exclusive rights and they form a consort pair. All of this is accompanied by a good deal of threatening and fighting among the males.

In accord with their generally placid orientation toward life, gorillas don't seem to get very excited about sex. Schaller observed remarkably few instances of sexual intercourse in the wild. From studies of captive gorillas, it is known that the female cycle is 30 to 31 days with a period of receptivity lasting 3 to 4 days. Marked sexual swelling is absent and intercourse is likely to be initiated by the female. Dominance is apparently not much of a factor. For example, Schaller observed a subordinate male engaged in intercourse with a female near the group's dominant male who took little notice of them.

The examples of sexuality in these three species differ somewhat, but the overall pattern is typical for the nonhuman primates. Sexual interest and sexual behavior, on the part of both males and females, is confined to the relatively brief periods of receptivity in the female cycle. The human sexual cycle is not characterized by such periodicity. Given some fluctuations in excitability, the human female is potentially receptive at all times and intercourse can and does occur at any point in her cycle. We are, thus, a much sexier species than any of our primate relatives, which is interesting since western religious beliefs tend to describe sex as a baser instinct—more beast-like than human. A fuller discussion of human sexuality must be delayed until later chapters. What is clear from a consideration of sexuality in monkeys and apes is that it is not a central force in their group life. It occurs too infrequently and it is obvious that social organization is maintained in its absence. But this is only true if we restrict the definition of sexuality to mating behavior between males and females. If we expand the definition to include a wider variety of pleasurable or *sensual* interactions between group members—that is, if we redefine sexuality as love and contact comfort—then we are talking about instinctual-emotional patterns that play a major role in the maintenance of primate groups.

Freud, whose views may lie at the root of the belief that sexuality is a central force within primates, uses the term in a very broad sense. Sexuality, in his theory, begins as the pleasurable sucking of infancy and progresses through a series of stages, each characterized by pleasurable stimulation of some particular zone of the body. Klein (1969) argues that *sensuality* is a more appropriate term for what Freud describes. When we redefine sexuality in this broadened fashion it becomes synonymous with love, with contact-comfort and other components of mother-infant interactions, with grooming—in short, with the many pleasurable, stimulating interactions that most monkeys and apes engage in. I am not arguing that we broaden the definition in this way, but, rather, pointing out the way the concept of sexuality has come to be used by Freud and later psychoanalysts.

A more accurate way to phrase these ideas is as follows: *Love,* consisting of a wide variety of pleasurable-sensual interactions, is a central force in binding primate groups together. Its most common and frequently expressed form is seen in mother-infant interactions—what has already been described as attachment. The components of these interactions include holding, touching, cuddling, rocking, looking at the face, cooing and other sounds, and playing. Of the various tactile, visual, and auditory interactions, the tactile are perhaps most important—"contact comfort" captures both the importance of touch and the pleasurable emotional state. In addition to mother-infant love, pleasurable-sensual interactions occur between other group members. Grooming is the most frequent of these activities, and it is not uncommon for animals to spend up to several hours a day in the intense tactile contact provided by grooming. Play also involves mutual contact, some of which is related to love, though most of it relates to aggression.

Sexuality (again in the sense of copulation between male and female adults) is not a completely separate system from the pleasurable-sensual interactions of love. In some species, such as the chimpanzee, copulation may be accompanied by an increase in grooming and other loving interactions, though in other species this is not the case. Harlow's monkeys who were deprived of love as infants were uninterested and inept at copulation, suggesting that mother-infant love is a necessary precursor to adult sexual behavior. Some components of specifically adult sexual behavior, such as the presenting motions of the female or the pelvic thrusts of copulation, are instinctually built in and released by hormonal stimulation and other cues; typically, however, these actions are practiced in play and depend on social experience for their normal development.

We can say that adult sexual behavior in the nonhuman primates is one partially independent subclass within the more general instinctual system of attachment-love. The many pleasurable-sensual components of love are a central force in binding groups together with specifically sexual acts playing a relatively small role. Species differences, as well as the differences brought on by changes in the environment should alert us to the possibility that specifically sexual actions may play a more important role in the human species. Of particular importance is the loss of estrous, a basic biological difference between the human female and her monkey and ape precursors.

Play, Curiosity, and Exploration

Anyone who has observed young primates, be they monkey, ape or human, cannot fail to note the considerable amount of time devoted to play and exploration. (Indeed, these activities are not restricted to primates, as those who have had a litter of kittens or puppies in their house can testify.)

Observation of monkeys and apes in the wild, as well as under controlled conditions, has shown that play and exploration are strongly motivated systems. Young animals spend more time engaged in play (when not eating or sleeping) than in any other activity. Play and exploration are not "secondary" to other motivated behavior such as eating or sensual pleasure; they are strongly motivated in their own right. Primates—and especially young primates—possess an instinctual-emotional system which causes them to: (1) seek out situations at particular levels of novelty and interact with them until they become familiar, and (2) engage in social play with peers and older species members. The emotions involved in exploration and play have not received as much attention from psychologists as anger or anxiety, but they exist and have been variously labeled interest, surprise, the joy of play, or excitement. Emotional reactions such as fear, anger, and love are also involved in play. In fact, the main function of social play is to *practice primate social skills* and, accordingly, much of this play consists of modified versions of separation, fighting, and dominance. Play can be divided into two categories: nonsocial play—including manipulation of objects and exploration of the environment—and social play. Activities in each of these categories are important to the survival of the group and the individual. Let us consider these adaptive or survival-related functions and then examine nonsocial and social play.

The Functions of Play and Exploration. There is a tendency, stemming from the puritanical overevaluation of work, to view play as something with no serious function or purpose. This is what the very word play means to many persons; it is defined as harmless fun; as the way one spends time when the serious work of life is completed. This view is incorrect in my opinion; it rests on too narrow a definition of work.

Since young primates spend a great deal of their lives playing and exploring, these activities are probably serving functions other than purposeless fun. The emotions that strongly motivate play and exploration are instinctual systems which are built in because of their adaptive importance to species survival. What important functions, then, are served by play and exploration?

Ethologists distinguish between animals whose survival depends on highly specialized structures and action patterns and animals who are "opportunists"—specialists in nonspecialization. Opportunistic species are more flexible and can change their way of life (within limits) as the environment changes; they can adapt to many different environments. Morris (1964) points to the restless curiosity of opportunists, their love of the new or novel, and the fact that they possess nervous systems which "abhor inactivity." Lacking highly structured or fixed behavior patterns, the opportunistic animal must sample each new environment, testing whether a novel object is edible, dangerous, a potential source of pleasure, or otherwise useful. Out of such sampling, exploring, testing, and playing, there gradually emerges a stable adaptation to a particular environment.

Primates are among the most opportunistic of species and, within the nonhuman primates, the chimpanzee is the most curious and playful. We can say that as one ascends the phylogenic scale, moving from less to more complex species, flexibility, the width or broadness of instinctual boundaries, curiosity, exploration, and play all increase. Within any species, the young have the most to learn and, hence, the greatest need to sample and test the environment with play and exploration. In addition, primates all have relatively complex social lives. Life within the monkey or ape group depends on an intimate and well-ingrained knowledge of the "rules" of social behavior: on what to do when the dominant male approaches, or a female in estrous presents; on how to groom and be groomed; on what noises signal the approach of danger. The play of young primates provides practice for all these social skills. Out of the many hours of social play that typifies the life of the growing monkey or ape, he literally learns how to be a well-functioning group member. Animals deprived of peer play experience are markedly deficient in adult social skills. Exploration and play are crucial parts of the flexible primate capacity to adapt to and utilize a variety of environmental opportunities. In addition, play provides the opportunity to learn and practice the social skills so central to primate life.

Nonsocial Play and Exploration. A good deal of nonsocial play helps to develop motor skills and perfect coordination with trees and other objects in the environment. We must remember that the large majority of monkeys and apes are arboreal; they live in trees and many are extremely skillful at moving swiftly about among the branches. Although equipped with bodies that permit swift arboreal movement—arm joints of sufficient flexibility to permit brachiation, prehensile tails, strong muscles, and excellent coordination—a good deal of practice is required to perfect these skills. Gibbons, for example, who are among the most graceful of primate acrobats, practice a variety of movements and postures in their youth. Swinging, climbing, jumping, running, somersaulting, manipulating of hands and feet in interaction with trees, branches, rocks or whatever is available is common to all monkeys and apes. In addition, the practice of nonsocial play familiarizes the young animal with the characteristics of his environment. The monkey learns which branch will support his weight or which creeper it is safe to fall on. Gibbons become so skillful that even if a branch breaks while they are swinging on it, they can move on without falling. Such extreme skill, perfected through many days of practice, aids the animal when approaching danger makes rapid flight a life-preserving necessity.

Exploration of the environment is another activity which, like play, is strongly motivated. One obvious function of such activity is the discovery of food sources; most monkeys and apes are incessant foragers who must seek out the variety of vegetation, fruits, and insects that make up their diet. In addition, exploration allows the animal to check the environment for dangers, and leads to that general familiarization with territory which makes a new area "home." In the earlier discussion of separation anxiety, I noted a relationship between the security of the familiar, as in clinging to the mother, and the excitement of the unfamiliar—the motivation of exploration. These two tendencies balance each other with fear or anxiety on the one hand, and interest and excitement on the other. The balance can be tipped either way depending on the level of novelty or familiarity that confronts the animal. Moderately novel stimuli motivate curiosity and exploration while extremely unfamiliar situations provoke fear and a seeking of security. Young monkeys, placed in a strange situation, will cling to mother until some of the novelty wears off and then they will make tentative forays into the new environment. A novel situation will gradually become familiar with sufficient exploration and eventually the monkey will become bored with it. In this way, a young animal progressively expands the sphere of his familiar territory until he acquires a thorough knowledge of his home area. One may think of the system as an interaction between the young animal's level of familiarity and the opportunities of the environment which stimulate or draw him forth to new interactions. Moderate levels of novelty motivate exploration by arousing the young primate's innate curiosity and interest. We see in this instinctual system the precursor of the balance between quest and rest so characteristic of human beings, the most opportunistic of primates.

So far, we have seen that exploration and a general interaction with the physical environment are useful in the search for food, the sensing of danger, the development of motor skills, and the creation of security through familiarization. As a final example of the adaptive function of nonsocial play, let me briefly discuss the use of tools among chimpanzees. Chimpanzees are the only primates who use tools in their natural environment. Lawick-Goodall observed them throwing rocks when angry, usually at random, but occasionally aimed. More common was the use of sticks to gather food. The chimps would modify a stick by picking off leaves and twigs until they had a clean pole. They would then "fish" for termites by pushing the pole into a termite hole, waiting until the insects attached themselves to it, and then withdrawing it and licking them off. Young chimps were able to learn termite fishing by imitating their mothers.[4] Their ability to learn by imitation sets them apart from other monkeys and apes and places them closer to humans who rely heavily on imitation.

Laboratory studies of tool use have also demonstrated the important role of play. Many years ago Köhler (1925) noted that chimps were capable of manipulating sticks and boxes in an intelligent fashion to obtain food. His ideas about the role of "insight" in such problem solving were more carefully investigated by Birch (1945). Birch studied the relation of free play with sticks to the use of these same sticks to solve problems such as raking in food that was beyond the animal's reach. Few of the chimps that Birch studied were able to solve the food-getting problem when they were initially presented with the sticks, unless they did so accidentally. Other animals were given the sticks for three days and, as is natural for chimpan-

---

[4] It is interesting to note that chimpanzees in captivity recognize and respond appropriately to their own reflection in a mirror; again something that is apparently beyond the intelligence of other monkeys and apes. For example, chimps become upset when they see colored markings that are placed on their head or face without their awareness. This suggests something like a "self-image" and shows, as does their ability to imitate, how their intelligence approaches that of human beings.

zees, played extensively with them. Out of this play experience, patterns developed in which the stick was used as a functional extension of the animal's arm. When the animals who had this play experience were presented with the problem of obtaining food beyond their reach, they all solved it within twenty seconds. The play had prepared them to use these tools in an adaptive fashion. It is reasonable to assume that the great amount of play with objects that young chimpanzees display in the wild serves a similar preparatory function in relation to the sort of tool use that Lawick-Goodall describes. It is logical to generalize the example of chimpanzees—the only nonhuman primate who uses tools—to man. As we will see when considering Piaget's theory of the development of intelligence, problem solving of all kinds grows out of the child's interaction, exploration, and play with the world of physical objects.

Social Play. The first social contact of the infant primate is its mother and we have seen the crucial significance of this attachment for later social functioning. As soon as the young animal is capable of moving about on his own, he begins to explore away from mother and it is not long before interaction with peers begins. The amount of time spent playing with peers rapidly increases until it becomes the dominant social activity throughout the child and juvenile periods, declining and giving way to grooming and other activities as the animal passes into adulthood.

If it is true that primate group attachment begins with the mother-infant bond, then play with agemates is the means by which this group attachment is fully developed. Peer play introduces the animal to the sights, sounds, smells, and, especially, the touch and feel of his group members. Through extensive play contact he acquires the rules and nuances of social communication. In Harlow's studies of early social isolation, the necessity for such social play was clearly shown. Rhesus monkeys who had peers to play with (but no real mothers) during early childhood were able to function as adequate group members when they grew up. Those who were raised with a normal mother, but without peer play, showed some of the same social deficiencies as monkeys raised in isolation or with dummy mothers.

Attachment to mother comes about via a number of interactions such as clinging and being held, sucking, looking, rhythmic moving, and so on. Attachment to agemates also involves a good deal of physical contact, though of a different form. The playing monkey or ape child is more mature than the clinging infant, and other systems, the most prominent of which is aggression, are involved in the physical interactions of play. A number of primate investigators agree that play is practice for later social interaction and communication. They also agree that the largest amount of such play is devoted to aggression and its control. Some sexual play, such as attempts to mount and pelvic thrusts, and some other forms of pleasurable, stimulating interactions have been observed, but by far the greatest amount of time is given to chasing, wrestling, mock attacks, and controlled biting. Some typical examples follow:

Juvenile male baboons spend practically all of their waking time chasing and fighting. An adult male is usually nearby and the play fighting is soundless. If one of the juveniles gets more seriously hurt—if a mock bite is carried too far—he breaks the silence with a squeal and the adult quickly interrupts the game. The large and dangerous canine teeth have not yet erupted in juveniles so that serious injury is unlikely. This play at aggression allows the juveniles to learn the rules before they are big enough—and before they possess their most potent weapons—to cause harm. Thus, they learn to express aggression within the controlled limits that make group life possible. The social play of young monkeys, chimpanzees, gorillas, and others are quite similar in this respect. Loizos (1967), in a chapter reviewing play behavior in primates, summarizes the findings of many field and laboratory workers as follows:

> In summary, social play between the sub-adult members of primate societies occupies the greater proportion of the time not spent in eating or sleeping. Patterns of social play are largely derived from those of agonistic (aggressive, combative) behavior, consisting of chasing, wrestling, tumbling, biting, dragging, and chewing. During play certain adjustments appear to take place which enable the young primate to function properly as an adult member of his species and to occupy a niche within the social organization of his particular group. Social play is generally agreed to contribute to the socialization process within each species. Young which have not had the opportunity for adequate play with conspecifics are, as Carpenter (1965) points out, faced with two options: "...to be 'maladjusted' within the group or to be excluded from the group." (p. 210)

Among the things that the young monkey or ape learns from aggressive play is the appropriate use of appeasement gestures which are so important in redirecting aggression or rendering it harmless. Chimpanzees show a particular expression, termed the "play face," in which the mouth is opened and the teeth bared. The play face, and related expressions and gestures, such as the "fear grin" let the other animals know that the action, while seeming aggressive, is all in fun. Baring the teeth for potentially dangerous biting would ordinarily arouse fear or counterattack, but the nuances of signals such as the play face let the other animal know that the attack is a game and that serious harm should not be expected. The play face and fear grin have their human counterpart in the smile, a baring of the teeth that signals friendship. When we smile at each other we, just like apes, are communicating, "See these dangerous weapons, I could bite you but I won't—you have nothing to fear."

Appeasement gestures, practiced and learned over the years of play, turn the aggression that could disrupt group living into a series of regulated exchanges that promote group cohesion. It is possible that the reason so much play is devoted to aggression and its control is that aggression is a more recently evolved system than attachment or anxiety. Because it is newer, it is not as smoothly functioning as these other systems. Aggressive primates must work at living in close groups and the "work" is accomplished through play aimed at perfecting the control and redirection of aggression.

SUMMARY

My purpose in this chapter has been to view primates from the evolutionary perspective and to develop a theory of instinctual-emotional systems. As complex species—the outcome of a long and many-faceted selection process—primates possess instinctual systems which set the limits or form the boundaries of their perceptions and actions. These instinctual systems are constructed in such a way that emotions—love, fear, anxiety, anger, pleasure, interest, and excitement—give special value to events in the animal's world and make particular actions likely to occur. In everyday terms, the animal's feelings tell him what to pay attention to and what to do.

Primates are social animals; from birth to death their lives are intimately bound up with the other members of their group. Because of this, and because they take a relatively long time to reach maturity, the specific shape of perceptions and actions is acquired through social experience. Primate instincts are flexible, compared to the fixed action patterns of simpler animals. The individual animal's development is influenced by his experience with his mother, his peers, the dominant males, and other group members.

The central social-instinctual areas—attachment-love, fear, separation anxiety, aggression and its control, sexuality, play, curiosity, and exploration—have been reviewed. Group existence is itself a major adaptive mechanism in primates, and bonds to the group are promoted in several ways. The first social relationship is that between the infant and its mother. Innate tendencies to cling, to suck, and to seek the pleasures of contact comfort interact with the maternal or caretaking responses of the mother to form this initial bond of love. Once attached, the infant experiences anxiety when apart from the secure familiarity of its mother. Thus, the primary social bond is promoted by the pleasures of love and the pain of separation anxiety.

The initial bond of love between infant and mother expands, via peer play, and is eventually seen as pleasurable physical contact between group members. Grooming is the most frequent form of contact between adults, and maternal behavior itself is an adult manifestation of strongly motivated physical contact.

Reactions of fear are displayed when the animal confronts unfamiliar situations, perceives the fear communications of other group members, and is confronted with threat gestures. A related emotion, anxiety, is evident when an attached infant is separated from his mother. With increasing social experience, attachment expands to include other group members and separation anxiety expands to become a general reaction to separation from the group.

Aggression is an adaptive characteristic; aggressive species are more likely to control territory (space and food) and to sire aggressive heirs by their control over sexual reproduction. Primates have evolved as a relatively aggressive group. Aggression between primates and other animals serves the functions of predation and protection against attack. Aggression between primate groups serves to space animals over a territory that is sufficiently large to support them. Both *interspecific* and *intergroup* aggression are less frequent than aggression within the primary group or troop. Since primates have evolved as group-living animals who, at the same time, are very aggressive, it was necessary that they develop a means of living closely together without tearing each other to bits. This is accomplished by the ritualization, redirection, and channeling of aggression within the group. Aggressive encounters between group members, although frequent in many primate species, are expressed within the structure of dominance hierarchies and rituals of display which usually prevent serious fighting or injury. The ritualization of aggression in dominance hierarchies is a major organizing principle in primate groups. In a sense, *dominance is the monkey and ape forerunner of government*. Groups are led by a dominant male who determines where they move, what they do when under attack, and a host of other actions that require the group to work together. The emotional reactions of anger and fear to threat must be added to the pleasure of love and the pain of separation anxiety, as powerful forces which bind and structure primate group life.

Although love is a central instinctual force, sexual relations between adults play a relatively small role in monkey and ape societies. Females manifest clear periods of estrus characterized by a swelling of the genital region and presenting behavior. Estrous periods are relatively brief, six to eight days out of the month, and sexual interest is low to nonexistent during the remainder of the female cycle. With some minor exceptions, monkey and ape societies are not organized around families—that is, around male-female pairs. This contrasts with human social organization which is structured around husband-wife pairs. The fact that the human female lacks estrus is an important biological difference which prepares the way for social organization that includes male-female pairs.

Primates are active explorers, "opportunists" who are prepared to take advantage of their surroundings. Exploration and nonsocial play are useful in the discovery of food, the development of motor skills, and familiarization with the environment. For example, play with sticks seems to be a necessary precursor to the use of such sticks as tools among chimpanzees. Moderately unfamiliar situations motivate exploration by arousing the animal's interest.

Young monkeys and apes spend a considerable amount of time playing with each other. This social play is the means by which attachment to the group is solidified. Most of the social skills necessary for normal adult functioning are perfected during the years of juvenile play. The majority of these play interactions consist of aggressive games; it is during play that the difficult task of channeling and redirecting aggression is carried out.

This completes the picture of our monkey and ape ancestors. We share many basic characteristics with them but also differ in important ways. We become attached to our mothers as infants, and experience anxiety on separation or in unfamiliar situations; as children we are curious explorers and spend much time playing with peers. And, certainly, our aggressiveness poses a perennial problem to group living and must be channeled and redirected.

The major differences stem from the increased intelligence made possible by the larger human brain. Earlier in this chapter I spoke of the three, interrelated components of emotion: physiological arousal, expressive action, and subjective experience. In gross ways, we do not differ too much from the other primates with regard to the first two components. Our internal physiology and autonomic and endocrine systems are similar; we also display some of the same facial expressions and body movements. We differ in that humans lack some of the body structures used to display anger and submission. It is in the area of subjective experience, however, that we radically part company with the other primates. Human intelligence and language make possible forms of experience and social life well beyond the capacity of even the smartest chimpanzee. The special evolution of the human brain has brought about one of those quantum leaps in species development—and it is to the special evolution of the human species that I now wish to turn.

chapter three

The Emergence of Man

Creatures intermediate between ape and man, who walked erect, used tools, and hunted in groups, have existed for some 2 million years. Members of the genus *Homo*—large-brained creatures who made more extensive use of tools, hunted large animals, and, sometime late in their evolution, acquired the use of fire—appeared at least 600,000 years ago. Man in his modern form, *Homo sapiens,* with a brain the size of ours, relatively well-perfected hunting techniques, cave art, burial and presumably other religious rituals, has existed for 60,000 years. Thus, the living monkeys and apes, whose social life we examined in the last chapter, are not the immediate ancestors of living men. There were a number of intermediary forms, missing links in the popular idiom, in the transition from ape to ape-man to man-ape to human being; forms which are now extinct.

Archeologists and paleontologists have done an amazing job in reconstructing the evolution of the human species from bones, tools, and other artifacts. Thanks to this work, our knowledge of the biological evolution of the species is relatively complete. Our knowledge of the social behavior of these early human and prehuman forms rests on much more speculative grounds, however. Customs, myths, family relationships, child-rearing practices, dominance, and other forms of social order leave no archeological records. Our speculations about the social life of early man must rest on other sources. We know the social behavior of the living apes, and can hypothesize that the chimpanzee is probably similar to the earliest ape-man. We can form hypotheses from such artifacts as stone tools, paintings, and burial grounds. And we know, of course, social life in existing cultures. Fortunately, a number of so-called primitive cultures—societies whose way of life may be quite similar to man of the last 60,000 years—have continued in existence until the present time. These hunting and gathering societies provide the most important data on the early forms of human society. Studies of these early societies give a picture of the basic forms of social organization from which modern culture has evolved.

The evolution of human society is a long and complex story and we must limit ourselves here. I will not attempt to trace human evolution or to review the archeological evidence, but will begin by discussing differences between apes and human beings and then move directly to a consideration of hunting and gathering societies. There will be no attempt at a comprehensive review of these societies nor of their evolution into the modern industrial state. Rather, I will examine them for the light they shed on the development of human culture over the relatively long time during which the hunting and gathering way of life was dominant. This review of early human culture will prepare the way for a general discussion of the dislocations introduced by rapid change which has, in a sense, outrun both our biological evolution and the evolution of our social customs. We can then examine man's social instincts: attachment, love, sexuality, fear, anxiety, aggression, play, curiosity, and exploration. All this will lead us to a view of the core conflicts of human life—those persisting issues that arise out of both biological and cultural evolution. The core conflicts—dependence-independence, pleasure and renunciation, aggression and its control—pose the issues that individuals and societies grapple with and attempt to resolve, each in their own way.

THE EMERGENCE OF MAN

The primate line that eventually led to the human species branched off from the other monkeys and apes several million years ago. A central innovation was the growth of the brain which has increased two and a half times in size over the last 2 to 3 million years. The earliest ape-men had brains of approximately 600 cubic centimeters (cc) volume—not much larger than that of the contemporary chimpanzee. The fire- and tool-using men of 600,000 years ago had a brain size of 1200 cc, while Neanderthal man of 100,000 years ago had a brain of 1500 cc, approximately the size of ours.

Change in brain size was interconnected with other changes in body and social life. The dexterity of hands, fingers, and thumbs improved. Fighting teeth and strong jaws decreased in size, and structures of display, used primarily in dominance, diminished. Language, made possible by a larger brain, came to replace these gestures in the communication of aggression, while tools took the place of fighting teeth and jaws.

The human brain is not only larger than the ape brain, it is less mature at birth and takes longer to reach its full size. For example, the brain of a human infant at birth is 24 percent of its adult size while that of the infant chimpanzee is 60 percent. The human brain gains 800 grams in weight during the first quarter of childhood while the chimpanzee brain gains only 110 grams (figures from Lenneberg, 1966b). This means that the human infant is less mature at birth and remains in a physically helpless state for a longer period of time. In addition, a slowly maturing brain remains open to certain kinds of learning—particularly the learning of language—that infants and young children show a special facility for. Adults can certainly learn new things after their brains have reached full size, but there does seem to be a critical period for language acquisition in childhood that is associated with the particular way in which the human brain matures.

The relative immaturity of the human infant necessitates more complex maternal skills on the part of the human mother. Human infants cannot cling the way baby monkeys and apes can. Their greater helplessness requires the mother to master complex skills of child care. These are learned within the context of human culture.

Culture is a very complex achievement that depends on the interaction of a variety of biological and social changes. Although growth of intelligence and language is crucial, other developments play their part. All living female monkeys and apes have brief, clearly signaled periods of estrous or sexual receptivity. Human females, on the other hand, are continuously receptive. This change in sexual physiology facilitates a form of social organization, the human family, that is different from that of monkeys and apes. Human societies are organized around male-female (husband-wife) pairs and this bonding together of pairs rests, in part, on the continuous sexual receptivity of the human female. The change in sexual physiology is related to the rise of stable families which, in turn, make possible a greater division of labor between male and female. And this, in turn, allows mothers the opportunity to care for their more helpless, slowly maturing infants.

The biological and social changes that we have been considering—larger brain, capacity for language and tool-use, more helpless and slowly maturing infants, loss of estrous, and capacity for social organization built on husband-wife pairs—are all interrelated. No one of them can be understood in isolation, and as we think of the gradual evolution of contemporary man, we must think of correlated changes in all these areas. For example, human culture requires a more complex system of communication than that found in any ape society. Language is this system and it, in turn, requires that the human infant be born in a less mature state. This, in its turn, requires some form of family organization in a social context which promotes and supports the adequate care of infants. Similar interdependencies exist with all of the evolving biological and social features. All of these changes eventually lead to human culture, a form of social organization at once similar and quite different from the ape societies that we examined in chapter 2.

Of all the changes brought about by human evolution, language is perhaps the most striking innovation. As Washburn and Hamburg (1968) put it:

> Just as the changed selection that came with tools led to increase in the parts of the brain controlling manual skills and to a reduction in the whole tooth-fighting complex, so the origin of language led to changes in parts of the brain ...and to a reduction or loss of most structures concerned with displays. In this sense the human body is in part a product of language and of the complex social life that language made possible. (p. 476)

As a way of approaching culture, let us look in a bit more detail at the contrast between language and the other systems of primate communication.

Primate Communication and Human Language

Communication among nonhuman primates can be very complex—more complex than that of any other mammal. At the same time, there is no form of communication among monkeys and apes that approximates language. Chimpanzees, the most intelligent of the living apes, do not use language in their natural environment. Baboons have a most complicated and well organized social life, a social life that requires a good deal of communication for its maintenance, but this is all accomplished without anything approximating language. Thus, it seems likely that nonlinguistic communication systems evolved as a necessary component of primate group living while language came later as a special adaptation of human beings. Since we continue to share the older systems of communication with monkeys and apes, a study of these will have a direct bearing on human communication and will emphasize the uniqueness of language. The following account draws on an excellent paper by Lancaster (1968) as well as the papers and reviews in Altmann (1967) and Lenneberg (1964).

Communication among monkeys and apes is accomplished with emotional display systems, the principal components of which are *facial expression, body posture and movement,* and *vocalizations.* These components typically occur together in patterns and their significance is dependent on the context in which the communication occurs. Nonhuman primates communicate information about their *emotional state;* for example, they assert their aggressive dominance, make known their fear of something in the environment, or grin to show appeasement. Communications around dominance-submission interactions are the most frequent kind among many monkeys and apes, in accord with the central role of dominance in their social organization. Many monkeys and apes vocalize only to draw attention to what they are communicating with their facial expressions and bodies—the vocalizations do not convey much specific information on their own. A baboon or chimp understands a typical emotional communication because it comes from another animal that he has had extensive experience with, usually in a situation that is familiar to both, and because information comes from several sources at once—that is, from facial expression, posture, gestures, and sounds.

Communication of emotional states using systems of display evolved early in primate evolution along with the development of group living. Although humans have lost many of the structures of display found in monkeys and apes, they are still capable of communicating emotional states—fear, anger, happiness, depression—in much the same way apes do. Prior to the acquisition of language, infants use these forms of communication which are, of course, transcultural. The parts of the brain and nervous system involved are phylogenetically "old" and are much the same in man and the other primates.

If monkeys and apes communicate a great deal of information about their emotional state, reference to the environment is extremely rare. In the wild, it is only found in special situations involving intense emotion such as predator alarms. The simplest form of reference to the environment is the naming of objects. Humans attach names to the important objects in their lives (*Mama, Dada, bottle*) as early as the first year of life. Although no monkey or ape uses even a rudimentary form of language in the wild, some experiments in teaching captive chimpanzees to use language are of interest since they highlight the differences in linguistic capacity between ape and man.

Some years ago, a psychologist and his wife (Hayes, 1951) adopted an infant chimpanzee named Viki whom they raised along with one of their own children. After six years of intensive effort, the Hayeses were only able to teach Viki four sounds that approximated English words. From this single experiment it appeared unlikely that a chimp could learn human language. More recently, the Gardners (1969) adopted a one-year-old chimp named Washoe. Reasoning that Viki's failure may have been due to deficiencies in the vocal apparatus that prevented her from speaking, rather than a lack of the necessary intelligence, the Gardners taught Washoe the sign language used by nonspeaking (deaf or deaf-mute) persons. Chimps have skillful fingers and Washoe mastered sign language sufficiently well to name a number of objects in her environment. What is more, once Washoe learned the name for something she could apply it in new or unfamiliar instances. For example, having learned the sign for *open* to a particular door, Washoe then used it for other closed doors, closed containers, a refrigerator, jars, and even the opening of a capped bottle of soda pop and a water faucet. Such intelligent generalization of object naming is typical of the early word use of human children.

The experiment with Washoe proves that object naming is not peculiar to humans. Chimpanzees seem to be intermediate between man and the other monkeys and apes in their ability to learn this first language skill, just as they are intermediate in their ability to use tools and in certain forms of their social organization.

Object naming is just the first step in the development of language, however. Although Washoe was able to master this step, the evidence indicates that this was as far as she got. In a discussion of the Gardners' experiment, Bronowski and Bellugi (1970) point out that shortly after a human child learns to name objects and apply these names more generally, his use of language progresses to higher and more complex levels. One important characteristic of the child's more advanced language usage is the way he separates the system of emotional communication from language. As we have seen, the great majority of monkey and ape communications are directly emotional. The early language of children is tied to emotional states—their desires, pleasures, angers—but it moves beyond this to a use of language for its own sake in many situations devoid of emotion. Washoe showed some ability to separate language use from emotional state; for example, she would spontaneously name objects when no one was about and was also observed practicing signs before a mirror. But her ability to do this was well below that of a two-year-old child.

The next big step in language development is the combination of names or signs into sentences. This involves the internalization of language as a form of thought, a complex topic that I will not attempt to discuss here. Washoe could not take this step. As early as the age of two, the normal human child begins to combine words to form simple sentences having what corresponds to a subject and a predicate (*baby go, mamma come, bottle gone,* etc.). From the simple two-word sentence, the child, with amazing rapidity, discovers the rules of grammar—not in the sense that he can state what is written in grammar books, but in the sense that his spontaneous usage displays the regularities of the language he hears spoken around him. From the examples he hears, the three- to four-year-old discovers the use of past and future tense, the asking of questions, negation, and the general ordering of sentences into their appropriate grammatical form.[1] As Bronowski and Bellugi point out, a young child says things like *he comed yesterday, it breaked, I falled, two mans, my foots, many sheeps.* The child has not heard these phrases, he is generalizing the past tense (as in *walked*) or the plural (as in *cats*) to additional instances. Such generalization, while not strictly correct, shows the intelligent application of the grammatical rules for sentence order, past tense, and plural forms.

Washoe, despite intensive training and exposure to human models, was not able to master any of these complex aspects of language. She seemed unable to arrange the names or signs she learned into any regular or consistent order. For example, she knew the signs for *me, you,* and *tickle,* but would use either *you tickle* or *tickle you* when asking someone to tickle her, or *me tickle* or *tickle me* to mean both someone tickling her and her intention to tickle someone else. Her failure to arrange signs in any consistent way demonstrates her inability to learn the sort of ordering that all human children master. By contrast, consider the tape recordings collected by the linguist Ruth Weir (1962) of the spontaneous monologues of her two-and-a-half-year-old son. His word play while alone in his crib consisted of spontaneous experimentation with sentence structure and grammatical forms. He would arrange and rearrange words into various orders, trying new words in established forms as he perfected his linguistic skills.

In addition to her failure to master word order, Washoe could not be taught to ask questions—which every three- and four-year-old never stops doing, or so it must seem to many mothers—nor could she learn to make negative sentences (*don't tickle me* or *no tickle me*).

In sum, Washoe was only capable of learning the first step of language, the use of object names. The chimpanzee apparently lacks the biological capacity to acquire the more complex aspects of language, including sentence structure, internalized grammar, and question asking. These aspects are of great importance since they are representative of complex human intelligence. When the three-year-old child shows, by his spontaneous word use, that he has discovered and internalized a set of grammatical rules, we see an instance of the peculiarly human capacity to construct an internal model of the world. Such models are the hallmark of human intelligence. This intelligence, which we will examine in more detail in subsequent chapters, rests on the unique evolution of the human brain. Let us now return to a topic raised earlier, the relationship of the two systems of communication: language and emotional display.

---

1 The child's mastery of language and the implications of internalized grammar, spontaneous use of new sentences, and so on for a theory of thinking are at the heart of the revolution in linguistics ushered in by Chomsky's (1965, 1972) work. See Slobin (1971) for an introduction.

The unique parts of the human brain involved in language have few connections with those centers involved in emotion. This suggests a specialized evolution for language and also points to the separation of the communication system of emotional display from that of language. Evidence (Lenneberg, 1966a) bearing on the development of language in young children also points to an initial separation of the two communication systems. Although the earliest use of language by children certainly involves an expression of things they feel strongly about, it is also true that early language is used for a *dispassionate* description of the world. The older emotional display systems, such as crying, smiling, or angry threat, precede language in both evolution and individual development. Language lends itself to a less emotional, more "intellectual" interchange with the world. As the child gets older, the two systems—emotional display and language—become increasingly conjoined. Primitive rage, crying, and so on are expressed more and more with words. Yet even in adulthood, when levels of emotion become intense, the systems may break apart; they may be used in ways commensurate with their earliest appearance. When this happens we express fear with a scream and trembling body, depression with crying and the facial signs of sadness, and anger with a yell of rage and the physical actions of fighting. Once language and emotional communication systems are conjoined, a greater flexibility of expression is possible than that achieved by apes. Displacement or redirection activities, observed with a greater frequency in the intelligent chimpanzee than in other monkeys and apes, take on a still wider scope in humans with the addition of language.

It is interesting to note that the two systems of communication are analogous to the "primary" and "secondary processes" described by Freud (see chapter 1). Like the primary process—which Freud tied to man's instinctual nature—the system of emotional display is mediated by phylogenetically "old" parts of the brain; is similar in monkeys, apes and man; is expressed through body, gesture, and facial expression in primitive ways; and, most important, is characterized by strong feelings which give it an imperative or driven quality. Analogous to Freud's concept of the secondary process, the system of language appears later in primate evolution—being unique to man—and later in the development of the individual child. It depends for its successful use on a separation from emotion and, to a certain extent, is less imperative or driven.

I do not mean to suggest that emotional display and language are equivalent to primary and secondary process, nor that language and thought are the same thing. Rather, I think these ideas about the two communication systems are an alternative model for what Freud was attempting to describe with his concepts of primary and secondary process—a way of talking about how the animal past lives on in contemporary man. And, as we have seen in chapter 2, a set of instinctual systems given force by emotion is a more inclusive model than the idea of a primary process driven by a pleasure-producing tension reduction.

The potential separation of emotional display and language makes possible many of the great accomplishments of human culture. It allows human beings to operate within a world of abstract symbols, separated from the press of immediate need. The word play of the three-year-old rests on the same capacity to manipulate symbols as do the inventions of science— from stone tools to the smelting of metal to the harnessing of nuclear energy. At the same time, man's potentially "independent" linguistic and intellectual capacities make possible some of the great tragedies of the human condition, ranging from the "rational" justification of the brutal treatment of other men, to the dissociations and schisms between thought and feeling characteristic of so many disturbed individuals. I will take up this topic of dissociation in detail in chapter 7; here it is simply interesting to note that the capacity to dissociate emotion from intellect results from the special evolution of language and related aspects of human intelligence.

In much of the preceding discussion, reference has been made to the concept of culture. It is now time to look more closely at man's unique social life.

EARLY CULTURE

As apes evolved into men, with ever larger brains, increased tool use, male-female pairing, improved group hunting techniques, and eventually language, a new form of social organization—human culture—came into being. The archeological evidence indicates that early man lived in small groups and obtained food by hunting game and gathering wild vegetation. Once evolved, the hunting and gathering society was remarkably successful and persisted for many thousands of years. Agriculture, the domestication of animals, and the use of metals are known to be only 10,000 years old. *Homo sapiens* lived by hunting and gathering for 50,000 years prior to agriculture and the earlier forms of man for several hundred thousand years before that. Lee and DeVore (1968) estimate that of all the men who have ever lived out a life span on earth, 90 percent lived as hunters and gatherers, 6 percent by simple agriculture, and the remaining 4 percent in industrial societies. Civilization, as we are familiar with it, is very recent; many basic cultural customs developed over thousands of years for a hunting and gathering way of life far different from ours.

Cultural practices evolve just as do the biological characteristics of a species. They are subject to more rapid modification in a flexible animal like man, but it is also true that when a way of life is successful for long periods of time, customs central to that way of life become firmly structured and resist modification. The hunting and gathering culture represents a successful adaptation over a relatively long period of time, though it has been eclipsed by even more successful agricultural and industrial societies. It is thus of great interest to examine certain of the basic aspects of hunting and gathering societies since they form such an important part of the human heritage.

Most of these early cultures are long since gone, leaving only relics for archeologists to piece together; however there are a number of them still in existence. From the study of these existing societies it is possible to reconstruct a fairly complete picture of man's early cultural life.

Many anthropologists have contributed to our understanding of cultures different than ours. The differences between these various "primitive" societies are more clearly understood today than they once were. An excellent source book which discusses these differences, points out revisions in earlier anthropological accounts, and above all, brings together material on a number of early cultures is *Man the Hunter* (1968), edited by Lee and DeVore. I draw heavily on this work in what follows.

Before presenting a picture of early culture some definitions and cautions are in order. What shall we call these societies? The term "primitive" has traditionally been used but this suffers from some limitations. Like "savage," it implies that these societies are inferior to our own. While they are certainly less advanced technologically, the question of whose social customs are inferior remains open. As we will see, they may have done a better job of channeling aggression and providing secure social roles than many later societies. "Primitive" reflects the ethnocentric bias of early observers. "Hunting and gathering societies" is an accurate, if somewhat cumbersome, label. I will use "hunters," as a shortened form of "hunting and gathering," but this too requires an explanation. In actual practice, the majority of early societies depended more on vegetable food obtained by gathering than on the meat obtained by hunting, but hunting, primarily a male activity, has almost always been more prestigious. Thus, it is their own male-centered view that is captured in the name "hunters." This is the way many of these people referred to themselves; it reflects an important cultural value.

Another point to keep in mind is that for most of their existence, the hunters were the only human societies; they had the world to themselves. There were never very many of them, relative to the human population of recent times, and they lived on land with abundant vegetation and game. With the rise of a new way of life based on agriculture and the domestication of animals, the hunters were gradually forced into less desirable living areas. This process has been tremendously accelerated since the rise of industrial nations until today—all that remains are small pockets of hunters living in arid deserts, dense forests, or above the Arctic Circle, lands that have been left because no one else wants them. In addition, many early cultures have become partially acculturated through contact with their tribal, agricultural, and industrial neighbors. So, in these ways, the hunting societies in existence today are not what they once were; their life is more arduous on poor land and they suffer the stress of culture change. Many of the disagreeable characteristics attributed to "savages" and "primitive" people by early explorers and unsophisticated observers were the result of cultures in the process of disruptive change or disintegration. Fortunately, it has been possible to reconstruct a picture of relatively uncontaminated early societies and, using this, to project backwards to a time when the hunting and gathering life was dominant.

As a final caution it should be noted that hunting societies have been characterized by great diversity. Just as chimpanzee groups adopt different modes of life in response to different environments, or the behavior of a gorilla troop is determined by the personal idiosyncracies of its dominant male, so hunting societies differ as a function of ecology, history, and the personalities of specific members.

Having voiced these cautions, let us now look at what life was like over the very long period when man lived by hunting and gathering. In what follows we will look at the economy, social organization, and expression of sexual and aggressive instincts in early culture.

Economy

Most hunting and gathering societies are *nomadic*; they do not possess fixed dwellings, but travel about within a defined area. In part this travel is determined by the seasonal availability of wild vegetation and game, but it should not be assumed that hunters make forced hunger marches. A good deal of the time they camp in one place, and moving may be dictated as much by the wish for a change of scene as by scarcity of food.

The lack of agricultural skills and domesticated animals means that hunters are not tied to a specific plot of land. In addition, the nomadic way of life requires that possessions be kept to a minimum. Hunters wear few clothes (the Eskimo excepted, of course); have crude shelters or sleep in the open; and carry the few tools—spear, bow and arrow, vessels—necessary to hunt, start fires, and transport food.[2]

---

[2] The Eskimo, in most respects a hunting and gathering society, is an exception to this description. Eskimos depend more on meat obtained from hunting than on gathered vegetation; they have a more developed technology of tools, clothes, and vessels; and they have domesticated the dog. This demonstrates the flexibility and inventiveness of early culture when confronted with extreme environmental demands. Still, it should be remembered that in earlier times the Eskimo lived below the Arctic Circle where there was more vegetation so that, in part, his present life results from his being forced into an extremely demanding environment.

At one time it was thought that the lot of primitive man was, as Hobbes put it, "nasty, brutish, and short." Anthropologists, sharing this view, spoke of the "marginal" subsistence of hunters or the "constant pressure" to find food or starve. More recent evidence indicates that these views are incorrect. Sahlins (1968) goes so far as to describe hunting and gathering groups as "the original affluent society." Studies of many early societies now show that within the terms of their own needs, these people have an abundant subsistence base. And this is true despite the fact that many have been pushed into less desirable environments by their technologically advanced neighbors. The key point, of course, is "within the terms of their own needs." Early cultural man usually has all he needs, but his way of life is such that he does not need very much. Hunters in the more favorable environments—and these are more representative of early groups—live well on two to four hours work per day. They know where food is to be had at different seasons and, since they cannot preserve extra food, they have no reason to accumulate a surplus. Although hunting is a more highly valued activity, the bulk of the diet of most hunters consists of fruits, nuts, roots, and other wild vegetation.

The !Kung Bushman of the Kalahari Desert in Southwest Africa will provide a representative example. Lee (1968) has done a careful study of the weight, caloric, protein, and vitamin composition of the Bushman diet. It is clear from this analysis that the !Kung have a constant supply of food that is rich in protein and vitamins and that most of this supply comes from gathered vegetation, primarily nuts. Two-thirds vegetation to one-third meat seems a representative figure for many early cultures.

The !Kung do not work very hard to maintain themselves. Lee estimates two and a half (six-hour) days per week are spent obtaining food. What is more, this is done by individuals between twenty and sixty years; children and the aged are not required to work. If they survive the hazards of infancy and childbearing in a culture without hospitals or medicine, the typical Bushman can expect a long, secure life. Lee estimates 10 percent of the group he studied was over sixty years of age. These old persons were respected for their knowledge and performed important ritual functions. The ease with which they maintain themselves without hard labor prompted one Bushman to respond, when asked why he had not taken up the agricultural methods of neighboring tribes: "Why should we plant, when there are so many mongongo nuts in the world?"

The paucity of personal possessions or property and the fact that food is not accumulated, tend to equalize individuals. Hunting and gathering societies depend on the sharing of food and the good fortune of one day's hunt is spread throughout the group. Sharing is an important cultural ethic in most of these groups. Since the food supply is more or less constant, and what is killed or gathered is shared, individuals need not be anxious about where their next meal is coming from. Indeed, many observers report a surprising lack of concern even when persons spend a day or two without eating. The lack of anxiety indicates that hunting and gathering people exist in a well-adapted equilibrium with their environment. Sharing is an important part of this adaptation; hunters do not always share because they like to or want to, but because sharing is a strongly built in, adaptive custom.

Social Organization

The family is the basis of early social organization. The simplest unit consists of husband, wife, and their children. Families are organized into larger social units called *bands*. A number of early anthropologists—notably Radcliffe-Brown (1931) and, more recently, Service (1962)—believed that all primitive bands were "patrilinial" and "patrilocal;" that is, that close male relations (brothers, and sometimes male cousins) lived and worked within their own territory and exchanged women with other male-centered groups. Much recent evidence, reviewed in Lee and DeVore, indicates that the male-centered form of organization is not universal among hunters. Bands are more loosely organized than was earlier supposed; their organization bears a shifting relationship to territory and the seasonal availability of food. That is, families may forage on their own during part of the year and come together in larger groups when a particular wild crop is in abundance or a large-scale hunt is to be undertaken. Bands may be defined simply by a common area and language; families may consider themselves part of the same social groups because they hunt in the same forest or live around the same water hole. The earlier anthropologists were dependent on informants rather than direct observation and, hence, their reports reflected certain cultural *ideals* of male-centered existence. As is the case with us, persons in early cultures do not always live their real lives as custom or ideal prescribes.

The flexible band organization of early cultures has its advantages and drawbacks. It allows social organization to adapt to shifting ecological circumstances. It also permits a certain amount of movement between groups and this, as we shall see, plays an important role in the control of aggression. At the same time, looseness is a form of disorganization or lack of organization and ultimately, hunting and gathering societies gave way to better organized tribal and agricultural groups.

In sum, the organization of early society is primarily *familial*. Members of a band think of themselves as brothers, cousins, aunts, uncles, and so on, even where this is not strictly true in a biological sense. Bands are defined in terms of *shared* habitat and language. Hunters are not "territorial" as some popularized accounts have suggested; that is, aggressive defense of specific land against other groups does not often occur.

There is a clear division of labor in early cultures: the men hunt and the women gather vegetable foods and care for children. Hunting is the more prestigious occupation and women's work, while more essential to survival, is monotonous and less highly valued. In this respect, the early woman who spends her time gathering roots, nuts or fruit is akin to her modern counterpart who feels tied to the monotony of housework while her husband goes off to his seemingly more glamorous job.

The prevalence of hunting as a male activity may be a carry-over of the male dominance so characteristic of monkeys and apes. Although certain biological differences between male and female are less pronounced in humans than in apes, the males are in general bigger, possessed of greater muscular strength, and more aggressive. Early woman is, of course, closely tied to nursing and caring for infants and young children. Whatever contribution comes from male versus female biology, however, is reinforced by the widespread cultural custom which defines the male as the hunter and killer of prey.

This review of economy and social organization shows that the life of persons in early cultures, far from being "nasty, brutish, and short," is secure, enjoyable, and long-lived. Even in the marginal areas where they are forced to live today, those hunters who are relatively free from disruptive cultural change live a healthy life with a surprisingly small amount of what we would call work. What is more, their dependence on naturally occurring food sources means they do not have to plan for the future, as even the simplest agriculturalist must. Thanks to this, they are, in a sense, free of responsibility. Given this freedom, and the small amount of time required for work, one can ask what *do* they do with their time? Again, let us look at the !Kung Bushman as a typical case. According to Lee:

> A woman gathers on one day enough food to feed her family for three days, and spends the rest of her time resting in camp, doing embroidery, visiting other camps, or entertaining visitors from other camps. For each day at home, kitchen routines, such as cooking, nut cracking, collecting firewood, and fetching water, occupy one to three hours of her time. (p. 37)

An actual hunt may prove more time consuming for the men, but they engage in it intermittently:

> It is not unusual for a man to hunt avidly for a week and then do no hunting at all for two or three weeks. Since hunting is an unpredictable business and subject to magical control, hunters sometimes experience a run of bad luck and stop hunting for a month or longer. During these periods, visiting, entertaining and especially dancing are the primary activities of the men. (p. 37)

As these quotes suggest, the !Kung and other hunters spend a good deal of time in various forms of socializing. An average for many of these groups would be: one-third time working, one-third time visiting, and one-third time receiving visitors. Dancing and other ritual activities, that play important roles in all early cultures, are included in the time not spent working. One sees the evolutionary forerunners of early socializing in the grooming of monkeys and apes that takes up several hours per day in adult animals. The forerunner of dance may be seen in the chimpanzee carnivals (with rhythmic drumming and a great deal of noise making). Persons in early cultures spend a large proportion of their time in intimate contact with their fellows, engaged in activities which express and satisfy primate social instincts. For a closer consideration of this point, let us now examine the ways in which sexuality and aggression are expressed and controlled.

Human Sexuality

Man is the only primate—indeed the only animal—to feel shame. Monkeys and apes do not cover parts of their bodies and feel no compunction over having sexual intercourse in public. All human societies, including the earliest ones, regulate the exposure of the genitalia in some ways, even when clothing is not worn for other reasons. Sexual relations between adults are normally private. The expression of sexuality in all cultures is governed by rules, customs, and taboos which limit the age of partners and prohibit sex with persons who are related in certain ways. The incest taboo—the prohibition of sexual relations between parents and children and between brothers and sisters, and other specified categories which vary from one society to another—is universal. From the primitive society which "regards incest as so horrible that they cannot imagine the necessity of having a rule against it" (Service, 1966, p. 30) to modern man, the taboo on incest is a most pervasive and strongly felt cultural custom.[3] Freud uncovered it as a potent source of guilt feelings in adults and it is related to a central aspect of psychoanalytic and postanalytic thought, the Oedipus complex, which we shall take up in chapter 5.

The taboo on sexual relations within the nuclear family sets the stage for one of the core conflicts of human life—the conflict between desire and its renunciation. Since the incest taboo is culturally universal we might expect that it serves some important purpose related to man's survival. Let us examine this taboo, noting its origin in the prehuman primates, and then focus on two interrelated functions that it serves in human beings—one psychosocial and the other biological.

---

[3] The fact that certain ancient emperors and some modern kings practiced inter-marriage does not contradict the universality of the taboo. The taboo was present in those societies and emperors violated it to demonstrate the power of their position.

Is there an incest taboo among monkeys and apes? The small amount of evidence available suggests that there is. Since mating is promiscuous, apes do not have "fathers" in the human sense so we must look at mother-son and brother-sister relations. Lawick-Goodall (1968a) reports definite avoidance of incest between mothers and sons in wild chimpanzees. As she puts it, "Up to the time of writing no physically mature male has been observed to copulate with his mother (p. 243)." This is not due to lack of opportunity, for when a female chimpanzee is in heat many adult males mate with her. Lawick-Goodall observed one instance in which all the males in the group copulated with a particular female *except* her two sons. Similar observations have been reported for two different species of monkeys by Tokuda (1961–62) and Sade (1968). The inhibition of sexual relations between sons and mothers probably results from what Sade terms "the reverberance of the role of infant (sons) in adult relations with their mothers." This is quite striking in male chimpanzees who remain tied to their mothers well into adolescence and show various forms of special "respect" for them. Translating into human terms we might say that sons avoid sexual relations with their mothers because they continue to feel like children in relation to them.

The case for an incest taboo between brothers and sisters is less clear. It probably does not exist among monkeys. But, even here, the socially advanced chimpanzee approaches man. Lawick-Goodall observed some copulation between known siblings but the females tried to escape from their brothers—something they ordinarily do not do with males when in heat—suggesting some sort of sibling incest avoidance. These findings suggest that the taboo found in all human societies is rooted in primate biology. Like so much else that comes from our primate past, the incest taboo takes on special forms in human culture.

As we have already seen, humans differ from the other living primates in the form and degree of their sexuality. Sexual relations between adult monkeys and apes are not a central force in binding groups together; rather, love—primarily between mother and offspring—and dominance serve this function. Love and adult sexuality are related but not as closely associated in monkeys and apes as they are in human beings. With the continuous sexual receptivity of the human female, a social system that includes fathers as well as mothers and children in close association, and the lessening of dominance as an organizing principle, love and sexuality within the family become coupled.

Early societies were familial: individuals had the most sustained contact and felt most comfortable, most at ease, with the members of their immediate families, and beyond this, with the members of their band. Each individual's history of pleasurable-sensual experiences is centered within his family, from the close attachment of mother and infant, to sibling play, to the admiration of children and adolescents for their fathers. All of these factors would seem to make sexual relations with members of the immediate family more likely. In contrast, monkeys and apes would not be likely to have sexual relations with their parents or siblings because troops are not structured along family lines—there is more random mixing—and because dominance plays a more decisive role in determining who has sexual intercourse with whom. Human beings, on the other hand, if left to their own desires, would most naturally have sexual relations with those family or band members they feel close to. The prohibition on these relations is thus somewhat of a paradox; why should all cultures have taboos which prohibit what is seemingly natural and desirable? Why is exogamy so prevalent—that is, why do so many societies force one to select one's husband or wife from among strangers?

The Psychosocial Function of the Incest Taboo. As apes evolved into men, structures of display disappeared and the regulation of relationships by dominance and threat declined. Human beings rely more on cultural rules and linguistic communications than on a dominance order enforced by emotional communications and gestures. The rules and taboos governing relationships within the family, thus come to serve some of the functions served by dominance in monkey and ape groups. For example, the taboo on incest serves to prevent open jealousy and disruption within the close, nuclear family. It regulates sensual relationships and helps promote an ordering of society. Every member of a primitive culture learns quite early what to be modest about, what sexual liberties are allowed, and what relationships are strongly tabooed. This learning is not always explicit—much can be communicated by customs of dress, the hiding of genitalia and sexual acts, and the many nuances that surround sexual and potentially sexual encounters. Although mediated by custom and language, emotions as powerful as those in dominance are involved in this uniquely human regulation of social relationships.

Most early cultures practice exogamy: they force young men and women to marry outside the local band. Exogamy reflects a broader incest taboo—the prohibition of marriage within the familial band. Its chief function is to promote political alliances with other groups. Service (1966) quotes the early anthropologist E. B. Tylor to the effect that:

> ...there is but one means of keeping up permanent alliance, and that means is intermarriage.... Again and again in the world's history, savage tribes must have had plainly before their minds the simple practical alternative between marrying-out and being killed-out. Even far on in culture, the political value of intermarriage remains.... 'Then we will give our daughters unto you, and we will take your daughters to us, and we will dwell with you and we will become one people,' is a well-known passage of Israelite history. (p. 36)

The Biological Function of the Incest Taboo. Biologists have long known that repeated inbreeding of animals or plants leads to weaknesses.[4] Outbreeding, on the other hand, counteracts biological deficiencies. It leads to the "hybrid vigor" that arises when new genes are introduced into a population. Lindzey (1967) reviews the issue of inbreeding within human populations. After considering several lines of evidence, he concludes that inbreeding within a relatively small number of generations would lead to marked biological deficiencies. These might appear as genetic malfunctions such as hemophilia, or lowered resistance to disease or other forms of physical weakness. It seems clear that any human culture which followed its natural desires and allowed sexual relations within the family would be at a marked biological disadvantage compared with other groups which did not inbreed. Thus, there is a powerful biological reason for the incest taboo—it prevents an inbreeding that would rapidly and seriously weaken the members of any society which practiced it. The fact that attraction within the family is strong necessitates a strong taboo; the biological consequences of inbreeding are severe enough that it pays all societies to prevent it.

One may ask how the taboo originated among early cultures who knew nothing of genetics, inbreeding, or natural selection and may not have even understood the relationship between copulation and pregnancy. The tendency for some forms of the taboo was already present in the prehuman primates and the advantages of exogamy and the regulation of relations within family and band probably gave great impetus to this social rule. Once established, the biological advantage of outbreeding was added to the psychosocial functions, giving those social groups that possessed the taboo a great advantage. This example shows that the principle of natural selection affects cultural customs in the same way that it does the physical characteristics of a species. The incest taboo is certainly one custom that was selected in this manner, and it is possible that the ethic of sharing, which is near universal among hunting and gathering peoples, is another.

In sum, the incest taboo has evolved as one of the most widespread and powerful of human customs for psychological, social, and biological reasons. Like many other aspects in the evolution of both species and culture, the various functions interacted with each other as the custom gradually took shape. Once evolved, the incest taboo set the stage for one of the central conflicts of human life, that between desire and renunciation. As surely as the unique evolution of human sexuality, nuclear family structure, and

---

4 This is primarily because most mutant genes are maladaptive, many are recessive in nature, and inbreeding increases the probability of offspring having a match of two recessive, maladaptive genes. For example, hemophilia—a genetic disturbance in which the blood fails to clot—is only manifest when the person has two recessive genes. Persons may have one recessive gene for hemophilia and not suffer from the disease. If these carriers of single recessive genes begin interbreeding, the probability of overtly hemophilic offspring immediately increases, as it did in certain European royal families who practiced inbreeding.

band organization arouses the sensual desire of mother, father, son, daughter, brother, and sister for each other, the incest taboo prohibits the gratification of these desires and forces sexual choice outside the family and the local group. The struggles of men and women with this core conflict are depicted in the Greek tragedies, in Shakespeare, and in the myths, legends, and fairy tales of many cultures over many historical periods.

Aggression in Early Cultures

In the preceding chapter we have seen the prominent role of aggression in monkey and ape societies. Aggression in man is both similar and different. As we have seen, human evolution led to the loss of fighting teeth and jaws and their replacement with a larger brain and fighting tools. A comparison of the functions served by aggression in ape and man will prove informative.

Man, even in the simplest of cultures, has no serious predatory enemies. His use of tools and fire and his organization into groups provide sufficient protection against being hunted. In this respect he is similar to the largest apes, chimpanzees, and gorillas, but the story is far different with regard to predation. Most monkeys and apes—including the large and powerful gorilla—are vegetarians. Chimpanzees engage in some predation; as in so many other respects they are midway between man and the other apes. But chimpanzee predation is sporadic. Of all the primates, man is by far the greatest hunter and killer of prey.

All primitive societies practice hunting, it is almost always a male activity, and it is associated with various customs which embue it with prestige. Man's biological heritage as an aggressive primate interacts with those cultural customs which teach and reward the hunting and killing of animals to channel aggression in this direction. Instinct and custom make it easy for men to become hunters and difficult to inhibit the killing of animals. Hunting remains a popular sport among many modern men who have no need for the food so obtained.

What about aggression in the service of territory? Some recent authors have made much of man's "territorial instinct," but the evidence here is much less clear than it is in regard to hunting. Contact between distant groups is infrequent. Given the low population density of hunters in their original state, there was probably not a great deal of actual fighting between groups. Distant groups are the recipients of a good deal of hostility and projected bad feeling, however. Service (1966) quotes an old Arab saying: "I against my brother; I and my brother against my cousin; I, my brothers, and my cousins against the next village; all of us against the foreigner (p. 58)." True to this sentiment, primitive man tends to direct his anger outward toward bands or groups beyond his own. The more distant the group the easier it seems to be to project all sorts of qualities onto them which justify hatred. This does not necessarily relate to the protection of territory, however. Territory as we understand it is not very important to hunters because of their nomadic style and lack of possessions. The direction of aggression toward members of more distant groups is useful since there is not much contact with these groups and hence, they serve as relatively harmless scapegoats.

It is essential, of course, to keep aggression under control within the family and band. As we saw with monkeys and apes, aggression within the primary group is potentially frequent and this necessitates the control and redirection of dominance hierarchies. Analogously, aggression within the human band is potentially destructive and it must be channeled and redirected. In place of dominance hierarchies we find cultural rules, customs, and taboos which serve to keep serious aggression under control. Angers, jealousies, resentments, quarrels, and fights are certainly a part of the life of hunters, as they are of everyone to some degree. Turnbull (1961) reports that the Mbuti Pygmies of the Congo forest—in many respects a typical hunting and gathering culture—deliberately provoke arguments and fights in camp, presumably for the hell of it. But they have well established ways of dealing with the aroused aggression. In extreme instances a Pygmy will simply turn around, thus ending the face-to-face confrontation so central to primate fighting. Other hunters will move their huts so they cannot see their "enemies" through the door. These are examples of a widespread and very important technique for the control of aggression. When anger and dispute reach a certain intensity, the hunter may simply leave and join another group or band. Lee and DeVore call this *fission*; in popular terms one "splits from the scene." The looseness of band organization and the customs of visiting and receiving visitors, as well as the lack of property and possessions, makes this easy to do.

When fission doesn't resolve aggressive disputes, most early cultures have established rituals and routines. The argument may be submitted to an elder, or a "song duel" or spear-dodging contest may be held. These rituals, like the gestures of dominance, allow aggression to be redirected in less harmful ways. One sees the remnants of such rituals in our athletic contests between different schools or between teams that represent different cities; but for the most part, these rites have ceased to satisfy the ritual function of aggressive discharge that they once served.

BIOLOGICAL EVOLUTION
AND CULTURAL CHANGE

Human biology and cultural customs evolved over long periods of time for a world that no longer exists. Many of the conflicts of modern life may be traced to this source. The social changes that began with the introduction of agriculture some 10,000 years ago have progressed so rapidly that neither our bodies nor our myths, rituals, or customs have had time to catch up. Ten thousand years may seem like a long time but from the perspective of evolution it is extremely brief. Even from the perspective of cultural evolution it is a very short span. Recall that the hunting and gathering way of life existed for some 50,000 to 600,000 years before the advent of agriculture. Add to this the fact that within the last 10,000 years we have progressed from the simplest tribal agricultural societies to the modern industrial state, and that change continues at what seems like an ever accelerating rate, and one begins to appreciate the problem.

The biological side of the issue is well known, the cultural side less so, since people tend to assume that cultural customs, being human creations, can be easily changed. In fact, cultural beliefs, values, and customs tend to have much more inertia than is frequently supposed. In some ways, bringing our customs into line with the present state of civilization is a more difficult problem than bringing our biology into line. Let us look at some examples, first from the biological side, and then from the cultural.

Early man obviously got a great deal more exercise than most of us do today. Biologically, the hunting and gathering way of life is extremely vigorous and these people, by and large, could run long distances and withstand extremes of heat and cold; they were, in short, in much better physical condition than we users of cars, houses, and the other creations of modern technology. Many other examples could be cited to show how the human body evolved for this early way of life and has not caught up with the changes brought about by advances in technology. Some forms of disease, particularly of the psychosomatic type, may be traceable to this discrepancy between our bodies and our present way of life. Humans are a generalized species, however. We are certainly not so specialized as, for example, dinosaurs were, and we won't become extinct because of this discrepancy. Analogous conflicts at the cultural level are much more serious, and in the case of aggression, do threaten the extinction of the human species.

Many anthropologists and other observers of early cultures are struck by the contented state of these people. The lack of anxiety about food, possessions, or property; the well-integrated way in which groups function; and the sense of oneness with the environment make this way of life very appealing. The contented and happy state of hunters is often contrasted with neighboring tribes who are moving into the modern era (see, for example, Turnbull's account of the Pygmies and how their life compares with their neighboring Bantu villagers). "Progress" is accompanied by a rise in drunkenness, selfishness, increasing exploitation of other people, and alienation from the environment; in short, life seems to become more sordid.

There may be a tendency to idealize "primitive" peoples—to see them as "noble savages"—but the view of their contented lot is fairly widespread among a number of observers. What is more, it makes good sense from the perspective of cultural evolution. Since the customs of hunting and gathering societies had a long time to evolve, they represent a very stable and successful adaptation. Early man feels at one with his environment and well-integrated within his familial-band society because his social experience and customs prepare him to function well in these spheres. In a way, the hunters are like Adam and Eve before the fall. Just as too much knowledge precipitated their expulsion from Paradise, it is the fruits of man's intelligence —the invention of agriculture and later of technology—that brought about the end of the "paradise" of a well-adapted hunting and gathering way of life. Many customs persist, or more to the point, we have not yet developed new customs which enable us to live as harmoniously within our world as the hunter's allowed him to do. Let us look at some examples of this disjunction between custom and reality.

With the advent of agriculture, people became increasingly tied to particular plots of land. Gradually the economy changed with the addition of surplus commodities and the increasing importance of personal property. These changes in human economy had many effects. Land and possessions became things to covet and fight about. The ethic of sharing, so central in hunting groups, and so important in the creation of an integrated, interdependent society, broke down. People in later cultures are not necessarily more intrinsically selfish; rather, the stable ethic of sharing which so successfully controlled greed in early cultures was disrupted by the rise of personal property. We are still searching for a stable ethic to take its place. Conflicts between the accumulation of individual property and the public welfare continue to plague modern nations.

Another effect of the rise of agriculture and property stems directly from the fact that individuals become tied to their land. This makes it more difficult to deal with aggression by fission. Faced with an unpleasant and potentially aggressive encounter, the hunter can simply leave and join another group. He sacrifices little by doing so; in fact the custom of mutual visiting has prepared both the visitor and the host for such a move. But with land and possessions it becomes more difficult to leave. One is tempted to stand and fight. Territorial disputes themselves become an additional and very important source of aggression. Man, tied to his land and possessions, is like a monkey caged in a zoo. The older customs and rituals which disperse aggression are more difficult to effect, and serious fighting increases.

The hunters channel a certain amount of their aggression toward distant groups with whom they have little actual contact. As I pointed out in chapter 1, early cultures are extremely ethnocentric—their words for the members of their own group are usually something like "the people" or "human beings," with outsiders viewed as barbarians or creatures slightly less than human. Like fission, this direction of hostility toward other groups is quite useful in preserving the peace within the local band. "I and my brothers and cousins against the foreigner" works well when one doesn't see the foreigner very often, nor have any serious way of affecting him. The rise of technology changes all this, of course. With increased mobility—even horses to ride on—increased communication, and most importantly, increasingly efficient weapons, it becomes easier and easier to put the hatred of "foreigners" into practice. From the crossbow to the rifle to the intercontinental ballistic missile, the direction of aggression toward others has become more and more destructive. Yet the old customs that support this practice are slow in changing. As Washburn and Hamburg put it: "...An aggressive species living by prescientific customs in a scientifically advanced world will pay a tremendous price in interindividual conflict and international war (p. 478)."

There is another way in which the rapid growth in the technology of killing deprives the old customs of their usefulness. In early societies, aggression is carried out on a face-to-face basis. If you want to harm or kill someone you must hit him with a club or throw a spear at him. Aggression at a distance was confined to techniques such as sorcery which were of dubious effectiveness. Appeasement gestures and inhibitory mechanisms make it difficult for most people, most of the time, to carry out the extremes of aggression in face-to-face situations. The customs which channel and redirect serious fighting evolved to deal with the face-to-face aggression of early man. Weapons that can kill at a distance deprive these inhibitory mechanisms of their effectiveness. When a man drops bombs from an airplane flying at 50,000 feet he has little sense of the human beings who are killed and injured. Again, this illustrates the failure of cultural custom to keep pace with technological change. We have still to work out myths, rituals, and beliefs that will allow us to channel aggression in less destructive ways.

Customs and rules governing sexual behavior provide another example of a disjunction that results from recent technological advances. Prior to the availability of contraception, sexual intercourse was likely to lead to pregnancy. Depending on its particular structure, each society had a stake in controlling pregnancies until the woman was in a position to care for the infant. In western culture, this usually meant until she was married and hence, our taboo on premarital sexual relations. This taboo has played its part in the creation of the excessive fear of sex and feelings of guilt so characteristic in western society. With the advent of effective methods of contraception, sexual intercourse need not lead to pregnancy. In this sense, the taboo on premarital sexual relations loses its purpose. Yet, to various degrees, the taboo persists, creating conflict and guilt in situations where there need be none. Again, we see an example of the disjunction of cultural custom and changing circumstances and the failure of cultural evolution to keep pace with technological change.

We need rituals, myths, and customs which will serve us as well as the hunter's served him. We tend to think of such customs as malleable since they vary from one society to another and can be changed. They can be changed, *but* the central customs and beliefs of any society change very slowly. The primitive religious beliefs of 2,000 years ago are still alive today; we have yet to develop adequate replacements; customs, and beliefs that will better integrate with the modern world.

SOCIAL INSTINCTS IN HUMAN BEINGS

It is now time to present an overview of the principal social instincts in man. In chapter 2, a model of instinctual systems—each given value or "driven" by its own emotion—was developed. We saw how these instinctual systems operate in our monkey and ape ancestors. The first portion of this chapter has traced the transition from ape to early cultural man and has indicated some important ways in which humans differ from the other primates. Following is a brief description of the principal human instinctual areas. Each instinctual system—love, fear, anxiety, aggression, curiosity, and play—has a characteristic emotion which gives it force, and each undergoes a long period of development. The detailed presentation of these areas will be reserved for the remainder of the book which will, in a sense, trace man's instincts through the life span.

Love

The forms of human love are as varied as the human mind can invent. At the same time, love in all cultures is bound up with certain central purposes—the attachment between infant and parents, sexual reproduction, and the bonding together of adult male and female into that basic unit of social organization, the nuclear family. As love and sexuality develop over the life span they become involved in the widest variety of strongly motivated human endeavors, areas so wide that Freud attempted to explain all motivation as a result of this "primary" source. Later work has proven his view to be over-inclusive—and even Freud did not stick with it, making a basic place in his theories for anxiety and aggression—but it is worth emphasizing the great importance of love, attachment, and sexuality in human life.

The centrality of love results from two factors. As we have seen, the human infant remains in a helpless state for the longest time of any primate. This helplessness requires a longer, closer, and more continuous bond between infant and his maternal caretaker. The second factor is sexuality. We are a more sexually motivated species than any of our monkey and ape relatives (which provides an interesting example of how we are more "animal-like" than the animals on whom we project our own qualities). The continuous sexual arousability of humans serves as an important motive in bringing male and female together and bonding them into families. Any species must be strongly motivated to reproduce, and an interest in sex serves this purpose as well. It takes humans a very long time until they reach a state of maturity where sexual reproduction is possible, however, so that the final form of adult sexuality is influenced by the great number of pleasurable, sexual-sensual experiences that occur on the passage from infancy through childhood to adulthood.

How is sexuality mediated through the long period of human development? What is common in the attachment of infant to mother, the love between young children and their parents, and sexual attraction between adults? In short, how does the instinctual system of love operate?

Freud grappled with this problem and solved it by postulating a source of sexual energy (libido) that drives everyone toward pleasure seeking. He assumed that this pleasure-seeking drive developed through a sequence of stages which he termed "psychosexual." In each stage, a certain area of the body—oral, anal, genital—was the focus of sexual pleasure. Freud's writings contain important insights, but the underlying theory is in need of modification. Erik Erikson (1950, 1959) and more recently, George S. Klein (1969) provide these modifications. Like Freud, Erikson focuses on the developmental course of sexuality, but he devotes more attention to the *meaning* of gratification or frustration at the various stages as opposed to the quantities of sexual energy. Klein carefully analyzes Freud's sexual theories and separates the useful insights from the outdated energy or libido model. The following discussion draws on the view that emerges from both Erikson's and Klein's reworking of the psychoanalytic theory of sexuality.

The central force of the motive system of human love is its *emotional* or *affective* quality. Attachment, love, and sexuality all involve qualities of pleasurable experience that arise from the stimulation of various parts of the body. This emotional experience appears in early infancy as the pleasure connected with sensorimotor activities—what Harlow describes as contact comfort. The pleasure derived from sucking—what Freud and later psychoanalysts term orality or oral pleasure—is one but not the only nor necessarily the main source of early sensorimotor pleasure. Following Klein, I will use the more general term *sensuality* to refer to this broad category of pleasurable experience. Stimulation of the genital or anal areas, or indeed of many areas of the body; rhythmic stimulation as in rocking; close holding or cuddling all are capable of eliciting sensual pleasure. Notice also that, as with Harlow's contact comfort, such pleasurable experience is normally interpersonal in its origins. Self-stimulation and pleasurable contact with inanimate objects such as soft toys or cloth may also occur quite early and play important, though usually secondary roles.

Let me make clear the difference between this view and that usually associated with the psychoanalytic theory of psychosexual development. The psychoanalytic view assumes that the physical locus of pleasure originates in the oral zone of the body and then moves through other zones as development proceeds. In each psychosexual stage—oral, anal, genital—the amount of pleasure received presumably determines the stage outcome with too much or too little leading to "fixation" or "trauma," while an optimal amount leads to a normal progression to the next stage. In contrast with this view, Erikson and Klein stress the psychosocial nature of the experience at each stage—for example, whether feeding is predictable or toilet training overly punitive—rather than the quantity of pleasure. Many zones of the body may yield sensual pleasure throughout the life cycle. It is primarily social regulations of the infant's maturing activities that determine the sequential order of psychosexual development. That is, the anal stage occurs when it does because the child becomes both physiologically and psychologically mature enough to be affected by the social rules governing toilet training and not because his anal region is any more or less sensitive to pleasure at a particular time than it was during the preceding, or will be during the following, stages. Indeed, the various zones of the body retain their sensitivity for sensual pleasure throughout life, participating in both the pleasurable stimulation of infancy and in sexual love between adults.

As development proceeds, the infant's intelligence expands and sensuality acquires a greater symbolic component. Childhood love and adult sexuality are intertwined with a variety of symbols and meanings that were not present in the sensorimotor attachment of early infancy. Still, it is the emotions and memories associated with sensual pleasure which give value to certain persons—most prominently mother and father—and certain experiences, though these become represented in increasingly complex ways.

One final point: an important characteristic of the sensual-pleasure system is its plasticity or malleability. Unlike strongly motivated activities such as breathing or eating, sensual pleasure is not fixed to a particular body area nor to a fixed time sequence. If one does not breathe or eat in certain ways one dies; not so with sex and related forms of pleasurable stimulation. One may engage in them for days on end or not at all for years; sensual pleasure may be elicited by self-stimulation (as in masturbation) or in a variety of situations with other people of either sex. Although society has a stake in promoting sexual interactions that lead to reproduction,[5] biologically a much wider array of activities are possible and do occur. Its very plasticity accounts for the fact that the sensual-emotional system can become

---

[5] At least this was the case before overpopulation and overcrowding began to threaten the survival of the species. Most social customs antedate the rise of overpopulation as a problem and they are difficult to change. This is another example of the disjunction between cultural custom and the changes brought about by technology.

entwined with such a wide range of meanings, conflicts, and neuroses and also be central to the bonds on which the family is built and the species perpetuated.

Fear and Anxiety

As one of the most "opportunistic" of primates, man must be extremely sensitive to novelty and change in his environment. This sensitivity manifests itself on a continuum that ranges from curiosity to fear. Moderately novel events stimulate interest, but that which is too different, too unexpected, is frightening. In addition to this general fear of the unknown, experiments and observations of primates suggest that particular sights, sounds, and events provoke innate fear. The threat gestures of other species members are one source of such fear and the sight of one's fellows, dead or mutilated, is another. As was true with love, the instinctual area of fear is broadly bounded. As the person develops, he may learn new fears and become inured to old ones.

Anxiety is an emotion that is closely related to fear, but one which has come to serve special purposes in primates. As animals whose existence is totally dependent on organized group living, a special instinctual system has evolved which promotes close social bonds by making separation from other group members the occasion for the very unpleasant emotion of anxiety.

Separation anxiety is a primary instinctual system in human beings. This point is worth stressing because various earlier theorists have viewed anxiety as secondary to other motives. Certain psychoanalytic writers assume, for example, that anxiety is a signal which heralds the rise of other instinctual energies, while a number of behaviorists have assumed that one learns to be anxious about events associated with actual pain. Although these sorts of things certainly happen, they should not obscure the fact that anxiety appears very early when the attached infant becomes separated from his mother. Separation anxiety is an important motive in maintaining the mother-infant closeness so important for the infant's survival. It is the primary source of interpersonal anxiety. *The basic prototype of anxiety is abandonment; its earliest state is the helplessness of the separated infant.*

As the person progresses beyond infancy, anxiety becomes symbolized in more complex ways and eventually is internalized. From the anxiety over actual loss or separation from mother, grows anxiety over loss of her love or approval. Later, the child comes to feel anxious about the general disapproval of the social group. The motive behind group conformity is closely related to separation anxiety; there is a sense in which the group comes to replace the parents, and anxiety about group disapproval replaces the earlier anxiety over loss of parental love which, in turn, rests on the still earlier separation anxiety of infancy. It is interesting to note that among most hunting and gathering societies, the common discipline for the infraction of group rules and taboos is some form of ostracism. The earliest cultures rely on the power of this instinctual-emotional system.

As the child progresses from separation anxiety to fear of parental disapproval to conformity to the group, rules, taboos, and standards are progressively internalized. Eventually he comes to feel a special form of anxiety —*guilt*—when he violates his own standards. The process of internalization and the problem of guilt are complicated issues and I will reserve more extended discussions for later, particularly chapters 7 and 8 which will examine the role of anxiety in dissociation and the internalization of standards and growth of conscience.

Aggression

Human beings are the only animals who regularly kill each other. The history of the modern world is a history of war. Despite these facts, the idea that aggression is instinctual in man is offensive or frightening to many persons. Our review of aggression in primates and in early cultures should clarify the debate over whether man's aggressiveness is instinctual or the unfortunate byproduct of civilization—a corruption of natural innocence by imperfect societies.

In part, this controversy stems from a misunderstanding of the concept of instinct as applied to human beings. As with love and anxiety, there is no fixed behavior pattern, built in at birth, that can account for aggression as we see it in children and adults. But this does not mean that important biological equipment is not present which sets boundaries and predisposes humans to develop specific patterns of aggression as they are exposed to the experiences of particular societies. As Washburn (1959) puts it:

> Man has a carnivorous psychology. It is easy to teach people to kill, and it is hard to develop customs which avoid killing. Many human beings enjoy seeing other human beings suffer, or enjoy the killing of animals...public beatings and tortures are common in many cultures.

There is now a good deal of evidence from several sources which points to the innate aggressiveness of primates in general and to the particularly strong propensity toward aggression that is part of the human heritage. Let me summarize some of this evidence. The chronical of human history is filled with war, brutality, torture, and the widest variety of aggressive treatment of human beings by other human beings. Richardson (1960) estimates that 59,000,000 people were killed in wars, murderous attacks, or other "deadly quarrels" during the period 1820–1945. Another 70,000,000 have probably been killed since then. It is only within recent times that torture and brutality have officially ceased to be a part of the legal treatment of criminals and suspects in the most "advanced" societies.

An unwillingness to look at the evidence, or perhaps a part of the justification for continued aggression, leads many persons to discount the brutal treatment of those not a part of their own group. For example, the American Indian was systematically destroyed by the white conqueror of North America, and even today is subject to a form of cultural annihilation —an aggressive victory celebrated over and over in the older "western" movies that are a part of our national mythology. Parallels may be found in the histories of almost all nations. The Spaniards in Mexico and South America, the English and French in Africa, and the United States in Southeast Asia all follow the same pattern; Indians, Africans, and Asian peasants have all been annihilated for one or another excuse. History certainly seems to justify the conclusion of Durbin and Bowlby (1938, cited in Freeman, 1964) that no group of animals is "more aggressive or ruthless in their aggression than the adult members of the human race (p. 111)."

But, some have argued, war is a modern phenomenon, the result of too much civilization. Primitive man is peace loving. Does the evidence on early societies support the idea of the peaceful savage? First, early man is a hunter who enjoys the killing of animals. This is certainly one form of aggression and it may serve as an important channel that helps redirect aggression away from other group members. Within the local group, one finds not so much the lack of aggression as stable customs which control and channel its expression.

The stable customs of hunting and gathering societies, so successful in channeling local aggression, were easily disrupted by the changes begun by the agricultural revolution 10,000 years ago. With the breakdown of custom and ritual there was an upsurge in aggression and killing, now made more effective by superior weapons. Viewing cultures on the continuum from hunters to modern man, one is struck by how easy it is for humans to resort to aggression and how difficult to successfully channel fighting and killing. The tribal and later cultures that replaced hunting and gathering societies were more openly aggressive, particularly toward members of other groups. If we keep in mind that "primitive" in the following quote should be taken to mean "post-hunter-gatherer," than the evidence supports Freeman (1964) when he states:

> The history of the more primitive peoples confirms the conclusions I have reached for the partially civilized. . . . "War plays a prominent part in the lives of most primitive peoples.". . . Primitive cultures also exhibit many bizarre expressions of human cruelty and aggression in sacrificial rites, ceremonies of initiation, ritual mutilations, headhunting and cannibalistic cults and murderous societies. These diverse forms of symbolic behavior are paralleled

by the highly aggressive fantasies to be found in mythologies throughout the world and in the frightful torments of the various hells of human religions. (pp. 112–13)

Fantasy, of course, is another way in which individuals may channel aggression. Clinical evidence, from psychoanalytic and other forms of psychotherapy, as well as the study of children's dreams and fantasies, points to the widespread presence of aggression in individuals who may not appear outwardly angry. It was, in part, evidence of this sort which eventually led Freud to postulate a separate instinct of aggression.

Evidence from these three sources—historical, anthropological, and clinical—points to the prevalence of aggression in human life and also to the diverse forms in which it finds expression. This evidence greatly strengthens the argument in favor of an instinctual base; it becomes increasingly difficult to believe that aggression is a byproduct of modern civilization when it appears in one form or another in practically all known cultures.

It must be stressed, in conclusion, that the instinct of aggression consists of biological boundaries and equipment—of a propensity to develop in a particular direction, the specifics of which are determined by experience in one's social environment. In man, as in monkeys and apes, play and social rewards shape the specific form that the instinctual tendencies will take. Monkeys and apes play at fighting and dominance just as they play at sexual relations. Depriving them of such play—as in the Harlow experiments—seriously interferes with their later ability to function in social situations. The same is true for human beings; the specific experience one has with aggression during the years of development shape its final form.

Like sensuality, love, fear, and anxiety, the human propensity for aggression is mediated through life by emotional or affective reactions; in this case those that we associate with anger and rage. Parts of the emotional system—facial expressions, posture and movements of the limbs, and patterns of physiological arousal—remain more or less constant, while the cognitive or symbolic component undergoes great elaboration. From the sensorimotor rage of infancy, to the complex intellectualized anger of the "civilized" adult, the instinctual system of human aggression poses a perennial problem for group living.

Curiosity, Play, and Human Intelligence

In the earlier discussion of curiosity and exploration among monkeys and apes, we saw that these activities were part of the opportunistic exploitation of the environment so characteristic of all primate species. There is a balance between the motive systems of curiosity and exploration on the one hand, and fear of the unknown on the other. Situations or events at moderate levels of novelty stimulate the animal to explore, manipulate, and generally familiarize himself with environmental possibilities. Those too different or unexpected provoke fear and a seeking out of the familiar and secure. Nonsocial play is useful in the perfection of motor skills and is an important precursor to the most intelligent ape activity observed in nature —the tool use of wild chimpanzees. Social play among monkeys and apes serves as practice for adult social relations and especially for the ritualization and redirection of aggression.

In general, these same purposes are served by the exploratory and play activities of man. However, the quantum leap of human intelligence gives far greater scope to exploration and exploitation of the environment, the use of tools, language development, and the play preparation for complex social roles.

Human babies explore their world, moving progressively away from the security of mother and home as they mature. Early man lives within a habitat he has made his own by thorough exploration. The territory of the earliest hunters is far larger than that of any monkey or ape; and of course, the territory of modern man is larger still, encompassing cities and even whole countries. Man shows a much greater flexibility in adjusting his territorial and exploratory habits to variations in the supply of food and other necessities. Whether it is !Kung Bushmen traveling miles to gather mongongo nuts or Eskimos following the migration of caribou herds, we see the greater scope made possible by man's intelligence.

Tool use provides another interesting comparison between ape and man. The large majority of monkeys and apes do not use tools in the wild, though they can be taught to do so by man. Chimpanzees do make and use rudimentary tools, as we have seen. The use of tools demonstrates the adaptive function of intelligent experimentation with objects. All primates exhibit such manipulation; all play and experiment with objects, familiarizing themselves with the object's properties and discovering possible uses. Man's intelligence, made possible by his large, more slowly maturing brain, allows him to go much further with this process. Human beings have used stone tools for at least half a million years, and fire for at least 60,000. And, of course, the last 10,000 years have seen a great upsurge in the exploitation and use of objects and materials. Claude Lévi-Strauss, the noted anthropologist, describes the rise of this early technology and gives an idea of the great amount of experimentation involved:

> Each of these techniques (pottery, weaving, agriculture and the domestication of animals) assumes centuries of active and methodical observation, of bold hypotheses tested by means of endlessly repeated experiments. A biologist remarks on the rapidity with which plants from the New World have been acclimatized in the Philippines and adopted and named by the natives. In

many cases they seem even to have rediscovered their medicinal uses, uses identical with those traditional in Mexico. . . .

To transform a weed into a cultivated plant, a wild beast into a domestic animal, to produce, in either of these, nutritious or technologically useful properties which were originally completely absent or could only be guessed at; to make stout, water-tight pottery out of clay which is friable and unstable, liable to pulverize or crack (which, however, is possible only if from a large number of organic and inorganic materials, the one most suitable for refining it is selected, and also the appropriate fuel, the temperature and duration of firing and the effective degree of oxidation; to work out techniques, often long and complex, which permit cultivation without soil or alternatively without water; to change toxic roots or seeds into foodstuffs or again to use their poison for hunting, war or ritual—there is no doubt that all these achievements required a genuinely scientific attitude, sustained and watchful interest and a desire for knowledge for its own sake. For only a small proportion of observations and experiments (which must be assumed to have been primarily inspired by a desire for knowledge) could have yielded practical and immediately useful results.[6] (1962, p. 14)

In this passage, Lévi-Strauss calls attention to the fact that the discoveries leading to the rise of technology over the past 10,000 years were made possible by man's interest, curiosity, and tendency to manipulate and experiment with the objects and materials available to him. The fact that most observations and experiments yielded no practical or immediately useful results means that experimentation was engaged in *for its own sake.* Experimentation for its own sake rests on the same sort of motivation that I discussed earlier as the *dispassionate* play with language. As we saw, language development in young children is initially separated from the other emotional systems; it develops as the child plays with words, sentences, and questions because he finds such manipulation of symbols interesting in its own right. Play and experimentation with objects is motivated in the same way. The source of this motivation is the intellectual interest and innate curiosity so characteristic of all primates and which simply takes a more complex form in man.

In the chapters to come, much more will be said about the development of human intelligence, drawing primarily on the work of Piaget. By way of preface, I might note that Piaget traces the origins of intelligence to the infant's earliest manipulation and experimentation with the physical objects available to him. The motive for this interaction with the physical world Piaget calls "the need to function." His extensive observations and experiments clearly show that there is an intrinsic motive system in humans which appears very early in life and which arouses interest and curiosity and gives value to experimental interaction with the world.

---

[6] Claude Lévi-Strauss, *The Savage Mind* (Chicago: The University of Chicago Press, 1962), p. 14. Reprinted by permission of the University of Chicago Press and of George Weidenfeld and Nicolson Ltd.

Social play is, if anything, more prominent and more important than play with objects. The human infant smiles, coos, and gurgles as it interacts with its mother. Young children play with each other, working out acceptable means for channeling aggression and perfecting the skills of social interaction that they will need to get along in the world. Children imitate adults and older siblings—boys play at hunting or driving cars, girls at dolls and "house." Such imitative play is practice for adult social roles. Although the perfection of social skills and practice at adult roles can be observed in the play of young monkeys and apes, it goes on longer and passes through more levels of transformation in human development because of our greater intellectual complexity. From age two or three onward, the play of human children is interwoven with language, fantasy, and related forms of symbolism. So we can say—as was true of all the other instinctual areas examined so far—that social play is similar in ape and human in its initial form and different as man's unique intellectual and symbolic capacities manifest themselves.

The role of play and fantasy in human development is a large topic and will be explored in greater depth in chapter 6. Here, we have traced its roots to the primate instinctual system of curiosity, exploration, and the need to function. This system has its own adaptive value: monkeys, apes, and men have evolved as opportunistic, information-seeking, playful animals because such motivation allows them to take advantage of environmental opportunities and to perfect social skills in ways that promote survival. Play and experimentation are not secondary to other motives such as hunger or aggression, though it is worth noting that these different instincts may become intertwined. That is, exploration of the environment may be motivated by *both* interest and the need for food, and a child's play by *both* curiosity and anger.

THE CORE CONFLICTS OF HUMAN LIFE

Man's biological evolution as a social, loving, sensitive, aggressive, intelligent, and symbolizing primate; the evolution of cultural custom, ritual and taboo; and the disjunctions between established cultural custom and the rapid changes brought on by technology all prepare the way for a set of core conflicts which each individual must face and work through within the opportunities and limitations of his society.

The core conflicts—*dependency and independence, pleasure and renunciation, aggression and its control*—are not resolved at any one time. They must be worked and reworked at each developmental level—infancy, early and late childhood, adolescence, and adulthood.

Dependency and Independence

The human infant is among the most helpless and dependent of creatures. His dependence on a maternal caretaker and later on other adults lasts for a good many years. This dependency, so crucial for the infant's survival, rests on the instinctual systems of love and attachment—which draw infant and mother together in a pleasurable and secure bond—and the system of separation anxiety which again draws them together as abandonment and helplessness give rise to intensely unpleasant feelings. Thus, the powerfully motivating emotions of love, pleasure, and anxiety all come into play in promoting dependency.

Curiosity and the attraction of the interesting world beyond mother impels the child to move away from his dependent position as early as the first year of life. The attraction of the novel and the lure of exciting new opportunities operate as primary motives throughout life. Too much security, too much of the same old thing, leads to boredom. To illustrate, Turnbull (1968) describes the contrasting myths of two neighboring hunting and gathering tribes, the Mbuti Pygmies and the Ik. The Mbuti, who live in a forest that provides abundant food, "treat their stable environment as though it were unstable, creating imaginary seasons of plenty and scarcity." The Ik, on the other hand, live on an arid plain where rapid climatic changes sometimes lead to scarcity of food. They "treat their highly unstable environment as though it were stable, and consequently bring upon themselves alternating periods of real plenty and scarcity (p. 134)." The Mbuti myths create excitement, breaking the boredom of their stable and well-provisioned lives. The Ik, on the other hand, use myths in an attempt to achieve security; they use fantasy as a substitute for what is sometimes lacking in reality. Whether it is primitive man inventing myths to make his life interesting, fifteenth- and sixteenth-century Europeans sailing their small boats into unknown seas, or contemporary man going to the moon, we see alternations between the poles of security and excitement.

Dependency-independence are the poles of a dimension that runs through life. At each progressive stage the person must reach some equilibrium between these two extremes—the security of a dependent position versus the excitement and accomplishment of a new independence. At the earliest stage the infant and young child must leave the security of the close bond with mother for the excitement of new achievements.

Familiar people such as parents and a familiar setting such as one's home are primary sources of the security of a dependent position. But they are not the only sources. Familiar customs, familiar social roles, in general a familiar way of life or *identity,* all confer security. Since all of psychological development involves the assumption of new roles and the abandonment of old ones, all development provokes a certain amount of anxiety and insecurity.

Beyond the level of the individual, cultural change itself may be disruptive. That is why rapid cultural change which produces disjunctions between traditional custom and new reality often leads to anxiety and a sense of alienation; of not being securely at home in one's world. Just as the individual must reach a balance of security and excitement, so societies must reach an equilibrium between stability and change.

Pleasure and Renunciation

The conflict between gratification of one's selfish interests and the renunciation of pleasure is another enduring human issue. Americans, especially, should be familiar with this conflict since our society has long presented a curious contrast between sexual-sensual denial or control on the one hand, and unbridled material greed on the other. In some form, the conflict between pleasure and renunciation is found in all societies.

Some cultures permit the nursing of babies for long periods of time and others force an early end to pleasurable sucking; some encourage thumb-sucking, masturbation, and self-stimulation and others consider these grave sins; some allow the infant free movement while others keep him tightly swaddled to a cradle board. There is a wide variety of ways in which the pleasures of the infant and young child may be encouraged or denied but at some point and in some way, all societies draw the line. In addition, all societies place some limits on individual selfishness. In some form, the individual has part of his energy channeled into work necessary for the common good. No culture approves of individuals who spend all their time simply gratifying their own pleasures, or devoting themselves solely to the accumulation of personal wealth. As Freud argues so beautifully in *Civilization and Its Discontents,* the very fabric of civilization rests on the renunciation of individual impulse.

The universal incest taboo, and the related Oedipus complex, is an important example of this conflict. In an earlier discussion, we saw how the history of pleasurable-sensual experience with close family members makes them natural objects of sexual desire. These desires are opposed by the taboo on incest. In the early years of childhood, as an interest and understanding of sexuality emerges, the young boy's desire for his mother or sisters and the young girl's for her father or brothers, is opposed by the taboo that prohibits these relationships. Already, in these early years the child must accommodate himself to the fact that certain pleasures, strongly desired, must be renounced. The persistence of Oedipal desires, the difficulty that so many have in coming to terms with this issue, attest to the power of the conflict between pleasure and renunciation.

Each of the core conflicts passes through a series of transformations as the person goes from one developmental stage to the next. The infant is forced to give up nursing or thumb-sucking, the child must renounce his Oedipal desires. Eventually, everyone must face the demands of an adult role; must take on more of the burden of work at the expense of childish fun and pleasure.

Aggression

There is little more to be added, at this point, regarding aggression and its control. We have seen how aggression arises from our primate heritage where it is controlled by ritual and gesture. The stable customs of hunting and gathering society allow aggression to be redirected into channels that are, for the most part, harmless. Fission (simply leaving the group and joining another), the direction of hatred toward outsiders, the hunting and killing of animals, and rituals specific to each culture such as song duels and spear-dodging contests, all channel and redirect potential destruction in more benign directions.

The rise of agriculture and technology and the resulting breakdown of hunting societies meant that the old customs no longer successfully channeled aggression. Cultural change of the past 10,000 years has been accompanied by a great deal of fighting, made increasingly lethal by improved weapons. We are groping for new customs, but so far none has proven too successful.

At the level of the individual, aggression manifests itself in different forms at different stages of development. The willfulness of the infant; the self-assertion of the two-year-old who battles his parents by continually saying "no;" the fighting between brothers and sisters that Alfred Adler labeled "sibling rivalry;" the often violent rebelliousness of adolescence and youth, each in its own way is a manifestation of the human instinct of aggression. And each must be met by a parental-societal response that controls, channels, and helps the person redirect it in less destructive directions. There is no easy way; excessive and harsh control may be so frustrating that it creates more problems than it solves. Man's aggressive nature sets the stage for this conflict and we all must struggle with it.

SUMMARY

Chapter 1 has outlined a general model of development that underlies physical growth, the biological evolution of species, the growth and change of culture and society, and the psychological development of individuals. The second chapter presented a model of instinctual systems, each given force by emotion which confers value on specific survival-related actions and perceptions. We then saw how these social instincts—attachment, love, fear, anxiety, aggression, sexuality, play, curiosity, and exploration—are manifest in our closest living relatives, the monkeys and apes. Chapter 3 then followed the course of these social instincts from ape to man, drawing on recent observations of hunting and gathering cultures. The unique features of man's evolution were noted, particularly the change in brain size on which language and culture depend. Human instincts were reviewed and certain central conflicts—dependency and independence, pleasure and renunciation, and aggression and its control—described.

Having set the background in these chapters, it is now time to begin our actual developmental journey. In the chapters that follow I will attempt to trace the major themes in the development of human personality. Two general formats suggest themselves: (1) a strictly chronological one in which the field as a whole is followed as if it were a developing individual moving from infancy to old age, and (2) a topic-oriented format in which substantive issues define each chapter. I will follow neither of these strictly, but will attempt a course which combines them. The overall sequence will be chronological, the next chapter dealing with infancy, the following one with childhood, and later chapters taking up problems of the adolescent and adult periods. Between these will be chapters dealing with fantasy, dreams, and play; consciousness and dissociation; and the development of self and morality, all of which occur, in differing forms, throughout the life span.

Let us begin with infancy.

chapter four

Infancy

Over the first year and a half of life the human infant develops from a state dominated by reflexes and emotional displays to one in which the world is increasingly symbolized and the beginnings of communicative language appear. Soon after birth, the infant shows he is a member of a social species by using the cry of distress and a little later, the smile of satisfaction or delight to communicate information about his emotional states. These first social communications involve emotional displays that are readily understandable to other species members. Mothers of all cultures recognize and respond to the infant's cry and react with pleasure to his smile.

The period of infancy precedes language—the infant cannot *tell* us what it feels like to be small and totally dependent or how it is to experience the whole world for the first time. Therefore, our understanding of the psychology of infancy rests on inferences that we make as adult observers. Young children or adolescents can tell us what they think and feel or how they perceive the world. Furthermore, adult memory extends back into these periods of childhood and adolescence so that we can fill in our understanding with memories of our own experience. Infants cannot talk to us nor does adult memory extend into this period. Hence, our understanding of infancy relies heavily on the theories or models of infant psychology that we create.

Because an understanding of infancy relies heavily on inference, there is a danger of distorting our theories of infancy in the direction of later stages. In chapter 1 I referred to this as "adultomorphism," a sort of adult-centered view of infancy. Many theorists attribute qualities to the infant—qualities such as the ability to fantasize or to remember things—that are not present, at least in the early stages. Given these cautions about the danger of adultomorphizing the infant, let me now discuss some theories of infant psychology.

THEORIES OF INFANCY

Every theory of infancy is based on certain observations which provide the data for the theory. In addition, the different theories contain ideas and assumptions about motivation and each has a particular view of infant phenomenology—of how the world is felt and perceived from inside the infant's mind. Some aspects of psychoanalytic, neoanalytic, and Piagetian theory have already been touched on in chapter 1. I will discuss selected portions of these theories to develop an overall model of infancy which combines features from Freud, Erikson, and Piaget. With this integrated theory as our guide we can then take up specific topics from the first year and a half of life.

The Psychoanalytic Model

Freud and his followers base their theories not on direct observations of infants, but on the recollections of adult patients in psychoanalytic therapy. Given the indirectness of this source of data, it is not surprising that a number of errors are found within their theory. At the same time, psychoanalytic theory has been valuable in calling attention to the importance of early experiences of pleasure (infantile sexuality) and more generally, to the crucial significance of early relationships and the emotions associated with them.

As we have seen in previous chapters, Freud attempted to construct a theory in which all motivation could be derived from a single source—the seeking of pleasure. He assumed that pain was based on an increase in tension and that pleasure resulted when this tension was released or discharged. The infant, according to this theory, is motivated solely by the desire for pleasurable tension release. Freud called this primary motive *the pleasure principle*. Associated with the pleasure principle is what he termed a state of "primary narcissism" or self-love. Pleasure comes from the infant's own body, hence he is focused on himself in a "narcissistic" fashion. Other people do not exist for the infant, or exist only as objects that can gratify his striving after pleasure. This means that the infant is essentially a nonsocial or selfish creature and that socialization must be forced on him. An example frequently cited by later psychoanalytic theorists such as David Rapaport is the infant nursing at his mother's breast. In this example, it is assumed that hunger causes an increase in tension which is "discharged" with the sucking that gives rise to oral pleasure. At first, the infant makes no distinction between himself and the "object" involved in the gratification of this pleasure-seeking instinct. Out of experiences of frustration, however, there gradually develops a sense of the boundary between self or ego and object or nonego.

The above is a brief account, but it points out the central features of the psychoanalytic model. Pleasure seeking is assumed to be the primary motive and the infant interacts with the world only when frustration forces him to. The theory contains the idea of an early state in which the self does not exist, or in which the boundary between self and other—between internal sensations and those from the outside world—is blurred or undifferentiated. This point is not always clear in psychoanalytic accounts, however, and sometimes a more advanced ego is attributed to the infant (for example, when it is assumed that he has the capacity to fantasize about past experiences of pleasure).

The emphasis on pleasure seeking as the primary motive is closely related to the model of psychosexual stages. Freud was always interested in giving his theories of motivation a biological basis, which is why he assumed that the locus of pleasure was successively tied to the oral, anal, and genital zones of the body. According to the theory of psychosexual development, the infant obtains his most intense pleasure from sucking and related stimulation of the oral zone. Infancy, then, is almost synonomous with "orality."

What can be said about these psychoanalytic ideas? First, a number of factors indicate that the model of motivation is in need of modification. The general model of instinctual-emotional systems, and the specific evidence bearing on attachment systems—discussed in chapters 2 and 3—indicate that the pleasure principle–tension reduction model is far too narrow. The idea that oral stimulation or sucking has a special significance is likewise too restrictive. The human infant is motivated to seek pleasure in a variety of ways, including sucking, clinging, rocking, and general contact comfort forms of stimulation. But he is not motivated solely by pleasure seeking. Other instinctual systems motivate forms of activity that go beyond a desire for passive tension release. The discussions in chapters 2 and 3 made clear that the human infant, like his monkey and ape relatives, is motivated to interact with many aspects of the social and nonsocial world. Let us look at some of these other systems.

Human infants and children are intrinsically active: they look at, touch, listen to, taste, manipulate, and in other ways actively engage the world around them. There is now ample evidence from psychological studies to support the view—of which any observant parent was already aware —that children actively engage the world and that such engagement is an end in itself. Nowhere has the older "drive" or the pleasure principle theory of motivation more clearly shown its inadequacies. Curiosity and exploration are not expressed only in the service of hunger or because they are related in some way to sexual or other pleasurable experiences. Nor is the infant active only when he is reinforced by social approval or reward. Quite the contrary, infants and children may be most active and curious when other needs are satisfied or when reinforcing adults are absent. And, as many parents know, there are times when children would rather play than eat— when it is all one can do to drag them away from hide-and-seek or baseball to the dinner table.

Simple drive theories of human motivation were never popular with investigators engaged in direct observational work with primates, especially young ones. Piaget has long stressed the motivating power of activity for its own sake. He posits a "need to function" as the driving force behind intellectual development. Harlow demonstrated that monkeys would solve puzzles and engage in related exploratory actions with high motivation simply because it was interesting or novel to do so. In a typical experiment, Rheingold (1963) was able to show that human infants as young as four months of age were motivated to touch a ball when this act was "rewarded" with a movie-show.

Mammals as a group tend to be active and curious, and some, such as primates, are much more so than others. Within all species, the young are especially curious and playful, no doubt because more of the world is novel to them. Curiosity and exploratory behavior are thus built in to the human species, and have as much instinctual force as pleasure seeking—interest and surprise are emotions which can be just as "primary" as anxiety or anger. As Hamburg (1971) points out, the long period of infancy would be maladaptive if there were not provision in the genetic code to cause the infant to attend to novelty, to venture forth, to explore, and to learn.

The orthodox psychoanalytic model of infant motivation needs to be reformulated in light of these factors. Erikson (1950) among others provides such a reformulation. He makes little use of the tension-reduction model and is quite clear that what is significant is the *quality* of the emotional relationship between the infant and his caretakers, rather than the *quantity* of oral pleasure. From the earliest period of life it is *social* relationships that are crucial, and this social aspect is structured into man's instinctual systems in a primary fashion.

Piaget's Model

Piaget bases his model on direct observation of and experiments with infants and children. His ideas and theories are thus more closely tied to the data than is psychoanalytic theory. Piaget's major concern has always been with cognitive development, though he states that his theories are meant to apply to the child's affective or emotional development as well. Because of this concern for the development of cognition and intellect, he has focused much more heavily on the motives which stimulate curiosity, exploration, and interaction with the environment simply because such interaction is interesting and expands the infant's understanding of the world. Unlike psychoanalytic theory, which depicts the infant as a passive creature who only reacts when painful tension builds up or when pleasure seeking is frustrated, Piaget sees the infant as intrinsically active—as a participant in shaping his place in the world. Although Piaget's emphasis on the active, information-seeking nature of infant motivation is supported by a good deal of evidence, it seems to go too far in disavowing the instinctual side of human nature. One sometimes gets the impression when reading Piaget that anger, anxiety, or sensuality have no special force in human life.

In its own way, this theory can be as unbalanced as Freud's. What is needed, it seems to me, is a view of human motivation that captures the valuable aspects of both the psychoanalytic and Piagetian theories—that makes a place for the special power of instinct and emotion and also endows the human infant with the motivation for intelligent action. The model of instinctual-emotional systems attempts to encompass the contributions of both Freud and Piaget. In this model, motivation is tied to man's biological past, not with a theory of energy discharge or special zones of the body, but with a view which places instinctual-emotional systems in the context of primate evolution. The special evolution of the human species has given a central place to the sorts of motives that Piaget focuses on; to the need to interact with and progressively understand all aspects of the stimulating environment. But it has also given a special place to systems of love, attachment, fear, separation anxiety, and aggression which give emotional value to these *specifically social* areas.

Infant Phenomenology. One of Piaget's essential contributions is the way he gets us to understand infancy from the infant's point of view. Piaget, as we saw in the first chapter, is a thorough developmentalist. He is least likely to adultomorphize the infant. In his model, it is clear that our experience of adult consciousness is the product of a lengthy development through the many stages of infancy, childhood, and adolescence. The infant is not only physically different from the child and adult, he also experiences life in a profoundly different psychological state. We are so used to the consciousness of ourselves, we so take for granted the existence of our bodies as independent things that exist in a world of other things, that it is difficult to even think about the radical difference during the first six months of life.

Initially, infancy is dominated by diffuse activity, given some order by basic biological rhythms, such as sleep-wakefulness, and reflexes such as sucking and grasping. The infant, during the first year and a half of life, cannot symbolize; he is incapable of evoking the image of persons or objects in their absence. His experience is dominated by momentary sensations and motor actions. For this reason, Piaget calls this first psychological stage "sensorimotor." This is the first important thing to note about infant phenomenology: unlike the symbols that we are used to—whether words, visual images, or memories—the infant can only "think" in a sensorimotor mode; all he has available to manipulate mentally are sense impressions and motor acts.

In the earliest months, the infant's experience of sensations and his own actions are relatively undifferentiated. He has no sense of self; not even the most primitive sense of his own body as a thing distinct from other things. So far, Piaget and Freud are together on this point: both posit an initial, undifferentiated, pre-ego, state. But Freud assumes that the sense of boundary between self and reality arises from frustration of the infant's attempts to achieve pleasure, while Piaget places it in the wider context of the infant's growing understanding of the physical world.

The infant begins his attempt at a practical, sensorimotor understanding of the world by "assimilating" everything into reflex "schemas." Each item in his world exists only as something to suck or to grasp, to look at or to hear. Assimilation, schema, and the related term, accommodation, are central concepts in Piaget's work and their meanings had best be clarified.

Piaget speaks of two major operations that characterize all mental life, *assimilation* and *accommodation*. Assimilation, which he derives from the broader biological concept as when an organism assimilates food and oxygen, is defined as the *incorporation of reality* (sights, sounds, events, and later, words and other symbolic input) *into existing mental structures or schemas.* The early reflexes of sucking and grasping indicate the presence of sucking and grasping schemas and when the infant treats everything as if it were "something to suck" he is assimilating reality to his sucking schema. Assimilation is interchange with reality that leaves the mind unchanged; if things don't fit they are assimilated anyway or distorted. For example, if a child has a schema on the basis of which he can recognize white dogs and black dogs and he sees a white dog and fits it into his existing category, he is assimilating a bit of reality into an established schema. If he sees a brown dog or a black cat and categorizes these as "black dogs," he is forcing a bit of reality to assimilate. If there are repeated experiences in which reality doesn't fit—that is, in which it can't be so easily assimilated because of the inadequacy of existing schemas—then the schemas will have to change. In our example, the child will have to add new categories for "brown dogs" and for "cats." *This modification of schemas is called accommodation.* The person accommodates to reality by changing the internal structures or schemas. Now, a word about schemas.

Schemas. A specific or exact definition of this concept is difficult and its overall meaning will only emerge from its use in a variety of contexts. One may think of a schema as an internal plan that determines the direction of action, thought, or fantasy. When we speak of the fixed action patterns that characterize the instinctual behavior of simpler animals such as insects, reptiles, or fish, we assume that instinctual schemas are built in to the animal's nervous system from birth or emerge after maturation with relatively little or no required experience.

Human instinctual systems can be thought of as those schemas having strong emotions connected to them. We can speak of them as potentiated or amplified by the feedback of emotional information. For example, schemas develop around that class of experiences associated with sensual pleasure, and the memories, anticipations, and sensorimotor acts involved. The distinctly pleasurable feelings or emotions connected to sensual pleasure become a part of these schemas and give them special value. When the sensual schemas are activated at later times—by external sights or sounds, memories, or actions—anticipation of pleasurable feelings is also activated and makes these schemas especially driving, demanding, or imperative. Indeed, that is why emotional schemas deserve the name "instinctual" in the common meaning of that term. Similarly, the schemas associated with anxiety or aggression have special motivating force due to that association or information feedback.

The discussion of instinctual-emotional systems in the previous two chapters should have prepared the ground for an understanding of the concept of schema. A schema is, after all, a *system,* an internal plan by which the person fits his experiences together. Instinctual systems or schemas are those associated with the core areas related to those adaptive characteristics of the human species.

You will recall that the emotional-display systems shared by man and the other primates are built in to relatively older parts of the brain and appear very early in development. This is the initial form of the instinctual-emotional schemas. Schemas also develop around the child's early experiences with other persons. These overlap greatly with emotional schemas (sensual and aggressive experiences typically involve others, of course) and Piaget (1951) speaks of "personal schemas" and "affective schemas" as if they were interchangeable.

In sum, schemas direct perception and action (assimilation), and certain types of experience force schemas to change (accommodation). Piaget's model implies an *interaction* between the guiding structures in the person and the modifying force of external reality. When the internal structures are dominant we have a preponderance of assimilation; when external reality is dominant, a preponderance of accommodation. All psychological development, in Piaget's view, is a balancing of these two tendencies; a balancing that Piaget terms *equilibrium*. These complex ideas have been briefly presented here, but they will appear again in several different developmental contexts which should further clarify their meaning. Let us now return to the problem of the differentiation of self or ego in early infancy.

Sensorimotor Egocentrism. We have seen that the infant initially assimilates the world to his sensorimotor reflexes; he has no awareness of objects that exist in space and that persist through time. Things are "real" for him only when he sucks, grasps, or looks at them. The world, to use Piaget's words, is a place "without objects, consisting only of shifting and unsubstantial 'tableaux' which appear and are then totally reabsorbed" (Piaget and Inhelder, 1969, p. 14). Since the infant cannot conceive of a permanent object that has a definite existence in space and time, he likewise cannot conceive of his own body—his sensorimotor self—as a permanent, substantial thing. The dominance of sensorimotor assimilation and the lack of differentiation between self and reality—or indeed among any objects—produces a profound narrowness of viewpoint which Piaget calls *sensorimotor egocentrism*.

In discussing the infant's first view of himself and the world, Piaget says, "... the child's initial universe is entirely centered on his own body and action in an egocentrism as total as it is unconscious (for lack of consciousness of self) (Piaget and Inhelder, 1969, p. 13)." "Egocentrism" refers to the infant's point of view: he is "centered" on his own fleeting sensations and actions and cannot view himself or the world from any other perspective. Egocentrism refers to the difficulty or inability to assume other perspectives. In a moment, we will see how interchange with the world forces accommodation and a decentering of this initial egocentrism. Here, it is worth referring to egocentrism as it was employed in chapter 1. There, we saw how cultures are centered on their own experience with an ethnocentric viewpoint, and how man's view of his place in the world has been developing from a centered to a progressively more differentiated, less centered perspective. The basic developmental progression from egocentric to less centered perspectives begins with the totally centered experience of the infant who assimilates everything to his sensorimotor schemas. This view of infant phenomenology is similar to Freud's: for example, both note the initial lack of differentiation between self and reality. But Piaget's model is broader; sensorimotor-egocentrism is not restricted to oral behavior but rather is the infant's total mode of experiencing the world. And it is not just frustration of pleasure, but his interaction in all modalities—grasping, sucking, looking, hearing, and so on—that forces accommodation and an eventual decentering. Here is how Piaget constrasts his view with the psychoanalytic position: " 'Narcissism' (in the sense of narcissism without Narcissus, i.e., without consciousness of the ego) corresponds to the complete egocentrism of the first year, during which the universe and the ego are one, because there are no permanent external objects (1951, p. 185)."

Permanent Objects. Gradually, over the first year of life, the infant comes to have a sense of the permanence and substantiality of things. He acquires the ability to conceive (in sensorimotor terms, of course) of things that exist apart from his fleeting sensations or momentary actions with them. In a way, one can say that repeated contact with the world forces the child to discover or invent the rudimentary principles of physics. Here are some simple examples. If an infant under six months of age is reaching for an object and one covers the object with a cloth, he stops reaching as if it ceased to exist (since he cannot see it). By nine to ten months the infant will not only look behind the cloth, but can remember which of two screens an object is hidden behind and search in the correct place. When he does this, he demonstrates that he has a permanent object schema; that objects have an existence for him even when he is not looking or directly acting upon them.

As a well established sense of permanent objects grows, so does the infant's sense of himself as a permanent object—as a thing distinct from other things in the world, a thing that is substantial and that persists through time. The sensorimotor nature of the infant's experience means that this early self or ego is almost entirely a "body-self," a coordination of sensations and actions from the different body areas.

I realize that this presentation of Piaget's model has been sketchy and brief, and that several important concepts—assimilation, accommodation, schema, egocentrism, and decentering—have been defined in a fairly short space. True to the developmental viewpoint, we will meet these ideas again and again as development proceeds and their meaning should become progressively sharpened.

Having outlined these theoretical ideas from Freud and Piaget, let me now move on to a consideration of issues of special importance from the period of infancy.

ATTACHMENT

In earlier discussions, we have seen how mother-infant attachment is part of an instinctual-emotional system of central importance to all primates. Young monkeys and apes are strongly motivated to cling to their mothers, to orient toward them, and, somewhat later, to follow and remain close to them. The mother, for her part, is also strongly motivated to hold, nurse, groom, and make sure her infant is close by. Periods of stress or threat intensify the need for both mother and infant to maintain closeness. Once the infant is securely attached to a mother figure, separation arouses anxiety and, if prolonged, grief and depression.

Human infants and their mothers show a closely related pattern of attachment, though there are differences due to the greater physical immaturity of the infant at birth, the longer period of time until he can cling and locomote on his own, and other features unique to our species. For both human and other primate infants, sensorimotor interactions with mother are of the utmost importance. Holding, contact comfort, and sucking are the only things the infant understands. Since he functions at a sensorimotor (as opposed to a conceptual or symbolic) level, sensorimotor interactions are the only ones that can affect him. Bowlby (1969) lists five species-specific behavioral patterns central to human attachment: sucking, clinging, following, crying, and smiling. The differences between human and nonhuman primates center on how this sensorimotor contact is brought about. Most monkeys and apes can cling to their mothers, either at birth or shortly thereafter. For humans, the mother must show more initiative and the infant must depend more on communicative crying and smiling.

Crying and other signs of distress on the part of the infant are typically cues which lead the mother to hold, cuddle, rock, and in other ways provide sensual stimulation to him. In the process, the mother becomes associated with the reduction of distress and the elimination of pain. Kessen and Mandler (1961) speak of *innate distress inhibitors,* such as rocking, which would normally be directed from mother to child. The consistent association of mother with the reduction of distress, along with her provision of sensual-pleasure experiences, play a role in establishing her as a principal figure to which the infant becomes attached.

Human infants have a readiness to become attached to that figure that provides visual cues associated with the face, contact comfort, and pleasurable holding, rocking, stress reduction, and playful and interesting sights and sounds. The critical period for this attachment process runs from approximately four months to one year of age. Although the emotional groundwork is being laid from birth onward, attachment to a specific mother figure cannot occur until the infant has the ability to conserve permanent objects. Prior to the development of this cognitive skill, mother, like everything else in the infant's world, exists as an uncoordinated set of sensations: she is only "real" at the time she is interacting with the infant, not before or after. As the infant acquires the ability to conserve permanent objects, he acquires a sensorimotor schema of "mother," made up of all those tactile, visual, oral, auditory sensations, and mutual interactions that characterize their relationship. This "mother schema" is of course the first and one of the most important human schemas to develop. Once it is firmly structured, other persons will be assimilated to it. To put it in more prosaic terms, we can say that if the infant loves and trusts his mother he is in a position to love and trust others. Conversely, if he cannot depend on her or comes to fear her as a source of pain and frustration, he will expect the same from others. Attachment to a specific mother figure occurs around six months of age, the same age at which object permanence is established. Separations and disruptions in the basic mother-infant relation will be more damaging in the second six months of life for this reason.

Attachment grows out of the sensorimotor relationship between mother and infant over the first months of life. It is dependent on the growth of cognitive skills, particularly object permanence. In any specific case, the form of attachment—whether it occurs early or late or is strong or weak— results from the type of care given by the mother interacting with unique qualities of the infant. A study of infants raised in a different culture will illustrate different patterns of attachment.

Cultural Differences in Attachment

Mary Ainsworth (1967) carried out intensive observations of mother-infant interactions among the Ganda of East Africa. For comparison, she also observed Ganda infants being raised by western methods in a nearby city. The infants raised in the bush experienced a great deal of physical contact with their mothers. They were carried about next to mother's body, slept next to her, and engaged in a good deal of physically stimulating play. The comparison group was cared for in the same manner as many American infants. They spent a fair amount of time alone in their cribs and experienced mother's coming and going, being with them and leaving. Overall, they received much less sensorimotor stimulation, particularly holding, rocking, and body contact. The more intense and consistent sensorimotor stimulation that the bush-reared Ganda infants received had several effects. Their general motor development was accelerated, compared to children reared by western methods. For example they crawled by twenty-five weeks as compared to the thirty-two weeks typical of American infants. Attachment to mother appeared earlier and was more strongly established. Ainsworth reports that some of these infants cried and attempted to follow their mothers as early as fifteen weeks of age. Almost all of them were strongly attached by six months. They showed a definite preference for their own mother, as opposed to the many other adults they were in frequent contact with, crying when mother would leave and greeting her return with smiles, uplifted arms, and sounds of delight. Infants raised by western methods showed these same signs of attachment at a later time, pointing to the important role of sensorimotor stimulation in the attachment process.

Components of Attachment

At this point, let us look at some of the components of attachment in more detail. General bodily contact and crying have already been noted. Since human infants cannot cling to their mothers during the early months of life other means of emotional communication such as *eye contact* and *smiling* come to play central roles. Several investigators (Wolff, 1963; Robson, 1967) describe the importance of mother-infant eye contact during the early months of life. Eye contact is a form of mutual communication that appears early and, as with pleasurable holding, endures throughout life as a component of human love. Infants are visually alert: they seek out their mothers' eyes and remain engaged. Mothers react to the infant's gaze as a sign of love and may experience the infant's failure or refusal to look as a sign of rejection. A purposeful avoidance of eye contact by the infant or young child is associated with disturbance in attachment.

Studies of infants in a wide variety of cultural and social contexts all agree that a clearly *social smile* appears by four months of age. It is preceded by the infant's attentive gaze and spontaneous or reflex smiling. The infant's smile is elicited by movement and complex configurations of stimuli. In the normal course of events, mother's face provides these qualities and the infant comes to orient and smile more at it, and less at other configurations. Mother, of course, typically reinforces the infant's smile, which brings pleasure to her. By the time the infant has attained the capacity for object permanence at six months or so, he is well prepared to smile selectively at that most important object, his mother's face. During the period from six months to one year, the infant becomes firmly attached to a single maternal figure and the social smile is selectively directed toward her. Thus, what begins as a reflex-like emotional display soon develops into a central part of the emotional communication system between mother and infant. The smile is almost universally rewarding to mothers who respond to it by directing attention to the infant, playing, babbling, picking him up, and so forth.

Babbling and *raising the arms* are forms of behavior related to eye contact and smiling that the infant displays from about six months of age.

Babbling typically serves as a cue for mother to babble in return; it is the precursor to language. The raising of arms is a signal of the infant's positive anticipation of mother's approach. The raised arm gesture is very similar in form to the clinging response of infant apes and is, no doubt, a later evolutionary development in which a response central to monkey and ape attachment now serves as a gesture or signal in the human attachment process.

Eye contact, smiling, and the raising of arms are all components of old—in the evolutionary sense—systems of emotional communication. Facial expression is particularly important as a means of communicating information about the infant's emotional state. As Darwin put it long ago: "The movements of expression in the face and body, whatever their origin may have been, are in themselves of much importance for our welfare. They serve as the first means of communication between the mother and her infants (1872)." A much more detailed treatment of all the components of attachment, along with a comprehensive review of the many available studies, may be found in Bowlby's book.

To sum up: the processes involved in the attachment of infant to mother lead to the establishment of initial human or personal schemas. These schemas are sensorimotor and consist of the mutual communication of information and emotion. The pleasure of tactile and kinesthetic stimulation, eye-to-eye contact, smiling, babbling, the raised arm gesture, and the corresponding maternal responses, all function to bind infant and mother together.

Harriet Rheingold (1970), a longtime student of mother-infant interactions, stresses that the infant socializes the parents more than the reverse. With his cries and smiles *he* communicates to *them* what to do and when to stop doing it. Rheingold points to crying, the infant's smile, and the related tender, pleasurable interactions between mother and infant as central in the development of the affectionate attachment that serves as a necessary prelude to later socialization. She also argues that "habit training" (schedules of eating and sleeping, breast versus bottle feeding, toilet training, and the like) has only minor significance in early socialization. These activities are, in her view, of more importance to the mother than to the infant.

Attachment is, thus, a complex process that takes some time to become firmly established in humans (ranging from five months to a year or even longer in some cases). Once established it is maintained by the strongest of emotional bonds. As Bowlby puts it:

> No form of behavior is accompanied by stronger feeling than is attachment behavior. The figures toward whom it is directed are loved and their advent greeted with joy.
> So long as a child is in the unchallenged presence of a principal attachment-figure, or within easy reach, he feels secure. A threat of loss creates anxiety,

and actual loss, sorrow; both, moreover, are likely to arouse anger. (1969, p. 209)

Once attachment to a specific mother figure is established, the characteristic separation reactions that Bowlby refers to make their appearance. Let us now look at these in greater detail.

SEPARATION

The strength of the infant's attachment to a mother figure can be gauged by his reaction to separation or loss. We have seen how the various components of attachment—the affectionate bond between mother and infant—are built into the human species because of their extreme importance for survival. Similarly, a number of characteristic reactions develop that function to maintain the mother-infant bond once it is established, or to bring mother and infant together if they become separated. These reactions involve the powerful emotions of anxiety, grief, and anger, and set the pattern for reactions later in life involving these same feelings. Because of this, a consideration of separation and loss bears importantly on our understanding of later emotional development.

The Protest-Despair-Detachment Pattern

A number of students of early infancy (Bowlby, 1960, 1961; see Averill, 1968, for a summary) have distinguished a characteristic pattern when the mother-infant bond is disrupted. This pattern, which occurs in three stages, becomes manifest after the infant is attached to a specific mother figure sometime during the second six months of life. The first stage, termed *protest* or *distress,* is characterized by anxiety, crying, a high level of activity, and rage. In most instances the infant's protest is successful in bringing mother back. In those cases where protest is ineffective, a period of *despair* or *despondency* follows. This is characterized by withdrawal, facial and body signs of depression, and a low level of activity. The despair phase may elicit caretaking from the mother figure, and also functions to conserve the infant's energy. Reunion at this point leads back to protest and excessive clinging as attachment becomes reestablished. In those instances where separation is prolonged, despair passes into *detachment,* a phase in which the infant is seemingly unresponsive to people. Detachment represents a serious disruption of the mother-infant bond which is difficult to heal and which may lay the foundation for psychological disturbance in later life.

Field and laboratory studies of monkeys and apes have shown the same pattern of reaction to separation, as we have seen in chapter 2. Infant chimpanzees, gorillas, baboons, and other species, all spend a great deal of time in close physical contact with their mothers. Separations are typically brief, with reunion rapidly following protest. Both protest and despair are observable in the wild, and laboratory studies such as that of Kaufman and Rosenblum (1967) have demonstrated the same anxiety-despair-detachment pattern in monkeys.

The study of attachment and separation in monkeys, apes, and humans points to the biological utility of the infant's reactions to separation. The crying and rage of the protest phase bring mother to the infant, while lack of activity during despair conserves energy. Separation anxiety, in general, serves as a powerful motive driving both infant and mother toward achievement of a goal—attachment—crucial to the infant's survival. The anger that is characteristic of the total reaction "punishes" the mother, making her less likely to leave on future occasions. This is not punishment in a conscious or willful sense but in the way that a biologically built in mechanism serves a goal because of the advantages it brings to survival of the species.

Separation Anxiety and Anger

Two important emotions are characteristic of the entire separation pattern: anxiety and anger. The unmistakable anxiety that the attached infant shows upon separation—commonly termed "separation anxiety"—is the first interpersonal anxiety, if not the first of any kind, that the human being experiences. The schemas amplified by this powerful emotion are the prototypes for later interactions involving attachment and loss. That is, when a symbolic or "conceptual" component is acquired, it functions within the sphere of schemas amplified by anxiety.

The infant derives his initial security from attachment, and disruptions in attachment may be thought of as the prototypes of insecurity. The other powerful emotion characteristic of separation is anger. Bowlby states, "... it is my belief that there is no experience to which a young child can be subjected more prone to elicit intense and violent hatred for the mother figure than that of separation... (1960, p. 24)." Other investigators have noted the intensity of direct rage, as well as the prevalence of indirect anger such as a refusal to look at, smile, or relate to mother. The infant's anger over separation is one of the earliest forms in which this emotion so central in primate social relations manifests itself. Bowlby believes the child's anger stems from the frustration of loss, but that it is also useful in getting needs met, including the need for reunion. Anger also serves to discourage the mother from abandoning the child on future occasions. As Bowlby puts it, "Looked at as a means that in other circumstances aids the recovery of the lost object and the maintenance of union with it, the anger characteristic of mourning can be seen to be biologically useful (1961, p. 321)."

As with anxiety, the anger present in the separation reaction is one of the earliest interpersonal expressions of this emotion. The form of the schemas, amplified by both anger and anxiety, is influential where later conceptual content is acquired. For example, the infant may acquire a characteristic way of expressing his anxiety and anger in early experiences of separation and loss. These emotional patterns will then be aroused when he reacts to later losses, whether these are actual—the loss of an important person—or symbolic, such as the loss of another's approval.

The infant's anger at separation is communicated in the sensorimotor modes characteristic of attachment. For example, Ainsworth and Bell, in their study of separation reactions, describe:

> Looking away behavior—ignoring the mother, or first starting to approach her and then turning away—[which] seem homologous with the behavior shown by some young children at reunion after separations lasting days or weeks. Investigators report that at reunion some children do not seem to recognize the mother, and that for a longer or shorter time they remain distant from her and treat her like a stranger...[this reaction] tends to succeed protest and despair reactions during separation itself, and may persist for a long time, even indefinitely, after reunion in cases of separations which are especially long and depriving or oft repeated. (1968, p. 10)

Grief and Mourning

Early reactions to separation are the prototypes for grief reactions throughout life. Investigators of grief in adults from varying social and cultural contexts (Lindemann, 1944; Engel, 1961; Averill, 1968) note a common underlying reaction pattern. Grief is typically initiated by loss, frequently the loss of someone close, such as a parent, child, or spouse. For example, Rogler and Hollingshead (1965), in their study of schizophrenic psychoses, found that the death of an infant or child was a main cause of breakdown among mothers who become psychotic. Symbolic loss, such as the loss of a job or of status, may also initiate the syndrome. The initial stage is one of shock and disbelief with thoughts and habits still focused on the lost object. This is followed by a stage of despondency and despair as the passage of time makes the awareness of loss unavoidable. Anxiety, guilt, hostility, apathy, withdrawal, and other signs of psychological disturbance are characteristic of the despair stage. Eventually, an adaptation is made to the loss and a recovery stage ensues in which new relationships may be established.

The pattern of grief varies in its specific form and intensity among individuals as well as among different cultures which have their own prescribed rites and rituals of mourning. Despite these variations, the basic pattern of the reaction remains constant. It is, essentially, an instinctual emotional pattern which promotes social attachment. As Averill puts it, ". . . the adaptive function of grief is to ensure group cohesiveness in species where a social form of existence is necessary for survival (1968, p. 721)."

The similarity between adult grief reactions and an infant's reaction to separation is apparent. Indeed, many writers speak of the two as if they were synonymous. This similarity illustrates how a basic, emotionally amplified schema—in this case, that which defines reactions to loss—sets the pattern for reactions later in life. Adult grief reactions involve conceptual or symbolic components not found in infancy. For example, the bereaved is preoccupied with thoughts, memories, and fantasies of his loved one; complicated ideas of a self-punitive nature are frequent and, eventually, a new love object may substitute for the lost one. All these facets involve forms of intelligence that the infant does not possess. Yet the form of the emotional reaction is the same in mother-infant separation and adult grief reactions. The similarity illustrates, in a clear fashion, the motivating power of this early instinctual-emotional system.

DISTURBANCE IN ATTACHMENT

The preceding discussion of separation has assumed the presence of some form of adequate attachment to a mother figure. Attachment is not always adequate and a consideration of disturbed forms is worth pursuing.

I have already noted how the greater intensity and constancy of mother-infant interaction leads to early and strong attachment among the Ganda. We have also seen, in chapter 2, how complete deprivation of a mother proves disastrous in the social development of monkeys. No human infant can be raised in complete isolation, but those instances of partial isolation provide information regarding disruptions in attachment.

Social Deprivation

Various instances of "feral" or "wolf" children presumably raised apart from human contact, as well as cases of children whose parents have kept them locked in attics or cellars or subjected them to other forms of severe neglect have come to public attention over the years. It is usually difficult to ascertain exactly what has happened in such cases, but there seems little doubt that both physical and psychological development are grossly impaired by experiences of isolation. Language and intelligence are grossly retarded, emotional responsiveness aberrant, and perceptual and motor abilities below par. As Lenneberg (1966b) puts it, "The only safe conclusion to be drawn from the multitude of reports is that life in dark closets, wolves' dens, forests or sadistic parents' backyards is not conducive to good health and normal development (1966b, p. 234)."

Children raised in public institutions such as orphanages or foundling homes have been studied with greater care. This work has made clear the effects of specific early experiences—or the lack of them—on infant development. One of the best studies is that of Provence and Lipton (1962) who observed seventy-five American infants raised in an institutional environment that provided adequate food and health care, but very little social or psychological stimulation. For example, the infants spent the first eight months of life in cribs where many were cared for by a single nurse or attendant. They were fed both milk and, later, solid foods from bottles propped up in their cribs. These infants experienced little of the play, holding, or other forms of human contact that is common to infants raised by their mothers. By four months of age they were already showing differences from noninstitutional infants. They cried and vocalized less and, in general, appeared less active.

From eight months onward, the differences were marked. The institutional infants were described as "emotionally bland." They did not cling or respond when picked up, and seemed uninterested in toys and the external environment. Language development was grossly retarded and the range of emotional expression restricted. Body rocking became common and anxiety to strangers was largely lacking. In all these ways, the effects of the missing or minimal social attachment impaired the infant's initial interpersonal schemas. Lacking the security of the mother-infant bond, as well as the stimulation of human contact, the infant's curiosity and exploration were curtailed. Perhaps most striking was the restriction of emotional expression. This failure to develop normal emotional expressiveness shows how the course of these patterns, whose foundation is instinctual, depends on continual interaction with other persons.

Cultural Differences

Let me introduce a note of caution at this point. The institutional conditions described by Provence and Lipton constitute an extreme degree of human deprivation. Findings from studies such as this do not mean that all infants must be cared for in exactly the same way. Studies of rearing conditions in other cultures show that a fairly wide range of early experiences can lead to a normal outcome within their own cultural context. Observations of children reared on the kibbutzes of Israel are interesting in this regard (Rabin, 1958; Rabkin and Rabkin, 1969).

Kibbutz children are raised in groups by special nurses from earliest infancy. As they grow older, there is a great deal of interacting with peers which apparently plays an important role in socialization. The kibbutz children develop normally and show none of the forms of disturbance reported for infants raised in institutions such as that studied by Provence and Lipton.

The normal development of kibbutz children is sometimes cited as proof that institutional rearing is not harmful to infants or that a mother figure is not really necessary. This view is not supported by the facts. The kibbutz mothers, who typically work, are given special time off when they have a baby and breast feeding is common. Both parents spend several hours each day, as well as most holidays, with their children. This is, of course, in marked contrast to the experience of institution-reared children who lack parents or, indeed, any other adults to interact with. It is clear that the kibbutz-reared infants receive adequate amounts of social and psychological stimulation. The kibbutz experience illustrates that a range of different early experiences can produce essentially normal emotional-interpersonal outcomes.

The relationship between early rearing experience and later social roles is also highlighted by the kibbutz studies. The intensely social nature of the kibbutz child's upbringing seems to prepare him well for life in contemporary Israel where great value is placed on cooperation for mutual aims. Indeed, although only a small percentage of the total population, the kibbutznik has personified the central values of Israeli society. Compare this with the experience of an American child without parents, raised in an institution. Not only does he lack the individualized early relationships to prepare him for life in a society which values individualism, but he must later cope with the stigma of having no parents—of being unwanted, an orphan—with all its negative connotations. Thus, we see that it is not only the experiences of individual versus group upbringing, or the amounts and kinds of social and psychological stimulation, but the meaning of these experiences to the child, a meaning that is culturally defined.

PLAY, CURIOSITY, AND EXPLORATION IN INFANCY

From the earliest weeks of life, the human infant is curious and explores his world to the extent that he is able. Lacking the ability to locomote, he relies on other modalities. He orients toward and attempts to fixate on the objects, sights, sounds, and people around him. Visual schemas develop quite early. For example, Fantz (1958) has shown that infants have a pref- erence for visual patterns of greater complexity as early as the second month of life. Even before they are capable of much directed movement, infants are visually exploring the world and attending to that which is more complex and more interesting to look at.

Even when he is asleep, the newborn infant's mind is active. A study by Roffwarg, Muzio, and Dement (1966) has demonstrated that from birth —if not in utero—the infant shows a cyclical pattern of rapid eye move- ment (REM) sleep interspersed with non-REM sleep. REM sleep is associ- ated with dreaming in older children and adults. Does the high percentage of REM sleep observed in infants mean that they dream right after they are born? This seems unlikely since they probably lack the ability to hold images in memory. What is likely is that REM sleep in infants involves the exercise of their newly forming sensorimotor schemas. I will return to the topics of REM sleep and dreaming in chapter 6 where we will consider its analogous functions in childhood.

Sucking is a reflexive action present from birth and central to feeding. As motor development progresses during the first six months, sucking, mouthing, and tasting come to be used in non-nutritive exploration. The young infant is as likely to examine a novel object with his mouth as he is with his hands.

As the infant begins to crawl about and gain coordination, his explora- tion of the world expands. Much is new and much needs to be learned; the normal infant or young child is an excited and highly motivated explorer. He is like a scientist confronted with novel data to be explained; with theo- ries of causation to be invented. As we have already seen, by six months of age the infant has achieved permanent object schemas. From his varied experiences with objects, such as fingers, bottles, or mother, the infant ab- stracts a sensorimotor "concept" transcending these particular experiences. He progresses from a stage in which he sees the world as fleeting images and acts, unrelated to each other, to one in which he perceives objects as having an independent existence in time and space. For example, he may experi- ence his fingers as handling things, as something to suck, or as moving objects to look at—all these at different times and in different contexts. Initially, the schemas involved are separate and limited to each separate sensorimotor occurrence. By six months the infant can coordinate these schemas, and, from this, emerges a new schema which represents "fingers" as more or less permanent things that transcend the immediate actions of touching or being sucked. This construction of reality is a crucial step away from the earliest reflex- and action-dominated stage of mental operations toward later symbolic or conceptual stages. And, as we have seen, it is crucial for the formation of attachment to a single mother object, as well as the formation of the sensorimotor sense of self.

Development occurs in all sensorimotor areas during the first year. For example, most infants engage in a good deal of babbling, both to people and to themselves. This occurs spontaneously at first, and has even been observed in infants who are deaf from birth, though it is sensitive to the social response it meets and will extinguish if not responded to. All normal infants babble when they are alone and this is the precursor to the play with words so central in early language learning.

The Maternal Figure and Play

Of all the objects to look at, explore, or play with, none are more interesting, varied, or inherently attractive than other human beings. They move, smell, make sounds, and provide tactile and kinesthetic sensations and sensual experiences. They are associated with feeding and the elimination of distress and, as we have seen, the mother figure is the natural object of the child's first attachment. The development of play, curiosity, and exploration is influenced by two aspects of the mother's relation with the infant: (1) the quality and amount of stimulation she provides, and (2) the security of the attachment bond. Let us examine each of these.

The infant is predisposed to explore and interact with his environment in a great number of ways. Although such activity has an instinctual basis, it is sensitive to the environmental response it meets. Infants in a more stimulating environment have more to explore, while those in a bland or dull environment may lapse into self-stimulation such as repetitive rocking, head-nodding, or sound-making. As we have seen, infants raised in institutions show much less curiosity and exploration and correspondingly more self-stimulation. A recent study (La Crosse, et al., 1969) has shown how specific types of mothers affect the cognitive development of their infants during the ages from one to three. The infants who were most advanced cognitively and who showed the highest levels of curiosity and exploration had mothers who provided a great deal of stimulation and who were closely attuned to their infant's capacities. They played appropriate games with them and talked to them a great deal at a level appropriate to the infant's capacity. At the other extreme were mothers who paid little attention to their infants. Those infants spent, on the average, forty-one times more of their life doing little or nothing—staring into space, rocking, and so on. Like the findings on institutional rearing, this illustrates the infant's need for supportive stimulation from the human environment.

The second major way in which the mother affects the infant's developing play, curiosity, and exploration is through the nature of their mutual attachment. As I stressed at the conclusion of the last chapter, dependence-independence is one of the core dimensions of human life. In infancy, this dimension makes its first appearance as the balance between secure attachment and exploration of the novel world away from mother.

Attachment and Exploration

On first thought, one might suppose that attachment to the mother and exploration of the unfamiliar are antithetical, that the child who is occupied in clinging and seeking closeness would be less likely to explore than the one who doesn't have his mother about. The evidence indicates just the opposite, however. Exploration and attachment are related but the latter seems a necessary prerequisite for the former. A study by Ainsworth and Bell (1968) provides an illustration. They observed some fifty infants, close to one year of age, in a situation that was novel and not too frightening. In some conditions, the infant's mother was present, in others she left, and in others her presence was alternated with that of a stranger. Thus, the infant's exploration of the physical environment and of a novel person were observed in relation to attachment to the mother. Ainsworth and Bell found that exploration was greatest with mother present and that her absence interfered with it. As they put it, there is a

> ...balance between exploratory behavior and attachment behavior. At the beginning, when the mother is present, the baby uses her as a secure base from which to explore the novel aspects of the situation and the balance is in favor of exploratory behavior. But when mother departs exploratory behavior declines and...proximity-seeking attachment behavior is heightened. (p. 6)

Observation of young apes and monkeys and other studies of human infants all support the view that exploration takes place in the context of secure attachment and that separation, or other factors that interfere with attachment, impede exploration. This provides one important illustration of a developmental sequence whose order must be maintained. The establishment of attachment has what might be termed an instinctual priority. When activated, the emotionally amplified schema of attachment is dominant and the infant engages in attachment-promoting behavior such as crying or seeking after mother. When mother is present, attachment can be taken for granted and the infant is free to move out from his secure base to explore the new and often frightening world. Observations of such exploration indicate that the infant repeatedly returns to mother when his exploration arouses anxiety; mother is, in this sense, the safe base from which to engage the world. Lacking this base, infants spend less time exploring, since they are either busy seeking the missing mother or attempting to deal with anxiety on their own.

Ainsworth and Bell also observed angry and ambivalent responses directed at the mother upon reunion after a brief separation. Thus, separation from mother heightens both aggressive and attachment-seeking behavior, as well as interfering with exploration and new learning. Again, we see how attachment has a built-in developmental pattern; when the pattern is disrupted a number of unpleasant consequences ensue. This is not surprising when we remember that the instinctual pattern evolved for a species in which mother and infant were in almost constant contact (as are nonhuman primates in the wild and most hunting and gathering people in their natural cultural setting). The infant's biology has not caught up with the innovations of civilization—houses, playpens, baby sitters—which make separations so easy for mothers in contemporary society.

Person Schemas and Fear of Strangers

In addition to exploring the physical world, the infant explores the world of other persons. Reactions to strangers will illustrate the role played by attachment and the mother schema. In the earliest months of life, the infant does not discriminate between persons. As object permanence and attachment become established around six months, he shows a clear preference for the mother figure. Around eight months of age, with attachment firmly established, he begins to display fear at the appearance of strangers. This fear, or "eight months anxiety," has been observed by many investigators, including Gesell and Thompson (1938), Spitz (1950), and others. What seems to occur is that the infant assimilates strangers to his mother schema and, if they are too discrepant, fear is aroused. With increasing experience in the months that follow, the "person schemas" expand. From the secure base of attachment comes an eventual growth of the infant's personal world, though it should be stressed that this process takes a good deal of time. Children show varying degrees of shyness for a number of years.

In much of the preceding discussion, I have spoken of "infants" as if they were all alike. This, of course, is an oversimplification and it will be worthwhile to note some of the dimensions on which individual infants differ from each other.

INDIVIDUAL DIFFERENCES

Most investigators of infant development call attention to the wide variations among infants in the age of onset and particular form taken by attachment, reactions to separation, play, exploration, fear of strangers, or any other dimension one cares to examine. Such variation should be expected given the genetic differences between infants, the long period of time during which development takes place, the inevitable variations in social environment, and the generally plastic or malleable nature of the instincts involved. Interestingly, there are widespread individual differences among infants even when they are raised in very similar environments. Consider some examples. (1) Infants differ widely in their general level of activity. Wolff (1966) did careful observations on newborn infants and noted differences in degree of crying and motor activity even in the first few days of life. These differences persist, at least through the period of infancy. (2) Attachment to a specific mother figure begins as early as five months but may not, in some infants, be clearly manifested until one year of age (Bowlby, 1969). Although cultural factors, such as degree of physical contact between mother and infant, have been shown to affect onset of attachment there are differences even within the same cultural setting. For example, while Ainsworth (1967) found that twenty-three of twenty-seven Ganda infants were clearly attached by six months, there were four who were still not showing attachment by eight months to one year. Other studies report similar variations (Schaffer and Emerson, 1964a). Schaffer and Emerson (1964b) studied the specific patterns of response to the physical contact involved in attachment. They found that infants differ widely in their degree of "cuddliness"—a difference that is apparent prior to specific experience with being held or cuddled. Some are content to be held and handled while others squirm and protest vigorously when their bodies are confined or their freedom to move curtailed. (3) Other aspects of infant behavior show similar variations including: the age of onset of fear of strangers (ranging from six months to one year); the degree and form of reactions to separation and reunion (ranging from mild protest to heated rage); and the age at which the infant is able to conserve permanent objects.

All of these individual differences, and particularly those involving the form and intensity with which emotion is communicated, shape the individual's style. They comprise what is meant, in one common usage of the term, by an individual's "personality"; namely, those ways in which he differs from others, has a unique life style, special patterns of action and reaction, or a unique way of being. These individual differences, interacting with the unique environment that each infant finds himself in, also play a central role in the development of psychological disturbances. For example, separation or maternal deprivation produces some form of distress in all infants, but much more so in certain cases. The infant who reacts with extreme protest and despair to loss of mother may subsequently have greater difficulty adapting to a new mother figure (say a foster parent or the nurses in an institution) which may then perpetuate a sequence of interpersonal difficulties. This is one example, and the reader may imagine others made possible by the wide variations among different infants, interacting with their specific environments.

SUMMARY:
THE INFANT IN THE SECOND YEAR

Let me pause here to survey where the infant is by the middle of the second year and to look at the areas of development that lie ahead. The initial personal schemas have been structured out of the infant's interaction with mother or other caretakers in the attachment process. The basic plans for loving others, and the characteristic reactions to disturbance in these affectionate bonds, have been structured by the experiences of attachment-separation, mutual communication of sensual pleasure or the lack of it, the provision of stimulation, mutual play, and related experiences. The infant, who enters the world with his own genetic predispositions in these basic emotional areas, has encountered a specific social-cultural world. Out of this interaction, he emerges as a person who loves or hates others in his own particular way, who is anxious or secure and who deals with this anxiety in terms of his central relationships.

Active exploration of the world begins early. The infant's ability to explore expands with his increased locomotor skills and by one year of age important confrontations begin to occur in which he must submit to social restraints on his curiosity. The age and degree at which social restraints are imposed varies widely among different cultures and families, but the confrontation is inevitable. It is the beginning of a form of parent-child interaction that assumes increasing importance in the coming stage of early childhood.

Intellectual development undergoes a tremendous transformation during the first year and a half of life. The infant's earliest mental operations are almost purely reflexive. These progress through a series of sensorimotor stages in which the infant, out of his own experience, gradually constructs a preliminary model of the world. By six months of age he can conserve permanent objects, that is, he has schemas for familiar objects and persons that allow him to conceptualize them through time and in space, independent of his momentary, discrete experiences. By approximately a year and a half, sensorimotor development is concluded and the infant begins what Piaget terms the stage of intuitive or preoperational thinking.

The development of language makes its appearance during the first year and a half of life, being preceded by the vocalizations—cooing, babbling, and sound play—characteristic of early emotional relations and private play. The earliest form of object naming is getting under way during this period ("ma-ma," "da-da," "bottle"), comprehensive as opposed to spoken language being even further developed in most cases. The intellectual-linguistic skill necessary for further self or ego development—the distinction between "mine" and "not mine," and the appropriate use of "me," "I," and "you"—is yet to come.

Self or ego, the initial form of identity, is primarily a *body* or *sensorimotor* self. That is to say, the infant has learned to distinguish his own body and the sensations and experiences that arise within it from the world beyond his skin. His earliest experience with others—the patterns of attachment and separation, of sensual pleasure and pain—lead to the earliest forms of the self schema and to early experiences of feeling good and bad about his own body. Again, this early form of self is preconceptual; it is structured along emotional and sensorimotor lines. At the same time it lays the foundation for the conception of self that begins to develop in the period of early childhood.

Putting it in different terms, we may speak of the early self as characterized by sensorimotor egocentrism. Because the infant is totally absorbed with developing a sensorimotor grasp of the world, and because he initially lacks the ability to distinguish between his own actions and the objects acted upon or between his will and wishes and those of other persons, he assimilates the world to his sensorimotor schemas. This is a primitive form of selfishness in which he is selfish because he does not yet know how to be otherwise. In fact, the next major step in the development of self will occur when this primary egocentrism clashes with the wills of others during early childhood.

All the experiences of the infant during the first year and a half lay the foundation for his feelings about himself and others. He comes to trust or distrust his caretakers, to associate his own body with pain or pleasure, to feel secure or fearful in new situations. Let me conclude this chapter with some comments on the emotional-personal orientation that emerges from the period of infancy.

The Sense of Trust

Erik Erikson (1950) describes the outcome of the period of infancy in terms of the development of a "sense of basic trust versus basic mistrust." This focuses attention on what we might call the primary orientation of the person; the initial sense of self or ego that will determine the direction of later self-development.

A sense of trust, structured largely along sensorimotor and emotional lines, arises out of the variety of interactions with maternal figures in which the infant's needs are met in a predictable and consistent fashion. These needs include holding, the mutual communication of emotion, sensual stimulation and gratification, stimulation and play, feeding, the elimination of distress, and comforting during periods of pain. Later, the mother aids the developing sense of trust by providing security for the infant's anxiety as well as a base for exploration. Such security derives from the consistent encouragement of curiosity and exploration as well as firm limits that protect the infant from external danger and from his own potentially destructive emotions and actions.

In the terms used earlier, the sense of trust refers to a particular structure of the personal and self schemas. Mother and others come to have a particular set of *meanings* for the infant, as do his own urges, pains, fears, and pleasurable sensations. Predictability, the association of mother with pleasure and the elimination of distress, attachment, and control all shape the schemas in a trusting direction. As Erikson puts it:

> Such consistency, continuity and sameness of experience provide a rudimentary sense of ego identity which depends, I think, on the recognition that there is an inner population of remembered and anticipated sensations and images which are firmly correlated with the outer population of familiar and predictable things and people.[1] (1950, p. 247)

Notice the stress on "sensations and images"; the infant has yet to have ideas and fantasies.

The sense of basic trust is the hoped-for outcome of the stage of infancy. As Erikson stresses, there is a wide range of cultural values and maternal practices within which such an outcome may develop. There are also values and practices which are incompatible with this positive outcome; which lead instead to a sense of mistrust of others and one's self. Infants who lack a consistent maternal figure or who experience crucial or repeated separations; those whose parents treat them sadistically or use them as pawns in games played out of their own unresolved conflicts; or those who are simply incapable of responding to the infant's basic needs, will come to view the world, themselves, and others through the schemas formed by such experiences.

I can think of no better way of summing up the chapter than by quoting Erikson on the development of trust versus mistrust:

> Mothers create a sense of trust in their children by that kind of administration which in its quality combines sensitive care of the baby's individual needs and a firm sense of personal trustworthiness within the trusted framework of

[1] H. Erik Erikson, *Childhood and Society*, 2nd ed., revised (New York: W. W. Norton & Company, Inc.). Copyright 1950, © 1963. This and all other excerpts from this work are reprinted by permission of W. W. Norton & Company, Inc. and of the Hogarth Press Ltd.

their culture's life style. This forms the basis in the child for a sense of identity which will later combine a sense of being "all right," of being oneself, and of becoming what other people trust one will become. There are, therefore (within certain limits previously defined as the "musts" of child care), few frustrations in either this or the following stages which the growing child cannot endure if the frustration leads to the ever-renewed experience of greater sameness and stronger continuity of development, toward a final integration of the individual life cycle with some meaningful wider belongingness. Parents must not only have certain ways of guiding by prohibition and permission; they must also be able to represent to the child a deep, an almost somatic conviction that there is a meaning to what they are doing. Ultimately children become neurotic not from frustrations, but from the lack or loss of societal meaning in these frustrations.

But even under the most favorable circumstances, this stage seems to introduce into psychic life (and become prototypical for) a sense of inner division and universal nostalgia for a paradise forfeited. It is against this powerful combination of a sense of having been deprived, of having been divided, and of having been abandoned—that basic trust must maintain itself throughout life. (1950, pp. 249–50)

chapter five

Childhood

Psychological development during early childhood—roughly from age one and a half to six—is so extensive, its impact on subsequent development so profound, and the process so complex, that it is clearly impossible to cover the topic in a single chapter. I will therefore limit myself to a discussion of the two major conflicts that emerge during the years of early childhood, how these are perceived and experienced from the child's point of view, and how the developing self is shaped by their resolution.

We may think of two major themes, each characterized by conflict between newly developing capacities of the child and opposing social forces. I will call these themes *emerging autonomy and the clash with authority* and *desire and its renunciation*. The first—the conflict between the child's new sense of aggressive independence and the imposition of social restraints —is characteristic of very early childhood, of the period from one and a half to three or four. It encompasses what psychoanalytic writers call the "anal" period, though, as we shall see, anality is part of a larger issue. During this period the child has his first major experience with limitations of his willful actions, with being controlled by others. This experience sets a direction for later encounters with authority, rules, and laws, for the internalization of self-control; and for the general human problem of individuality versus obedience.

The second theme, desire and its renunciation, comes to prominence during the years from three or four to six. As the child's intelligence grows, he begins to form a rudimentary sense of his own *sexual identity*. This early maleness or femaleness combines with the pleasures of attachment and leads to a heightening of desire within the family. Sensual desire within the family—the love of the boy for his mother, girl for her father, and attractions between brothers and sisters—conflicts with the incest taboos so prominent in all societies. This is the conflict that Freud called Oedipal. It produces a major frustration of pleasurable longings and a blow to egocentric pride. Like the clash between autonomy and authority, the frustration of desire sets a course for later experiences—in this case those involving love, sensual desire, and the choice of partners. Both of these issues are destined to be repeated in later childhood, adolescence and, still again, in adulthood.

Both conflicts may be resolved in healthy or unhealthy ways. A severe stifling of early autonomy can interfere with later independence and initiative; it can cause the child to feel overly apprehensive about his own aggressiveness. Too little control, on the other hand, may lead to selfishness. The Oedipal complex may lead to later anxiety over one's identity as male or female. Shame and anxiety over sensual feelings or one's own body may also have their origins here. Healthy resolution in both areas involves an active identification and growth of the self. Following a more detailed discussion of the two conflict areas, we shall look at some examples of healthy and unhealthy conflict resolutions and discuss the principles of active identification and dissociation implicit in these two directions.

In the earlier discussion of infancy I stressed the importance of seeing the world from the infant's sensorimotor point of view. It is equally important that we gain some understanding of how things seem from within the young child's mind. To this end, I will delay consideration of the two conflict areas and first discuss mental development during early childhood. With some basic ideas of how the world is perceived by the child, we may then look at the conflict areas from both his perspective and ours.

THE CHILD'S POINT OF VIEW

To a one- or two-year-old, the world must seem populated by giants. The people around him are bigger, more powerful, more competent, all wise and all knowing. This is true in one sense, but we may also be projecting our adult perspective, for such a view implies that the very young child has concepts of "bigness," "power," and "competence" with which to evaluate himself and others. At the early stages, at least, he has still to discover these.

The mind of the child undergoes a tremendous development during the early childhood years. The gap between one and a half and six is probably greater than that between six and twenty.

At one and a half the child is just emerging from infancy where thought is dominated by sensations and actions. From the pure sensorimotor egocentrism of early infancy, the baby has, through repeated interactions with the physical world, acquired a firm sense of objects, space, time, and his own body-self as a unique object. From a generally diffuse or undifferentiated state, there has grown a well-differentiated set of schemes which permit a balanced interaction with the world. But, again, this is all at the level of sensations and action.

The major development of the next phase is the child's acquisition of the *symbolic function*. The sensorimotor infant can only deal with "real" things and acts; the young child gradually acquires symbols—mental representations of these things and acts—and can increasingly manipulate these. Piaget terms this whole period of mental development "preoperational" since it stands between the sensorimotor thought of infancy and the concrete operational thought of later childhood. He also uses the term "intuitive" to refer to the way the child first uses symbols in a private or intuitive manner.

What can we say, then, about the way the young child uses symbols? We talk and think with a complex symbolic system—language—in which words not only stand for things and acts, but can represent complicated ideas and theories. The child, during this early period, learns the language spoken around him and by age four or five can manipulate this linguistic symbol system with considerable skill. An earlier development of the symbolic capacity precedes this, however. As he grows out of infancy, his first use of symbols develops from sensorimotor thought; the first symbols are *imitative acts*. Here is an example: a two-year-old goes for an exciting ride in a car. The next day he moves a toy car across the floor while making "vroom-vroom" noises. He is obviously recreating the car ride in his play, the toy symbolizing the car and his own movements and noises symbolizing the movements and sounds of the ride.

Very young children engage in a great deal of play in which they imitate the sights, sounds, and actions that have captured their interest. They mimic eating, going to sleep, and later play out interpersonal encounters, fights, frustrations, pleasurable experiences, and conversations. Piaget notes that what begins as a pure action symbol can become an internal image—a thought—which the child can manipulate in his mind in the absence of external sensations or actions. That is, from playing with symbols of car, movements, and noise, the child can eventually visualize or imagine these symbolic gestures. This ability to imagine marks the transition from sensorimotor to intuitive thought. In sum, the young child's earliest use of symbols are imitative gestures which gradually become internalized as images.[1] The child imitates, plays, and imagines a wide variety of things and actions; such play is, of course, the natural way in which children spend their time.

The early play and imagination of the child possesses qualities that color intuitive thought for some time. Because it is only emerging from its sensorimotor origins, early intuitive thought has a physical cast to it. The young child does not clearly distinguish actions from images, thoughts from things, his games and play from reality. The game with the toy car may be as real to the young child as the actual ride. Let me state this another way. Piaget makes the distinction between *symbols*, which have private meanings, and *signs*, whose meanings are socially shared. The child who plays with *his* particular scrap of cloth as a symbol for his blanket—or to recreate his feelings of comfort while going to sleep—is using a private symbol. The word "blanket," on the other hand, is a social sign; it is a symbol whose meaning is shared by all speakers of the English language. The child begins with a preponderance of private symbols, employed in the sphere of play. Even language, when the young child first acquires it, is made over into a private symbol system. "Mama" is a word with a shared meaning (an abbreviation of "mother" referring to a class of women with children), but to the intuitive child "mama" does not represent a class, it is a private symbol for *his* mother—her face, body, actions, and the things she does for him. As Piaget puts it: "Actually, play cannot be opposed to reality (in the young child) because in both cases belief is arbitrary and pretty much destitute of logical reasons. Play is a reality which the child is disposed to believe in when by himself, just as reality is a game at which he is willing to play with the adult and anyone else who believes in it (as quoted in Flavell, 1963, p. 161)."

From sensorimotor play with objects and his own body, the child progresses to intuitive play with private symbols. These symbols are action-dominated at first and evolve into the internal images of early intuitive thinking. The private nature of intuitive thought calls our attention to the recurrence of egocentricism at this phase of development. Just as the newborn infant assimilates the world to his sensorimotor, egocentric perspective, so the child, at the beginning of the intuitive phase, assimilates the world to his newly developed, symbolic perspective.

As I pointed out in chapter 1, there seems to be a general human

---

[1] It is interesting to note an important difference between Piaget and Freud on this point. For Piaget, action precedes the image; the capacity to manipulate internal images comes after sensorimotor thought. For Freud, the image comes first in the form of the "hallucinatory wish-fulfillment" of primary process thinking and is later replaced with the realistic actions of secondary process thought. The evidence favors Piaget: images and the ability to think imaginatively follow the imitative gestures which come at the end of the sensorimotor period.

tendency to overextend oneself at each new level of thought—a tendency termed "overassimilation." It is as if the child, in the glory of his newly discovered intuitive symbols, attempts to encompass the whole world with them. As he pushes this new skill forward, of course, he realizes his limitations. The initial overassimilation becomes tempered by contact with reality. Increasingly, the child will recognize the difference between his private symbols and social signs, especially language. He will be forced to accommodate his intuitive thought to reality, and to take into account the perspective of others who do not always use symbols in the same way he does. Such accommodation is seen very clearly in the changing way language is employed. At first, the child uses words with no concern for the listener's comprehension. It is as if he thinks, "I know what 'mankey' (his private symbol for "blanket") means, so of course everyone else must understand it in the same way." Gradually, over the years from two to six, the egocentrism of intuitive thought gives way; his private symbols become tempered in a social direction. He continues to employ them but he knows the difference and can more and more take the other's point of view. The cycle is: Egocentrism and overassimilation→contact with social reality→accommodation→equilibrium.

The general point to keep in mind in considering the major conflicts of the period is that at the beginning, the child does not differentiate his own intuitive point of view from the perspectives of other people. This is what egocentrism means. Let me conclude this discussion by mentioning some other qualities of intuitive thinking.

Certain qualities have already been discussed: the physical or action-like nature of early intuitive thinking and the egocentric use of symbols. In addition, the young child tends to be centered on the present. He lacks a differentiated time perspective. Reality, from his point of view, consists of a string of succeeding "nows." He has yet to acquire the more complex time perspective that will allow him to place these "nows" in the context of past and future. This present-centeredness has several consequences. One is that he can feel very good or very bad about himself or others, almost from moment to moment. If he accomplishes some new feat—walking or using words—he feels like a tremendous bigshot, only to stumble, hurt himself, and come crying to mommy as a baby a few moments later. Lacking a differentiated time perspective, he is not bothered by the inconsistency between his bigshotness and his babyishness. Or, if mother and father discipline or frustrate his wishes, he "hates" them; at that point in time they become the archetypical bad parents and he the innocent, persecuted victim. But a short time later, they are again mommy and daddy and he the loved child.

Present-centeredness—a narrowness of perspective with regard to time

—combines with the young child's egocentrism—a narrowness of perspective with regard to the views of others. From *his* point of view, mommy is bad when she treats him in ways he does not like. Badness isn't one of her temporary qualities; she is, at that moment, a physically real, bad object. She will, later, be many other things to him. But it will be a very long time until he begins to see that there are other ways of viewing things than from inside his present-centered self.

The gradual modification of the child's egocentric, intuitive mode of thought comes about through those continuing experiences in which he is confronted with the views of others. Flavell, summarizing Piaget on this topic, puts it this way:

> One of Piaget's firmest beliefs, repeated over and over again in scores of publications, . . is that thought becomes aware of itself, able to justify itself, and in general able to adhere to logical-social norms of noncontradiction, coherence etc., and that all these things and more can emerge only from repeated interpersonal interactions (and especially those involving arguments and disagreements) in which the child is actually forced again and again to take cognizance of the role of the other. It is social interaction which gives the ultimate *coup de grace* to childish egocentrism. But this is a development the preoperational child has yet to undergo. (1963, pp. 156–57)

Psychoanalytic theory describes this same process in terms of the way the frustrations of reality force primary process thinking to give way to secondary process thinking. In this theory, the change from one process to the other occurs in infancy. Piaget locates the process more accurately in a later phase of childhood. He captures, with more precision, the general idea that Freud and later psychoanalysts have recognized: that there is a stage early in life in which fantasy and reality are undifferentiated, in which the differences between the private and social worlds are not clearly grasped.

The clash between childish egocentrism and social reality breaks down the overassimilation of intuitive thought. A closely related process is going on in the area of self-development and social relationships. As infancy and the phase of primary attachment pass, the young child's growing capacities lead to an overextension or egocentrism in the emotional and social, as well as the intellectual, spheres. With some understanding of how the child views himself and the world, we may now examine these areas.

AUTONOMY AND AUTHORITY

The problem for both child and parent in this period is comparable to that of a government which must find a course between anarchy and tyranny. As the child develops new skills he pushes them to their limits with a growing sense of his own importance. He becomes willful and demanding. If unchecked, like persons in a state of anarchy, he would make living very difficult for the others around him. On their side, the parents meet his growing competence with some mixture of encouragement and the imposition of social restrictions. Their problem is to impose authority in an equitable manner; to be restrictive without being tyrannical.

Emerging Autonomy

Early in the attachment phase the infant begins to explore and to do things on his own. Young primates are instinctually curious and playful, being motivated by interest, the innate attraction of novelty, and aggressive self-assertion.[2] By one year of age, if not sooner, the feeding situation may consist of a battle over who holds the spoon, almost to the neglect of eating. Even earlier than this, the infant can express independence in his resistance to being held or overly confined.

Autonomy and self-assertion gain momentum after age one due to maturing physical and psychological capabilities. The toddler's legs carry him farther, his fingers get into and manipulate more, and his mind can conceive of more to do. Increasing experience with the world means increasing expansion of schemas and the constant need for new stimuli. The more the infant masters, the more he needs experiences at a level of novelty which will not be boring. The ability to locomote on his own not only feeds his sense of importance, it opens up new worlds for exploration.

It should be stressed that this new independence is balanced with dependency and the need for security. The young child not only remains attached to mother, but becomes attached to certain objects—a blanket, a doll, or a teddy-bear—from which he derives comfort. These objects can be carried around, so they fit in more with his independent actions than does the earlier need for exclusive physical contact with the mother. Such security objects play their part in the transition from the primary attachment to mother to increasing independence.

2 Several major theorists have stressed these motives, using different terms. Alfred Adler broke with Freud over what he felt was Freud's exclusive emphasis on sexuality. Adler stressed the motivating power of aggression and self-assertion, in his terms the "striving for superiority." A number of writers in the neo-Freudian group—Karen Horney, Erich Fromm, Abraham Kardiner, and, of course, Erik Erikson—espouse similarly broadened views of motivation. Robert White (1960, 1963) presents a detailed discussion of this issue. He draws attention to "competence," the motivation behind autonomous actions, exploration and attempts to master the world, and argues persuasively that competence motivation be given equal weight along with sexuality and aggression. The earlier discussion (chapters 2 and 3) of curiosity, interest, and exploration place these tendencies within an instinctual system of primary importance.

The child also derives security from rituals and repetitious actions, as many parents discover when asked to play peek-a-boo or tell the same story many times in a row. This parallels the child's behavior during the earlier attachment period. There, we saw how the secure base of attachment—which means repetitive experience with the most familiar person—is necessary for exploration and mastery of the novel. At the later childhood stage, we see a similar balance between *exploration of the new and a return to the security of the past*—themes that will recur throughout the life span.

Although independence, curiosity, and self-assertion are intrinsic motives, their further expression is influenced by the social response they meet. A variety of environments can satisfy the young child's need for novelty, particularly if others—usually parents—have time and inclination to interact. Environments differ and these differences may have important effects on the child at this stage. The particular form and direction in any individual child results from the interaction of intrinsic and environmental factors.

The child is developing in several areas at the same time. He learns to walk, to climb, and later to run. Simultaneously, he is developing increased manual dexterity. In the intellectual area, he begins to manipulate action symbols and, later, internalized images. Language skills burst forth with great increases in comprehension, vocabulary, and the ability to speak in more complex sentences. All of these increases in competence combine with the general overassimilative tendency of a new stage to produce an aggressive overemphasis on his new independence. This is characterized by overdoing newly-discovered skills; by refusing to comply with parental demands and insisting on doing things "by myself;" and by insisting on having things his own way. This phase of development results from the clash between the early egocentrism of the infant—expanded now in the form of his newly-acquired motor, cognitive, and linguistic skills—and his increasing perception of his relative smallness and powerlessness made possible by this same dawning intellect. The child's new independence is set on a collision course with the wishes and wills of others.

The Battle of Wills

As the child pushes his independence to its limits, he is forced to rely on those techniques within his capabilities. Since parents frustrate his wishes by saying "no" to him, and since intuitive thought rests largely on the imitation of gestures, it is only natural that he turn their "no's" against them. This is part of the negativistic behavior so typical of the period from one and a half to three or three and a half.

The negativistic behavior of the child during this period is well-known to mothers and pediatricians; it may be found in descriptive accounts of the period (Gesell and Ilg, 1943), though it occupies a small to nonexistent place in the writings of many personality theorists. Early negativism is enhanced by the child's general egocentrism, his inability to take any side but his own in disputes with others. His newly-acquired skills and the praise and attention typically lavished on them by parents, enhance this egocentrism and contribute to an initial state of ego inflation (Freud's primary narcissism)—a feeling of the "big me," of being the "baby-king" of the universe. As White puts it:

> ...the child begins quite directly to try out his social competence. The sharp-eyed Sully (1896) pointed out a "sudden emergence of self-will" around the age of two. Stern chose "willfulness" as the proper term to characterize this phase of development. Words such as "obstinacy" and "defiance" are also common in the literature. Gesell, who sees these tendencies as reaching their peak at two and a half, feels certain that parents would vote this time "the most exasperating age in the pre-school period."[3] (1960, p. 117)

The child's negativism is important in establishing a separate sense of self—what some psychoanalysts refer to as "ego boundaries." With his negativism, the child differentiates himself from his mother; his ability to resist and refuse helps him feel like a separate entity. Parents and child move into a phase of attempted control and resistance. The conflict grows as parents and others impose restraints on his emerging autonomy—as the many "no's" and "don't's" are visited upon him—presumably to protect him from the dangers of modern civilization or to prevent his doing those things that make parents anxious. His newly sensed competence then becomes pitted against the parents' power and the battle of wills is underway. Since the young child lacks the size and skill of the parents, he must rely on other techniques such as noncompliance or turning their "no's" against them. What he lacks in size, he makes up for in devotion of time and effort; after all, what else has he got to do and what is more important? Some young children are capable of amazing obstinacy during this period and one gets a real feeling for the strength of the human spirit of independence.

Negativism frequently becomes exaggerated as the child, with increasing intellectual appreciation of his real weakness and incompetence in comparison to parents and siblings, attempts to affirm what he senses is an impossible position. That is, the peak of negativism during the second year tests the limits of the child's unrealistic overevaluation of himself. When this test fails, he is then ready to move on to a new stage in the development of self, one characterized by a great deal more compliance. This new stage is also made possible by his more advanced intellectual, imaginative,

---

[3] R. W. White, "Competence and the Psychosexual Stages of Development," in M. R. Jones (ed.), *Nebraska Symposium on Motivation,* 1960. This and all other excerpts from this work are reprinted by permission of the University of Nebraska Press.

and linguistic abilities. He now has additional means of dealing with the frustrations and anger aroused by his smallness and by external restraints, than the relatively primitive, negativistic noncompliance.

The way the battle of wills is met and resolved by parent and child has a great deal to do with the structuring of authority relations throughout life. This does not mean that the parental response determines the child's relations with authority for all time, but, rather, that it sets the initial direction or pattern. This pattern, which involves both child and parents, is likely to be reenacted as authority conflicts arise in subsequent stages.

Many observers stress the necessity for a parental and societal response that strikes a reasonable balance between control and freedom. Since the child's autonomy is newly emerging, it is important that it not be too harshly restricted nor that it be blocked by meaningless or arbitrary rules and regulations. At the same time, the child, lacking the ability to control himself—especially his own violence—needs the reassurance of parental limits and controls. Without these, his demanding willfulness and exaggerated sense of self-importance may become semipermanent ways-of-being. The parents' ability to impose limits and controls is strongly influenced by their own feelings about authority, submission, and independence, and by their own position in society with respect to these issues. Persons with a tenuous hold on their own angry rebelliousness may react in extreme ways to signs of defiance, or even independence, in their children. Some may subtly encourage the child to express defiant anger while others may overcontrol the child's slightest sign of self-assertion. Fathers who must behave submissively on their jobs or individuals who live their lives in frustrating, authoritarian situations, are likely to have difficulty striking a fair and reasonable balance with their child's emerging autonomy.

Erikson (1950) describes the outcome of this conflict in terms of "autonomy versus shame and doubt." A reasonable balance between freedom and control leads to a realistic sense of autonomy within the child—a state in which he can accept the limitations of his smallness and feel protected against his own destructiveness while, at the same time, feeling competent for his age and having a sense of where his autonomous actions can take him in the future. The negative outcome, which Erikson describes as a sense of shame and doubt, may take many specific forms. In its simplest form, the child comes to incorporate parental restrictions and complaints into his self-image. He feels that he is somehow intrinsically "dirty," "messy," "bad," or "uncontrollable." In a more complicated form, the child's negativism—his willful self-assertion at a stage when he has few other ways of expressing his autonomy—becomes encapsulated and continues into adulthood as a means of self-definition, a way of maintaining self-esteem. In extreme cases, this appears as the negativistic refusal of the catatonic to speak or physically comply. It is also observed in obsessive-compulsive individuals who negate, in one way or another, most of what is demanded of them. Obsessive neurosis is a complex outcome of the conflicts between autonomy and authority. There is, typically, a lifelong ambivalent battle with authority; the obsessive person wages a continual struggle between "giving in" (which usually means doing what is socially required), and saying "no" or rebelling. Freud's insight into the connection between obsessive-compulsive characteristics in adults and certain early experiences have been of great importance. At the same time, the typical psychoanalytic account is phrased in terms of "anality." Let us look at this account of the anal period and attempt to fit it into the larger conflict between autonomy and authority.

The Anal Phase

Freud's views on anality consist of two parts: the first is his attempt to encompass the conflicts of the period within his theory of psychosexual development, and the second his astute clinical observations on the connections between anal conflicts and later character structure. By clarifying certain problems with the first we will be better able to make use of the second.

Freud attempted to link the conflicts of this period with sensual pleasure, with what he termed "anal eroticism" This led him to postulate a special erotic or sensual sensitivity of the anal region. Frustration of this sensual pleasure, he thought, led to conflict between child and parents. This attempt to subsume anality under psycho*sexual* development was a mistake that arose from Freud's attempt to reduce all motivated behavior to the single pleasure-seeking or sexual instinct. What seems more in keeping with the facts is a model in which anality—the battle over when and where defecation and urination will take place—is a specific instance of the more general conflict between the emerging autonomy and willfulness of the young child and the social restraints imposed by the parents. As Robert White puts it:

> It is worth noticing at the outset that direct observation does not give the libido theory the kind of support it provided in the oral stage. To be sure, there is plenty of evidence, even in the pages of the clean-minded Gesell, that children are interested in anal functions, that they play with feces, and that they experience frustration and conflict over the process of training. But direct observation would never suggest that these happenings were the central preoccupations of the second and third years, nor would introspection convince us that retaining and eliminating could have anything like the intensity of oral pleasures. The evidence for a stage of predominant anal libido thus rests heavily upon the reconstructions that occur in psychoanalytic treatment. On the other hand direct observation has long recognized a sharp and significant crisis in human relations, usually called two-year-old negativism. This could

be, of course, a displacement from bowel training, but the competence model suggests another possibility. We may be dealing here with a profound *intrinsic* crisis in the growth of social competence. (1960, p. 115)

As White suggests, there is little evidence for a specific sexual sensitivity of the anal zone. Sensual stimulation of the anus may or may not be pleasurable during various stages depending largely on what it *means* to the person. It is the *meaning* of anal experiences that Freud's clinical observations alerted us to. Let us look in more detail at the connection between the so-called anal character and toileting experiences.

In treating obsessive-compulsive adults, Freud was able to trace a connection between their ambivalent concerns with neatness, stubbornness, and compulsive rituals to unresolved conflicts from this early childhood stage. It was as if they were still secretly fighting the battle with their parents over keeping clean. Their outward concern with neatness and order betrayed, by its very excessiveness, wishes to be dirty or messy. Perhaps more significant were unresolved conflicts with authority. While outwardly compliant—often overly so—the typical obsessive-compulsive person struggles continually against the wish to rebel, to fight back, and to resist doing what is required of him. The unresolved nature of these conflicts is what qualifies them as neurotic. Neatness versus messiness, stinginess versus generosity, compliance versus self-assertion, giving versus holding back—these are the ambivalent conflicts of the "anally-fixated" or obsessive-compulsive individual. In tracing these conflicts back to childhood, Freud frequently came upon a neurotic nucleus of anal concerns. He was then able to show how the adult characteristics of the anal personality derive from this nucleus of unresolved early conflicts.

The argument connecting early experience and later character is often quite convincing. At the same time, it does not necessitate a theory of "anal libido." The reason these adult characteristics are so frequently "anal" is because our culture—and this includes Freud's European society—so often imposes a stringent toilet and cleanliness training right in the midst of the conflict between the child's emerging autonomy and parental authority. It is not that anal experiences of pleasure or frustration cause the crisis of the period, but that any issue between parent and child can get caught up in the more general conflict of autonomy versus authority. In our culture, eliminating or retaining one's bowel movements or, more generally, being "dirty" or "clean" become a frequent battleground.

Erikson's account of the period is particularly illuminating. While giving the zones of the body their due, he goes on to describe the general conflict of this stage as one in which the child can "hold on" or "let go," that is, as a conflict between autonomy and compliance. His account of the Yurok Indians (1957, pp. 166–86) is particularly important since this group shows a number of "anal" characteristics as adults despite a lenient and relatively conflict-free bowel training. The Yurok rules and regulations which become caught up in the conflict between autonomy and authority concern eating and the way food and other material goods are obtained and handled. Insofar as the imposition of these rules occurs during the period when the Yurok child is expressing his early independence, they become involved in the typical conflict of the period and lay the groundwork for later personality traits of stinginess, compulsive ritual, and hoarding—traits which, in our society, are associated with bowel training.

It is not uncommon, in our culture, for the bathroom to be the battleground in the struggle of wills with the child negativistically refusing to comply and parents attempting to force obedience. Withholding feces, or playing dumb and dirtying oneself, both fall within the child's range of ability and lend themselves to his assertive-rebellious purposes. I recall one young boy whose parents had spent many hours trying to get him to use a small toilet seat. He approached it one day, pulled down his pants, put one foot on the seat, and triumphantly urinated on the floor. He thus demonstrated that he understood what their attempts at training were aimed at and that he was not going to give in. The pleasure involved here is not sensual or sexual but the pleasure of self-assertion, of an autonomous action or an aggressive victory.

A variety of actions, objects, substances, and parts of the body may come to symbolize the different sides of the conflict typical of this phase of development. Recall that the child's ability to symbolize is still dominated by action and body. Feces, toiletry, and related actions are frequent symbols within our culture. "Piss on you" or "shit on you," symbolize a rebellious noncompliance while the many jokes and "dirty" words of childhood pertaining to urinary and bowel functions attest to the emotional conflicts involved. For example, the *Dictionary of Slang* lists an amazingly large number of definitions for the word "shit," ranging from disgust and things generally dirty or undesirable to substances such as certain illegal drugs, which are desirable but forbidden. The exclamation, "Sheet, man!" among segments of the contemporary black population illustrates an interesting compound usage. It expresses a shared rebelliousness against the social prohibition on feces—affirming the goodness of the prohibited—just as the emphasis on blackness attempts to affirm the value of the very characteristics depreciated by white society.

Such an affirmation of characteristics negated by parents or society is one direction open to the child who is faced with restrictions that allow little room for freedom or the development of autonomy in alternative directions. That is, some children begin to affirm their "badness" at this stage; they react to excessive frustration and restrictions with an overemphasis on the very qualities prohibited, as if they are saying, "You think I am dirty, well

I will *really* be dirty!" This sort of "negative identity" is more apparent in later stages, especially adolescence. What one sees here is the crucial importance of an *organized identity*. The child who develops a negative identity does not do so because he necessarily likes being that way, but because he comes to feel that being a consistently "bad" or "dirty" or disobedient person is the only meaningful way to be *somebody*. A negative self seems better than no self at all—better than being a pawn at the mercy of meaningless external rules and forces. Negative identity may begin in this period and play an important role in a variety of later life styles.

In summary, the central conflict of this stage revolves around the child's emerging autonomy and the frustrations it meets. Such frustrations typically produce rage and aggressive reactions. We see in this conflict, remnants of primate dominance-submission patterns. The young child pits his newly discovered skills against parents and siblings, asserting his still egocentered self with negativistic noncompliance when other means fail. Toiletry and cleanliness training frequently become the battleground for this conflict since our culture is preoccupied with these matters. Indeed, a child can be made to feel that he is a "dirty" or "messy" or "uncontrollable" person because of attempts to enforce a meaningless hygiene too early in life.

The psychoanalytic account in terms of anality is valuable, especially in calling attention to the typical body and action symbols of the period, but it is important to remember that what is central is the *meaning* of such human functions as giving in or maintaining autonomy; holding on or letting go; being controlled or cooperating. Such meanings are manifest in the young child's self-view, which may be crucially shaped by the experiences of this period. The dangers lie in stifling early autonomy, in laying the seeds of an authority-ridden self, or in failing to control the destructive potential of the child's rage.

EARLY IDENTIFICATION

The previous section has presented typical conflicts of early childhood and hinted at some of the problems that can arise during this period of development. I have said little about positive outcomes, about ways in which the child's self develops to new levels as the earliest conflicts are resolved. These must be discussed since a resolution of early conflicts leads not only to growth of the self but also sets the stage for the sexual conflicts of the next developmental stage.

We have seen how the child's egocentrism conspires with his emerging skills and new aggressiveness to form a spirit of independence that becomes pitted against parental restrictions and social prohibitions. Ausubel (1950) likens the child's ego at this stage to the pre-Copernican view of the solar system. The egocentric child feels like the center of the universe with the rest of the familial system—parents, siblings, and others—revolving around his wishes and actions. The realization of his own relative smallness, which occurs with the growth of preoperational thinking, combines with the frustrations of self-assertion to heighten resistance and negativism. Like post-Copernican man, he must face up to the fact that the sun doesn't revolve around him but that he is a satellite. Eventually, the stage of negativism passes, to the great relief of many parents, and the child enters a new stage of compliance. This new stage is accompanied by a change in self-view, by a new phase in ego development. Where before the child conceived of himself as the center of the family universe, he now begins to recognize that he is more like a planet or satellite attached to the more powerful and competent parents. His more advanced intelligence and imaginative capacities allow him to conceive of the advantages of this position as well as to accept its limitations. If he cannot be the sun, he can at least be a satellite of the sun and bask in its warmth and power.

The development of play and imagination is extremely important in this process. We saw how the very young child imitates gestures and begins to internalize private symbols. As he becomes accomplished at this, he can use his play to compensate for frustrations received in reality. Where at two, he maintained self-esteem by saying "no," at four and five he can play at being mommy or daddy saying "no" to dolls or playmates. *Imitation has begun to be identification—an incorporation of parental roles into the self.* Increasingly, the self will be shaped by identification, by imitating and internalizing aspects of parents, siblings, and other adults and children.

Ausubel describes the early form of identification in the following way:

> . . .as the world stoutly resisted Copernicus's theory, the child resists accepting a comparable revision of ego organization, and only succumbs after putting up a last-ditch battle which characterizes the resistant behavior of 2½ to 3½. Threatened by the complete loss of an ego status he is loath to relinquish, despite its untenability, he asserts its dominant characteristics even more aggressively and vigorously than before. In the face of greater threat, tolerance to restraint and frustration reaches a new low. Uncompromising and petulant self-assertiveness, frequent temper tantrums, tyrannical ordering about, and insistence upon 'baby ways' become familiar response patterns in the daily behavior routine, reaching a peak and then declining as the new ego organization begins to take root. What makes the final yielding easier is the compensations inherent in the new position. Surely if one cannot be the sun, what could be better than becoming its satellite and enjoying its benefits and protection? But this attitude is the end result and not the immediate reaction to ego devaluation. Initially there is only the furious opposition of a threatened ego reacting with all of the accompanying overtones of rage that are associated with the frustration of self-assertiveness. (1950, p. 802)

The child's new self-view as satellite has several consequences. He is, of course, more compliant and easier to live with. He is more open to social learning, more willing to follow rules and to acquire the host of social skills —eating and dressing in prescribed ways, speaking correctly, being more polite with others, and so on—that each society teaches in its own way. He is, in short, more loving and more lovable.

Perhaps most central, his recognition and acceptance of the greater power of the parents is part of a more complex identification with them. He is open to the idea that the way to competence lies in becoming like the more skillful older siblings and adults. More and more, the child in the years from four onward, experiments with the roles of those important others in his life. He plays, fantasizes, and dreams himself into roles that are, in reality, beyond him. The little boy with his stick horse and gun, the young girl ordering her playmates around in an exaggerated version of mommy's bossiness, games with adult clothes, and the imitation of speech and gestures all show the child trying out new roles and expanding his sense of self by an incorporation of the characteristics of others.

Motives for Identification

A good deal has been written about identification, from the early work of Freud, through Piaget, to contemporary workers in the field of child development. There is general agreement that the process is important, though different writers emphasize one or another aspect in describing how it works. Without attempting to review the different theories or the evidence, let me briefly summarize the major motive systems involved in the identification process.

A simple form of positive identification occurs when the child tries to be like someone he loves or admires. We noted the precursor to this in early imitative behavior. If one needs to make a distinction between imitation and identification, one can say that imitation consists of the reproduction of specific acts, gestures, or sounds while identification is the use of these specific acts in the reproduction of a total *role*. When a child runs across a room with arms outstretched making a loud roar, he is imitating an airplane. When a little girl wants to wear clothes like mommy, plays at cooking or the tending of baby dolls, and does this persistently, she is identifying with her mother, incorporating a more complex role—with the motivation to be like a loved person.

Competence refers to another class of motives that play an important part in the identification process. As anyone who has observed young children knows, they are almost uniformly motivated by a wish to be "bigger," to have the skills and power of the giants around them. Making oneself over in the image of the bigger, more powerful people in one's world is perhaps the most common form of identification. Here, it is the power of the model and not one's love for him that is central, though these may obviously be combined since family members, who are the natural recipients of the child's love, are also the main power figures in his life. As the child gets older, he encounters a host of other children, adults, and mythical figures (characters in cartoons, stories, movies, and television), who possess powers that he wishes were his. And, as he moves into the world beyond his home, he experiments with being like these powerful others.

A special form of identification occurs with experiences of loss, particularly if the losses are severe or repeated. As we saw in earlier chapters, the loss of a loved person arouses the powerful motive system of separation anxiety. The child's ability to imitate and use imaginary symbols permits a new mode of coping with loss. The infant can only cry and express related emotions, but the child can increasingly use his new symbolic and play skills to cope with loss. In the absence of a loved, attachment figure, the child can play at mothering himself; he assumes an imaginary mother role as a way of alleviating the anxiety aroused by separation. This is identification based on anxiety.

Finally, we must note what has been termed "identification with the aggressor." This arises when one is controlled, frustrated, or mistreated in situations where there is no escape. For example, Bettleheim (1934) describes the way some prisoners in a Nazi concentration camp, after several years of torment and extreme mistreatment, began to model themselves after the very guards who tormented them. They sewed bits of the guards' clothing onto their own shabby garments and copied their sadistic behavior toward other prisoners. Such behavior is extreme, of course, but it illustrates a process that occurs, in milder form, in the lives of all children. Frustrated and enraged by parental restrictions, yet trapped by his dependence on these same parents, the child attempts to gain their power by making himself like them. Identification of this sort is illustrated when young children tell themselves not to do this or that forbidden activity, frequently employing the parent's voice: "Don't hit the baby!" "Keep your hands off the glass!" "You've dirtied your pants again!" "Eat with your spoon, not your fingers!"

Common to all the forms of identification described is an expansion of self by the imitation, assumption, and eventual internalization of new roles. All the forms are interrelated; they occur as shifting mixtures since the child, at different points in development, models himself after parents and others whom he loves and hates, who make him feel both good and anxious, whose power he envies, and whose control he chafes under. The motivational power of the different forms stems from the arousal of those emotions —love, anger, interest, and anxiety—that give force to the primary instinctual-emotional systems discussed earlier. Identification based on love or the

wish to gain the power and status of others leads to a fairly straight-forward
growth of the self. On the other hand, identification based on anxiety and
anger introduces complications that have profound effects. These effects are
complex and will be treated in greater detail in later chapters. Let me, here,
just describe the problem briefly.

Ambivalence

When a child has his anger aroused by a parent whom he also loves,
admires, and is dependent on, we say his feelings are *ambivalent*. Separation
and loss not only arouse anxiety but also—especially when repeated or prolonged—intense rage. The necessary frustrations of socialization imposed by
even the best-intentioned and loving parent, arouse anger in the child. Some
degree of ambivalence is the normal state of affairs; all children feel both
love and hate, joy and anger, need and resentment toward their parents;
the mixture and intensity of emotion vary with the individuals involved and
the specific experiences they share. A child who is constantly abandoned or
beaten is going to feel more anxiety and anger toward his parents than one
who is not, but some mixture of feelings is the rule.

Since identification involves an internalization of an external relationship (a change in self by the incorporation of a new role), it follows
that the child will feel the same way toward the new part of himself as he
did toward the parent he is identifying with. When he adds the role of a
parent out of love or the wish to be powerful, he comes to love or be proud
of this new part of himself. But when he adds new roles out of anxiety or
anger he will experience these emotions in regard to parts of himself. Identification of this sort leads to an *inner ambivalence*. A simple example may
be helpful.

A young boy is jealous of a new baby sibling who has usurped his place
as the favorite. In anger he tries to injure the baby but is thwarted by
mother who becomes quite angry at him. The situation becomes charged
with dangerous emotions—anger directed at the baby, anger between boy
and mother, and anxiety over the loss of mother's love. Identification provides a solution. If he cannot defeat mother, he can at least pretend to have
her power. He identifies with the very mother who is controlling him. In
her absence, he controls himself as she previously did in reality. He has
internalized an aspect of her role—in this case, the "mother who makes
him behave and not hit the baby" aspect—into himself. When he does this,
that part of himself—his jealousy and wish to hit the baby—becomes the
target for the anxiety and anger previously directed toward mother. Four of
the motives that promote identification—love, envy of power, anxiety, and
identification with the aggressor—are involved in the foregoing example,

but it is the mixture of love and hate—the external ambivalence—which produces an internal ambivalence. We see here the childish origins of self-control and morality, of guilt feelings and conscience.

Much more will need to be said about the process of identification and the development of conscience through the later stages of development. What begins with satellization and early identification is destined to be repeated as the child progresses through later stages of childhood, adolescence and early adulthood. But, it is worth stressing again that identification frequently involves ambivalent emotions and that the internalization of this ambivalence lies at the root of *internal conflict*.

Sex Role Identification

The infant cannot differentiate self from the external world. One and a half years of interaction leads to a sensorimotor self, centered on bodily experience. With the growth of intuitive thinking over the next few years, the child's self-conception makes corresponding progress. A little before age two, a beginning sense of individual possession emerges with the use of "mine." By age two, the average child can refer to himself in the third person—using his new found ability to name objects, he labels himself as an object. Finally, around 27 months of age, the use of "I" appears and is used with increasing frequency, being fairly well established by age three (average ages taken from Gesell and Ilg, 1943). From three to four, as we have already seen, the child's initial egocentrism and negativism has passed and he is beginning a process of identification in which he conceives of himself as satellite within the family universe. With the passing of the more diffuse emotional reactions, fantasy assumes a more prominent place in his attempts to cope with the frustrations inherent in his position. For example, the four-year-old may work through feelings of aggression in fantasy, a mode of adaptation that continues for many years (as the popularity of comic books, television, cartoons, and movies all evidence). Violent fantasies are safer than real aggression, since they don't hurt anyone, and at the same time, are potentially more "destructive," since anything is imaginable. Along with the growth of this imaginative ability there is often a corresponding increase in anxiety—particularly since the lines between fantasy and reality are not clear, nor are the boundaries between the permissible and the forbidden.

In addition, four-year-olds display social laughter; they have a sense of humor and some are able to laugh at themselves. This, along with other advances in language, the seductiveness of some little girls, and the athletic skill of boys, allows the growing child to cope with parental demands and to find new solutions to the obstacles in his life. He can plead or put on a show to distract mommy's attention from a transgression, or turn a stern father into a laughing friend.

The use of humor, as well as the clear appreciation of child and adult roles, is nowhere more evident than in the laughter of a four-year-old when he is jokingly called by a parent's or sibling's name, or when mommy or daddy pretends to be a baby. That which was cause for deadly combat at two and a half is now a big joke. As the child perfects more and more of these intellectual and social skills he develops a clearer conception of himself as an individual related to other individuals within the family. At the same time, he begins to puzzle over the nature of these relationships. What does it mean to be younger or older? Who has power and control and who must submit? And, increasingly, who is man and who is woman; what differentiates them and how do these differences fit into the pattern of human relations within which he lives?

Most parents treat their infants differently, depending on whether they are male or female. The father buying baseball equipment for his yet unborn son is a cultural stereotype. But the infant has not reached a stage of intellectual development to be much affected by these responses to his maleness or femaleness, at least not affected in ways that the parents would like. Not until he has acquired some skill with symbols—that is, well into the preoperational stage of three or four—will he be markedly affected by the differential treatment that each society prescribes for males and females. Several different influences are at work here, including biological, social, and those stemming from identification.

The biological differences between the sexes have important early effects on levels of aggression and activity. Experiments with primates have shown a clear relationship between male sex hormones and aggressiveness and dominance. In all monkey and ape species, the males are bigger, physically more powerful, more aggressive, and dominant. Although these gross differences are not found in humans, the relationship between maleness and aggression remains. Many mothers know that baby boys are more likely to be "difficult"—hard to control, more vigorous, and less cuddly—than baby girls. These are average differences with a good deal of overlap; that is, the correlation of masculinity and aggressiveness holds for many boys and girls, but there are still a number of relatively passive baby boys and relatively difficult baby girls. The other biological differences between the sexes—male versus female genitalia—are apparent at birth and determine the initial sex-typing of the infant, though it will be some time before he or she begins to become curious about the way his or her genitalia compare with those of other males and females. Secondary sex characteristics, of course, do not emerge until much later.

The principal determinants of masculine and feminine identity, however, arise from the social response the young child encounters. This does not mean that the biological differences between the sexes are unimportant, but that their significance is determined by the social—and this means primarily parental—interpretation and response to the infant as a biological being. One comes to feel and think of oneself as boy or girl largely as a result of being treated like a boy or girl by one's parents and other social agents. Studies of gender identity, homosexuality, and rare cases of mixed chromosomes all confirm the fact that one's sexual identity is powerfully shaped by the social and interpersonal response to biological maleness or femaleness.[4]

Two general sorts of influence are at work in this process: the relatively straight-forward effects of reward, social response, and expectations on the one hand, and the less direct effects of modeling, imitation, and identification on the other.

With increased conceptual and imaginative skills, the child at three or four is receptive to the impact of sex-role training. Society, through the parents and, later, teachers and others, reinforces prescribed sex roles in a number of ways. It dresses boys and girls in different clothes; provides them with different toys; lets them know directly such things as "You are a boy and boys shouldn't cry so much," or, "Little girls shouldn't fight," and, in a host of subtle (and not so subtle) ways, teaches, rewards and conveys society's sex role expectations. As we have seen, the satellizing child is relatively eager to comply, which helps sex-role learning proceed rapidly.

In addition to direct learning, the child begins to imitate the behavior of older siblings, friends, and parents. He models aspects of their behavior and fantasizes himself into the roles of big brother or sister, mother or father. A variety of things are imitated, from speech mannerisms to the actions used in games, to more general dispositions to "be like" an admired older child or parent. Practicing being a boy or a girl, playing "dress-up" games or dolls in which one assumes a maternal attitude, aggressive tricycle riding ("like daddy driving the car"), or being maternal toward pet animals are activities that begin to appear around age four and continue throughout childhood in changing forms. Dollhouses may be exchanged for clubs, tricycles for bikes, and later for cars, or the infamous game of "doctor" for adolescent petting, but the process of experimenting with adult roles continues.

Experimentation with different sex roles is affected by biological sex differences, and is increasingly subject to social influence as childhood progresses. Biologically, many boys naturally gravitate toward more aggressive, "masculine" activities. Socially, parents, teachers, and other adults become less and less accepting of behavior and attitudes that are not appropriate to

---

4 A review of the issues and evidence bearing on sex and identity may be found in Rosenberg and Sutton-Smith (1972).

defined sex roles. Societies differ as to which aspects of sex-appropriate behavior are most rigidly enforced. American society, for example, has traditionally made more rigid demands for masculine behavior from boys than it
does for feminine behavior from girls the same age. Boys just don't wear
dresses, and many parents feel threatened if their sons play with dolls or
other feminine games even as early as three or four years of age. Girls, on
the other hand, may engage in masculine games up until adolescence with
relatively little censure. Being a tomboy is much less objectionable than
being a sissy.[5]

Imitation and modeling may become involved in conflict depending
on the particular social response that they meet. Another conflict is looming
on the horizon, however: one based on attempts to imitate mommy or
daddy that are carried too far. As the child's concept of himself as male
or female becomes more firmly rooted, his desire for appropriate sexual
gratification, as he understands it, grows. He moves toward the next great
conflict of the childhood years.

DESIRE AND RENUNCIATION

Stages and crises in human development are never sharply separated.
Rather, the central interpersonal concerns of dependency versus independence, love and aggression, or fear versus exploration wax and wane. The
stage dominated by one side of these pairs recedes as the other side advances.
Crises occur at one point in development, are resolved allowing new concerns to come to the fore, only to reappear later in new forms.

The course of sensual development illustrates this cyclic recurrence of
a central human problem—the seeking of pleasure and its frustration. As
we have seen, pleasurable interactions are central in the earliest relationship
between mother and infant. Many areas or zones of the body are capable
of yielding a uniquely pleasurable form of sensation that we later associate
with sexuality. These areas include the lips and mouth (as in sucking and
kissing), the genital area (infant males have erections during the first year
of life), the anal orifice, and practically all areas of the body surface

---

[5] A loosening of sex-role definitions seems to have begun in the late 1960s, most
noticeably in the dress and grooming of young people. It is also seen in the
abandonment of some of the old taboos on male-female relations in the adolescent and post-adolescent years. The long hair of young men, the jeans and tee
shirts of young women and their greater freedom in sexual expression are examples. The demands of women for equal rights and equal treatment, as seen in
the women's liberation movement, also illustrates challenge to the existing sex
role stereotypes. All of these are initially greeted with horror by the older generation whose sex role values are more firmly set.

(though some parts are more sensitive than others). In addition to the pleasure of direct body stimulation from touching, rubbing, or kissing, sensual pleasure may be aroused by rocking or other movements, temperature changes (as by warm baths), and certain sounds and visual patterns, though these would seem less potent during the early years.

Sensual pleasure becomes associated with other people who provide the stimulation, with parts of one's own body—thumb sucking, masturbation, and general self-stimulation—and, finally, with favored objects such as soft blankets or teddy bears. For the normally attached infant, the mother and other caretakers are the major figures associated with the unique pleasures of sensuality, because of innate preferences and because of the many interactions of feeding, rocking, cuddling, playing, holding, and comforting.

Emerging autonomy causes a certain amount of "disattachment." As the child tries out his new skills, he must inevitably move away from the mother and at the height of the negativistic period, anger and defiance are prominent in parent-child interactions. This means that the pleasurable component moves to the background, but it does not disappear; we are talking about the relative balance between closeness and independence, between sensual-loving interactions and self-assertive, aggressive ones. The balance is tipped in favor of love during attachment, swings over to self-assertion during the stage of emerging autonomy, and then back toward love with the new compliance that comes with early identification.

Attached infants show some self-assertion and even the most negativistic two-year-old is still a dependent baby who requires parental love. And, of course, there are wide differences between infants and children on all these dimensions. Thus, what is being described is a general pattern of development, the specific form of which will vary depending on the infant's nature and the social milieu.

As the child moves into the compliance phase, he masters more of the social roles expected of him. He begins to take pride in being a "good" boy or girl with special emphasis on the male or female aspect of such "goodness." He or she enjoys displaying the masculine or feminine characteristics that make him or her "just like daddy" or "just like mommy," or like big brother or sister. He is certainly not interested in being "like baby"—infantile habits are taboo; thumb-sucking, bed-wetting and other carryovers from babyhood must be abandoned, especially as school approaches. The emphasis, then, is on both "bigness," in the sense of approximating adult behavior, and on appropriate sex actions. These combine in the powerful wish to be a "big boy" or "big girl."

During this period, there is a general advance in competence, particularly in the realm of social play. These are the years when play with peers begins in earnest. There are, in addition, continuing advances in communicative skill, in motor coordination, and in imaginative capacity. All these accomplishments, and particularly those that make the child lovable and earn him praise for bigness and for masculinity or femininity, propel him toward the other family members as his romantic partners. The love involved in these relationships is different from that which existed during the stage of attachment, though it is based on that earlier version. The love of a five- or six-year-old boy for his mother, or girl for her father, is much closer to adult love; it contains a conceptual component—including fantasies and jealousies—that combines with the sensorimotor components of sensual pleasure. The love between infant and mother during attachment is physical, gestural, and emotional; it consists of pleasurable holding, looking, kissing, and cuddling—and little else, from the infant's side. By five or six, with a conception of individual identity, of maleness or femaleness, and of family relationships, "love" for the child has new dimensions undreamed and unthought of in infancy. Individual possession, rivalry, jealousy, accompanying ideas of getting rid of one's rival, and the expectation that he might do the same, are all possible. Particularly important is the child's skill with imagination and fantasy. He is able, at this stage, to construct dreams in which any or all of these things may happen. His new imaginative skills bring new fears; these are the years when fear of the dark and "monsters" and "boogey-men" first appear. The child can project his feelings of love and jealousy, rage and destruction, into fantasy with such skill that he frightens himself.

The great advance in social competence along with praise from parents help build the new sense of pride and encourage expectations of success. "Why shouldn't I be able to have mommy as my partner in love—doesn't she keep saying what a wonderful boy I am; doesn't she obviously love me?" Combined with this expansion of skill and expectations is the fact that pleasurable sensual experiences have a history within the family. The child comes naturally to direct his desire toward those who have most frequently and consistently been associated with its gratification in the past. As Lindzey (1967) puts it, human beings seem to be "wired for sexual choice along dimensions of proximity and similarity."

Freud's description of the Oedipal conflict[6] is essentially an account of

---

6 Underlying the discussion of the Oedipal stage, as well as the preceding stages already presented, is a reformulation of Freud's theory of psychosexual development. Freud's theory rests on a mixture of outdated biology and astute observations of human relationships. At the level of abstract theory or "metapsychology," he postulates a reservoir of instinctual energy or "libido" which is centered in different body zones at different times; initially in the mouth (oral stage), then the anus (anal stage), and then the genitals (phallic stage and Oedipal conflict). The assumption is that stimulation of these different body areas is uniquely pleasurable during the successive stages. At the level of clinical observation, the focus is on human relationships—between mother and dependent infant, or between socializing parents and resistant young child. The events of the Oedipal stage are clearly interpersonal. As a number of psychologists have

the conflict between the child's newly developed masculine or feminine desires and the cultural prohibition on incest which forbids their gratification.

The Oedipal Conflict

Oedipus is the hero of Sophocles' monumental Greek tragedy, *Oedipus Rex*. Banished from his family as an infant, Oedipus returns to his homeland, "unknowingly" kills his father the king, marries his mother and assumes the throne. When the true nature of his identity and deeds become known, he gouges out his own eyes in an act of retributive guilt.

Freud recognized that the theme of this enduring tragedy had deep roots in the structure of the human family, an insight he initially derived from the fantasies of his neurotic patients and the analysis of his own dreams. From these sources he inferred a crisis that occurred in the childhood of everyone at a particular stage of development, the stage to which he gave the name "Oedipal."

In its simplest form the Oedipal conflict consists of the desire of the young child to exclusively possess the parent of the opposite sex with accompanying rivalry and jealousy directed toward the same-sex parent. Thus, the young boy becomes a miniature Oedipus who wishes to do away with his father and have mother's love all to himself; while the young girl, like Electra in another prescient Greek tragedy, is a rival with mother for father's love. Accompanying the anger and rivalry, and assuming more importance as the drama unfolds, are the child's fantasies of what the rival will do to *him*. In many psychoanalytic cases this is "castration anxiety," the boy's fear

---

pointed out (Holt, 1965; Klein, 1969) the libido theory is a failure on several counts, not the least of which is that nowhere are there observations of libidinal energy nor is there any evidence for the differential sensitivity of body zones at different periods. (See Chodoff, 1967; and especially the comments by Wolff on pp. 61–64).

What determines the nature of successive stages are changes in interpersonal relationships and in self-conception interacting with biological characteristics and physical and cognitive maturation. Thus, "attachment" is a more appropriate term than "oral" for the first stage and "emerging autonomy" and "negativism" are preferable to "anality." "Phallic" may be dropped since, like "oral" and "anal," it is an attempt to define the stage in terms of the body locus of "libido," (it also excludes the female half of the human race). The term Oedipal may be retained since it refers to dominant interpersonal-psychological events of the period.

Erikson's account of psychosocial and psychosexual development is consistant with that put forward here. He defines stages in terms of the dominant actions of the child and the principal psychological crises of each period, though out of loyalty to his background as a psychoanalyst, he still places a special emphasis on the traditional body zones.

that his father will castrate him. Although this fantasy is one way for the boy to symbolize his fears—a way that is probably frequent because of the equation of self with body and the child's preoccupation with the physical differences between the sexes—it remains a symbol of the more general anxiety over loss of the parent's love. This more general fear harkens back to the instinctual system of separation anxiety.

Freud's account of the effects of the Oedipal conflict and its outcome is a complicated matter. The young child is torn in two directions, for although he feels jealous rivalry with a parent, he is also desirous of that parent's love and protection. The relations with both parents are *ambivalent* —a feeling present in earlier conflicts, and one that continues throughout life to varying degrees. The ultimate frustration of the child's sensual longings for his opposite-sex parent necessitates the redirection of love outside the family. The way in which the Oedipal conflict is resolved does much to shape future relations of love.

At the beginning of the period of increased compliance and lovability, the child may not make the distinction between mother and father on the basis of sex. Rather, he directs his expectations of sensual gratification and love toward the caretaker or caretakers with whom he has had the most experience. Since this is frequently mother, she is likely to be the first romantic choice of both boys and girls. Two factors combine to change this in the years from four onward. The first is the growing sense of sex role identity in the child. As he comes to learn more about what it means to be male or female, he (or she) moves toward a romantic choice that is appropriate for this new self-conception. The second force arises from the parents themselves. Mothers typically have a special affection for their sons and fathers for their daughters, stemming from their own sexual identity. The impending Oedipal conflict has two sides to it: mother and father must give up, in some sense, their romantic attachment to son or daughter just as the child must. The conflict between desire and renunciation can be a powerful one within mother and father that affects many aspects of the parent-child relationship beyond the purely loving or sensual ones.

Specific experiences within the family have much to do with the intensity of the Oedipal conflict. The only son and his mother, objects of each other's exclusive affection, are likely to have a harder time giving each other up than the pair who have shared love among many siblings (see Philip Roth's tragicomedy *Portnoy's Complaint* for a good example). But, whatever the family constellation, it is almost certain that the child will direct his love toward those whom he knows best, who have provided sensual gratifications in the past, and who love him the most. And this will, in most cases, be mother for the young boy and father for the young girl. While both boy and girl also direct their love toward the same sex parent, the newly acquired sense of male or female identity propels them toward the opposite sex parent with a special force.[7]

It is easy to minimize the force of such love during childhood; our society doesn't take it too seriously and many of the adults involved have a stake in ignoring it. But it is very real and very intense for the child. It is, in fact, this intensity which makes the inevitable frustration of the initial romantic attachment the central life conflict that it is. Since sensual and romantic attractions most naturally occur between members of the same family, we must ask why society—any society—prohibits their fulfillment.

The Universal Incest Taboo

Study of the world's cultures has uncovered an amazing diversity of customs, social standards, and rules of conduct. Habits of dress, forms of government, modes of agriculture or the lack of them, and family structure itself are found in a variety of forms. Despite all of this diversity, there is no society—no culture—which does not prohibit sexual relations between siblings or between children and parents within the same family. The taboo on incest is one of the clear universals of cultural life. The taboo exists for both biological and psychosocial reasons, as the discussion in chapter 3 has shown.

Every culture has its own rules for enforcing the incest taboo, rules which focus on one or another aspect and emphasize, to differing degrees, the reprehensibleness of the many thoughts, acts, gestures, and fantasies involved. The problem for the developing child is the same, however. His past experience of sensual enjoyment, the many positive loving or rewarding interactions with other family members, his new sense of bigness and male or femaleness all drive him toward mother or father as a natural romantic choice. And just as these forces become strongest in the years from four to six, so do the social prohibitions on incest. Mothers become upset by the too frankly sexual approaches of their too "big" sons; fathers become anxious over the seductiveness of their daughters. As Klein points out:

> Complicating the learning problem is the fact that the mother is a source of both sensual and of permissible non-sensual pleasures (for example, rewards and satisfactions), and these have early to be distinguished by the child. A mother gratifies in all sorts of ways, but the linking of sensual experience to

---

[7] An important difference between the model presented here and that favored by many psychoanalysts should be noted. In the present account, sex role identification begins as early as age three and it is precisely because the young child can clearly and accurately conceive of himself or herself as boy or girl that rivalry and jealousy within the family becomes prominent. In the typical psychoanalytic account, sex-role identification comes after the Oedipal conflict and is, in fact, a result of its resolution. The present model is also favored by Kohlberg (1969) who reviews the evidence in greater detail.

her person as a specific source is not acknowledgeable as such beyond a certain age. Other pleasures, as for instance what White (1963) calls "effectance" pleasure, are likely never brought under so severe a rule of severance. These distinctions pose an uncommonly difficult task, one that is often complicated by the mother's own conflicts and her emotional stake in blurring these distinctions. It will happen, therefore, that the child's feelings on the subject of his relationship with his parents and their attitudes toward his body and person are destined to become deeply divided.

Nevertheless, preparations for the required, eventual heterosexual separation long precedes the actual maturing of genital sexuality in the child. Admittedly, the matter deserves more study than it has had but there is good reason to suppose that a mother's handling of the infant boy is different than that for a girl, guided by a subtly inbred, culture supported premonition of the inescapable sensual estrangement that is to come. (1969, p. 151)

Oedipal Dislocations

The Oedipal conflict is a universal human problem; it is not, as some critics have claimed, peculiar to Freud's Viennese society with its sexual prudishness. The specific form of the conflict may vary from culture to culture and from family to family. Greek drama depicts the plight of Electra and her father, and Antigone and her brother who, like Oedipus, are caught between their desire for a close family member and the taboo on incest. The playing out of the many thematic variations in myth, drama, and literature is voluminous. This, along with evidence from many other sources, indicates that the conflict captivates human interest and that strong emotions remain attached to it. At the same time, the lack of direct recognition of the problem—indeed, the attempts by many societies, including our own, to purposefully ignore its importance—indicates that some form of repression is usually involved in attempts to resolve the conflict. Freud's contribution lies not only in demonstrating the universality of the Oedipal conflict but in detailing many of the ways that it has been kept out of awareness, purposefully negated or defended against. As Lindzey puts it:

> If psychoanalysis could boast of no other achievement than the discovery of the repressed Oedipus Complex, that alone would give it a claim to be included among the precious new acquisitions of mankind. (1967, p. 1057)

The "repressed" aspect of the Oedipal conflict brings us to a consideration of the various ways in which the child may resolve the problem. In one sense the problem facing the child is similar to that during the period of emerging autonomy and the clash with authority. His new skills lead him to overreach himself, to a position where he exaggerates his capacities. He then faces a potential defeat, a blow to pride and self-esteem. In the earlier stage, the child's willfulness must give way to compliance with parental-social demands; in the Oedipal stage, immediate desire must be renounced and eventually redirected. Another similarity between the two stages is the form that conflict resolution typically takes. Many variations are possible including a refusal to "give in" or to renounce the desired family member, various partial compromises and, perhaps the healthiest course, an active identification with the same sex rival that grows from the child's eventual realization that he cannot really win—cannot exclusively possess his mother or father.

For a variety of reasons, a healthy resolution of the Oedipal conflict seems difficult to achieve. In the earlier conflict between autonomy and control, gratification of the child's aggressive impulses brings pain to the victim —a lesson that even a young child comes to understand when aggression is visited upon him. The Oedipal dilemma must be much more difficult to understand since a gratification of impulse here can, seemingly, bring nothing but pleasure to both parties. Even with his new intellectual capacities, it must be hard for the child to comprehend why he is prohibited from a form of pleasure he so strongly desires. And it is difficult for the loved parent to enforce the prohibition since he or she also must give up a form of pleasure.

The dislocations and rapid changes of modern society create additional difficulties. Rapid changes in social and sexual mores lead to a sense of uncertainty—a lack of conviction—over how to be a man or woman, and a corresponding uncertainty over how to shape the sex role of one's children. The stress of contemporary living is reflected in various ways within the family—high divorce rate, difficulty in communicating from one generation to the next, and so on. Children raised by one partner (usually the mother) of a divorced pair will have a special experience of male and female roles. What is more, it is not uncommon for women without husbands to turn their affection toward their sons, making them the "little man" in the house, much to the child's later regret.[8] Or a parent may turn against the child as a means of overcontrolling his or her own incestuous desires, inflicting punishments that retain a sensual component. Many other patterns exist that lay the seeds for anxiety, guilt and ambivalence about one's body, one's sensual experience, the meaning of being a man or woman, and the choice of adult sexual partners. Let me now present some examples of problems that stem from the Oedipal stage.

Disturbance in sexual and other relations of intimacy can often be traced to this period. We find neurotic young women who remain ambivalently attached to their fathers or boys to their mothers. Seductiveness on the part of the parent frequently keeps such relationships going. It is as if the

---

[8] For an interesting example, see the case of "Roger" in our book, *The Effect of Stress on Dreams* (Breger, Hunter, and Lane, 1971).

child is led to expect sensual gratification in his or her relations with mother or father—and indeed may be receiving it in subtle ways such as permissible ministrations during "sickness"—while at the same time being made to feel guilty over violations of the incest taboo. Many neurotic symptoms symbolize such conflicts. Disturbances in sexual function, frigidity, excessive guilt feelings over sexual thoughts and fantasies, the repetitive seeking out of partners who are rejecting or "ineligible" (such as prostitutes) may all represent an unresolved ambivalence toward mother or father.

Let me introduce a note of caution regarding the too literal use of the Oedipal concept by many writers influenced by Freud and psychoanalysis. Although it is true that sensual attraction within the family and the incest taboo pose a universal conflict, the specific forms that it may take and the types of resolution are many. A feature of sexual motivation is its plasticity —we humans can obtain sensual gratification in a wide variety of ways. Attraction may shift from parents to siblings or may be symbolized by objects such as clothing, or acts such as looking, while feelings of guilt may become connected with a variety of ideas and fantasies that have become associated with sexual conflicts.

Many of these patterns represent what might be called a partial or compromise solution in which the child splits himself into an outward compliance and a world of private fantasy in which he or she refuses to renounce the sexual attachment to mommy or daddy. This splitting is more natural for the child at the preoperational level of thought since he has difficulty distinguishing thought from action. The fantasies of the period have much to do with shaping the meaning of sex, of later romantic involvements, and of pleasure more generally. For example, some young women— on whom psychiatry has placed the fancy label "anorexia nervosa"—must deny themselves the pleasure of food because the forbidden "sexual" meaning of pleasure has become so extensive that they feel guilty when eating. For others, the pleasures of eating take on a different sexual meaning, one in which a sexualized eating arouses less guilt than heterosexual relations and hence becomes a substitute for such relations (see the case of "Hal" in Breger, Hunter, and Lane). In this regard, Schachter (1971) has shown that food consumption in obese overeaters is unrelated to physiological hunger. Such individuals seek the gratification of food, not when they are hungry, but when aroused in some other way, such as sexually.

The meaning of heterosexual relationships themselves is, of course, profoundly affected by the interpersonal events of the Oedipal period. Some men may only be able to enjoy sex with women who are degraded in their eyes, while being impotent with women whom they perceive as "normal" or virtuous. What seems to be operating in cases such as these is both a particular structuring of the meaning of sex—it is "dirty," degrading, and associated with guilt—and also a particular categorization of women—they are either "virtuous," like mother, and hence sexually taboo, or not in the same category as mother and hence acceptable as sexual partners (see the case of "Joseph Kidd" in Robert White's *Lives in Progress,* 1966).

A common form of male homosexuality illustrates the way in which experiences with parents during this period determine the meaning of sensuality and sex role identity. Homosexuals differ widely and no one cause can explain all cases. They do not all suffer from "unresolved Oedipal complexes," but for purposes of illustration, I will cite a form commonly uncovered in psychotherapy (Bieber, 1965). These young men experience their mothers as much more powerful and interested in them during childhood than father, who is frequently absent or personally distant. At the same time, mother is overcontrolling and there are rage-filled memories of her interfering with the young boy's sensual play and masturbation as well as other areas of his private life. These experiences with mother structure the meaning of women and sexuality in special ways. One patient in psychotherapy described a recurring image of a vagina with fish-hooks while another— during a time before he adopted homosexuality—could not touch his girlfriend's genitals because they seemed like the spiders and squids of his nightmares. These specific, emotion-laden images were the symbolic residues of relationships with ensnaring, spider-like mothers.

Women as destructive, powerful creatures, and sex with them as a frightening, injury-producing experience, illustrate how the experiences of the Oedipal period, mediated by the fantasies of childhood and the later experiences of adolescence, can determine the meaning of sexual relations in adulthood. The young boy's perception of mother as more powerful and the distant father (particularly important seem to be memories in which father failed to protect him from mother's intrusive control) make identification with the male role less likely. Thus, some boys with this particular constellation of family experiences incorporate the ambivalent relationship with mother into themselves; they attempt, as homosexual adults, to become the powerful woman they hate.

In sum, the vicissitudes of the romantic-sexual experiences within the family lead to many later patterns. Some neurotic or disturbed outcomes stem from a failure to fully renounce the initial, within-family romantic choice. Such a failure can come about in many ways, and the parents own role in keeping son or daughter bound within the Oedipal dilemma plays a crucial role. In other cases, there may be an inability or unwillingness to give up the pleasures obtainable immediately for the possibility of pleasure with future partners. Highly disturbed outcomes, as in the example of male homosexuality just described, result from parent-child relationships of intense ambivalence which are so often produced by overcontrolling, rejecting, intensely anxious or disturbed mothers and fathers.

Summary: Renunciation and Identification

Like the earlier blow to autonomous pride, facing the Oedipal renunciation is potentially a great blow to the child's sense of adequacy and self-esteem. And, as in that earlier crisis, identification offers a way through the crisis that softens this blow and opens the way to the future. When the little boy renounces his desire for mother and faces up to his inadequacy in comparison to father, things must seem bad indeed. But when he is able to identify himself with this same father, when he can take him as a model and fantasy himself capable of the same accomplishment, there is hope. Such identification is an active process in which the child embarks on the road to greater maturity. It is, given the inherent limitations of the Oedipal conflict, the most *hopeful* solution.[9]

Identification does not take place at some precise turning point: the child does not make a decision to give up his claims and start identifying. Rather, the process is a gradual one. Over a period of several years most children try out a variety of paths including many neurotic, unrealistic, or fantastic resolutions. The child plays many roles; tries out many fantasy selves. The reaction of the parents to these new roles is important. For example, a mother, out of her own ambivalence over losing a son may, in subtle ways, discourage his identification as an independent male. Although there are many problems there are, as well, forces within the child, and sources of support within society, which promote healthy development.

Identification is not just an end to the Oedipal conflict; it is a process that—in combination with earlier satellization and sex-role learning—launches the child into a host of new opportunities and difficulties. Some of these will be taken up in future chapters; so, in anticipation, let me end this chapter by indicating where development is heading.

The conflicts of the Oedipal period are not resolved all at once; one may best think of identification as a process that appeared in earlier stages, takes a specific form here, and continues throughout childhood, adolescence, and the adult years. But there is a sense in which the Oedipal crisis "passes"—for those children and parents who don't get stuck there in some disturbed fashion. As it does, the child's energies and attention can then shift to other areas. In the psychoanalytic account, the years between the Oedipal conflict and adolescence are called the "latency period," presumably because sexual energy is inactive or latent. But since there is no sexual energy, this makes little sense as theory. Erikson, more meaningfully, de-

---

9 The identification of this stage has important implications for conscience, or what Freud called "Superego," development, but this topic will be delayed until chapter 8.

scribes the period as a "moratorium." The child is allowed by social custom to take time out from heterosexual demands; to engage his drive toward competence in the many tasks and opportunities of the early school years. In our culture, and apparently many others, one sees the formation of same-sex groupings which allow boys and girls in middle and late childhood to solidify and push their sexual identities to their limits. One frequently observes overassimilative tendencies, for example, the bravado, machismo, and toughness of preadolescent boys who, at the same time, are very uncomfortable around females. The girls have their cliques and groups, too, but they usually do not defend as strongly against heterosexuality, perhaps because a prohibition on love and tenderness is not a part of the stereotype of female identity.

Sullivan (1953) presents one of the better accounts of social development during a period of life that is far from "latent." Thus, the "passing" of the Oedipus Complex that Freud speaks of is really a passing of the peak of its intensity. With this passing, the child begins a process of identification which is destined to shape his self and his moral development in profound ways. Much of this process is revealed in play, dreams, and fantasy, and it is to these topics that I now turn.

chapter six

Play,
Fantasy,
and
Dreams

Play and fantasy are the child's natural ways of dealing with emotional and interpersonal concerns. Children are not "taught" to play; fantasy and games are not dependent on reinforcement or parental approval. They are spontaneously interesting human activities. It has been established that everyone spends approximately 20 to 25 percent of each night dreaming, something that "happens" without the individual's having to try. Educators often attempt to devise means by which the "serious learning" of the classroom can be made as interesting or motivating as the games and fun of the playground. These examples highlight the intrinsically motivated nature of play and dreaming. Children, and the rest of us too, must be made to work; play is what we do when we have a choice, a day off, a holiday.

The reason for the strong intrinsic drive toward play and fantasy is found in their connection with the core instinctual systems described in chapter 2. In that earlier discussion, we saw how our primate heritage has defined a set of social instincts that includes curiosity, exploration, and play. Each instinctual area is amplified by emotions—pleasure, anxiety, fear, anger, interest—which make the thoughts and actions associated with it especially driving or imperative. As the child develops past infancy, the core instinctual areas and the emotions associated with them are increasingly expressed in play and fantasy.

We saw earlier how the play of young monkeys and apes serves as practice for dominance and the redirection of aggression, for sensual-sexual relations, and for channeling curiosity and experimentation with the environment. The process is similar in human children. Early play involves love and separation anxiety, aggression and its control, sensual contact and exploration. In addition, imitative play and modeling are central to the process of identification.

If play and fantasy are so important, why has American psychology, with a few notable exceptions such as Henry Murray, paid so little attention to them? First, our culture has a puritan background—fun for its own sake is taboo. We are a work-oriented people who somehow manage to convert even lesiure activities, such as camping or weekends at home, into work. Goffman (1963) comments on our implicate social rules against "doing nothing" in public. If one wishes to daydream, he usually rationalizes it as "fishing" (from a pier where fish are rarely caught) or "getting a tan." Second, fantasy and dreaming are, by their very nature, private activities. As long as American psychology under the influence of behaviorism, restricted its subject matter to so-called observables, dreams and fantasy fell under the same ban as other mental content. Finally, there is probably a certain amount of what Freud termed resistance—or at least of personal uncomfortableness—in examining too closely, topics so intimately concerned with social taboos, anxiety, and feelings of guilt, or with a time of life during which one felt small, weak, and inferior; a time of life which many power and success oriented Americans would just as soon forget about. This neglect of the topics of play and fantasy does not reduce their importance in human life. Like infantile sexuality before Freud drew attention to it, the importance of play and fantasy is obvious to children and to their more discerning caretakers.

The special characteristics of preoperational or intuitive thought facilitate the connection of play and fantasy with the expression of emotion. Instinctual actions are expressed with facial expression and gesture. These are central to play and to the visual images of fantasy. With the emergence of the symbolic capacity, the early physical expression of emotion acquires a symbolic component. But, as we have already seen, the preoperational child does not differentiate between symbol and action; his thought, just emerging from the sensorimotor stage, does not clearly distinguish between emotional gestures and their symbolic representation. Nor is he capable of differentiating the spheres of private play and fantasy from socially defined reality. In a sense, intuitive thought *is* the thought of play and dreams.

The play of the infant is hardly different from the play of young monkeys and apes. With the growth of symbolic capacities, including language, crucial differences are introduced. Let us turn now to an examination of the similarities and differences.

PRIMATE PLAY, CHILDREN'S GAMES, AND HUMAN LANGUAGE

Anyone who has observed monkeys or apes for a sufficient period of time is impressed by their spontaneous play. This is especially true of infant and juvenile monkeys who, like their human counterparts, are more playful than adults. Much of this play seems to be simply exercise—swinging about in the trees, chasing, and the like. Closer observation shows that monkey games are more than random exercise, however. For example, Schaller (1963) describes the young gorilla versions of "chase," "king of the mountain," "tug of war" (usually played with tree limbs and branches), and "follow the leader." These games utilize gestures that are destined to become part of the dominance-submission rituals that regulate gorilla society. Games such as "king of the mountain" and "tug of war" have an obvious relation to dominance. Similar observations have been reported by Lawick-Goodall for chimpanzees and by Washburn and De Vore for baboons. A great deal of the play of young monkeys and apes consists of the specific gestures and movements associated with dominance and submission. There is a good deal of snarling, mock biting, aggressive gesturing, and play fighting. Since dominance-submission rituals are so central in preventing serious aggression and in maintaining social order in these primate groups, it is likely that play is preparation or practice for adult social roles.

Young monkeys also play at adult sensual and sexual actions. Grooming—in which animals clean each other's fur—takes up a good deal of time among both young and old animals. Pleasurable tactile activity that has no relation to reproduction is widespread among the nonhuman primates, while acts and gestures specific to reproduction can be observed in the play of young animals, including mock "mounting" and simulated sexual intercourse. As with dominance, the sensual-sexual games are practice for instinctually important adult actions. It is interesting to note that Harlow (1971) observed marked distortion in both sexual and dominance behavior among monkeys raised in isolation. In contrast, monkeys raised without their mothers, but who were able to play with peers, functioned normally in these areas. Harlow points out that juvenile play at dominance, sexual, and related social behaviors are crucial antecedents to adequate adult functioning.

The play of young monkeys and apes also involves interaction with physical objects and an exploration of the environment. Motivated by a driving curiosity, the young animal gradually familiarizes himself with more and more of the world around him. As he moves beyond infancy, his exploratory activity pushes him away from the bond of attachment to mother, preparing him for his eventual independence.

The play of human children is similar to that of monkeys and apes. It is motivated by the emotions of pleasure, anger, interest, curiosity, anxiety, and fear. Children's play prepares them for adult functioning in areas of instinctual importance. When mother and baby play "peek-a-boo" they are making a game out of attachment and separation anxiety. Later in childhood, nothing seems so exciting as a game of "hide and seek" (or "kick-the-can" or whatever the local variant may be). Like the earlier peek-a-boo, separation anxiety and mastery of the unknown play motivating roles, as does a more general aggressive competitiveness.

Sensual-sexual play is common in young children as are a variety of mock and more serious forms of fighting. Much of the fighting between siblings—so-called sibling rivalry—is similar to the dominance struggles of monkeys and apes. Competitive games of many kinds—from simple races to spear throwing to basketball—also illustrate aggressive play. Through games and play, the individual learns to channel his aggression into socially acceptable forms. Human children who are deprived of such experience, like Harlow's isolation-reared monkeys, may become disturbed adults.

Play is also central to intellectual development. As Piaget demonstrated, the child moves to increasingly sophisticated levels of thought from his continued interaction and experimentation with the objects around him. Curiosity and interest—what Piaget terms the "need to function"—motivate play of this sort.

To sum up, we see how the play of young primates, both monkey and human, is the natural way in which instincts are expressed. The propensity to play is built into all primate species in such a manner as to assure its frequent occurrence. It is this feature that accounts for the strong intrinsic motivation behind the play of the young. The actions and gestures involved in much of primate play are emotionally amplified—games arouse and are maintained by powerful feelings of interest, surprise, and joy, and by *tempered* separation anxiety, fear, anger, and sensual pleasure. Although monkey and human children share this base of strongly motivated play, the unique symbolic capacity of humans introduces important differences. Let us now consider these from the perspective of human evolution.

Symbolism and Language

Communicating emotion through facial expression, sound, and gesture evolved as an integral part of primate group existence (as we have seen in chapter 3). These instinctual systems are old in an evolutionary sense; they appear in much the same form in monkey, ape, and human child. The systems that communicate fear, joy, anger, and surprise were well entrenched in primates long before the evolution of human beings. Little new was needed in these spheres and a great deal of our social communication can be accomplished by essentially prelinguistic means.

Complex symbolic capacities, including language, appear late in primate evolution and are unique to the human species. The development of the human individual parallels the evolution of the species: nonlinguistic, emotional communication appears first and only gradually gives way to language. By the time the baby learns to talk and engage in the intuitive manipulation of symbols, his social relations are already structured in the "language" of emotional expression and gestures, of cries and smiles, of rages and pleasurable goos and gurgles, and of tactile contact. As we saw in the last chapter, the child's capacity to use symbols and language emerges around age one and grows steadily over the next few years of childhood.

Preoperational thought develops from its sensorimotor precursor and is used, initially, in an egocentric manner. The very young child does not distinguish the private or personal meaning of his symbols from their existence as public or socially agreed upon signs—to him, they are *his;* they are akin to personal possessions. Language, when it first appears, is used in the same way. Words are treated as private symbols. But at the same time, language and related forms of symbol use are also capable of a curious form of independence from the emotional communication systems.

I mentioned earlier that individual development parallels species evolution, that the communication of social need is well established in the baby before he learns to talk. When he does begin to speak he uses words to name objects in the environment. The symbolic capacity is largely focused on what might be called the intellectual sphere, the emotional sphere being well taken care of by the older system of communication (see Lancaster, 1968). What this means is that language intially develops as an independent system for understanding the world—a system set apart from the press of immediate need. The partially independent nature of the language system is seen in its rapid development. It is as if a separate genetic program exists that governs language. And, in fact, something of the sort seems to be the case.

Eric Lenneberg presents an excellent summary in his paper "The Natural History of Language" (1966b). He points out that speech and language development have their own built-in maturational sequence of invarient stages. These stages are relatively unaffected by environmental variations and appear in the same order in diverse cultures and in children with very different language environments—for example, those with deaf and dumb parents. The stages, in summary form, are as follows:

1. Coos and chuckles at four months;
2. Babbles ("Ma," "Da"), reduplicates sounds, from six to nine months;

3. Knows small number of words, follows simple commands and responds to "no," from twelve to eighteen months;
4. Vocabulary increases from 20 to 200 words, comprehends sentences and forms two-word phrases, from eighteen to twenty-one months;
5. Vocabulary increases from 300 to 400 words, has two- and three-word phrases, and uses prepositions and pronouns, from twenty-four to twenty-seven months;
6. Shows big increase in vocabulary; uses three- and four-word sentences; word order, phrase structure, and grammatical agreement approximate language of surroundings, but still makes unique utterances, from thirty to thirty-three months;
7. Has vocabulary of 1,000 words or more, has well-formed sentences using complex grammatical rules, grammatical mistakes less frequent, about 90 percent comprehensibility, from thirty-six to thirty-nine months.

Thus, by the time he is three, the child has mastered the fundamentals of his native tongue. Later learning is largely a matter of adding vocabulary. This is a truly amazing accomplishment; the more amazing, perhaps, since children in all cultures and diverse life circumstances—barring extreme isolation from other people, injuries that interfere with the speech or hearing apparatus, or certain brain defects—acquire their language in this manner. Language development, like play and fantasy, will occur without directed teaching, reinforcement, or adult approval, though these no doubt influence the process.

The separate nature of the language system means that the child, and later the adult, can engage in the sort of thinking and experimentation that has led to the accomplishments of human culture, including the development of agriculture, technology, and science. It is precisely because language is free from the imperatives of emotion that it lends itself to thought of an experimental or abstract nature.

Language and Play

The separate evolution and development of the systems of play, fantasy, and language suits them to different purposes. Play and fantasy express emotion and are centered in the social-instinctual areas. Language is suited to the comprehension and communication of complex information that cannot be dealt with by the older emotional systems. Because of this, it is initially separated from emotion and strongly felt, personal interactions. This separation sets the stage for some of man's greatest accomplishments in the fields of science and mathematics which, of necessity, develop in an abstract, impersonal realm, and for some of our greatest tragedies—stemming from the unfeeling or dehumanized use of the products of scientific achievement. What I am presenting here is a speculative hypothesis: that the particular evolution and development of human language and intelligence makes possible the separation of thought and feeling, a separation that appears in many guises. We see it in the many religions, philosophies, and belief systems that separate "mind" and "body," "heart" and "head," or "cognitive" and "affective." In psychoanalytic theory it appears as the distinction between primary and secondary process—the first a system closely related to sex, aggression, and fantasy and the second a system bound to socialized thought and action. As we will see in the next chapter, the potential separation of these two systems has its advantages and dangers.

Although thought and feeling may be separable, it is possible to make too much of the distinction. In the normal course of child development, thought and feeling, language and play, become intertwined. Even in the early years, the child uses language in his play. By three or three and a half, the typical game is an interwoven combination of movement, emotional expression, and chatter. Language becomes a part of personal interactions with "I love you" and "I hate you" added to facial expression and body movement. The symbolic abilities that language exemplifies, and which are a part of thought, become a part of play and imagination. That is, play and fantasy do not remain at the less complex levels of infantile emotional display. By stressing the initial separation and separate purposes of the emotional-play-dream system and language, I merely wish to suggest why emotional and interpersonal concerns, problems of power relations, conflicts over sensual gratification and the like, fit so easily into the play and fantasy modes and why it is relatively easy for these modes to become *decoupled* from language and intellect in later life. There are other differences between the two systems, a central one being the public-private distinction to which we may now turn our attention.

PUBLIC AND PRIVATE

Language, play, and dreams may be ordered on a continuum from public to private. A unique feature of speech is that the speaker hears his own words at the same time, and in much the same way, as the listener does (see Klein, 1965). Language is thus a *public* mode; you and your listeners are equally well informed about your discourse. Play is less well observed—many young children prefer to play alone, they become offended or embarrassed if watched. In addition, the player and observer do not share the same perspective; one is not instantly aware of how one's facial expression looks to another. Dreams are private—nobody can see the dreamer's visual imagery but he and, what is more, dreaming occurs during a time and in a place when observation of any kind is not likely.

In the early stage of preoperational thought the child cannot clearly distinguish between his private thoughts and his public actions; words are egocentric or personal symbols. The public to private continuum suggests that a public mode such as language lends itself to much more rapid differentiation and socialization than does a private mode such as dreaming. The fact that speech provides instantaneous feedback to both listener and speaker plays a crucial part in the rapid socialization of language. As the data on language development show, the child has incorporated the enormous complexity of language and is speaking correctly by a little over three years of age. The instantaneous feedback of speech is one feature that facilitates such rapid socialization. We come to expect a demanding exactness in language usage; even small errors in young children are treated as mistakes.

Dreams, at the other extreme, remain unsocialized to a certain degree throughout life. No one else sees them and, with some exceptions, they are rarely communicated or even remembered. They are experienced as an unreal, undifferentiated blend of private symbols and public signs.

Play stands between the extremes of public speech and private dreams. It may be more or less solitary; it makes use of language, imagination, gesture, and movement. Play with peers, although social, is not necessarily observed by adults and is thus free from that source of censure or demand for compliance. *An important consequence of the private nature of play and dreams is that they become ideal modes to deal with those life areas in which socially appropriate actions are not possible, arouse anxiety or fear, or lead to conflict with parents and other adults.* When the child feels small and inferior, he has no wish to expose these feelings to public inspection. But he can play a game or have a dream in which the socialized conventions of reality are suspended and he—or some imaginary stand-in—becomes big and powerful. A few years ago, a popular book about childhood appeared entitled *"Where Did You Go?" "Out," "What Did You Do?" "Nothing"*— a commentary on the child's wish to keep his world of play private, at least from parents. The less socialized nature of visual imagery, the lack of instant and symmetrical feedback, the development of play and fantasy as practice for social roles, and their tie with instinctual systems, all contribute to make these modes natural ones for working on central emotional and personal concerns. Piaget (1951) takes a similar position in stressing the preponderance of assimilation over accommodation in play and, even more so, in dreams. He states that dreams are "pure assimilation," indicating that no attempt is made to accommodate to social demands. Information is processed entirely within the individual's existing schemas.

Because play and dreams are private and less subject to the demands of social reality, they may be much freer, more experimental and creative. The wide range of symbols, gestures, speech, and movements, and the suspension of constrictive social demands allow the child to experiment freely with different situations and roles; he can play at being different people or imagine himself in all sorts of situations. This freedom to experiment, along with the features already noted, make play and dreams natural modes for working on the many problems that the child encounters.

In this way, the child is like a scientist experimenting with models of the world. Just as the scientist sees the world through the eyes of his theory or paradigm, so the child perceives things through his fantasy paradigms. Like a scientist creating models in the laboratory so that he can manipulate, in analogue form, the phenomena he is interested in, the child's world of toys, peers, and dreams contain models of the central concerns in his life. He experiments with these in the safer, more manageable world of play. Piaget's summary of this issue is particularly cogent:

> Symbolic play is the apogee of children's play. Even more than the two or three other forms of play which we shall discuss, it corresponds to the essential function that play fulfills in the life of the child. Obliged to adapt himself constantly to a social world of elders whose interests and rules remain external to him, and to a physical world which he understands only slightly, the child does not succeed as we adults do in satisfying the affective and even intellectual needs of his personality through these adaptations. It is indispensable to his affective and intellectual equilibrium, therefore, that he have available to him an area of activity whose motivation is not adaptation to reality but, on the contrary, assimilation of reality to the self, without coercions or sanctions. Such an area is play, which transforms reality by assimilation to the needs of the self, whereas imitation (when it constitutes an end in itself) is accommodation to external models. Intelligence constitutes an equilibration between assimilation and accommodation.
>
> Furthermore, the essential instrument of social adaptation is language, which is not invented by the child but transmitted to him in ready-made, compulsory, and collective forms. These are not suited to expressing the child's needs or his living experience of himself. The child, therefore, needs a means of self-expression, that is, a system of signifiers constructed by him and capable of being bent to his wishes. Such is the system of symbols characteristic of symbolic play. These symbols are borrowed from imitation as instruments, but not used to accurately picture external reality. Rather, imitation serves as a means of evocation to achieve playful assimilation. Thus, symbolic play is not merely an assimilation of reality to the self, as is play in general, but an assimilation made possible (and reinforced) by a symbolic "language" that is developed by the self and is capable of being modified according to its needs.[1] (Piaget and Inhelder, 1969, pp. 57–59)

Piaget's view of the emotional-social determinants of play and fantasy provides a concise statement of the position I have been trying to state:

> It is, primarily, affective conflicts that reappear in symbolic play, however. If there is a scene at lunch, for example, one can be sure that an hour or two afterward it will be re-created with dolls and will be brought to a happier

[1] J. Piaget and B. Inhelder, *The Psychology of the Child* (New York: Basic Books, Inc., 1969). This and all other excerpts from this work are reprinted by permission of Basic Books, Inc. and of Routledge & Kegan Paul Ltd.

solution. Either the child disciplines her doll more intelligently than her parents did her, or in play she accepts what she had not accepted at lunch (such as finishing a bowl of soup she does not like, especially if here it is the doll who finishes it symbolically). Similarly, if the child has been frightened by a big dog, in a symbolic game things will be arranged so that dogs will no longer be mean or else children will become brave. Generally speaking, symbolic play helps in the resolution of conflicts and also in the compensation of unsatisfied needs, the inversion of roles (such as obedience and authority), the liberation and extension of the self, etc. (1969, p. 60)

PLAY AS MASTERY

The idea that play and fantasy serve important functions in the child's adaptation to reality is not new. One can find it in Freud—though it is usually overshadowed by the competing idea that dreams serve to fulfill infantile wishes—and in the work of Piaget and Erikson. As Erikson puts it, "to hallucinate ego mastery and yet also to practice it in an intermediate reality between fantasy and actuality is the purpose of play (1950, p. 212)."

Although the mainstream of psychology in this country has largely ignored play, a number of investigators in the early part of the century were interested in it. These included G. Stanley Hall and later Gardner and Lois Murphy, Henry Murry, and some of their students. An important study that demonstrates the functions of play and fantasy is Ruth Griffiths' *A Study of Imagination in Early Childhood,* published in 1935 and largely neglected since that time. Griffiths studied the process of play and imagination in different groups of five-year-olds using observations of play, dream and daydream reports, free drawing, responses to ink blots, and interviews. She worked intensively with each child (up to twenty sessions) establishing a comfortable relationship in which the children were free to engage in their normal form of play, almost as if she were not there. This was important since she wished to study the natural form of imaginative activity. Examples from this study will be cited later; here let me quote a statement from her concluding discussion:

> The whole of the position worked out in this book emphasizes the *value* of the phantasy method as employed in children's thinking, the fact that it is the child's own method, his means of overcoming emotional difficulties, his route to the resolution of intellectual problems. When faced with a difficulty he clothes it in symbolism, and experiments in the newer medium. Temporarily leaving the real problem which he cannot overtly work out to its logical conclusion, he develops an analogous situation at the phantasy level. Here he can safely experiment subjectively, that is in 'play,' and himself discover (though not necessarily with full conscious realization) the sequel to his attitudes. (1945, pp. 325–26)

The young child, in the preoperational stage of thought, has a natural use of metaphor which facilitates the poetic, creative aspects of play and fantasy. Several points in Griffiths' statement are worth further comment. Note that she sees play as the child's *natural* mode and, also, that she points particularly to "emotional difficulties" as well as intellectual problems. Typical of the emotional problems described in her study were: concerns with smallness and power relations with parents; jealousy and rivalry with siblings; fears of abandonment, separation, and loss; and concern with birth, death, and the origins of things. Note also that Griffiths sees play as experimentation in the medium of symbolism. The symbols of dreams and play are not a "disguise;" they are a means of expression by which the child can actively engage that which is frightening or difficult. Symbolism, in which a toy or dream image represents some important person or force in the child's world, permits a kind of manipulation akin to that of a scientific experiment. Let us examine a few examples of play as mastery.

Griffiths presents the case of a young boy who fears being hit by cars and is terrified of crossing streets. In his play, he "...is never content unless pushing little toy cars around and causing accidents among them. In this harmless way he gradually overcomes his fear and gains a sense of power over the object (p. 164)." In this example, the symbol or analogue is direct —toy cars for real cars. Similar forms of direct symbolism are seen in doll play in which the older sibling plays out jealousy by aggressing against a baby doll or plays at being mother or father. Less direct symbols are also frequent: animals, for example, are extremely common in children's dreams and fantasies. Aggressive and frightening lions or alligators, uncontrollable and independent cats or birds, small and weak mice, large and powerful elephants, all make natural symbols for the child to work with aggression, fear, control, dependency, and power relations.

In addition, play and dreams are characterized by a great deal of freedom in the exchange of roles. The child playing out a family situation with dolls easily slips back and forth—being first the naughty baby, then the scolding mother, then the aggressive older sibling—in each role assuming the appropriate tone and gestures. Dreams, of course, are characterized by still greater freedom in role exchange; fantastic roles, magic heroes, and miraculous powers are all imagined in the private world of sleep. And it is this privacy—the freedom of play and dreams from the social rules which define the right and wrong ways to do things—that allows such creative experimentation. Children are, in many ways, quite conservative in their outward behavior. A child of six might strongly wish to be a baby again, but feels he must keep up appearances and be a "big boy" who doesn't suck his thumb or cry. In play and dreams he may indulge this wish in safety, partly because it is private and partly because it is, after all, "only a game."

Converting Passive to Active

Let me present a further example of play as mastery—an example with special significance. It is taken from *Beyond the Pleasure Principle* (1920) in which Freud develops his formulation of the principle of mastery. Freud observed a boy of one and a half whose principal game consisted of taking any small object or toy he could find and throwing it into a corner or under the furniture. This was accompanied by interest, satisfaction, and a "long-drawn-out 'o-o-o-o' " sound which proved to be the baby's version of the German word "gone." In another version of the "gone game," the child would throw a toy attached to a string over the edge of his crib, uttering his expressive "o-o-o-o" and then pull it back, greeting its reappearance with a joyful "da," ("there"). In still another variant, the child would make his own reflection in a mirror disappear while uttering "baby o-o-o-o!" Freud noted that the child was very attached to his mother and very upset on those occasions when she left him. In the gone game, which was clearly connected with her leaving, he seemed to be repeating, over and over, this centrally upsetting experience, using toys and his mirror image as symbols. But why repeat at experience that was obviously unpleasant? In answering this question, Freud suggests an important principle of mastery—the conversion of a passive experience into an active one. As he puts it:

> At the outset he was in a *passive* situation—he was overpowered by the experience [of his mother's leaving]; but, by repeating it, unpleasurable though it was, as a game, he took an *active* part. These efforts might be put down to an instinct for mastery acting independently of whether the repeated memory were in itself pleasurable or not.[2] (1920, p. 15)

In further examples, Freud notes how a child converts a frightening experience, such as being examined by a doctor, into a game in which he "passes over from the passivity of the experience to the activity of the game;" that is, he plays at being doctor with a friend, a younger sibling, or a doll.

Freud's view of the role of play in mastery fits closely with the view developed in our earlier discussion, and with the ideas of Piaget and Griffiths. What constitutes a problem or a passively experienced trauma is typically something that the child feels strongly about—it lies within an instinctual system; attachment and separation in the example of the "gone" game. That which is frightening, arouses separation anxiety, or arouses anger that the child cannot directly express, all motivate such play. The fact that the child is in a passive position means that he is incapable of doing any-

---

2 Loevinger (1966) cites mastery as one of the three major principles in all of psychoanalytic theory. It appears in a number of places in the work of Erikson, but has been relatively neglected by many within the orthodox psychoanalytic group.

thing about the actual situation; the baby cannot make his mother reappear, nor can the child effectively aggress against the doctor who hurts him. This state of affairs is dealt with in a symbolic world where he *can* do something. We have here the basic prototype for a wide variety of play, dream, myth, and rituals. Writing a story, acting out a drama, and the myths and rituals of primitive peoples are all concerned, to some degree, with attempts to gain control over the world, with mastering the "slings and arrows of outrageous fortune."

CHILDREN'S DREAMS

We saw earlier that language, play and dreams can be ordered on a dimension of public to private—of socialized to unsocialized—and that this ordering carries with it certain implications. Play permits a greater range of symbolism, a greater freedom in experimentation with social roles, and a potential for practice at mastery not found in the more tightly structured mode of speech. Dreams are still more private and less subject to the conventions of social acceptability and, because of this, exhibit still greater freedom for expression and experimentation. An examination of some actual children's dreams will illustrate this and, at the same time, provide further examples of the preoccupations and emotional concerns of the child.

I wish to devote some attention to the presentation of actual children's dreams reported in several studies by David Foulkes and his students, and in a study of mine. In these studies, dreams were gathered using techniques of monitoring sleep through the night, and it may prove helpful to describe these methods briefly before presenting the case material itself.

In the early 1950s, workers at the University of Chicago discovered a relationship between dreaming and rapid eye movements of the sleeping subject. A great deal of work was spurred by these initial discoveries and is summarized in a number of publications (see Foulkes, 1966; Jones, 1970). It has been established that sleep is a cyclic phenomena during which the person passes from physiologically "quiet" to "active" phases. Dreaming is most likely to occur during those portions of the sleep cycle when the brain is most active (as measured by an electroencephalogram or EEG); the eyes are moving rapidly as if looking at the dream images; indicators of emotional arousal such as heart and respiration rate are active; but the external muscles are relaxed. The phase of sleep (referred to as REM, for rapid eye movement sleep) takes up about 20 percent of a typical eight-hour night.[3]

---

[3] It is interesting to note that the percentage of REM sleep is much higher in neonates, and still higher in premature infants (Roffwarg, Muzio, and Dement, 1966). It declines progressively through the childhood years and stabilizes at around 20 to 22 percent of sleep time by age five or six. It again declines in later life. In another paper (Breger, 1967), I discuss the hypothesis that the

The indicators of dreaming can be monitored through the night, so that an investigator can awaken a subject toward the end of each REM period and obtain a report of the ongoing, or just completed dream. This method of obtaining dream data allows one to obtain a vastly superior sample of dream material; a sample that includes sequences of dreams from a single night, a number of dreams across nights and reports from individuals who might not, under other circumstances, be able to recall their dreams. Dreams obtained from appropriate nighttime awakenings are longer and more detailed, more "dreamlike" or bizarre, and, in general, very rich imaginative products. They are closer to those processes involved in the creation of the dream—private, unsocialized modes of thinking—and less influenced by the public, socialized modes of waking thought and speech. The monitoring methods introduce problems too, since the subject must sleep in a laboratory or quasi-laboratory situation and knows that his usually private dreams are being observed. It is possible, however, to minimize the intrusive effects of the methods by taking care to establish a close working relationship with the individual.

Several studies have used these methods to gather dreams from children and I will summarize them here since they are, in many ways, the best evidence available on what children dream about. Foulkes, Swanson, and Larson (1968) studied dreams in a small group of boys and girls between three and five years of age. These young children dreamed about events and concerns from their everyday life. For example, one young girl had expressed interest in a neighbor who was nursing her baby, asking her mother how women give milk and related questions. Some of her dreams were of "a man milking a cow," "a farmer milking a chicken," and "a lamb drinking milk." In addition, some of her rivalrous feelings for a six-year-old brother were expressed in a dream of a "rattlesnake getting a six-year-old boy." Foulkes and his students have published two other studies (Foulkes, et al., 1967; and Foulkes, 1967) in which the dreams of boys in the six to ten age range are presented. In general, Foulkes emphasizes the realistic as opposed to bizarre qualities of the dreams and views his data within an Eriksonian model of psychosocial development. The following summary quote is illustrative:

> The dreams of the pre-adolescent consist, to a surprisingly large extent, of content fitting under the rubric of "anticipatory socialization." He is looking forward to what he would like to be in terms of his physical, emotional, social, and psychosexual development, or, perhaps, even more accurately, to what

need for processing information via the dream mode is highest in infancy and declines as more of the world is mastered—a hypothesis which fits the data on percent of REM through development, and which is confirmed in several studies by Greenberg and his collaborators. (Greenberg, 1970; Greenberg et al., 1970).

he would like to *do* in the world about him—and he is doing so with a generally realistic appraisal of the difficulties involved. (1967, pp. 96–97)

Foulkes' conclusions are quite close to those of Griffiths, cited earlier. Dreams are a mode in which the child experiments with social roles, confronts his fears, sometimes in fairly direct ways, and less directly when fear is more intense. For example, one boy, seven years old, reported the following dream.

> It was on the Fourth of July. [My big brother] had a big firecracker, and he put it in a tin can and lit it. It made a pretty big dent in it. [My little brother] had one and lit it, and he thought it would make a great big bang except it just made sizz...[firecrackers] called snakes. You light them with matches and they grow. I was lighting some of those, and some firecrackers too. Sometimes they went bang and sometimes sizz. My Dad was watching us do the firecrackers. (p. 91)

The dreamer is concerned with his relative potency in relation to siblings (and father, as his other dreams reveal), and with the problem of attaining adult status (the "firecrackers that grow"). The firecracker symbols realistically place him between younger and older brother. Foulkes reports similar concerns in the dreams of the other boys though each is focused on those aspects of his life most central to him. One is still preoccupied with "a lingering emotional attachment to mother, with concomitant fears of a castrating father." He is still in the midst of the oedipal dilemma. Others have moved beyond the peak of the oedipal conflict and are working out identification with the male role. The wish to become a masculine adult was, in fact, the most pervasive characteristic of all the boy's dreams in Foulkes' study. Let us now examine in detail the dreams of one young boy collected as part of a study of mine.

Jake: A Case Study

The subject, whom I will call "Jake," was seven and a half years old at the time his dreams were first collected. He slept in his own home and dreams were collected on four nights (spread over a one-month period) during which he was awakened near the end of each REM period (the complete sample of dreams and more extensive discussion of methods may be found in Breger, 1969b). The project was carried out with the participation of his parents.

Jake is the second of three children with a sister one and a half years older (who served as a dream subject before him) and another sister six years younger. He is an extremely active, aggressive boy who was, for some years, fairly difficult for his parents to manage. At the same time, he possessed considerable charm and was getting along quite well in school and with persons outside the family. His relationship with his older sister was close and very ambivalent: he was admiring of her intelligence and social competence, but also jealous and competitive. At the time the first set of dreams was collected, he was dealing with his baby sister mainly by ignoring her existence. In the general sequence of psychosocial development, we might expect a boy of this age to have passed the peak of the oedipal conflict and to be struggling with his identification as a male. Let us look at some of the twenty-one reported dreams to see what concerns him, how his conflicts and hopes are symbolized, and then relate this material to Jake's life situation. The dream reports are exactly as he gave them when awakened out of REM sleep.

No. 4 (The fourth dream on night one):   Once there was a sticker bush and this man lived in it, under it, you know, where all the dirt is and he got all dirty. One day he turned the Empire State Building on the tippytop of the top and then one day he threw it into the sea. He wasn't very strong, but he could do it. So he got put in jail and then he sneaked out by his pen. It x-rayed through the wall and then he took the capitol and threw it in the water again and then President Eisekler put him in prison again. [President?] Yeah, he died and I keep dreaming this over and over again, and then the last time he threw both things; he threw them both over at the same time and he got put in jail, but he couldn't find his pen. [Who was he?] Just a man. [Who did he look like?] Like Dad when he goes to work.

No. 7 (The second dream on night two):   There was a football game on TV and we were watching and in the middle of the game I went to get some crackers and as I got up I flied through the TV and I went there right on the field and I raced back some steps and had to stay there, and I couldn't find my dad then. [Who was with you when you were watching TV?] My dad was. [How did it feel to go into the TV?] Bad, you know, getting cut, real, real, real bad ones. Real bad, a hole, real deep in. [What part of your body?] All over.

No. 10. (The fifth dream on night two):   Once upon a time this boy had a talking finger and it goes everywhere because it was off and now he doesn't have a thumb anymore, because that was the talking finger. And the talking finger went all over and one day the talking finger went to this park where this boy was, and the boy was sleeping. The talking finger was magic, so the talking finger turned the boy into a chair and then the talking finger laid on it and then the talking finger was like me and went to sleep, and when he went to sleep, the boy woke up and when he woke up, turned him on his back and spanked him. And then the finger went home and he went to bed. (Who was the boy?) A little boy, you know. (How was the feeling? Angry, sad, or happy?) Happy, kind of happy and angry.

No. 14 (The third dream on night three): Once opon a time there was a little man, he was going to eat dinner. And one night he starts to eat some fish. And when he was a little done he went to take a shower. And when he was done he went to bed. And in the night there was this man saying, "I want my finger back, give me my finger back." So the man didn't know what.., so he jumped out of the window and killed himself. [And then what happened?] The finger man went to bed. [How feel?] Pretty good. [Recognize the man or the finger man?] No.

No. 16 (The first dream on night four): Once there was this man who had no fingers. And he just walked down, down and had nothin' to eat or nothin'. One day there was this little boy who walked around the block all the time. And he had the same thing...no fingers or no nothin' to eat. One day they met each other and said "Hi!" and shaked. And then they went back to live together and in the house they went to bed. And the man got scared by nothing and he jumped out the window. And then his stomach grew and grew and grew. So then he climbed back up and he was still alive. And the boy was glad. That's all. [Recognize anyone?] No. [How feel?] Pretty good—funny.

No. 18 (The third dream on night four): Once there was a little boy who ran and ran all the time, who never stopped for his whole life. One day he was a very old man and he had a grandson. And he ran and ran for the rest of his life and he was old. And he had a grandson, and he had a grandson, and he had a grandson. And they all ran. One day, in a million years, the other man had a grandson and he didn't run. So all the other grandsons came up to his house and shot him. And then all the other ones went back and they went to sleep...and near nighttime that grandson who got shot woke up, and he went over to the house and shot the other grandsons. [Recognize anyone?] No. [How feel?] Kinda good. [Did you like it when he got shot?] It was kinda funny, he looks...[What did he look like?] My dad. [Who?] The man, cause they all looked the same, kinda.

These dreams, like a number of others collected from Jake during this time, present certain consistent themes and symbols. Many of them portray the plight of a weaker, younger child or son figure in relation to a more powerful adult or father figure. Aggression between child and adult is common, as is injury and deprivation ("no nothin' to eat"). Dream No. 4 was preceded by a dream in which a powerful "fat man" cuts open a "magic flower" only to find "nothin' " inside. Dream No. 4 deals with the general issue of rebellion against authority. Feeling weak and helpless in the hands of more powerful figures in the preceding dreams, Jake creates a fantasy in which a hero who resembles his father combats still bigger authorities (the Empire State Building, the capitol, and the president). We see here the process of identification at work in fantasy. The hero is clearly a blend of Jake and father and, initially, is successful in his aggression. But eventually, he goes too far and must suffer punishment.

Dream No. 7 presents Jake and father in a situation from his actual experience, watching football on TV—they also play football together—which emphasizes father's physical superiority. In this context, and perhaps because he tries too much too soon, assuming a place as an adult football player, Jake suffers serious injury.

Dream No. 10 represents a blending of the core conflicts, fears, and solutions seen in many of the other dreams. The cut off finger—once a part of the boy but now leading an independent and powerful life of its own—is an excellent symbol for the adult, masculine power that Jake desires, as well as the attendant dangers of acquiring such power. The symbol also represents the role of his own aggression in creating the anxiety in these dreams. That is, the powerful finger which turns on the boy represents what can happen if his own aggression gets out of control—the danger of killing the adults he depends on or, more realistically, losing their love.

Notice how the symbol is alternatively referred to as a finger and a thumb. Jake used to suck his fingers as a baby and subsequently his thumb. This suggests that the finger symbol and the desire to assume adult power necessitates giving up the security of babyhood. The pain of giving up the comfortable baby role contributes to the fear of injury and deprivation. The cut off finger and the cuts in dream No. 7 (and injuries that cause him to go to the doctor in dream No. 8) all symbolize this pain. He did, in fact, visit his doctor during the week preceding these dreams, and it was the same doctor who treated him the previous year for a severe cut on his finger and, later, a severe cut on his chin. Jake inflicted both injuries on himself while engaged in independent, aggressive action. The identification aspects of dream No. 10 appear in the confused blending of boy and finger—a purposeful confusion that Jake achieves via use of the vague "he," "him," and "his" which permit boy and finger to be almost interchangeable in the telling of the dream.

Dreams Nos. 14 and 16 continue the theme of conflict and aggression. The finger symbol appears again, as does the attempted solution via identification. In No. 14 the theme may be stated as, "if one appropriates the power of a man (takes his finger) one is retaliated against." The victim and aggressor are, in some ways, blended together, as in "a little man." The retaliation includes deprivation—there is the suggestion that assuming adult power is frightening, not just because of a conflict with adults, but because it means giving up a position of nurturance. The conflict between receiving nurturance and being powerful and aggressive is continued in dream No. 16 which again experiments with identification with father as a possible solution. Boy and man share the same fate—no nurturance ("nothin' to eat") and no power ("fingers," again). The man is killed but regains life in a way that implies both power (return to a large size) and nurturance (a full stomach). One may view this dream as an experiment in identification with the father. It is as if Jake fantasizes what would happen if he became the father and says to himself, "we are both stuck with the same problem but being big may solve it." There are additional hypotheses that one might entertain here regarding the large stomach as a symbol of pregnancy (Jake saw his mother pregnant with his baby sister just a year and a half previously). Men, for all their toughness, need mother's love, which may be why a swelling stomach is selected as a symbol for power.

Jake is very much torn between the gratifications of babyhood and the wish to be big and powerful. Although desirous of father's adult power he is by no means certain if it is worth it; father is portrayed as not receiving nurturance and perhaps Jake has yet to understand clearly what gratifications—heterosexual, for example—are available to male adults. Being a "tough" male and being loved are incompatible in Jake's mind, as they are for many American boys in middle childhood.

Dream No. 18 expresses, quite poignantly, the theme of becoming a man. In his view, it takes forever and when he defies the system, tries to be aggressive and independent too soon, he suffers retaliation. The theme of generations is very cleverly used to represent the boy becoming the father who was once a boy. We saw the same theme of identification in dream No. 16, in which boy and man share the same fate, and it appears in dream No. 21 in which Jake and his father actually change into each other. Note that the "man" looks like his dad and that all the figures look the same, supporting the interpretation that the dream deals with identification. Note, also, that the boy seems to win this one, though at the end it is not clear if he is a boy or a man who looks like his father. This suggests that winning, or successfully solving the conflict, is tied to becoming the father, as it was in several earlier dreams.

Shortly before these dreams were collected, Jake wrote an autobiography in his second grade class in which he described himself with the following words:

> ...I have two sisters and no brothers. I like hippies and comics. I don't like girls. I get into things.

He added the drawing of himself reproduced in Figure 6.1.

FIGURE 6.1

The autobiography reveals the prohibition on love and tenderness so common in boys of this age ("I don't like girls"), and the most interesting, gratuitous comment "I get into things." The drawing speaks for itself; the long arms and large, multiple fingers dominate Jake's self image. Along with the self-descriptive, "I get into things," the drawing represents Jake as an aggressive, perhaps troublesome boy. Note the ambivalence symbolized by the mouth which is both smiling and frowning. He is, in fact, an aggressive, active, athletically talented boy, who finds it difficult to sit still very long. His fingers are frequently tapping out a rhythm on whatever is near and his energy and curiosity do, indeed, cause him to "get into things." He was, for some time, difficult and rebellious toward both his mother and father. Outwardly, he shows little fear or babyishness and is usually quite confident with peers, particularly in athletics and other active play. A sociogram, done at the end of the year in second grade, revealed him as the most popular boy in the class.

Thus, in his outward behavior, he is a tough and successful masculine figure. The specific use of fingers and arms in the figure drawing is very interesting since this is a recurrent symbol throughout the dream series. There, the themes and affects refer to power and independence; for example, the "magic finger" in dream No. 10 that "can do anything," and the

frightening aggressive "arms" in dream No. 20 that even a policeman's
bullets cannot stop. At the same time, these symbols suggest an opposite
theme, with cut off fingers (dream No. 16) representing a feeling of smallness, fear of harm, and lack of nurturance; that is, they emphasize his dependence on adults. An examination of some specific experiences and
memories will show why the image of a cut off finger is particularly suitable
to represent these two shifting sides of his developing identity.

In Figure 6.2, I have tried to relate as many elements as possible to
the finger symbol.

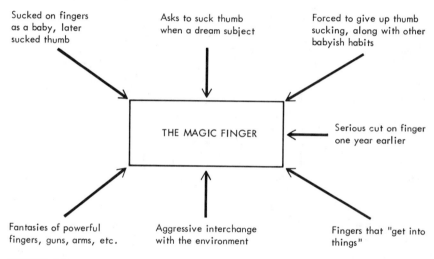

FIGURE 6.2

On the bottom of the diagram are listed elements related to fingers as
instruments of aggressive, independent interchange with the environment.
In addition to the usual fantasies of power associated with such phallic objects as guns and pens, Jake reported specific daydreams in which his finger
would take off and "bop" classmates on the head. There is, also, the image
of himself as mostly long arms and multiple fingers that "get into things."
The top of the diagram shows his other side. As a baby, he sucked the two
fingers on his right hand and later sucked his thumb. These babyish habits
persisted and only in the last year or two, with the onset of public school and
the additional pressure to be a big boy, did he give them up. In time of
stress they tended to reappear. For example, when he was a dream subject
he asked to suck his thumb to help him fall asleep in this new and somewhat
threatening situation. We might assume that the memories associated with
thumb sucking were reactivated in the dream-subject situation. Thus, thumb

and fingers are associated with the comforts and gratifications of being a baby, while giving up thumb or finger sucking is associated with the loss of such gratification made necessary as he grows up.

A specific experience one year previous to the time these dreams were collected was an additional determinant of the finger symbol. Jake was cutting out a Halloween costume, using a scissors in his usual aggressive and careless way, when he cut a rather large piece of skin from one of his fingers. There was a deep wound, a good deal of blood, a rushed trip to the hospital emergency room where the doctor appeared, replaced the cut off skin and dressed the injury. Over the next month there were a series of visits to the doctor to check on the wound. Although the finger healed completely, there is no question that the experience was a very frightening one for Jake, involving injury to his body and his reduction to a position of helpless dependence. About nine months later he fell off his bike while trying to skid through a puddle of water at high speed. He cut his chin severely and received eight stitches from the same doctor. Interestingly, he had been to this doctor with a minor flu prior to the second dream night, so that the memories associated with both injuries may have been activated by this more recent experience. Note dream No. 7 in which he gets cut "real bad, a hole, real deep in," which sounds like the actual finger injury (dream No. 8 refers to going to the doctor because of a fever, his actual, recent experience). Dream No. 10 on that same night then presents the symbol of the "magic" finger.

Thus, for a variety of reasons, the cut off finger (or thumb, or the powerful "arms") all symbolize Jake's central life conflict. The finger and thumb as "cut off" represent the nurturance of babyhood, metaphorically "cut off," as in giving up thumb sucking. These dream images are associated —in both the same dream and in dream sequences within a night—with the feeling of endlessness, a feeling tied to his sense of smallness. This theme is also related to lack of nurturance, symbolized as being empty inside or having nothing to eat. Both the specific symbols and the related emotions are present in dreams with a consistent theme. Thirteen of the twenty-one reported dreams represent a child in this particular conflict with a male adult while several of the remaining eight can be similarly interpreted if one allows some inferences.

I have gone into detail regarding these symbols to illustrate how specific experiences come to determine the selection of symbols related to a life conflict. The conflict itself is a very general one. Jake is torn between being a man and being a baby. His curiosity and aggressiveness impel him toward the adult role: he desires the power of adults and frets under the constraints of an endless smallness. At the same time, he fears giving up the gratifications of babyhood and has doubts about his ability to succeed as a big boy.

This fear or insecurity merges with his fear of retaliation—a feeling that appears in those dreams in which he comes closest to appropriating adult power. We see here, the fantasy blending of fear of his own aggressiveness and retaliation by adults, and the related feeling of being unloved because of this same aggressiveness—because he is a *boy* and not a baby or a girl. Recall that he has two sisters—an older one who gets by with charm and sweetness and a younger one who is loved as a baby. Perhaps the extent to which he exaggerates his aggressive maleness stems from a need to differentiate himself from his sisters.

The dreams may be viewed as fantasy experiments in which Jake tries out various solutions to his identity problem. For example, in some dreams, he experiments with being all toughness and power, only to discover that the consequences are unpleasant. Running through the series of dreams is a central solution: the various and ambivalent attempts at identifying with his father. This reveals, in dream form, the process of identification at work. In different dreams Jake (1) appropriates father's strength or power, (2) becomes physically like him, (3) shares a common fate, (4) is protected from still worse aggression, and derives comfort from this protection. Although some of these attempts are ill-fated, leaving him injured, helpless, or with no way out, others clearly suggest progress toward resolution. Particularly striking is dream No. 18 with its endless chain of men and their grandsons. Here, there is the beginning realization, in fantasy, of the boy's place in a series of men who can have some effect on the world.

In the dreams collected at this point in his life, Jake seems to be struggling with his identification as a boy-male, breaking away from the remnants of babyhood and exploring ways in which he could be like the father who he resents, fears, loves, and admires. Observation of his waking behavior supports this view. Jake was frequently at loose ends during this time, not knowing quite what to do with his energy—too old for "baby stuff" and too young for athletics. Thus, the emotional state of an endless waiting, of being stuck with no clear way to a goal, was one he frequently experienced as he hung around the house with "nothin' to do." His relationship with his father, and mother as well, was clearly ambivalent: loving from time to time and frequently rebellious. Over the course of the year he seemed to move more and more in the direction of the positive identification presaged by the dreams. He became much easier to live with, more cooperative and loving, and less openly defiant. A spontaneous self-portrait, done just thirteen months later speaks for itself (Figure 6.3).

Jake is apparently going to be a man of extreme commitments, either all fingers or none. Actually, the dreams collected at this later time indicate that the peak intensity of the baby-man conflict had passed and that he was more clearly committed to his identification with the male role. His ability

FIGURE 6.3

to engage his aggressive energy in socially approved athletics and the increasing ability to play with peers combined to make this later period of his life a more comfortable preparation for the future.

FANTASY AND REALITY

The private world of fantasy provides opportunities for the child to experiment with new roles and solutions to life conflicts. Identification, the process whereby the child imitates and models himself after those who are more competent and powerful or who have access to things he desires, begins in this private sphere. He is free to assume the power and positions, or to symbolically engage in the desired actions, of his models. Imagining himself as his models, he becomes them, as long as he remains in the fantasy world.

But one cannot live entirely in a world of fantasy. For identification to become more than just wishful thinking, the roles and solutions that the child experiments with in fantasy must be tested in the world of reality. We saw before how mastery is a process whereby passively experienced events are mastered by active repetition. It is also true that dreaming, the purest mode of fantasy, occurs when the person is most passive (sleeping with the least muscle tonus). Dreams are typically experienced as "just happening," as something beyond the dreamer's control. Thus, dreams may present creative solutions to conflicts, but in order for these to become involved in mastery or growth-related identifications, they must be translated into action in the world. Piaget makes a similar point when he states that dreams are "pure assimilation." It is only in interchange with the world that accommodation occurs, and schemas only change when accommodating. His stress on the equilibrium between assimilation and accommodation parallels the interdependence of fantasy and reality that I wish to discuss here.

For example, a child of three or four may want very much to be a "big boy" and may dream and fantasy himself as such. He is also faced with certain real demands and opportunities to become "big;" he can give up thumb sucking or bed wetting or baby talk, learn to ride a trike or go to nursery school "by myself;" increasingly separate himself from his mother; and, in all these ways, actualize these wishes and fantasies in reality. This is necessary for progressive identification to occur because fantasy and reality are interdependent. Let me discuss this last point in more detail.

In an earlier section I discussed the private to public continuum on which dreams, play, and language fall. The public and private modes are interdependent. Dreams are constructed from memories of the preceding day's events and memories from the past. These memories are manipulated and experimented with according to the mode or "language" that characterizes private, visual imagination. Although dreams permit free experimentation, they are also limited by the material—the memories—on which they are based. Without new material from new experiences in the world, fantasy will degenerate into an endless repetition of the same story, which is what seems to happen in certain withdrawn psychotics. An analogy is with a writer who constructs novels or plays, applying his style and imaginative skill to events and images from his experience. If he locks himself away from life and ceases to experience active interchange with the world, his work, no matter how carefully crafted, will become an endless retelling of the same story. He will become stuck or fixated; he will cease to develop.

The same holds true for the relation between fantasy and reality. Although solutions and roles can be invented in the fantasy mode that are not dreamed of in the more constricted social sphere they must be translated into action in some way, at some time. This action will then produce its own consequences which, in turn, will provide new material for one's dreams. When dream and reality interact in this fashion, a progressively expanding growth is made possible.

The foregoing does not mean that "idle dreams" must be immediately transformed into "real" actions. Quite the contrary, I wish to stress the necessity for both experimentation in fantasy and mastery via action. Each mode makes a unique contribution—one creative, the other practical. In children, the process probably goes like this: the child, confronted with an emotional problem or conflict which he cannot solve by direct action or with his existing skills, begins to experiment with new solutions and to try out new roles in dreams. This then overlaps into his private play—those games where children move their cars or dolls or blocks around, talk to themselves, and assume different roles. In early childhood, of course, fantasy and reality are not clearly differentiated by the preoperational child. Increasing experience leads to increased differentiation. Private play becomes social play. Here, engaged with peers, the new roles and solutions are subject to further experimentation. As the child proceeds, the roles and new ways-of-being become more and more a part of himself. What begins as imitation and imaginary identification moves to role playing and eventually becomes a part of the child. As he incorporates new roles, his self or ego moves to new levels of development.

This process takes a number of years as the child moves through a succession of stages and conflicts. Fantasy solutions may be experimented with and then put aside because of lack of competence, only to be revived at a later time when the child's body and social skills catch up with his desires. Something like this occurs with the sensual desires of the oedipal phase; that is, they are put aside until after puberty.

The case of Jake provides a specific example of the interrelationship of fantasy and actualization in the social world. At seven and a half, Jake was very much in the midst of a conflict; torn between the comforts and gratifications of being a baby and the attractions of being a male adult. The intensity of his fears indicate that, in a sense, he had not made up his mind whether the change was worth it. This ambivalence could be seen in his social functioning—he still sucked his thumb on occasion and in other ways revealed the baby under his tough veneer. Also, many of his forays toward maleness and adulthood were overdone; in his experimenting he became too aggressive, causing a further loss of his parents' love and approval. This is seen in those dreams where his attempts at identification—throwing over the Empire State Building, killing enemies, becoming all power and toughness—although gratifying to him, are rather one-sided. Over the next two years, Jake found a socially acceptable channel in athletics, especially football (which was presaged in his dreams at seven and a half—see dream No. 7). He became a habitué of the after school playground and a favorite of the coaches. In his own fantasy life, he strongly identified himself with these coaches (he was so identified with a young Negro coach at one point that he unconsciously drew himself as black in a self-portrait done in school). By spreading his male identification among men other than father, he escaped the confines of home with its connotations of babyhood and dependency. His bedroom walls were adorned with magazine pictures of sports heroes and each night before bed he would arrange and rearrange his "football cards."

A number of factors made this an ideal identification for Jake at this time in his life. Becoming a football player is socially approved and strongly supported by male peers, and he was skilled enough to receive a fair amount of praise. His father had been involved in athletics and spent some time playing with Jake and encouraging him. Thus, he was able to find a fantasy identity that he could act on in the social world and, in this way, make progress in mastering the baby-man conflict. These real accomplishments built self-esteem in a more profound way than fantasy alone since they entailed accommodations of the self. And, in turn, the actual accomplishments gave him new material to dream about.

In sum, as the roles and plans of fantasy and play are tried out in active interchange with the world, mastery and growth of the self occur. Each child masters his particular version of life's recurring conflicts in his own way; developing a certain style, certain expectancies, and certain identifications. Many of these are temporary or will be changed or absorbed into others as self-development proceeds. In all likelihood, Jake will not grow up to be a professional football player. But the fact that his solution to a core conflict at age seven to nine took the form of this particular set of goals and identifications will shape his development in different directions than if he had devoted his energies to stamp collecting or playing the piano.[4]

THE SOCIAL MILIEU

There is a tendency, when focusing attention on the individual or his dreams and play, to assume that reality is some sort of constant outside the child. Of course, it is not. The development of self is always an interaction between the individual—with his unique skills, fears, desires, fantasies, and hopes—and the opportunities presented by the social world he lives in. Since this is a book about individual psychological development, there is a tendency to overlook or minimize the importance of differences in the social world. To counter this, let me briefly mention some important social factors.

It is useful to remember that birth control is a relatively recent human invention. In addition, the discussion of early cultures in chapter 3 indicated that our small, relatively closed, nuclear family is atypical for most human societies. The usual experience of human children for many societies throughout history was to be surrounded by older and younger brothers and sisters and to have various other adults—grandparents, aunts, and uncles—share in their upbringing. Many customs and practices of child rearing evolved to fit this earlier state of affairs.

---

[4] For an example of childhood experience that contrasts markedly with Jake's and leads to a very different sort of adult personality, see Jean Paul Sartre's autobiographical *The Words*.

The structure of the family, and the child's place in it, makes up a specific social reality which shapes, and is influenced by, the developing child. Alfred Adler (see Ansbacher and Ansbacher, 1956) was one of the first to note the specific influence of family structure on personality development. Adler describes what it means to be an oldest child or the last of many; to be a middle child surrounded by a favored first born and a pampered baby; a boy with only sisters, or the reverse; and so forth. Such factors as sibling position and sex in relation to siblings interact with each other, as well as with other factors such as the social or economic status of the family.[5]

Many factors may play a role in determining parents' feelings and actions toward their children. As just one example, compare, from the child's point of view, growing up in a relatively stable family where mother has time and inclination to attend to his needs, and some degree of harmony prevails between parents and other children, with that of the child in a typical slum situation. Here, in addition to the stress of poor food, clothing, and living conditions—which bring with them the stigma of being second-rate in a highly competitive society—social life itself is typically disordered. Father is either absent or does not seem to exist. Racial discrimination is perceived early by the child. Robert Coles, in *Children of Crisis,* an excellent study of black children in the South, shows that by the time he reaches school age, the black child's self-image is already shaped by the racist attitudes to which he has been exposed. Coles' black children view themselves as small, ugly, and generally inferior to their white peers.

The stress of ghetto life, poverty, and discrimination produce a high incidence of psychological breakdown among slum parents. Having a disturbed mother, or losing her periodically to a mental hospital, becomes one more factor for the developing child to deal with. Much of the actual upbringing of these children may be in the hands of their older siblings who, however much love they may have, simply lack the skill and authority to do a good job. What is more common is a pattern of abuse in which younger children become targets for the frustration of their older siblings, with no parent to protect them. The novels of Charles Dickens give an excellent picture of children in the slum environment of nineteenth-century England. The *Autobiography of Malcolm X* and Claude Brown's *Manchild in the Promised Land* describe conditions from the point of view of the black ghetto child in contemporary America, while Oscar Lewis' works (*Five Families, Children of Sanchez*) provide an excellent picture of poverty life in modern Mexico. Let us turn from this consideration of general social conditions and examine a few of the intricacies of parental reactions.

The specific ways in which parents treat their children constitutes the

---

5 Several studies have confirmed the importance of place in the family birth order and sex in relation to siblings on adult personality (reviewed in Janis, Mahl, Kagan, and Holt, 1969, pp. 549–55).

immediate social reality against which the child tests his roles and identifications. Childhood is a period of trial and error, of testing various ways of being, and the people in the child's life become the reality that he tests against. In part, this involves a fairly straightforward communication of standards—letting the child know that growth in certain directions is desirable and in others it is not. Baby ways are discouraged and more mature actions encouraged. During the oedipal period, it is made clear to the child that his sensual desires cannot be gratified within the family; in cases where this is not done (for example, by seductive parents), lasting conflicts may result. Aggression is controlled and directed into acceptable channels. Boys are rewarded for acting like males and discouraged for acting like females and vice versa for girls.

Since childhood is a time of experimentation, much is to be gained if standards are not enforced too severely and rigidly—if parents and others respect the child's attempts to find a way to maturity and maleness or femaleness through his own efforts and in his own way. Some adults, for example, communicate social standards as if the child is at fault for not knowing how to be mature, male or female, or how to control his impulses. In short, they react as if childhood were not a time of experimentation but a phase in which certain "bad"—immature, babyish, uncontrollable, sexual, aggressive—qualities or habits must be eliminated as rapidly as possible. Such a view is communicated to the child as he is shamed or punished and made to feel intrinsically bad for being what he is. Excessive guilt over sensual desire or experiments with the opposite sex role, and excessive embarrassment over smallness and immaturity may be inculcated by such a parental or social response, and these responses make mastery of developmental conflicts and progression to new stages difficult for the child.

Erikson (1950) points to another aspect of the parental response to the child's development. We have seen that parents should communicate standards in a reasonable way and serve as a social reality against which the child can test new roles and experiment with new styles. In addition, in their response, the parents can communicate their expectations for the child's future. For example, in letting the child know that his intrusive exploration is destroying too much valuable property—that he "is going too far"—a parent can communicate an expectation that such exploration will later prove a virtue—that when he is bigger "he will go far." Or when rejecting the child's romantic overtures within the family, mother or father can still make the child feel loved, can communicate that he or she will find a loving partner at some future time. The same sort of positive expectations may be communicated in other areas. Such expectations pose a set of positive goals for the child to live up to. While he may be small, rejected, or filled with anger now, he, through his parents' expectations, can envision a time when these conflicts will pass. Negative expectations, which are communicated by a parental response that treats the child's experiments as manifestations of his "badness," set negative goals for him to live up to. And certain children oblige by living up to them, much to their parents' and their own dismay.

SUMMARY:
FANTASY SCHEMAS AND LIFE PLANS

Throughout childhood and adolescence the child continues to experiment with roles and ways of being. Freud is sometimes quoted as believing that personality is fixed when the oedipal conflict is resolved, but such a view is too restrictive. Erikson, Sullivan, and others trace important personality changes in adolescence and in later life. Yet, while personality may not be fixed for all time by age five or six, Freud's observation calls our attention to a valid point. If we think of developmental stages and crises as a series of opportunities which determine the direction of personality, then it is true that the resolution of each stage makes alternative resolutions more difficult or less likely. The freedom of the individual to change becomes increasingly restricted as he resolves each crisis-stage in one direction to the exclusion of others. The form of resolution at each stage also determines one's freedom to change in the future. The child may face a developmental crisis and work it through in a manner that we think of as "healthy" or he may fail to work it through and become stuck with the problems and conflicts of that stage. In other cases, the conflicts may prove so difficult for his capacities that he can only resolve them by a rigid form of overcompensation which precludes freedom of experimentation in subsequent stages. Such directions in personality development are at the root of many psychological disturbances in later life.

As the various developmental crises are worked through, the child's self, interpersonal style, and emotional reactions become increasingly structured. He becomes a person who is confident or insecure, assertive or withdrawn; who acts toward and expects certain things from men, women and peers; who is more or less loving or aggressive, dependent or independent; with particular interests, and a special style. In short, he becomes someone with an individual personality.

Since play, dreams, and fantasy have played a central part through the years when personality was developing, much of the record of this development is stored in the plans or schemas that guided play or fantasy in the past and that continue to guide dreaming throughout life. Recall, too, that these schemas are connected with strong emotions since they involve instinctually important areas of life; areas such as loving or aggressive relations with other people, patterns involved in care and nurturance, or the expression of curiosity and exploration. In an important sense, *the schemas of childhood play and fantasy are the way the child lives on within the adult.* These schemas direct dreaming and may be most clearly inferred from a study of dreams; hence Freud's dictum "Dreams are the royal road to the unconscious."

The unconscious is also a way of talking about those parts of the person that remain unchanged from childhood. In an earlier discussion, I stressed the necessity for the interaction of the private mode of fantasy and the public mode of mastery. As children move through the conflicts of childhood, they encounter difficulties which make mastery more or less difficult: anxiety, experiences of loss, rejecting parents, or harsh social circumstances may all tip the balance in favor of an overreliance on private fantasy. A child with a preponderance of these experiences will be more likely to withdraw from the world and not experience those interactions that lead to an expansion of competence. In short, he will have less experience at *active mastery* and the schemas of childhood will become unbalanced. Such people, to a greater or less extent, remain stuck with the residues of poorly resolved childhood crises. They are forever seeking the infantile love they missed, or attempting to recreate an ambivalent family romance too literally with their adult partners. They may be so paralyzed with anxiety or guilt that meaningful relations and experiences are difficult, only a fantasy-like creation of a past that never was.

These considerations lead us to a new set of questions centered on the relative openness of the personality to change. We come now to the topics of consciousness and the unconscious, repression and defense; the preservation versus the transformation of self; topics which will be taken up in the next chapter.

chapter seven

Anxiety, Dissociation, and the Growth of Self

We are what we pretend to be, so we must be careful about what we pretend to be.*—Kurt Vonnegut, Jr.

We are so in the habit of wearing disguises that we end by failing to recognize ourselves.—La Rochefoucauld

As one progresses through life's stages, from the security of infantile attachment to the overblown independence of the early years; from Oedipal closeness to the conformity of middle childhood; from there to adolescence, young adulthood and beyond; certain core conflicts repeatedly appear. These conflicts are intrinsic to the human species and human societies; they are our heritage as aggressive, sexual, curious, group-living primates, each of whom begins life in an extremely helpless state and lives through a long period of dependence on others. These core conflicts may be labeled, with some overlapping: dependence-independence; security-anxiety; aggression and its control; love-hate; sensual pleasure and its renunciation; excitement-boredom. As I have attempted to show in the previous chapters, these conflicts wax and wane during the different stages of development. Each comes to the

---

* From *Mother Night,* copyright © 1961, 1966 by Kurt Vonnegut, Jr. Used by permission of Seymour Lawrence/Delacorte Press and Donald C. Farber, New York.

fore at a particular time, reaches a peak intensity, is worked through or put aside as another conflict builds up, only to reappear in a new form later on. For example, the two-year-old, coming from the stage of infancy where he is completely dependent on mother—a dependence so profound that initially he could not differentiate his own body as a separate object—struggles to define himself as an independent being, one who can say "no" and "do it myself." Breaking free from Oedipal attachments is a later version of this same conflict, but a version that appears in a new form. The Oedipal age child has secured the independence of his body and basic locomotor actions; he has had some few years of experience eating, dressing, playing, and relating to others by himself. But now it is his emerging social role, his self-conception or identity as male or female, around which the struggle of dependence-independence is waged.

As the Oedipal conflict passes, the child enters a period in which struggles over independence are less intense—they do not disappear, the latency period is not *that* latent—but the next significant eruption does not usually take place until adolescence. At this time the child begins the task of defining himself as an adult, independent of his family and, sometimes, even from the fact of his own childhood.

At each point in his struggle with independence the child or young adult is different. Struggles during the early intuitive, or later concrete operational periods are different from those in adolescence when abstract thought is possible. What is more, the conflicts are different at each stage because of what has gone before. The two-year-old has no experience being independent, but the adolescent has gone through earlier versions of the struggle and the residues of these versions have their effects on his perceptions and actions.

What is true for the cyclic encounters with dependence-independence is true for the other areas as well. Fresh bursts of aggression and sexuality, stimulated by new challenges and temptations, must be dealt with again and again as life progresses, and as new skills and opportunities stimulate curiosity and excitement. As we have seen earlier, there is a tendency to overdo things at the onset of a new stage, to overassimilate and push new skills and opportunities to their limits. Overassimilation leads to conflict with others, it is countered by social constraint which forces accommodation and a balanced or, in Piaget's terms, "equilibrated" outcome.

The very process of self-development is itself a source of conflict. As we have seen, imitation, modeling, and identification are the major ways in which the person develops. One incorporates new roles by identifying with those one loves or needs, envies or admires, or whose control one chafes under. *The growth of self by identification implies that external conflicts become internal conflicts.* The aggressive child who acquires self-control by internalizing parental restraint of his aggression, thereafter carries the conflict between the impulse to aggress and the prohibition of this same impulse, inside himself. I am talking here about conscience or what Freud called the superego. The process by which internal control or morality develops is more complicated than this brief example suggests, and I will present a fuller treatment in the next chapter. Here, I simply wish to make the point that all the core conflicts between the child and others can, to one degree or another, become conflicts within the person.

I have reviewed the material on core conflicts and identification as a way of introducing the topic central to this chapter: the means by which the person deals with conflict and the effects of conflict resolution on self-development. The perennial conflicts of human life involve growth and change, but they can also lead to psychological disturbance. Persons who fail to deal adequately with conflict have been called "disturbed," "neurotic," or "psychotic." They are said to rely too heavily on "defenses," to be "repressed," or to have relegated conflicts to "the unconscious." Alternately, such individuals have been described as "rigid" or "anxiety-ridden," as having "symptoms," or as "regressing" to infantile patterns. All of these descriptions come from psychoanalytic or neoanalytic sources. Those who favor other theories speak of "low self-esteem," a lack of "integration" or a "divided self;" of "schizophrenia" or "depression;" or of chronically disturbed "interpersonal relations." Adequate resolution of conflict has been termed psychological "health," "normality," "sublimation," "awareness," "progression" rather than "fixation," an "integrated self," the absence of symptoms or crippling anxiety, or a minimum of defensiveness. Although all of these descriptions have some theoretical connotations, many of the terms are used by psychologists and psychiatrists in an atheoretical or pantheoretical fashion. That is to say, workers of different theoretical leanings rely on terms such as anxiety, disturbance, normality, and health and seem able to agree with each other at the level of description.

Many of the major theories and terms were developed from experience with disturbed persons. In addition, concepts such as repression or defensiveness, rationalization, projection, or the use of anxiety and guilt as explanatory terms ("He only acts nice because he feels guilty.") have passed into common usage. Orthodox psychoanalysts, neoanalysts, self-theorists, existentialists, certain behaviorists, and educated laymen use concepts, descriptions, and explanations such as these in overlapping ways. The widespread use of such concepts implies either a great deal of agreement or a great theoretical muddle. In fact, while things are a bit muddled, I believe that the strands of a consistent theoretical account exist. In this chapter, I will try to sort through these different concepts with the hope of arriving at such a consistent theoretical and descriptive account. We will see that the developing individual resolves conflicts in one of two general ways, which I will term *dissociation* and *integration*. Dissociation involves a splitting off of conflict-producing or anxiety-arousing thoughts, impulses, feelings, or actions from one's self-conception. It encompasses the phenomena of repression, defense, and the unconscious. Adequate conflict resolution involves an integrated growth of the self. Whether the dissociative or integrative course is taken at any particular point in development is a function of the individual's skills, past experiences, opportunities in the environment, and crucially, of anxiety. Anxiety is a key concept in the thinking of so many writers who deal with psychological disturbance and health that we can best begin a theoretical synthesis with an examination of this concept.

ANXIETY

Security versus anxiety is one of the core conflicts that recurs through different developmental stages. But this conflict also underlies the entire process of psychological development. All development involves change, and change means giving up the security of the known for an uncertain future. Let me review the concept of anxiety, trace it from its early appearance to its later transformations, and then see if this developmental view can encompass the usage of the term by Freud, neoanalysts, existential writers, and others.

Separation anxiety is one of the basic primate instincts. Once an infant is securely attached to his mother, separation arouses anxiety which, at this stage, we infer from screams, facial expressions, and body movements. This emotional reaction pattern is found in all primates, as the earlier review of monkey and ape data demonstrated. The maintenance of mother-infant attachment has been crucial for the survival of infants and, thus, for the species, and separation anxiety strongly promotes attachment.

Several aspects of separation anxiety are worth emphasizing. First, it is a primary social instinct. Anxiety does not arise in a secondary fashion when other drives (hunger, thirst, sex, aggression) are frustrated, though it becomes interconnected with these drives later in development. Anxiety comprises an early-appearing, independent system. Second, the earliest form of anxiety is interpersonal. It is provoked by the loss of mother, her care, and all that this means to the infant in his sense- and reflex-dominated state. Again, this points to the primary *social* quality of anxiety. Third, we should note that early anxiety is tied to the infant's state of helplessness; it does not arise, for example, from traumas or pain-producing injuries. Accidents and traumas certainly occur and cause reactions in the infant similar to anxiety. But they are often transitory and of little lasting significance. Attachment to and separation from the mother is a pervasive and continuing part of the infant's life; the helplessness of separation and loss is almost always a more influential source of "trauma" than accidents, sickness, or injuries. In sum, the prototype for anxiety is *helplessness arising from the disruption of a vital human relationship.*

Attachment comprises a state of familiarity; mother's face, voice, and actions are the human world the infant knows best. Separation from this world plunges him into an unknown situation, so even at this level we see the prototype for the security of the familiar and fear of the strange. Fear of strange persons—"stranger-anxiety"—commonly appears in the latter part of the first year and illustrates this phenomenon. Exploration of the new gets underway at this same time, but involves overcoming the anxiety of separation. The very young child is drawn forth by his curiosity, but he will explore best from his base of secure attachment. In strange situations the baby will cling to mother and, a bit later, to familiar symbols of sensorimotor care such as blankets and dolls.

Before considering the later forms of anxiety, let me try to restate what I have just described as the prototype of anxiety in a slightly different way. The attached infant and his mother are, from the infant's point of view, one person. The term symbiosis is sometimes used to describe this intimate relationship. The early self is a symbiotic self. Much of the struggle for independence in the next two years is an attempt by the very young child to define himself as a separate being. The implication of the symbiotic self—of the oneness of attached infant and mother—is that separation is not simply perceived by the infant as the loss of an external source of supply or gratification. *From the infant's perspective, separation is like the loss of a necessary part of himself.* Keep this in mind because, as we shall see in a moment, a later form of anxiety may also be described as a "loss of self."

Loss of or separation from loved ones is a potential source of anxiety throughout life. Adult grief and mourning following the loss of a parent, child, or spouse are similar in pattern and feeling to separation anxiety. While this is so, it is also true that the infant detaches himself from the symbiosis with mother and becomes, with increasing security, less anxious over separation. This new independence is made possible by his expanding motor and intellectual skills which will eventually enable him to carry his security around inside himself. This is another way of saying that the external relationship, characterized by some balance of security and anxiety, becomes an internalized state in which the person feels secure (good about himself, a sense of "basic trust," high self-esteem) or anxious about what exists "inside," about what he *is*. Let us see how this transformation comes about.

From Loss of Love to Fear of Impulse

As the young child moves out more on his own, both love and control come more from a distance. Earlier the mother could interact with direct physical contact, but later, verbal expressions, requests, rewards, praise, and admonitions come increasingly into use. Eventually both love and control will be internalized—the person will carry his own versions of them inside himself.

During the important early years the child learns that certain of his actions lead to parental disapproval. Such disapproval may be expressed by punishment, scolding, reprimands, a withdrawal of privileges, or frowns and angry words from parents. The overall impact on the child is the same. From his present-centered and relatively undifferentiated view, mommy doesn't like *him* or he is *bad* when engaged in the forbidden activity. Parental restraints or negative reactions are experienced by the child as a loss of love and a threat to self. And this loss of love, of course, is simply a later version of separation—it arouses the same sort of anxiety as earlier threats to the vital relationships. To put this another way, loss of love— withdrawal of affection, parental disapproval, threats, and punishments— symbolize separation to the young child. The basic source of the anxiety is helplessness; loss of love derives its emotional or instinctual force from its connection with separation anxiety. Some examples will illustrate the force of experienced loss of love.

A young child is angry and strikes out at his mother. She reacts by withdrawing her love and affection—a threat of abandonment which triggers separation anxiety. From repeated experiences, the child learns that his anger and impulse to aggress are signals of an approaching danger, the danger of loss of love. Consider an example from later childhood. The child, glorying in a newly acquired masculine or feminine role, is sexually attracted toward mother or father. But these advances are rejected; the child is made to feel that the very sensual ideas and feelings that make the parent an object of romantic desire, lead mother or father to reject him. Again, the impulses are signals of a threatened abandonment, and, because of this, are capable of arousing intense anxiety. It is because such sexual or aggressive impulses can be signals of a threatened disruption of vital human relationships that they arouse anxiety.

These examples trace the process from separation anxiety, to anxiety over loss of love, to fear of the internal cues—such as the impulse to aggress or sensual arousal—which become signals for a threatened abandonment. The internalization of this process is the next stage in the transformation of anxiety.

Identification and Internalized Anxiety

When the child reacts to his own impulses as cues of a threatened loss of love, anxiety has become an inner process. That is, the child can feel anxious when no threatening parent is present simply because his own wishes, actions, or thoughts are danger signals. The process of identification greatly enhances this process of internalization.

During the years of childhood, imitation, modeling, and identification play large parts in the growth of self. Love and anxiety are two of the powerful motives for such identifications. In simple form, we may say that the child comes to love himself modeled after the way his parents have loved him. This is another way of stating what many writers on the self or ego—from the social theorist George Herbert Mead (1934) to the interpersonal psychiatrist Harry S. Sullivan (1953)—have stressed: the self is social; it is a precipitate of interpersonal relations. One's sense of self is shaped by the way others treat one.

Identification describes the growth of self by the internalization of external relationships. Parental love becomes internalized in the form of a secure self-image, a sense of trust, or high self-esteem. Once this internalization is firmly structured, then departure from this image—from what one has come to feel one is—arouses anxiety, since it is an internalized version of separation or loss of love. Maturation, changing social demands, in short, all psychological development, provokes and requires that the person change. The well-loved baby must become the seeking and assertive two-year-old; home must be abandoned for school and later for work and one's own family. Each of the many crises in personality development demands some transformation of self; thus each threatens security and arouses anxiety. Just as the child must move beyond the security of mother's arms, so he must move beyond the security of his early versions of self. And just as a secure early relationship provides the base for later growth, so does the internalized version of this relationship.

The child also uses identification as a means of coping with the anxiety aroused by separations and loss of love. For example, when a child is abandoned by his mother, he tries to cope with the aroused anxiety and anger by providing himself with the lost love. He does this by playing a mother role with himself, whether this is enacted with toys and dolls, other children, or in private dreams and fantasies. Since the real mother is the model for such identifications, the games and fantasies contain the anxiety and anger—the latter a strong emotion that is typically aroused by abandonment—present in the actual relationship with her. The child attempts to come to terms with his feelings by playing out the conflict on an internal stage in which part of him pretends to be the loved-hated mother and part the anxious-angry child. If abandonments are repeated or prolonged, this inner ambivalence may become a more or less permanent part of the self. Just as the child who is loved by others comes to love and feel secure in his sense of self, so the child who is abandoned comes to feel anxious and angry toward himself.

The development of a stable sense of self—an identity built on identifications—becomes a prime source of security. This is true even if one's identity contains severe internal anxiety and ambivalence. Some sense of self is always preferable to none at all. Just as it is better to have a parent that mistreats one than no parent at all, so a self divided by conflict, or prone to anxiety or other unpleasant feelings, is better than being nothing.

The foregoing is only an outline of the complex developmental course of anxiety. In the older child, adolescent, and adult, anxiety arises from within—from internalized conflicts or external threats to the sense of a coherent self. In a way, this development has come full circle. From the initial threat to a symbiotic self, to fear of loss of love, to anxiety over dangerous impulses, the source of anxiety has increasingly come to reside within the self, as it did at the beginning, though of course in a very different way. As Erik Erikson puts it:

> As the fear of loss of identity dominates much of our irrational motivation, it calls upon the whole arsenal of anxiety which is left in each individual from the mere fact of his childhood. (1950, p. 413)

As Erikson and others have stressed, adult identity contains a host of factors in addition to the models of childhood. People, to various degrees, derive a sense of security from their identification with their spouse, children, and family group; with kings, presidents, and movie stars; with nations, flags, and ideologies; and with religious or ethical beliefs, church, and God. But this is getting ahead of the story. In the preceding discussion I have presented an account of anxiety that is based on, and synthesizes, central aspects of the major theories. It would require a good deal of additional discussion to demonstrate that this model is, in fact, a comprehensive integration. Since a scholarly effort of this sort would detract from the task at hand, I will make do with a few remarks and some illustrative quotes and leave further checking to the interested reader.

Freud's Views on Anxiety and the Ego

Most of the ideas on the origin and transformation of anxiety presented above, as well as many contemporary theories, derive directly or indirectly from Freud. At the same time, certain complications or contradictions exist within the usual psychoanalytic account due to Freud's tendency to formulate new ideas and models without revising earlier ones. There are several early theories of anxiety and repression and these coexist alongside the later theory of anxiety and "ego defense" which is based on a much broadened psychoanalytic experience. Without attempting anything like a complete historical analysis, let me try to sort out these different theories.

Freud's early patients suffered from hysterical symptoms such as paralyses, loss of memory, and various inhibitions of their sexual and other functions. Using hypnosis and early versions of the "talking cure," he was able to link a number of these symptoms to traumatic events of a sexual nature which the patients were unaware of or had "repressed." Always formulating hypotheses to explain his observations, Freud at first thought these patients had suffered an actual sexual trauma—that they had been seduced by a parent, for example—and that the pain or anxiety of this traumatic memory caused the repression and neurotic symptoms. This was one of Freud's earliest models of anxiety, as well as his first model of repression, a concept that was later elaborated into a whole list of "ego-defenses" such as intellectualization, projection, regression, and reaction formation (see Anna Freud's *The Ego and the Mechanisms of Defense* [1936] for the best-known description). A conception of anxiety related to the early trauma theory followed soon after.

As Freud constructed his theory of sexual energy—which I have commented on in earlier discussions of the psychosexual stages—he began to view anxiety as arising from ungratified sexual impulses. He came to believe that his hysterical patients did not suffer from actual traumas but from fantasies which led to sexual inhibitions. These inhibitions prevented a "discharge" of sexual energy, and this undischarged energy was experienced as anxiety. It was as if the patient, lacking the outlet of sexual intercourse, became anxious as the unexpended sexual energy built up.

Although these early psychoanalytic ideas about anxiety and repression were based on important observations which linked together sexual experience, anxiety, and neurotic symptoms in new ways, the theories also contained the excess baggage of the energy model. Among other problems, anxiety was seen as secondary to pain or to a "primary" sexual drive. Never completely disavowing his early models, Freud formulated a different theory in his later work, particularly in *Inhibitions, Symptoms and Anxiety* which he published in 1926. The model that he presents here is almost identical with the synthesized view I attempted to outline in the preceding sections. Some quotes will demonstrate the similarities:

> Only a few instances of the expression of anxiety in infancy are intelligible to us; we shall have to keep to these. Thus, the three situations of being left alone, being in the dark, and finding a strange person in place of the one in whom the child has confidence (the mother), are all reducible to a single situation, that of feeling the loss of the loved (longed for) person.... It decidedly seems as if this anxiety were an expression of helplessness, as if the still undeveloped creature did not know what else to do with his longing.[1] (pp. 75–76)

---

[1] Sigmund Freud, "Inhibitions, Symptoms and Anxiety," in J. Strachey (ed.), *Standard Edition of the Complete Psychological Works of Sigmund Freud* (London: Hogarth Press, 1959). This and all other excerpts from this work are reprinted by permission of the publisher.

Freud, as this quotation makes clear, sees the basic source of anxiety as separation and the attendant state of helplessness. All the characteristics of this source—its primary social character, and so on—apply to Freud's view. He then traces the later transformations of anxiety, as follows:

> Object loss as the precondition of anxiety now has some further implications. For the next transformation of anxiety, the castration anxiety which makes its appearance in the phallic phase, is a separation anxiety also, and is similarly conditioned. (p. 78)

> The various steps in the development of the child, its increased independence, the sharper differentiations of its mental apparatus into various agencies, the appearance of its new needs—all these cannot remain without their effect upon the content of the danger situation. We have followed the change in the content of the latter from loss of the maternal object to castration, and we now see the next step therein as caused by the power of the superego. With the impersonalization of the parental authority at whose hands castration was feared, the danger becomes more indefinite. Fear of castration develops into dread of conscience, into social anxiety. It is now no longer easy to state what it is that there is fear of. The formula, "separation, exclusion from the horde," applies only to that more lately developed portion of the superego which was patterned after social models, not the nucleus thereof which corresponds to the introjected parental authority. Expressed in more general terms, it is the anger, the punishment, of the superego, the loss of its love, which the ego apprehends as a danger and to which it responds with the signal of anxiety. (p. 79)

The only way in which this account differs from our earlier summary is the special emphasis Freud gives to castration. If we take the liberty of expanding this notion—of seeing castration as one, but not the only, source of threatened rejection in middle childhood—then the two accounts are very close. In the last quotation above, Freud clearly describes the process by which an external relationship becomes an internal one; the way in which the love and fear between parent and child becomes love of oneself and anxiety over impulses or fear of conscience.

While Freud's revised ideas concerning anxiety find clear expression in his later writings, the same is not true for his concept of the ego. In his work after 1900, Freud speaks of the unconscious as a repository of instinctual impulses, governed by the tendency or striving for immediate gratification. He called this "das Es," the "it," typically translated in English as the *id*. What he had earlier called consciousness or the preconscious he now replaced by the part of the personality which develops in opposition to the id's instinctual striving; the part associated with purposeful, realistic interchange with the world. To this he gave the name "das Ich," the colloquial "I," which has come to be translated in English as the *ego*.

This marks the beginning of an "ego psychology" in Freud's work, an approach that relates the problems of internal conflict to one's ego or self-conception. Unfortunately, a clear or unambiguous description of the role of self in neurotic conflict is hard to find in Freud since his concepts of id and ego continue to be encumbered with the mechanistic energy theory.

The permutations and convolutions of the ideas of consciousness and the unconscious, of repression and defense, of id, ego, and anxiety, both in Freud's writings and those of many who followed him, is a tangled thicket. At the risk of oversimplifying, I will reduce the complications to two broad directions and suggest that one of these, if followed, will provide a resolution of many of these complications and will lead to a view compatible with that outlined earlier.

We must remember that Freud stands between two traditions: the nineteenth-century scientific outlook which led him to formulate his ideas in terms of mechanisms, forces, and energies, and that of a new psychological viewpoint which he did much to initiate. In this later view, observations can be stated in terms of purposes and meaning (conscious or unconscious), thoughts, wishes, impulses, symbols, and inner conflicts. Many of the changes in Freud's formulations of repression, consciousness, anxiety, and the ego paralleled his evolution away from a mechanistic theory towards a view expressed in terms of purposes and meanings. Discussions of these concepts, however, are found throughout Freud's writings in forms consistent with both the mechanistic and the psychological models. We may say that the orthodox psychoanalytic view—which one finds in Fenichel's (1945) influential book on neurosis, and in the writings of Freud's most orthodox followers—is aligned with the mechanistic position. In this view, the ego is comprised of a variety of "mechanisms," such as the defense mechanisms, with which it controls or directs the id. Nondefensive functions of the ego such as "sublimation," are mentioned, to be sure, but they assume a secondary position. If the ego can synthesize things, this is but one of its functions—the "synthetic function of the ego," as one theorist puts it—conceptualized in the same mechanistic model as the defenses. This is an approach which emphasizes the relative power of the id and the relative impotence of the ego, which stresses the centrality of unconscious forces while minimizing the role of purpose and conscious intention. Anxiety, in this view, is the fear of id impulse erupting rather than a primary social instinct. Perhaps most central, this view substantializes the personality into entities; it speaks of *the* ego and *the* id, of the ego's doing things to the id's impulses, as if it were a gatekeeper in the mind.

The other view casts the same observations of anxiety, defense, neurosis, and ego in a framework closer to human experience. We have already seen how this is true with respect to anxiety. Freud's terms for "ego" was "I;" he was perhaps speaking of one's concept of *self* which is certainly something different from, or more than, an assemblage of mechanisms or functions. If we follow the path in which ego refers to one's *experience of self,* the observations of symptom, defense, and neurosis may be cast in a way which eliminates the cumbersome and untenable mechanistic-energy model while still maintaining the essence of Freud's insights. What is more, this conceptualization is close to human experience, and may be coordinated with the views of many neo-Freudian, existential, and phenomenological theorists. Indeed, a major contribution of this group of post-Freudians—the ego-psychologists, Horney, Fromm, and, particularly, Sullivan and Erikson—has been to elucidate the role of self and identity in internal conflict.

As early as 1910, Freud described repression as follows: "The incompatibility of the idea in question with the 'ego' of the patient was the motive of the repression, the ethical and other pretensions of the individual were the repressing forces (p. 22)." One may read this clearly in terms of self and the dissociation of ideas incompatible with self-conception. The neurotic has "pretensions" to virtue and purity; he has a stake in maintaining a certain picture of himself. Certain "impure" ideas threaten this picture and must be disowned. In the important *Inhibitions, Symptoms and Anxiety,* Freud recognizes the dangers of substantializing ego and id as entities, as the following quotation reveals: "To return to the problem of the ego. The apparent contradiction is due to our having taken abstractions too rigidly and attended exclusively now to one side and now to the other of what is in fact a complicated state of affairs. . . . The ego is, indeed, the organized portion of the id (1926, p. 97)." Still, it is hard to talk about nouns preceded by "the," in the English language at least, in a way that does not imply that they are material objects. For linguistic, as well as for theoretical reasons, things might have gone better if "das Ich" were translated as "self" rather than as *the* ego.

Self is related to purposeful action: to interchange with the social world which takes account of reality; to organized functioning; in short, to all those ways we think and act that go along with an experience of self, of "I am doing this," or "This is happening to me because I put myself in this position," or "I am thinking these thoughts." *Repression and defense refer to a class of thoughts, actions, feelings, and impulses which are experienced as nonself.* In a related way, Sullivan speaks of "dissociation" from the self when describing defended phenomena. The repressed hysteric cannot remember events in her own life; it is as if they did not happen to her. The intellectualized and emotionally isolated obsessive reacts to his own wishes and ideas as if they were foreign invaders of his mind—obsessive ideas "just come into" his head and he cannot keep them out. The paranoid experiences his own aggressive intentions as coming from others: "It is not me who thinks that, it is him!" In all these examples, the person's ideas, impulses, or actions are treated as if they are not his own; they are experienced as *alien;* as done *to* me rather than done *by* me; as *passively suffered* rather than *actively initiated.* An examination of psychoanalysis as therapy will provide a further example of these two versions of psychoanalytic theory.

Psychoanalytic Therapy

In his early treatment of patients it was clear that Freud, coming from a medical background, viewed them as the helpless victims of illness. The goal of treatment was to rid the patient of symptoms and various authoritative means—hypnosis, suggestion, and even trying to force "insights" about his unconscious on the patient—were used. This model of treatment derives from the same sort of thinking as the early model of repression and anxiety. The patient was thought of as a machine that was not functioning correctly due to past "traumas" (or undischarged libido) and the psychoanalyst's job was to fix it (him) by removing the effects of such traumas. Part of the appeal of this thinking stemmed from the success of conventional medicine, of course. Viewing the body as a machine was a part of the germ theory of disease and the development of many forms of successful treatment. But it did not work so well with psychological disturbance.

Freud made an important break with his mechanistic-medical background when he gave up hypnosis in favor of free-association. Rather than the doctor telling the patient what to say or do, the patient was now free to say whatever came to his mind. From a passive object of "treatment," he became an active participant in his own cure.[2] The goals of treatment also changed. Instead of focusing on the removal of symptoms, or the uncovering of specific traumas, Freud came to view the goal of psychoanalytic therapy as "making the unconscious conscious" or, stated another way, "where id was there shall ego be." While this goal moves beyond the early mechanism of symptom removal, traces of the earlier thinking persisted in orthodox psychoanalysis. That is to say, "making the unconscious con-

---

[2] This oversimplifies things, as Robert Holt has pointed out to me. When Freud introduced free association it was in the form of a "basic rule" to say whatever comes to mind; the patient is, in a sense, ordered to be a passive spokesman for his unconscious. And many patients do not feel free, especially in relation to the analyst's "authority." I think the point is, that since analysis involves a struggle with the patient's dissociations, he will not feel free until he is "cured." Thus, feeling like an active participant becomes a long-range goal: as the patient overcomes resistances, defenses or dissociations he feels increasingly free, both from his "neurosis"—the dissociated side of himself—and from the analyst's "authority" which he discovers was largely of his own creation, that is, what Freud called "transference."

scious" or replacing "id with ego" have been interpreted with either a mechanistic or a psychological emphasis.

In the orthodox view, still tinged with mechanism, making the unconscious conscious refers to the recovery of forgotten memories. Replacing id with ego may mean nothing more than tinkering with defense mechanisms or allowing impulses, formerly repressed, to be "sublimated." In a completely psychological view these traces of mechanism are dispensed with. Anxiety is a social or interpersonal motive with an internalized aspect. Repression and defense are ways in which the person dissociates or disowns ideas, wishes, actions, and even parts of his own body, which he senses are reprehensible by external or internal standards. That is, he attempts to split off such reprehensible aspects from his sense of conscious self or ego. When we view repression and consciousness—id and ego—in terms of dissociation from self, then bringing the repressed to consciousness involves much more than a recovery of forgotten memories. *To become "conscious" of a dissociate complex is to own up to it—to comprehend its meaning as part of one's self.* This view fits well with the thrust of Freud's ideas which were concerned with truthfulness and the exposure of hypocrisy, whether the latter was society's denial of infantile sexuality or the neurotic's defensive covering over of his motives and intentions. When we equate the "ego" with self and the "id" with disowned impulses, then the purpose of therapy —the meaning of "where id was there shall ego be"—becomes *the integration of alien parts into a whole.* The goal, in fact, becomes the development of a whole person, one who does not experience certain of his core feelings, ideas or acts as alien.

Freud spoke of the ego as "the organized part of the id." The present view enables us to broaden this idea. The ego as integrated self is synonymous with organization. To put it another way, the ego *is* organization, it is the person's experience of himself as a coherent, whole organism. That which does not fit must be actively disowned. For example, if sexuality is felt to be impure, dirty, or sinful it must, for these reasons, be dissociated from one's self-view, in spite of continuing erotic arousal. Once dissociated, it will be experienced as arising outside of the existing organization of self. "I can't understand why these filthy thoughts keep coming into my mind," says the obsessive; while the hysterical woman can't understand how she so often finds herself in erotically-tinged situations with men—but no matter, an attack of nausea or a fainting spell will come to the rescue. Impulses, wishes, forbidden feelings and acts continue to exist, but only outside the organization that *is* ego or self. The neurotic or dissociated person experiences these as beyond his control, as compulsions, symptoms, unexplainable emotions, or unconscious acts. The goal of therapy is *re*organization; it is a form of ego or self-development whose goal is the inclusion of the dissociated aspects in a new structure of self.

Reconceptualizing repression, ego, id, and the process of therapy in terms of dissociation, self, and reorganization has two advantages. It is a closer descriptive fit with the clinical data from which these ideas originated and it is phrased in a less technical, more psychological or experiential language which facilitates communication with the patient. It is difficult to talk with a patient about what his ego is doing to his id. But one can talk about the way his symptoms or ideas are experienced as not a part of his sense of self. Freud's early case studies and analyses of dreams are, in fact, close to this language of psychological experience. Suppose we ask ourselves the question, "What was Freud observing and attempting to explain with his concepts of repression, the unconscious, id and ego?" The answer is, "All those small and large ways in which people deceive themselves, pretend to feel other than they do, carry social niceties to parodied extremes, or cover up those acts which they are ashamed of." Repression is not the same as simple lying, to be sure, but it is very close to the way in which covering up old lies becomes a way of life. Defensiveness is comprised of forms of lying and pretense in which the unwanted or distasteful is separated off from one's conception of a polite, nonsexual, or unaggressive self.

To understand fully how lying or pretending, which we all engage in to some degree, can become dissociation, we will have to trace the process through development, for it is only in its developmental context that dissociation can be comprehended. This journey will reveal dissociation—all those ways in which thoughts, impulses, acts, and parts of one's body, are experienced as alien—as one of two major ways in which developmental crises are resolved. The other, for which I will use the general term integration, will emerge as a way of resolving crises by active participation: a mode that incorporates experiences into an expanding self as opposed to splitting them off or dissociating them. As we will see, this view of integration is quite different from the view of "sublimation" as one of many possible "ego defenses." In the present view, interpersonal crises may be resolved in two major directions—dissociation or integration. Resolution in the direction of integration is almost synonymous with what the experienced self *is* or becomes.

Before examining integration further, however, we had best complete the account of the way the present formulation of anxiety, self, and dissociation fits with various neo-Freudian and existential theories.

Neoanalytic and Existential Theories

In the preceding section I have tried to show how a formulation of psychoanalytic theory in terms of meaning and organization—one which is couched in terms of anxiety, self, and dissociation—is preferable to the theory which speaks of id, ego, and sexual energy. This reformulation already goes a long way toward integrating psychoanalytic, neoanalytic, and existential accounts. Many postanalytic theorists such as Sullivan, Horney, Fromm, and Erikson have attempted to reformulate psychoanalytic ideas in ways similar to those just presented. (This is no accident, of course, since my integration draws heavily on the work of these authors.) Rather than reviewing their ideas in detail, I will present a small but representative sampling.

Harry S. Sullivan (1953) places his primary emphasis on the social or, as he terms it, "the interpersonal" aspect of personality development. He defines anxiety as an interpersonal emotion communicated directly from mother to infant. As such, it is very close to separation anxiety as a primary motive. The self, in his view, is a coherent system which tends to perpetuate itself. Things which arouse anxiety are dissociated from the self-system, in Sullivan's view. These ideas, of course, are consistent with the account of social anxiety, the security of a known self or identity, and dissociation, previously outlined. Dissociation is, in fact, a term borrowed from Sullivan.

This same use of anxiety is found in the work of other post-Freudian thinkers. Erikson, for example, stresses the role of social and cultural forces, and an earlier quotation has shown how he connects threats to the personal-cultural identity of the adult with infantile helplessness. Frieda Fromm-Reichmann summarizes the confluence of ideas from several schools of psychoanalysis as follows:

> In going over the literature on anxiety in children and adults, from M. Klein, Sharpe and Spitz, to Ferenczi and Rank, Freud, Rado, Sullivan, Fromm, Horney and Silverberg, it seems that the feeling of powerlessness, of help-lessness in the presence of inner dangers which the individual cannot control, constitutes in the last analysis the common background of all further elabora-tions on the theory of anxiety. (1954, p. 718)

This summary quotation draws attention to both the state of helplessness characteristic of separation anxiety and loss of love, and the later, inter-nalized version of this state: anxiety due to "inner dangers," fear of impulse, and threats to identity.

R. D. Laing, whose insightful analysis of schizophrenia is having increasing impact on contemporary psychology, describes himself as an "existential psychoanalyst." His book *The Divided Self* presents a descrip-tion of schizophrenia as experienced from the inside and an account of anxiety and splitting of the self that is very close to the present discussion. Laing is quite clear in locating anxiety in the self; his term is *ontological insecurity*—ontology referring to the basic sense of "being," the core of self or identity. Here is how he puts it:

> Such a basically *ontologically* secure person will encounter all the hazards of life, social, ethical, spiritual, biological, from a centrally firm sense of his own and other people's reality and identity. It is often difficult for a person with such a sense of his integral selfhood and personal identity, of the permanency of things, of the reliability of natural processes, of the substantiality of natural processes, of the substantiality of others, to transpose himself into the world of an individual whose experiences may be utterly lacking in any unquestionable self-validating certainties. (1960, p. 39)

Laing goes on to show how the schizoid person suffers from ontological insecurity, from a basic anxiety that prevents his feeling secure, even about his own body. Much of the behavior and thinking of the schizoid person becomes understandable as attempts to come to terms with this basic anxiety or ontological insecurity. "The divided self" refers to the way the ontologically insecure person splits himself into real and fantasy selves, into mind and body, and how he hides behind a false self-system, plays roles within roles, all in a futile attempt to gain the security that he so desperately seeks. For example, Laing states:

> In the schizoid condition here described there is a persistent scission between the self and the body. What the individual regards as his true self is experienced as more or less disembodied, and bodily experience and actions are in turn felt to be part of the false-self system. (p. 78)

Such splitting of the self is an extreme form of dissociation; it differs not in kind but in degree from the defensive dissociation of the neurotic person. Both neurotic dissociation and the schizoid splitting of self are motivated by anxiety and both represent attempts to deal with this anxiety by disowning or dissociating a part of the self—by relegating it to the category that Sullivan calls the "not me." The schizoid person is more intensely anxious, he carries dissociation further, or, alternatively, we can say that more of the self is involved in the dissociative process.

Much more could be said about these complex issues, but this brief discussion should be sufficient to show how Laing's existential-psychoanalytic views are consistent with the present model of anxiety, dissociation and self.

There are a number of other thinkers aligned with the existentialist label, from the psychotherapists Rollo May and Victor Frankl to the novelist-essayist Albert Camus and the novelist-playwright-philosopher Jean Paul Sartre. Again, space does not permit a presentation of many ideas associated with existentialist thinking; the interested reader is referred to the works of the above authors. An excellent general source is Herbert

Fingarette's *The Self in Transformation* which reviews a number of these ideas and shows how the existential concepts of anxiety and being may be integrated with psychoanalytic ideas.

Following Fingarette, we can say that ego is "being" or "meaning" and anxiety the other side of ego, "nonbeing" or "meaninglessness." The "despair" that existential writers such as Kierkegaard describe, or the loss of a sense of reality and meaning so acutely portrayed in Sartre's novel *Nausea,* are akin to Laing's ontological insecurity. They represent the anxiety of extreme dissociation, of a splitting of self carried so far as to disrupt the security of one's basic identity.

In summing up his integration of psychoanalytic and existential theories of ego and anxiety, Fingarette states:

> There is no genus-species distinction between neurotic anxiety and ontological or existential anxiety. There is anxiety, and there are the ways we face it and respond to it, and the latter may be analyzed in terms of a variety of dimensions of experience and modes of language use. "Anxiety" may be taken into the existentialist vocabulary or into the psychoanalytic one. When anxiety is taken up in the context of psychological language and theory, it is "psychological" anxiety. When it is taken up in the context of existentialist languages, it is "existential" anxiety. When the response is evasive, we speak, according to our orientation and conceptual scheme, either of psychological defense or of lack of spiritual courage, of the "inauthentic." Where the response is reparative, expansive, realistic then we speak either in psychological terms (sublimation, realism, maturity) or in existential terms (authenticity, courage). (p. 96)

Anxiety and Self: A Summary

Anxiety begins as the helplessness experienced by the symbiotic infant when the vital oneness with mother is disrupted. The self develops beyond symbiosis with the eventual internalization of external relationships. Anxiety is experienced as loss of love, and later becomes connected to those internal cues which signal a potential loss of love. In short, one comes to feel anxious about impulses, wishes, and ideas. Similarly, the security of external relationships becomes internalized as the security of a known identity. Threats to this identity provoke defensiveness. The core conflicts, and the very fact that development occasions continual change, both assure a constant provocation of growth and anxiety. I elaborated Freud's theories on anxiety and the ego at some length with the hope of showing how his views —if taken psychologically rather than mechanistically—are consistent with the present interpretation of anxiety and self. This general model also fits closely with the thinking of neoanalytic and existential authors such as R. D. Laing.

Throughout the foregoing analysis of anxiety and self, reference has been made to the two general modes of conflict resolution—dissociation and integration. I have suggested, for example, that self or ego *is* organization and wholeness, and that symptoms, unconscious fantasies and defensive acts are parts of the person split off from the whole, dissociated from the experience of an integrated self. With a general model of anxiety and the self completed, we may now take a more detailed look at the two modes of crises resolution.

DISSOCIATION AND INTEGRATION

The problem that the growing child faces is how to become something different and still retain the security of the past. Psychological growth and change pose a threat to identity; they demand an abandonment of mother's love, of the security of babyhood; the child is propelled into new, challenging, and frightening situations with peers, in school, and in the world— situations in which his old skills and ways of being are not necessarily effective. In short, change and growth, although inevitable and exciting, also produce anxiety. The attraction of novelty, innate human curiosity, the pleasures of competence, the "need to function," all provide the motivation *for* change. The security of the known, the tendency for self once structured to perpetuate itself, the anxiety of separation, all pull *against* change; they are motives for the maintenance of sameness. Piaget's terms are "accommodation," in which adjustment to novelty results in change or growth within the person, and "assimilation," in which the novel is dealt with via established ways. He stresses the necessity for an equilibrium that includes both processes.

In discussing these two motives within different psychological theories, Loevinger notes: "There are people dominated primarily by one or the other, those who seek the Lost Paradise and those who seek the New Utopia. There are psychological theories built on one model, tension reduction, or its contrary, striving for competence and self-realization. But normal life is built on both models; indeed, their alternation provides the rhythm of the day (1969, p. 130)."

Development, especially, intensifies the conflict between the security of the past and the satisfactions of new growth and accomplishment. The child is faced with a number of opportunities and, at each of the various stages of development, must deal with them in one of these two general ways—either by relying on the established modes of the past or by trying new ways and, in the process, changing himself. He can dissociate or integrate. The choice of one or the other is closely tied to the dimension of anxiety-security. As a general rule, we can say that the greater the anxiety the more likely dissociation, and the greater the security, the more likely integration.

Dissociation From Self

The essence of dissociation is that conflicts are dealt with in such a way that this "dealing with" is not experienced as actively initiated. This sounds as if "the self dissociates part of itself from itself" and confronts us immediately with a paradox. For if it is the person who does the dissociating, how can he be "unconscious" of it? The developmental model rescues us from this paradox. It reminds us that there are states such as play, fantasy, and dreaming during which the sense of an active self is diminished, and there are times of life (early childhood in particular) during which these private fantasy states predominate. The essence of dissociation, therefore, is to be found in the typical ways in which a child meets a conflict he cannot resolve in reality; that is, by splitting himself off from such reality and "solving" conflicts in play or fantasy. When he does this he experiences his ideas and acts as not actively initiated. Fantasy solutions to conflict involve an abandonment of a direct or "real" solution for a "pretend" or imaginary one. Let us consider some examples:

A child is disciplined by father or threatened with a loss of love by mother. Striking back directly doesn't work because the parents are bigger and stronger, and because it will simply lead to more loss of love. What can the child do? He can give in and accept the parental discipline, becoming outwardly a "good child," and express his frustrated anger and wishes in fantasy. Games are played and dreams dreamed in which father dolls are run over by cars or are vanquished by the masked marauder, the avenger of injustices to the weak. Versions of this specific fantasy are found in a number of cartoons, comic books, and fairy tales. Heroes such as "Superman," "Batman," and "The Lone Ranger" are interesting examples. The symbolic tie of these heroes with childhood is represented in one way or another, as in Batman's child companion Robin, or Superman's weak and ineffectual other self, Clark Kent. One of the comic book heroes from my own youth, Captain Marvel, was a young boy in his "other life," who changed into a superhero by saying a magic word. These hero figures are thus not "supermen" but "superchildren;" they are fantasy representations of the child's typical wishes and identifications.

The superhero represents both an identification with adult models and an attempt to dethrone the adult and usurp his power (in a manner quite similar to "Jake" in the preceding chapter). The typical plot of hero stories illustrates these themes of competition and identification. There is usually some injustice perpetuated on weak or innocent people, symbolizing the way the child feels in reality when adults make him do things he does not like, or when they discipline him. Adults appear in two guises; they are either the evil figures whom the hero must fight or the inept authorities who call on the hero because they are incompetent to deal with evil themselves. Again, this represents the child's wish to outdo adults as well as his identification with desirable adult characteristics; that is, in fantasy he outdoes them by becoming a bigger, stronger, purer version of themselves.

Comic hero stories are close to the preoccupations of young boys—perhaps because they are written by men. Certain fairy tales represent some of the typical conflicts of young girls and their fantasy solutions. For example, when a young girl's desire for her father is frustrated by mother, conflict ensues in which daughter feels humiliated, cast aside, or not worthy of love. In reality, there is little she can do about this state of affairs—except wait until she grows up, when she can have a man of her own. But in fantasy, anything is possible and the young girl may play and dream herself as Cinderella or Snow White, cast aside by the unfeeling mother figure, but winning the handsome prince after all. Like the superheroes so common to the fantasies of young boys, the Snow White or Cinderella figure is better or more virtuous than the evil adult (typically a "bad mother" portrayed as a witch or step-mother). This again shows how fantasy combines competition and identification.

These examples illustrate the way in which the child turns to fantasy as a means of dealing with conflict. The child's retreat to fantasy is almost always accompanied by outward compliance. It is precisely when he feels he must "give in"—do what adults want, or publicly renounce his rebellious or selfish goals—that a turn to fantasy becomes most appealing. *The contrast between outward compliance and fantasy gratification is one important prototype for a splitting of self.* That is, one of the roots of dissociation as a response to conflict lies in the child's division of himself into an outward, socially compliant, good boy or girl, and an inward or fantasy self who overcomes frustrations and social constraints. Recall also that young children think intuitively—they are centered on the present and do not clearly differentiate fantasy from reality. A splitting of self is thus more natural in early childhood and it is only later, with the appearance of more advanced modes of thought, that dissociation becomes more clearly pathological.

Pretending, putting on an outward show of goodness and compliance, acting as if one feels differently than one did a few moments before, and playing roles, all are childhood prototypes of dissociation. Let us look at the process more closely. First, there is the act of pretending itself. The essence of pretense is that one actively does something and, at the same time, actively denies doing it. Angry older brother hits the baby but pretends baby hurt himself; the child with his mouthful of cookies asserts that it was really someone else who raided the cookie jar. "I didn't start the fight, he did!" "What are you doing?" "Nothin'," and so it goes. Such lies and pretending are common enough in childhood and we accept them as excusable to various degrees. They will be more frequently used when parents are particularly intrusive or controlling, or when they subject the child to conflicting demands or double messages. Research on the families of schizophrenic persons, which I will discuss in a later section, has shown that contradictory messages are a common part of the communication system of such families, a system that leaves the child few options other than a pervasive splitting of himself.

When the child moves into the world of fantasy as a way to resolve conflict, he is pretending in two ways. Outwardly, he pretends to feel other than he does—he ceases to be angry, demanding, or selfish. Inwardly, he pretends that things are other than they are—he creates fantasies in which his anger can be expressed or his demands gratified. When he creates such fantasies, the child takes both (or all) parts to the conflict. He becomes the punitive parent and the punished child, the victorious child-hero, and the vanquished adult-villain. Such pretense and fantasy is "unconscious." The child does not connect his enjoyment when reading about Superman with the way he feels towards his father.

Passivity. The world of fantasy is both private and, in an important sense, passive. It is private by design; the child has a stake in appearing outwardly compliant since this represents part of the solution to adult demands. If he is to use fantasy as a way of reaching desired but forbidden goals, then he certainly doesn't want to expose his fantasies to those who do the forbidding. The passive quality arises from the conditions under which fantasy occurs. Dreaming during sleep is the purest form of fantasy and it occurs during a time when the person is most passive. Not only is he sleeping, but dreams take place during a phase of sleep when there is the least amount of muscle tonus, when the body is most limp. Dreams are, of course, private since they occur during sleep and are typically not communicated to others. Daydreams and other fantasies occur when the person is awake but are also associated with a quality of passivity. The day dreamer stops "doing things" and simply lets images and fantasies float through his mind.

Both qualities, privacy and passivity, along with the pretend features noted earlier, make it likely that fantasy solutions will be experienced as unwilled, as "nonself," or dissociated. Let me expand on this statement. When the child outwardly complies, he is assuming a passive stance vis-á-vis the parents; he "gives in" and accepts control from them. This is likely to be experienced as letting one's self be willed by another. The other side of self—what the child "really" wants—retreats to the world of fantasy. But here too, the child is likely to experience himself as passive—he is just a dreamer to whom images appear, as if unbidden. This *is* the quality of dreams. Along with these passive experiences goes the more active form of dissociation. If the child's desires manifest themselves in action, if he strikes out in jealousy at the baby, for example, and is caught, he may try to pretend that it was not *he* who did it or, more accurately, that it was not he who *willed it* to happen (that is, it was an "accident," or someone made him do it). The similarity between such "pretend" actions and their fantasy counterparts lies in dissociation from self. In both examples, the forbidden or anxiety-arousing or conflict-producing thoughts, feelings, and actions are experienced as "unwilled" or as not "owned" by oneself. They "just happen" or are attributed to other causes or people that "made me do it."

Passivity, Emotion, and Dissociation. The words "passivity" and "passion" are both derived from the Latin *pati,* meaning to suffer (the Greek *penthos,* signifying "grief"; the English *pathos,* that which arouses feelings of sympathy, pity, or sorrow). Passion refers both to the experience of strong emotions and to the suffering or enduring of pain, as in the passion of Christ—his suffering on the cross. These etymological links call our attention to important psychological connections between emotion, passivity, and dissociation from self.

Passion, in the sense of strong emotion, refers to experience within the instinctual-emotional systems—love, fear, anxiety, anger, and interest. The importance and pervasiveness of emotions makes them specially "driving" or imperative and, particularly in childhood, they are often experienced as coercing behavior, as "taking over," or guiding action in a manner that the child cannot stop. Indeed, a central problem for the child is learning how to deal with his anger, demands for love and gratification, jealousy, or intrusive curiosity; how to bring these imperious emotional states under self-control. This state of emotional domination is surely what Freud is describing when he speaks of "the id" as a seething mass of excitation pressing for discharge.

Passion as emotional domination is not confined to childhood; we speak of adults in a "fit of rage," "blinded by love," or "driven by fear" to express this same quality—the taking over of behavior by powerful emotion. Children and adults differ markedly in the manner and degree to which they are capable of controlling their emotional states. An infant lives more directly by emotion, and children are generally closer to the expression of feeling than are adults. Insofar as this is true, they are more likely to experience their fears and joys, their rages and pleasures, as just happening to them, as passions which they enjoy, endure or suffer. In sum, the closeness of childhood with the direct experience of emotion is one way in which the child is passive, in which he experiences himself as compelled to act by his feelings. Let us look at some other ways.

The most obvious factor contributing to the child's sense of passivity, that he is "one to whom things happen," is his real lack of power and competence in comparison to older children and adults. The child is often at the mercy of persons whom he cannot control and whose actions he may not understand. He is made to do things that adults want and must curb his own desires. He sees the giants around him doing things that he envies and yet cannot accomplish. Such feelings of smallness and incompetence are a part of every child's life to some extent, but they will be enhanced by certain types of parental response. For example, I earlier referred to research on the patterns of communication in families of schizophrenics. A striking characteristic of these families is that the child is much less able to influence what happens to him in any meaningful way. The parents do not respond in understandable ways to his needs or communications. The way they treat him stems from their own unresolved conflicts and is often incomprehensible or contradictory. Thus, the child's natural tendency to feel at the mercy of forces he cannot influence is much greater in such families, making dissociative life patterns more likely to occur.

As a general rule, we might expect that those factors in the child's actual situation which make him feel helpless, which make him the victim of forces he can do little to effect, will reinforce dissociation. Being abandoned, treated with inconsistent love and abuse, and being subjected to contradictory communications all contribute to the child's sense of helplessness.

As a further example, consider illness and physical injury. Do you remember what it was like to be sick as a child? One feels like a victim of fate, struck down by painful circumstances that just do not make sense. "Why me?" "Why now?" Feelings of helplessness, rage, and abject dependence are all common. These responses to illness are not confined to childhood, of course, though they are more intense at that time. Illness is not the child's fault, yet there is little he can do to influence it. It is, thus, another example of passive suffering, a precursor to dissociation.

The similarity of experienced illness to emotions and psychological events that the child cannot control may form the basis for the widespread view that psychological disturbance is a kind of "sickness' or "mental illness." That is to say, the person who is mentally disturbed feels "sick;" he experiences his anxiety and conflicts as forces beyond his control, as unpleasant happenings which he can only suffer. Thomas Szasz (1961) cogently argues that the idea of "mental illness" is a myth, that only harm will come from misconstruing anxiety, unresolved conflicts, and interpersonal difficulties—what he terms "problems in living"—as if these were the same as illness due to germs or malfunctioning parts of the body. His arguments are well taken. Many psychologically disturbed persons feel as if they are sick. As we have just seen, the conditions which foster dissociation, as well as dissociation itself, are experienced as passive suffering which the person cannot do anything about. When psychiatrists or other official representatives of society label such psychological suffering as "illness," however, they are aiding and abetting the disturbed person's dissociative tendencies. It makes a great deal of difference whether *you* treat yourself as a helpless, "sick" person or your psychiatrist does!

Psychological Disturbance and Childhood

Many authors concerned with psychological disturbance attempt to connect such disturbance with factors in the person's childhood or infancy. Let me apply the concepts of anxiety and dissociation from self, as I have developed them here, to this problem.

The first thing to note is the similarity between the "symptoms" of a neurotic or psychotic and the normal experiences of children. Young children are centered on the present; they do not necessarily integrate past memories into their present self. In a related way the neurotic who relies on repression does not integrate his past. The repressed person's motto is: "I don't remember, hence it did not occur or I didn't do it." Young children have difficulty distinguishing fantasy from reality: the real world from the world as they would like it to be. Obvious parallels are found in the withdrawal to fantasy which is so much a part of schizophrenia, and which is found in most forms of psychological disturbance, to some degree. The child feels pushed around by persons he cannot control, compelled to do what others tell him. In a related fashion, the obsessive-compulsive neurotic is compelled by internal forces; he feels at the mercy of his symptoms and emotions. In a more extreme form, the paranoid feels literally persecuted by external agents and forces. Physical or "somatic" symptoms will provide an important further example of the tie between childhood experience and dissociation.

When a young child is hurt, it is not uncommon for him to deal with the injured part of his body as if it were not his. He tries to cope with the pain by disowning it from himself. This is particularly common during the phase of intuitive thinking. During the early phase of a new mode of thought there is a tendency to overassimilate, to push the new mode to its limits. In the early intuitive phase, the child is just learning to differentiate himself from others and to distinguish "inside" from "outside." Central to this differentiation is a conception of his own body and its boundaries. In early childhood, when these differentiations are coming into being, the child naturally experiments with the boundaries of his body and pushes them in different directions. As part of this process, he pretends that good feelings are inside him and bad or painful feelings a part of the outside that is not him. When his own body, or some part of it, causes pain, he tries to disown it, to pretend that it is out there or "not me." If a finger is pinched or an arm bruised, the young child talks to it, "Bad finger, why are you hurting me?" "Arm go away, I wish I didn't have you!" Again, let me stress that dissociating parts of the body, like the other forms of childhood dissociation, are normal features of intuitive thinking. At the same time, the process of somatic dissociation provides a developmental model for related forms of dissociation in later life.

Physical or somatic symptoms are a part of many forms of psychological disturbance. The hysteric suffers paralysis or loss of sensation in different parts of the body—these body parts are thereby relegated to the realm of nonself. The anxiety that is central to all forms of disturbance has frequent somatic manifestations as, for example, nervous stomach, shakiness, headache, feelings of weakness, and pains of various kinds. All of these manifestations of anxiety are experienced as inexplicable sickness arising outside the self. An earlier quote from R. D. Laing called attention to the severe splitting of self characteristic of the schizoid person. Here the entire body can be experienced as an unreal "thing" that moves through a world "out there," a body-thing to which events "happen." In these ways the person attempts to dissociate the pain-producing body from the sense of self.

In sum, the various forms of dissociation common to childhood provide patterns for dissociation as a means of dealing with later pain, anxiety and conflict. Common to dissociation at any age is a state of passivity, a sense that one is a victim on whom misfortune is visited, a feeling that one is driven by emotion, or must endure sickness—in short, an experience of helplessness which, as we have seen, is the essence of anxiety.

Now, it should be made clear that children are not miniature neurotics or psychotics. The parallels I have just outlined indicate that disturbed adults show distorted and exaggerated forms of processes that normally occur during childhood. While I have made a few suggestions, I have still to explain why certain persons become stuck with the dissociative solutions and feelings of childhood while others do not. Let us consider this question next.

Fantasy and Reality Testing

An important feature of dissociative attempts at conflict resolution is its private character. Once a conflict goes underground (becomes dissociated from the outward self) it is no longer subject to social influence. The term "reality testing" refers to attempted solutions that involve interchange with the social world; interchange in which the child tests his actions against the reality of other people. Dissociation, insofar as it is private and passive, does not permit such reality testing. Once a dissociative direction is taken, it is likely to be maintained. This is what Freud is getting at when he says, "The Unconscious is timeless," and what Piaget means when he states, "Dreams are pure assimilation." The dissociative solutions embodied in pretense and fantasy maintain the *status quo* of self until such time as active and public efforts are made at self-transformation; until assimilation is balanced by accommodation.

Dissociation, passivity, and a retreat into fantasy are all common in childhood since every child experiences conflicts that he cannot master at particular developmental stages. As I attempted to show in the preceding chapter, the use of imagination has its own values; it can be very creative and is a first step in internalization and identification; the process by which the child acquires new aspects of self—new roles—by creating internal or imaginary copies of other people. Insofar as the child realistically cannot have or do what he wants at a particular age, it makes sense to settle for a fantasy or pretend gratification.

Putting aside one's wishes in fantasy until such time as one is capable is the normal or adaptive thing to do in many circumstances. Erikson calls this putting aside a *moratorium*. For example, the moratorium on hetero-sexuality during the years between Oedipal conflict and puberty allows the child to engage in much of the social learning within his capacity precisely because the heterosexual behavior that is beyond him is put aside until later. Or, it makes sense for the two-year-old to put aside his aggressive ambitions and submit to the greater power of the parents precisely because this will enable him to learn from the parents how to be more realistically ambitious at a later point in his life. Thus, moratoria at various points in development are necessary, and temporary dissociation from self is a normal occurrence. Neurosis or disturbance in development occurs when dissocia-tion becomes fixed, when moratoria do not get reopened, when one becomes what one pretends to be. Thus, neuroses are not caused by "unconscious fantasies" as one version of psychoanalytic theory maintains; such fantasies are simply representations of old, dissociative solutions to conflict which will continue to occur until the person can do something different. Schemas will keep assimilating until forced to accommodate.

The general answer to the question of why certain individuals remain stuck or fixated with dissociative solutions is that excessive anxiety has become connected with the original conflicts, that this anxiety was the original motivation for the dissociation, and that attempts to reopen the area to nondissociative reality-testing rearouses the anxiety. For example, the child who is abandoned or suffers frequent losses is likely to have exces-sive amounts of separation anxiety aroused by these experiences. He deals with these by creating passive fantasy substitutes for his lost love—fantasies that also vent the frustration and anger aroused by separation. In extreme cases, fantasy relationships may become more important than real ones. The expectation, based on the earlier experience of loss or abandonment, is that real relationships will be too painful and will arouse too much anxiety. Such a person may then become permanently "fixated" with dissociative rather than real relationships. To put it another way: early experiences of anxiety and dissociation plant the seeds for later disturbed complexes. Establishing real relationships as an adult then rearouses anxiety which motivates further dissociation.

Obviously this example is an oversimplification. But it should serve to illustrate the basic pattern of: anxiety⟶dissociation⟶lack of reality-testing ⟶fixation of self. We will consider some more detailed examples in a moment, but first it is time that we explored the other mode of conflict resolution: integration.

Integration

Integration grows from attempts to act on problems. If dissociation is passive and private, integration is active and public. Where dissociative solutions turn away from reality and abandon the testing of oneself in social interchange, integration involves active engagement with others. Where dissociation leads to stasis and a protective preservation of self, at least for periods of moratoria, integration involves the transformation of self and the expansion of horizons. Perhaps most important is the way these two modes are experienced. Where dissociation is experienced as nonself, as "happening to me," integration is the essence of self; it is associated with the experience of "done by me." Existential thinkers would say that integration *is* ego or self while dissociation is nonself, nonbeing, or meaninglessness.

We have seen how the qualities associated with the dream and fantasy state, as well as the adoption of pretense and overt compliance with the will of others, can contribute to a sense of nonself. In contrast are those experiences where the person bumps up against reality and, instead of retreating from it, attempts to engage problems by alternative means. An important example was presented in the previous chapter: Freud's observation of the child who masters the anxiety of being left by his mother by actively repeating what he passively suffered. Consider a few additional examples. A child has his aggression controlled and suffers a blow to pride and self-esteem. The dissociative solution is to assume an appearance of outward compliance while continuing to express aggression in fantasy and by various "unconscious" acts, for example, by accidents or mistakes. The integrative solution is to actively repeat the conflict of aggression and its control in some other situation. Play is the most likely and the child can master the blow to self-esteem by taking the role of parent toward a younger sibling or playmate and controlling him. When he does this sort of thing, the child is identifying with the parent in a positive or growth enhancing way.

Play is the great laboratory for the child's integrative experiments. In its early forms, play stands half-way between private fantasy and public accommodation. From about age four onward the child is increasingly capable of social play. With the onset of school, peer play and true coopera- tion become possible and by age seven or so, the child can play games with rules. This social play allows him to experiment—to put his fantasies to the test of reality—in the important instinctual-emotional areas. Love, aggres- sion, anger, friendships, exploration, overcoming fears—all the important emotion-laden relationships—can be tempered and shaped in the crucible of peer play. Such play is public, as opposed to the privacy of fantasy and dreams, though the audience is drawn from the relatively safer world of other children. What is more, play is active.

The active quality of social play contributes to a sense of self in quite the opposite way that the passivity of dissociation leads to a sense of non- self. That is, one experiences acts or thoughts as one's own when they are self-initiated, when they are done under one's own will power. In addition, the feedback from one's own body in active play, or one's voice in social interchange, both contribute to a sense of ownership of acts and intentions central to the experience of self. What is more, play with peers is free from the direction of parents and other adults. The child plays be- cause he and his friends *want* to and not because mother, father or teacher *make* him do it. This freedom from adult compulsion further contributes to a sense of active self-direction.

Another important quality of integrative experiences arises from the fact that certain kinds of sensorimotor actions are intrinsically antithetical to anxiety. We saw earlier how anxiety originates in separation, becomes tied to loss of love, and, later, to fear of those impulses, thoughts, and actions that threaten such loss. Closely tied to abandonment and loss is the experience of helplessness which is, of course, the state of the young infant who is separated from mother. Thus, a prototype of experienced anxiety is the passively helpless infant who lacks mother's sensorimotor care. Such care, the natural antidote for anxiety, involves active social interchange, as in clinging, holding, rocking, and the like. Even at this early level, activity is associated with a primary experience of anxiety reduction. So it is in later stages. Activity is, in general, incompatible with anxiety. Dissociative solu- tions, insofar as they are passive, perpetuate the feeling of helplessness. Integrative experience, insofar as it is active, contradicts helplessness. One can easily think of examples from everyday life: the intense anxiety before a public performance which is lost when one is actually doing it, sometimes to appear later when one is again in a passive state. Anxiety of this sort is almost always worse in anticipation than in actuality; doing something is always better than doing nothing, as many primitive, childish and compulsive rituals illustrate.

It is important to note that certain forms of action may be relied on to dissociative degrees. Some people must keep continually busy; anxiety causes a dissociation from fantasy, dream or introspection. Such action has a compulsive quality to it and is to be distinguished from the *active engagement* of integrative development. The concept of *integration* implies a balance, an equilibrium where various aspects—action, play, instrospection, and dream—can all find their place within the structure of self.

These thoughts concerning activity bring us back to a consideration of reality-testing. Insofar as a person relies on dissociation, the conflicts which arouse anxiety remain in the realm of anticipation—hence, the anxiety may never diminish. When one overcomes anxiety and attempts an active and public encounter, anxiety is lessened immediately because of active engagement, and, in the long run, because actuality can prove anticipation excessive. This assumes that reality will, in fact, prove benign though, of course, that is not always the case.

We may now consider, in more detail, the factors that predispose the person toward one mode or the other. "Why does one person dissociate where another can integrate?" Or, within a single individual, why are certain relationships—for example those which arouse sexual feelings— dissociated while areas such as work or career are actively engaged? To answer these questions we will have to look more closely at the circumstances in which the dissociative or integrative directions are first taken.

Dissociation or Integration

For purposes of discussion we may conceive of two sorts of factors which, acting in concert, determine the choice of dissociation or integration. The first set of factors is environmental, the most important environmental force being the parents and the love, conflicts, anxieties, and strengths they bring to the task of child rearing. The family exists in a wider social-cultural-historical context which shapes and reinforces the specific ways in which parents and, later, peers, teachers, and others act toward the individual. Parents, friends, social values and beliefs, institutions such as schools, codified practices surrounding sex, or the expression of aggression or dependency are the sorts of things that make up the environmental side of the equation.

The other set of factors comes from the child. Children differ, even from early infancy, on such dimensions as intellectual potential, placidity-activity, aggressiveness and amount of rage displayed to frustrations, cuddliness and lovability, and so forth. Since every child exists in a social context, it is impossible to separate environmental from individual factors. They are always interacting and influencing each other. Thus the child of high potential intellect encounters parents who stimulate and encourage his brightness or those who blunt it by neglect. The active-aggressive child meets frustrations and a lack of consistent control which encourage these tendencies in him, or an environment which does not overstimulate his anger and which helps him channel it in useful directions. Many more examples could be cited to make this point: that individual and environmental influences do not exist separately; every real child has his own unique predispositions and, at the same time, his own particular social environment within which these predispositions develop into permanent characteristics. In what follows, it may sound from time to time as if environmental factors create the person, as indeed they seem to when their extremity fosters dissociation: calling attention to the interactive nature of individual and environment should warn us against taking such examples literally.

The developing child always encounters a certain number of frustrations, rejections, and blows to pride and self-esteem. The scheme of human life consists of inevitable conflicts between dependence-independence, disire and renunciation, the need for excitement versus the wish for security, aggression and its control. In addition, the child's smallness, his relative lack of power and competence, are further sources of frustration. This state of affairs occasions a certain amount of dissociation in everyone.

An examination of the experience of individuals who rely on dissociation to excessive degrees—individuals who are labeled disturbed, neurotic, or psychotic—reveals an excessive amount of conflict and anxiety. They have typically experienced, in their core relationships, excessive frustrations, separations, or experiences which intensify feelings of smallness, lack of competence, and helplessness. These traumatic life conditions are often coupled with parental responses that block mastery, fail to reward competence, or, in other ways, make the choice of dissociative solutions more likely, on the one hand, and active engagement difficult or impossible, on the other. This states the matter from the environmental side. Whether dissociation or mastery emerges as a predominant way of life depends on what the individual child brings to his particular life situation. The strengths of the individual are important. Some children are able to overcome adverse environments and may grow stronger in the process. Traumas, when successfully mastered, can be growth enhancing. The final outcome in any real case results from the interaction of child and environment.

In what follows I will describe some typical examples of life situations which foster dissociation. Bear in mind that these are, of necessity, mere outlines of what takes place in actual life.

Sources of Anxiety and Dissociation. Separation or the loss of important figures are among the most basic sources of anxiety, as our earlier discussion of the attachment-separation instinctual system would lead us to suspect. Separations are extremely difficult for infants and young children to deal with. Loss of parents through death or divorce, and various degrees of partial abandonment through neglect make integration difficult and dissociation more likely. This is so because such experiences arouse levels of anxiety that the child is unable to deal with in any realistic fashion. If the parent is not present, no amount of crying or pleasing social action can affect him. Prolonged separations, particularly when these occur at crucial ages, can lead to a lasting sense of helplessness.

A parent need not be physically absent for a child to feel abandoned. Mother may be present but too preoccupied, or depressed, or drunk, or involved with other matters to attend to the child which, from the child's point of view, constitutes abandonment. The crucial factor is whether the child, through his own action, can affect mother and the social world. If there is no mother present or if she does not respond in any consistent or meaningful fashion to the child's communications, he will eventually learn that people do not provide comfort and he will turn away from social reality in his search for security.

There are many forms that the retreat from reality can take depending on the child, his specific talents and limitations, and the stage of development at which anxiety becomes prominent and the turn inward is initiated. In the earliest stages, with certain special children, the result may be infantile autism or childhood schizophrenia—conditions marked by a serious lack of positive relationships with the human world and a substitution of self-stimulation such as rocking, repetitive sounds and gestures, and attachment to nonhuman objects. Disruptions in the attachment-security sphere at later stages plant the seeds for psychotic and neurotic disturbances which may not become apparent until later life. In all such cases, the child learns that he cannot trust mother or others to allay his anxiety; in this sense he has tested reality and found it lacking. He then turns away from the social world to the private sphere of dissociative fantasy.

There are many other sorts of parent-child interactions that reinforce dissociation and thereby lay the foundations for disturbance in later life. Let me briefly describe a few of these. There are parents who take out frustrations on their children and others who seek compensation in their children's lives for that which is missing in their own. For example, a parent may express the anger and frustration aroused in his relationships with other adults by frankly rejecting, criticizing, or belittling his child. More subtle forms of this pattern include the parent who is conflicted about being male or female and who deals with this conflict, not by looking within himself, but by reacting in peculiar ways to the child's emerging masculine or feminine traits. Such a parent may cause the child to feel there is something wrong or bad about his or her penis, vagina, breasts, menstruation, or masturbation. The child may acquire excessive guilt over sexual fantasies or the normal sexual experiments of childhood and adolescence.

A related pattern involves the general control of impulses, whether these are sexual, aggressive, or just plain spontaneous excitement. Certain parents have a tenuous hold on themselves; it is as if they can only keep their impulses in check by maintaining a kind of internal police state. For such individuals, the child's anger, sensual acts, or excitement are threatening signals; these parents are likely to overreact and, in the process, cause the child to feel that he is bad, angry, or unmanageable.

Families and Schizophrenia. Studies of parent-child interactions that lead to schizophrenia—in many ways the most severe form of dissociation —shed a great deal of light on the genesis of dissociative disturbances in general. Several investigations, each done independently, point to a common pattern of communication and human interaction in families with schizophrenic children. Laing and Esterson (1964) present a series of cases based on extensive interviews with mothers, fathers, and their schizophrenic and normal children. These interviews, which are very illuminating to read, show the way parents, and sometimes brothers and sisters, direct confusing messages toward the "sick" family member while, at the same time, showing a bland insensitivity to his own expressions of feeling. The parents frequently speak of doing things for the child's "own good" and simultaneously belittle or ignore him. The families are typically preoccupied with maintaining a facade of normality. Conflicts, anger, and other open expressions of emotion are threats to this facade and must be ignored, distorted, or attributed to the "sick" family member as a sign of his "mental illness."

Similar patterns are described by other investigators. Bateson, Jackson, and their collaborators (Bateson et al., 1956) present the *double-bind* hypothesis. This refers to contradictory messages directed from parent to child, as when a mother says, "Come and give me a hug if you love me," while, at the same time, stiffening and making a face of disapproval at the child's approach. When the child withdraws in response to these nonverbal cues, mother then says something like, "I don't understand what's wrong with *him,* he doesn't love me." Wynne and his coworkers (1958) speak of the "pseudo-mutuality" which is characteristic of relationships between members of such families. Additional evidence is supplied by Lidz and his group (1958) and by some striking cases presented by the anthropologist Jules Henry (1963, 1971) who lived in the homes and directly observed parents relating to their young children in ways similar to those described by the other investigators.

A common characteristic, described in slightly different terms in all these studies, is the way in which conflicts within the family—for example, between husband and wife or between the wife and her parents—are denied, distorted, or masked by pretense and a "normal" exterior. How can the growing child understand what is going on, who is angry with whom, or indeed, how anyone really feels, including himself, with all this lying and pretending? In short, the families are characterized by a great deal of dissociation and it is little wonder that this leads to schizophrenia in some of the children. Let us now turn to an actual case which will illustrate many of the parental communications described in this, and the preceding, sections.

The Sins of the Mother: A Case Example.   A woman, whom I will call Mrs. Flynn, grew up on the fringe of respectability in a small town boarding house run by her mother. No father was present and Mrs. Flynn, though her memory was hazy, seemed to recall a fair amount of drinking and vaguely illicit dealings between her mother and the railroad workers who frequented the boarding house. In the small town atmosphere, she was afraid the immoral reputation of her home would rub off on her—that others would see her as "her mother's daughter" in an immoral sense. Her red hair and outgoing nature caused her concern in this regard; she sensed the danger that she might fit the stereotype of a "hot-head," someone who was quick-tempered and sensuous. Although she was these things, in some ways, she was more concerned with living down the "bad reputation" implicit in the stereotype.

Her adult identity was one of those compromises in which the dangerous side is dissociated while finding indirect expression in a "neutral" form. She presented herself as good-natured but dumb. She was less educated than her husband and many of their friends, but was certainly not stupid. Yet she used this "dumbness" as an excuse for her fears and impulses, just as she fell back on parts of the old "hot-head" stereotype. Her occasional angry outbursts were explained away as touches of blarney due to her comical Irish nature. If she acted in ways which hurt her children or husband, this was not really her fault but due to her "dumbness." She did not like being this way, but also felt there was little she could do about it.

The man she married was a civil servant with many outward signs of stability and respectability. Being an overly inhibited person himself, he obtained gratification from his wife's gregarious, if at times unpredictable, nature. They seemed to have worked out one of those relationships in which each partner expresses the dissociated side or secret longings of the other.

All went well in the marriage for a while: the first child, a son, was bright and easygoing. Then, a second child, Karen, was born. Karen was difficult from the early months—she did not sleep regularly and feeding was a problem. One day, when she was under a year old, the infant's body went rigid in her mother's arms, her eyes closed, and she lost consciousness. Mother was terrified and sought out the doctor. Eventually, epilepsy was diagnosed and Karen placed on anticonvulsant medication.

The medication successfully controlled her gross seizures and, given the limitations of her handicap, she might have grown up to a more or less normal life. That is, if her mother was capable of the special understanding that her condition required. But just the opposite was the case. Mrs. Flynn's initial terror was, in part, the reaction that any mother would have felt when her infant had a seizure. But her anxiety did not diminish once the seizures were controlled. For her, Karen's seizures—or even the thought that she might have them—aroused intense anxiety. As one listened to her talk about Karen, it became clear that the damaged daughter, prone to what the mother saw as potential mental retardation, loss of control, and breakthrough of impulse, was a living symbol for those parts of her own nature that she most feared. Having controlled her sexuality and anger and lived down her "bad reputation" only with great effort, she now saw these same dangers reemerging in her epileptic daughter. Her own dumbness, a comforting joke which hid her more serious fears, was now too literally emerging in Karen. Karen was, after all, her own flesh and blood, and Mrs. Flynn seemed to operate on the unstated belief that the sins of the parents are visited on the children.

Because her attitude toward her own impulses and intellect was intensely ambivalent, her attitude toward Karen showed this same ambivalence. She loved her and was concerned and upset for her health. But, at the same time, she was possessed of a furious hatred for this child who symbolized all those parts of herself that she had struggled so long to overcome. Her ambivalence led her to treat Karen in ways which made no sense to the young girl since they arose from mother's internal conflicts and not from Karen's own person or actions. For example, the epilepsy itself was dealt with in the worst possible way. Throughout her childhood Karen was never told about her condition. This was done, of course, "for her own good." Mrs. Flynn went to great lengths to disguise the required daily medication by secreting it in Karen's food and then hovering about to make sure the food was eaten, even if it tasted bad or Karen was not hungry. Karen's social activities were constantly being restricted because of mother's fears that she would lose control while, at the same time, no sensible reasons were given for the restrictions. When Karen was ten, Mrs. Flynn would not let her play outside with other children because she was certain that Karen would lose consciousness and might be raped by some passing male. Again, none of this was explained to Karen; rather, she was given a shifting and inconsistent series of excuses and evasions, many of which referred to her "retarded" condition.

These examples show that Karen's epilepsy was more than a disease in Mrs. Flynn's mind. Her reaction to it, and her treatment of Karen, betrayed her deep sense of shame and guilt. The damaged daughter who "lost control" of herself aroused great anxiety in the mother who had dealt with her own tendency to lose control by a tenuous dissociation. Where mother played dumb to cover her impulsiveness and anger, her daughter seemed a punishment in which this pretense became real.

Needless to say, Karen grew up a deeply disturbed girl. The only sensible inference that she could draw from her mother's treatment was that some bad presence—unexplained and unexplainable—lurked inside her. Her mother's restrictions and ambivalent overconcern were a constant frustration to Karen. When this led to angry outbursts, attempts at rebellion, or even self-assertion, it only confirmed mother's fears and daughter's self-image—her anger "proved" that she could not control herself, that she was specially bad and stupid.

By the time she was twelve, Karen was rather firmly enmeshed in her own web of dissociations. Finding only frustration in her attempts to relate meaningfully with her mother, and largely denied social experience with peers, she had turned more and more to the world of fantasy. She spent a good deal of time listening to the phonograph in her room, drawing what little security she could from hearing the same record again and again. Occasional forays out of her increasingly private world led to more and more violent confrontations with mother. As she entered adolescence, her budding sexuality and greater physical strength only intensified mother's anxiety over what her daughter represented. By this time, Karen had become what her mother feared: retarded and unable to control herself—though the sensitive observer could see from occasional flashes of intelligence and the peculiar form of her fantasies that the "retardation" was due to a schizoid withdrawal from the world and not from a lack of intellectual potential. To paraphrase the Old Testament saying, "The sins of the fathers shall be visited upon the sons," we might say of schizophrenics, "The dissociations of the parents shall be visited upon the chidren."

Much more could be said about Karen and her mother, but the pattern represented by their relationship should be clear by now. When a parent's response to a child is determined by the parent's internal conflicts, ambivalence, anxiety, and guilt; and when, as is typically the case with such conflicts and feelings, the parent must deny, distort, or disown them, then the child will experience the response as senseless frustration, criticism, double-binding communication, or rejection. Such parental responses preclude meaningful action on the child's part and, hence, make an integrated development of self practically impossible. Dissociation of one sort or another remains as the child's chief means of gaining security.

The case of Karen illustrates, in rather extreme form, the effects of a parent who projects her own conflicts and fears on her child. Earlier, I mentioned abandonments, separations, and parents who use their children as compensation objects. The common feature in all these examples is the inability of the child to meaningfully affect his parents and, through them, the larger social world, by his own actions. A surly or angry father who demands that his child toe the line and punishes small infractions may be no fun to live with. But, if he consistently acts this way and, of great importance, if the local society defines this as appropriate paternal behavior, then his children will adjust to it. Strictness, parental anger, or other unpleasantries do not lead to dissociations or psychological disturbance in later life. At the least, the child can fight back and may even be rewarded for doing so. It is when children are denied their status as individuals, when they become screens for the projection of parental dissociations, that difficulty ensues.

DISSOCIATION AND SOCIETY

The account of dissociation so far has focused on the individual. Even the consideration of the environmental side was stated largely in terms of individual parents. We must remember that the individual lives in a social context, and that real parents find support or opposition from the surrounding society which defines parental roles and practices. Every society has features which enhance integration in some spheres of life while promoting dissociation in others. This is done through values, beliefs, ideologies, and shared images which define ideal types of men, women, and children and which encourage or prohibit certain actions and fantasies. In this section, I will present a few observations concerning the ways in which contemporary American society fosters dissociation.

Dissociation involves pretense and a denial of the full reality of human life. We may look, therefore, for social practices which aid and abet individual pretense and denial. There are several major areas here, including sexuality and the human body, anger and violence, aging, death, and deviations from psychological "normality." All of these are shaped by the pace of change characteristic of modern society.

It has almost become commonplace by now to cite the psychological stress caused by the rapid changes of modern civilization. Still, the point is worth emphasizing. In chapter 3 we caught a glimpse of the well-adapted life of hunting and gathering societies—cultures which evolved as stable systems over many thousands of years. During this relatively long period of time there were few, if any, disruptive technological changes. The ways of being a hunter or a mother, the free play of children under the loose but adequate surveillance of visiting-gossiping adults, the sense of oneness with the physical environment, all these changed only gradually, if at all, from one generation to the next. Life conditions in hunting societies made it easy, relative to our culture, for men to grow up hunters and women mothers, and for both to feel secure within these identities.

The advent of agriculture and the domestication of animals introduced major changes, but even these were slow compared with what has occurred since the rise of industry and modern technology. Mass transportation—from the railroad to the supersonic jet; the rapid dissemination of information—from the printing press to television; the rise of medicine and improved agricultural methods leading to the prolongation of life and overpopulation all have been so rapid that cultural customs and psychological practice have not had time to catch up.

At the psychological level, the rapid changes wrought by technology make the road to a stable adult identity a most difficult one to follow. Nowhere is this more evident than in the differences between each succeeding generation. It is the rare child in America today who can, with the ease and simplicity of earlier generations, follow in his father's or her mother's footsteps. The gap between generations is one of experience and values; it makes parents—ordinarily the natural models for identification—suspect or unacceptable. On the parents' side, rapid change and shifting values complicate the task of child rearing. Should they be permissive or strict? Attempt to impose the morality they learned (under similarly changing conditions) from their parents, or adopt a modern code within which they are not quite comfortable? And what will the world be like that these children are growing into? Won't rapid change make any course obsolete? This overstates things somewhat, but it seems certain that the basic fact of rapid change is itself a primary source of stress. Insofar as people derive security from familiar physical surroundings, from known values and beliefs, widely shared by other members of their group, and from the relationship with previous generations, then rapid change produces anxiety. This "social-change anxiety" becomes a general burden which adds to the anxiety that is a part of any particular child's life.

The anxiety of social change is world wide and not specific to America, though we are leaders in that paradoxical form of progress that can pollute the psychological, as well as the physical, environment. Let us turn now to a consideration of some specifically American problems.

Sexuality and the Body

The prudishness and sexual inhibitions of Western society are well-known. America was founded by Puritans and other overly inhibited Europeans, and restrictions on sex, excessive camouflage of the body, and shame and guilt over sensual pleasure are as much a part of our heritage as the flag. Although sexual taboos and restrictions are currently being relaxed (I will make some comments on that in a moment) the older doctrines are still firmly entrenched in the minds of many Americans. It is not sexual restrictions themselves that lead to conflict and dissociation, but the inevitable hypocrisy involved when these central life areas are excessively inhibited or suppressed.

As we saw in chapter 3, sex and sensual pleasure are parts of instinctual-emotional systems which promote attachment and reproduction. Human beings are sexier than their monkey and ape relatives; the loss of estrous, the continuous receptivity of the female, and close bonds within a family structure all play a part in the arousal of sensual pleasure. The infant's bond with his mother and, later, with others, is largely based on such pleasure. Infants and young children are, of course, innocent of social taboos. They seek pleasure through contact with others and the stimulation of their own bodies, for example, in thumb sucking and masturbation.

Society's restrictions on sensual pleasure become pitted against the powerful human drive for sensual pleasure. Some restrictions are necessary, of course. Almost all societies cover some parts of the human body, usually the genitalia of adults. The earlier discussion of the incest taboo and Oedipal conflict brought out a central cause for the renunciation of desire within the family. Given the necessity for some modesty and some controls, however, it still seems clear that our society has, in the past, gone far in excess of the requirements. It was not so long ago that Western missionaries went about the world bringing Christian "purity" to the heathen. Of much greater significance, it was only a generation or two ago that many American parents played the role of missionary within their own homes, attempting to stamp out the heathen sensuousness of their chidren.

The older attitudes toward infantile sexuality are revealed in an interesting study by Martha Wolfenstein (1953). Dr. Wolfenstein surveyed the government pamphlet *Infant Care*, from the first edition, published in 1914 through several revisions, to the 1951 edition. These pamphlets were put out as guides for parents and represent the expert opinions of their day regarding the care and rearing of infants and young children. *Infant Care* has been the most widely circulated child-care publication, at least of the pre-Spock era. It thus serves as a retrospective poll of average, widely disseminated opinion.

In the early editions, infantile sensuousness is viewed with horror and excessive restrictions are recommended. In 1914–24, "the danger of masturbation, if not promptly and rigorously interfered with, would grow beyond control and permanently damage the child. While he was in bed, he was to be bound down hand and foot so that he could not suck his thumb, touch his genitals, or rub his thighs together (Wolfenstein, 1953, p. 121)."

The direct repressiveness of this early period is muted in the later editions but the attitude of basic antagonism to the child's sensuality appears in other guises. During the period 1929–38.

> ...it is bowel training which must be carried out with great determination as early as possible. Severity in this area increases as compared with the previous period. This is accompanied by a pervasive emphasis on regularity, doing everything by the clock. Weaning and the introduction of solid foods are also to be accomplished with great firmness, never yielding for a moment to the baby's resistance. (p. 122)

In the subsequent editions, the emphasis on severity and the need to strictly control the child's impulses lest they run wild largely disappears in favor of tolerance and permissiveness. But there is a curious quality to this tolerance. The child's sensual impulses are not accepted, rather their existence is ignored:

> Autoerotic activities become even more harmless and negligible. Sucking is a permissible though low-grade pleasure (a poor substitute for being held or fed or talked to).... Masturbation is mentioned only in connection with toilet training (in 1951). While on the toilet, the baby may touch his genitals. This does not amount to anything, not even pleasure, but if it bothers the mother she may give the child a toy. (p. 122)

A deeply conflicted attitude toward the child's natural sensuality is evident whether this manifests itself as outright fear and disgust (masturbation is an "injurious practice"—it "easily grows out of control...children are sometimes wrecked for life") necessitating severe control such as tying the baby's arms and legs to his bed, or sewing up shirt sleeves to prevent thumb sucking—or a bland denial of the pleasure involved and recommendations to slyly shift the child's attention away from his body to "harmless" toys.

Treating the normal sensuality of infancy in this fashion can only result in conflict; first, because a strongly felt impulse is needlessly thwarted and second, because the infant, functioning at the early levels of thought, has no way of comprehending the reasons—such as they are—for these practices. From his sensorimotor and intuitive perspectives, these restrictive practices mean unpleasantness, rejection by caretakers, and anger; they imply that something is bad or wrong with his body and feelings. This sets the stage for the dissociation of pleasurable feelings for, insofar as they become categorized as bad or painful, the young child will tend to deal with them in the same way he deals with physical pain; he will try to dissociate them from himself. As in the case of Mrs. Flynn and Karen, we see how the conflicts and dissociation of one generation are passed on to the next.

Taboos on sexuality are not confined to the younger years. Our society makes stringent demands that children cover their bodies, not stimulate themselves openly, nor engage in too frank forms of mutually affectionate play. The taboos spread out into many related areas such as cleanliness and grooming. Our taboo on the natural odors of the human body supports thriving soap and deodorant industries. Other areas include "manners," speech (words or phrases referring to sexual acts and parts of the body are "dirty"), and other practices. The normal masturbation of later childhood and adolescence is still shrouded with guilt and not openly acknowledged by many. In sum, our society's attempt to suppress, deny, cover up, or distort the natural impulse toward sensual pleasure has caused generations of children to feel bad, anxious, and guilty about their bodies, their pleasurable feelings, and the acts related to these.

The power of these impulses is such that excessive repression inevitably leads to hypocrisy—prudish "upstanding" citizens carry out their sexual affairs in secrecy. The sexuality that the white middle class dissociates from itself is projected onto blacks or foreigners. The whole structure is, of necessity, shot through with hypocrisy and is therefore a breeding ground for dissociations in the next generation.

Now let me say a few words about the "new sexual morality" that some see on the increase among young people. It is seen in the relaxation and greater comfort with which young men and women relate to each other. College age couples enjoy sex together more openly and with less guilt than was true in earlier generations. The taboo on sex before marriage—making less sense than ever since the advent of effective means of birth control—is gradually lessening in strength. The stringent differentiation between the sexes, a central part of the old sexual morality, is giving way as boys and girls wear each other's costumes and hairdos. Related changes can be seen in a greater acceptance of infantile sensuality, the relaxation of standards applying to hygiene, neatness of dress, and conventional manners.

There is little doubt that a new morality based on acceptance of the pleasures obtainable through stimulation of the body will prove beneficial. The vicious cycle, in which conflicts and dissociations are passed from one generation to the next, can be broken and needless anxiety and guilt avoided. Already, some of the artificiality and phoniness of boy-girl relations is passing. Perhaps, in the future, sexuality and bodily pleasures will become a source of gratification less shrouded in frustration and conflict. The course will not be smooth, however. As is true of developmental change on the individual level, there is a tendency to overassimilate when a new social or value level is reached. This is especially true when a new set of values and practices arises in opposition to an overly restrictive or suppressive set of older views. We see this in the zeal and excess of many political revolutions in their early stages. Overassimilation in the area of sexual practice can be seen now in various experiments at "sexual revolution"—from the total nudity of plays and films, to experiments at group sex and orgiastic practices, to attempts to completely abandon marriage and family. Recognition of the tyranny of the old morality does not automatically lead to a new set of beliefs and practices that can be integrated into a harmonious social structure, including provision for the care of children, and meaningful adult identities. From the extremes of sexual repression and free sexual experimentation will eventually emerge, one hopes, a more balanced sexual morality.

Anger and Violence

Somehow, over the course of our history, Americans have acquired the belief that we are a peaceful, innocent people who fight only when provoked or attacked. Nothing could be further from the truth. We believe in our innocence in spite of the fact that we are among the most intensely competitive, driving, success-oriented people that ever lived; that we literally wiped out the native Indian population of this continent in the process of settling the country; that we have been almost continually involved in wars of one kind or another, from the Revolutionary War to Vietnam; that racism and the brutal treatment of various ethnic and racial groups, not to mention the poor, has been, and continues to be, a central part of the American way of life; that an incredibly large number of Americans presently own guns whose main purpose seems to be to shoot at their fellow citizens; that we drive around at high speeds in overpowered, oversized cars endangering our own lives and those of others; and so it goes. The instinctual system of aggression has boundaries which set upper and lower limits. Within these boundaries, social custom, value and reward determine the extent and form of expressed anger and fighting. An honest look at American history shows that, as a society, we have both stimulated and rewarded high levels of aggression while, at the same time, denying that this is so. It is no accident that the governmental agency involved in one of the most brutally destructive and least justified of wars—Vietnam— is called the "Department of *Defense.*"

When an area of life with a strong instinctual base is both encouraged and denied by society, we have a situation ripe for dissociation. The case of aggression is not quite the same as that of sexuality. Aggression has always been more open; Americans are encouraged to fight and kill, providing they justify and rationalize their acts. Indians were openly shot as late as 1900, Negroes openly lynched until the 1930s, and violence and brutality in films have never been subject to the taboos and censorship directed against nudity and sexual acts. Still, the rationalizations are indicative of conflict and dissociation. American violence has long been accompanied by a sense of guilt.

The problem for the young child is similar in the areas of sex and aggression. He has trouble comprehending hypocrisy and adjusting his own behavior and beliefs to it. The contrast is very clear in the public elementary schools, our major institution for the socialization of children from age five or six onward. The classroom situation makes great demands for the inhibition of aggression. Rambunctious boys must sit quietly, raise their hands to speak, and *never* yell, jump about, or fight! At the same time that their natural aggressiveness or, if you prefer, their natural excitement and creative energy, is being overly inhibited, they are expected to become competitive in those ways that can lead to later success. Surely a better way to do this would be to openly recognize the child's aggression and energy and to channel it, from the beginning, into socially productive, nonviolent avenues.

Aggression, unlike sexuality, is a potentially destructive instinctual system that will always require a great deal of control and redirection. The distinction I am urging is between control that openly recognizes human aggressiveness and anger and that which attempts inhibition by denial, projection, and other forms of dissociative distortion. The first can lead to a more balanced solution while the second perpetuates guilt and the kinds of excess characteristic of American history.

As is true with the new sexual morality, there has been a new awareness of the problem of aggression in this country. Young people are less willing to accept the old rationalization for war or the treatment of blacks, other minorities, and the poor. This change in perception and values is only just getting underway and, as of this writing, has had only minimal impact on society at large. Some of the same overassimilative tendencies that occur in the breakdown of sexual repression have appeared here in the form of excessive passivity—for example, the attempt to "love" everyone while abolishing all aggressiveness from oneself. Dealing with the problem of aggression in this fashion leads to its own form of dissociation since, like the rationalizations of the dominant society, it rests on a denial of powerful human emotions.

Aging, Death, and Deviations from "Normality"

If an anthropologist from another planet came to this country and sampled our prevalent myths and images as they are displayed in films, popular novels and on television, he might get the impression that Americans never grow old, and that they do not die except under exciting or romantic circumstances. The violence of our myths frequently leads to death, but it is an unrealistic form of dying. Being gunned down in a shoot-out at the O.K. Corral is not the same as growing old, losing one's strength and abilities, one's position and friends, and dying of some debilitating disease. The first is glorious and thrilling, the second all too painfully drab and realistic. The reality of aging and death is kept from our awareness.

Our emphasis on growth, and the concomitant disparagement of middle and old age, is seen in a number of ways. Standards of feminine beauty are tied to youth—as women grow older they fight their wrinkles, dye their hair so the gray doesn't show, and even undergo surgery with the aim of restoring a youthful appearance. The really old are an uncomfortable reminder of what we all will become and our society tends to isolate them, to put them off someplace where they won't be seen.

A similar segregation takes place with those individuals who deviate from a rather narrowly defined image of normality. Those of lesser intelligence are kept in institutions for the retarded, those who express bizarre ideas are incarcerated in mental hospitals. We are so used to this sort of segregation that we never think it could be otherwise. Yet it was not always so. Mental hospitals and institutions for the retarded are relatively recent social inventions. In earlier periods, death was more visible and old people more an integral part of society. The paintings of Breughel give an impression of life in the late Middle Ages in which the young and old, the crippled and deformed, all mingle together.

What, you might ask at this point, is wrong with the segregation of the old, the dying, the feebleminded, the insane, the crippled, and deformed from us "normals"? Aren't they better off in their own places? Why should we have to look at them? The answers are not simple, but in general, one can say that such persons are not well treated in their special institutions, and that the rest of the society is not necessarily better off with them hidden. Segregation of the deviant is a way of dissociating ourselves from a portion of human reality. The reality doesn't go away; we just pretend that it does. Everyone of us has parents who will grow old and die, just as we will ourselves. To pretend that most people can be beautiful and young, that retardation or the many forms of psychological disturbance only happens to others, is to make up a world that never was and never will be.

From the child's point of view, the effect of segregation of deviants is to make him feel that something is unexplainably wrong when he discovers any of these qualities in himself or his family. It is as if everyone has a crazy old grandmother whom they hide in the attic, pretending to others that their family is "normal," yet feeling secretly guilty because they are taken in by everyone else's pretense while knowing that they themselves are not what they pretend to be. The child with a retarded sibling, a dying parent, a crazy aunt, or more to the point, with surges of violence, lust, and occasional craziness, feelings of stupidity, or ugliness within himself, comes to recognize that he must hide all these and dissociate them from his public image.

The general pattern is the same for sexuality, violence, aging, death, and deviations. All are recurring aspects of human life that cannot be escaped. All provoke anxiety and become caught up in conflict. In American society, a good deal of hypocrisy surrounds these areas. We deal with them by suppression, rationalizations, pretense, and segregation. This prevents a balanced integration of these areas into our ongoing lives. When an American's life does become caught up in one of these areas, he is likely to experience his involvement as due to alien forces. He feels victimized, smitten with the "cruel hand of fate," or "struck down by mental illness." Aging and death, the range of intellect or attractiveness, and the inevitable crises and emotional stresses of life are experienced as if they were symptoms of illness or neurosis, foreign intruders which arouse shame and guilt and must be hidden or disguised. Again, we see how the dissociations of society become the dissociations of the individual.

CONCLUSION: HUMAN DUALITY

Dissociation and integration, the two ways in which persons deal with the stress and anxiety engendered by development, suggests the wider theme of human duality. The central dimensions of human life—what I have earlier called the core conflicts—are bipolar. Individuals, families and whole societies tend to emphasize one pole and deemphasize the other. To be independent one must give up the gratifications of dependence; to satisfy curiosity and the need for excitement, one sacrifices security. People desire love and admiration, yet their very ambition, sensual longings and aggressiveness bring about disapproval and the loss of love.

As we have traced the core conflicts through several developmental periods, it has been apparent that vacillation between the poles of the major dimensions represents healthy experimentation. The overassimilative characteristic of a new stage, on the social as well as individual level, allows a testing of the new by exploring its most extreme possibilities. Play, fantasy, dreaming, social interchange: experimentation can and should take place in all these forms. Moratoria—the putting aside of gratifications and opportunities—submerge one pole of a conflict dimension. The lack of outward heterosexual interest so common in American children, especially boys, through middle childhood, is an example of a temporary dissociation, a moratorium. Like other forms of dissociation, this involves an exaggeration of one pole and a concomitant submersion of the other. In this case heterosexual interest is submerged and an exaggerated version of male or female identity emphasized. Similar dissociative trends operate in other areas. The child who wishes to be "big" must severely limit his dependent desires. Societies which demand excessively masculine behavior from their men encourage these same men to hide their "feminine," tender, or sensitive qualities. Excessive protestations of innocence mask underlying guilt, bravado, secret fears. All development involves such swings from one extreme to another, the extent and form being determined by individual talent and social pressure. Moratoria are normal at particular stages of development as are hyperaggressiveness, or an overreliance on fantasy, hyperindependence, or excessive conformity. All represent the search of the developing person for an identity within which the different aspects of his nature can be integrated with social demands and values.

The fateful question for psychological health versus disturbance is, then, what determines the extremity and permanence of certain dissociations? Why are some individuals able to reopen moratoria when others remain stuck with the one-sided solutions adopted out of childhood fear and lack of knowledge? Our discussion has implicated certain parental and social actions which, in interaction with the characteristics of the individual child, arouse excessive anxiety, on the one hand, while failing to encourage active identification, on the other. When a child has grown up in this sort of interpersonal environment, dissociations become deeply ingrained and are rearroused on those future occasions which recreate the original emotional situations. For example, the child who has experienced repeated separations or abandonments will be anxious and untrusting in future relationships, expecting them to turn out the same way. The boy with a seductive-controlling mother will interact with women in the same manner as he developed in this earlier relationship. In short, the earlier interpersonal experiences become the plans for later relationships. Dissociation will be maintained when: (1) it has become well established by repeated experiences in childhood, and (2) when the painful emotions—anxiety and its derivatives—are so intense that the working through of new modes cannot be tolerated. This second point means that reality-testing, developing new skills through active interchange, will be less likely when previous experiences have led to the connection of strong and painful feelings with certain classes of experience. These painful emotions—anxiety, guilt, threats to self-esteem—can become so imperative as motives that their arousal causes an immediate flight to the quick "solution" provided by established dissociation.

In contrast to these dissociative solutions are those interpersonal experiences during childhood that have supported active engagement. The central factor is a parental or social response that facilitates a direct as opposed to highly ambivalent identification. Clearly, an adult must be available, which he is not in cases of extreme separation or loss. In addition, there must be sufficient positive components to the relationship—love, treatment that makes the child feel valued as a person, a lack of features that cause intense anxiety—so that he is drawn toward the parent and perceives value in becoming like him. When conditions of this kind exist, conflict may be dealt with by active engagement leading to progressive integration and transformation of self. This class of actions, in contrast to dissociation, is experienced as actively initiated, as willed or owned, in short, as part of oneself.

Both dissociation and integration have their internal versions; which is to say that both produce changes in the self. But the qualities of these internalized versions are quite different. Parent-child interactions that arouse anxiety, that create a sense of vulnerable passivity, of the futility of action, or of victimization, all lead to dissociation. The person then feels helpless and victimized by the internalized version of these relationships. This may be experienced as being propelled by internal emotions or forces which one does not understand, or being coerced by "symptoms," or feeling the victim of uncontrollable actions, thoughts, compulsions, or fears. Repeatedly attempting to dissociate these, the individual is left with a feeling of fragmentation, meaninglessness, or uncontrollability.

Integrative social exchange produces active identifications. The child internalizes the parents' love and respect, their consistent control and limits—in short, their honesty and lack of ambivalence. Having done so, he can then love and respect himself. He can control his impulses in a more consistent fashion, accept his sexual role—he has less need to hide, to split himself into inconsistent roles, or to pretend to be other than he feels.

It is fitting that the discussion should come around again to identification, to the process whereby the self develops through internalizing relationships. For this topic is central to the broader question of how the child acquires the standards and values of his society and it is to this topic that we turn in the next chapter.

chapter eight

Conscience
and
Moral
Development

The Widow Douglas she took me for her son, and
allowed she would sivilize me; but it was rough living
in the house all the time, considering how dismal regular
and decent the widow was in all her ways; and so when
I couldn't stand it no longer I lit out. — Huckleberry Finn

Adults are always trying to "sivilize" children and a boy of Huck's spirit can hardly put up with it. He flees from the constraints of foolish rules and manners, seeking a life where he can be *free,* where no meddling Widow Douglas can tell him what to do. In *Huckleberry Finn,* Mark Twain captures a dominant theme of childhood—the resistance to authority and the related fantasy of freedom from all control and supervision. To Huck Finn, and the many children he represents, rules and control are "out there"; they are burdensome things that one submits to, puts up with, or rebels against. By running away, Huck expects to escape rules and authority, but as his journey progresses he finds that even he has some restraints "inside." It is not long before the Widow Douglases, Aunt Pollys, and Judge Thatchers are replaced by an internal voice—his own conscience.

Huck's companion on the flight to freedom is Jim, a runaway slave, whose basic decency and love set him apart from the other adults in the novel who are either suffocatingly "moral" and proper like the Widow; venal and cruel like Huck's drunken "Pap"; or self-serving crooks like "the King" and "the Duke" (confidence men with whom Huck and Jim share their raft for a time). With the eyes of childish innocence, Huck can see Jim's basic virtue, yet he takes for granted the prejudices of his time and place: Jim is pretty good "for a nigger-slave." Huck unthinkingly accepts the laws of slavery and feels guilty for helping Jim escape. At one point, the Duke and King are ready to turn Jim over to the authorities in order to collect reward money, placing Huck in a crisis of conscience. Should he act to save Jim—who is clearly the better person and who he knows loves him and would never do such a thing to him—or should he go along with the Duke and King, those symbols of bogus authority who he knows would turn on him in a moment if they saw a profit in it? Should he act out of love and respect for a fellow human being or obey the law? There is no widow or judge around to tell him what is right and Huck finds himself torn in two directions. "Conscience," he moans, "just won't let a person be."

Many of the themes and issues I wish to take up in this chapter can be found in Mark Twain's masterful novel: the passage from childhood innocence to the world of adult corruption; the conflict of individual freedom with social restraint; the internalization of rules "out there" (embodied in authority figures or laws) into rules inside (within oneself in the form of conscience). The issues are alive today; the earlier scheme of American life—of rapid change represented by the expanding frontier and the contradictions between democracy and slavery—exists in new forms. Young men who see the contradiction between democratic values, or the simple moral belief that it is wrong to murder those who give you no cause, on the one hand, and laws which force them to fight in unjust wars, on the other, face a dilemma similar to Huck's. The legacy of slavery exists in our mistreatment of minorities. America is once more, or still, in the midst of a moral crisis.

We are all familiar with conscience; with nagging feelings of guilt when we don't meet some standard, and with the inner source of control that causes us to act morally even when there is no possibility that our misdeeds will lead to punishment. Powerful feelings may be caught up in the struggles of conscience; men have gone to jail or sacrificed their lives for their moral beliefs, while in others, a "righteous morality" serves as justification for brutality and violence. In both cases intense emotions—love, anxiety, rage—can give conscience and moral belief a special force. How is it that feelings of guilt, in extreme instances, can cause individuals to engage in masochistic or self-destructive behavior or, in a more general sense, why is conscience such a special burden to civilized man? To answer these questions I will return to the ideas of Freud and later psychoanalytic thinkers. The motives of conscience and morality will be traced to the process of identification—a topic touched on briefly in the account of childhood (chapter 5) and which will be elaborated here.

The child does not begin life with a readiness to obey, or even understand, social rules and laws. He must be socialized—"sivilized"—a complex affair that we will examine in a later section, following the discussion of the motivation of conscience. The infant begins life with a completely egocentric view of the world. One result of this view is a sort of naive selfishness. Moral development involves a decentering—an overcoming of self-centeredness—and an increasing appreciation of the views and rights of others. To comprehend this process we will trace the development of morality though the major stages and crises of childhood. The earlier account of intellectual development has sensitized us to the fact that the child thinks and perceives differently at successive stages. Because of this, his understanding of social rules and customs will be different at each stage. The ideas of Piaget will prove useful in comprehending the role of intellectual stage in relation to moral development. More recent work by Lawrence Kohlberg, a contemporary psychologist who has extended Piaget's earlier speculations on moral development, and the work of Jane Loevinger on ego development, will lead us to an expanded outline of the major stages of moral reasoning.

MOTIVES FOR CONSCIENCE

Let us approach this topic by looking at the motives underlying social regulation in our monkey and ape relatives. As we saw in chapter 2, all primates are highly social; their group life is extensively regulated. This regulation is achieved by bonds of love and affection, on the one hand, and patterns of dominance-submission, on the other. The social bonds and patterns rest on the powerful emotions of love, interest, anxiety, anger, and fear. These emotions are constantly being communicated between group members via facial expression, physical contact, and related means. Consider an example: a group of monkeys arrive at a watering hole. The more dominant males assert their right to drink first by a few ritualized gestures —bared teeth, brief assumption of a fighting posture, and so on—which are responded to with corresponding gestures of submission by the less dominant animals. These gestures are then passed down the line, organizing the group's drinking behavior. Such interchanges are repeated many times everyday of a monkey's life around a host of situations. Consider another example: a young monkey is separated from his mother. He makes the characteristic screams and facial expressions of separation anxiety which bring forth maternal responses from his own mother and other group members. Related forms of maternal holding and caretaking are also seen in the ritualized grooming behavior which keeps so many monkeys in contact with other monkey bodies for hours each day. These examples illustrate the central role of emotions and direct physical action in the maintenance of social order. Loss of contact with or ostracism from the group is a powerful, emotional sanction among all monkeys and apes.

When we turn to humans we observe crucial similarities and equally crucial differences. Among infants and very young children, social bonding and control is accomplished by emotional expression and physical action. The infant needs the physical presence of his mother to feel secure; when a two-year-old is told to "Stop that!" it is as much the tone of voice (one can almost see the bared teeth and fighting posture) as the meaning of the words which arouses his fear of the more dominant adult. Social control in the early years of life is based on direct emotional expression and the physical presence of the controlling agent. Children learn to inhibit those actions which are deemed undesirable in their culture because adults stop them, speak to them in disapproving tones, withdraw affection, or punish them. Again, this is similar to the way social control is maintained among monkeys and apes.

Although apes never progress beyond this level of "morality," we humans do; or at least some of us hope to. As early as the time he starts school, the child is expected to control himself, which means he must inhibit socially undesirable actions in the absence of constant external threat and reward. By the time one is an adult, social control is largely internalized. The big difference between the morality of young children and that of adults is that adults can understand and obey rules and laws in the absence of direct threats, loss of affection, or the physical presence of authorities. Indeed, some too civilized persons are so scrupulous that they demand more of themselves than any reasonable external agent might. Unlike our ape brethren, adult humans do not need threats, signs, and constant reminders to support and maintain their social behavior; the whole process becomes *internalized*.

Internalization is made possible by the intellectual and linguistic skills of humans, skills which apes do not have. Yet social order—both positive bonding and the control and inhibition of aggressive and other disruptive actions—is as crucial to the survival of the human group as it is for other primates. As we have seen, social patterns which are important for species survival typically have emotions connected to them. Thus, although we progress beyond the stage in which social bonds and control are maintained by constant emotional expression and physical presence, our more complex forms of morality must still be maintained with the strength and imperativeness of those earlier forms seen in apes and young children. *Internalized standards must have the same emotional force as the primate emotional patterns which bind and control group life.*

One of Freud's great insights illuminates this problem for us. In his account of *identification* he shows how the child develops by internalizing the emotionally-charged relationships in his life. As this progresses, the feelings of love, respect, anxiety, fear, and anger—characteristic of relations between child and adult—become internalized and give emotional force to inner social regulation. Conscience and morality derive their motivational power from the emotions originally a part of external relationships.

Identification and the Growth of Conscience

Identification, as we have seen in chapter 5, is motivated by all the emotions characteristic of human social life. A person may attempt to make himself over in the image of another who he likes or admires, or who appears more skilled, or who possesses desirable qualities. Young boys copying the gestures of athlete heroes, children wearing the clothes of their older siblings, young women affecting the latest fashions of desirable or glamourous models, or the mutual identifications of the adolescent peer group, all exemplify a straightforward identification motivated by love, a need for group belonging, or the striving for competence. Kohlberg (1969), in his account of the motivation for morality, stresses these factors, almost to the exclusion of other motives.

Competence and admiration are very important motives and they play their role in the growth of conscience and morality. Young children obey rules and eventually internalize such obedience out of love and respect for their parents or because it makes them feel good to act like those bigger individuals who possess desirable qualities.[1] If this were the whole story, life would be simple and pleasant indeed. But, just as social life is characterized by conflict, anxiety, aggression, and anger, so do these human acts and emotions play their part in the identification process. Although development is motivated by love and competence, it also arouses anxiety and threats to security. Conflicts between dependence-independence, aggression and its control, and sensuality and renunciation are an integral part of human social growth. Each of these conflict areas arouses ambivalent emotions and, when identification is involved in the resolution of these conflicts, the ambivalence becomes incorporated into the structure of self. Let us look at each conflict area, in turn, taking its first appearance in the

---

[1] Indeed, a whole school of psychology, the behaviorist or S-R (stimulus-response) group which explains all this in terms of rewards and punishments or "reinforcements," limits its conception of conscience and moral development to such external factors.

life-cycle as a prototype, and examine how the process of identification operates.

Dependence-Independence. As we have seen in earlier chapters, the infant begins life in a state of symbiotic dependence. During his first six months he cannot differentiate his own sensations and actions from the external world. During the first year, symbiosis becomes a more differentiated attachment to the mother figure, characterized by sensual enjoyment, pleasurable contact, and anxiety upon separation. As the infant acquires more skill and security he increasingly seeks to expand his competence and to express his independence. During the years from one to three a crisis develops between the earlier symbiotic-dependent organization of self and the new push toward individuality, a push augmented by parental encouragement of new independence and the concomitant withdrawal of some of the immediate gratifications of baby needs. As the crisis takes shape, the young child attempts first to obtain the best of both worlds; initially he tries to get what he wants without changing himself. If it were possible he would retain the satisfactions of infancy along with the prerogatives of emerging independence. Separation anxiety also operates as a powerful motive pulling him back toward the earlier, dependent state. New skills, competence, the desire to master, and the pleasures of new accomplishments all combine with social rewards for independence (walking, talking, etc.) and withdrawal of nurturance, urging a new independence. Opposed to these is the wish to retain the pleasures of infancy; the tendency for self, once structured, to maintain itself and the anxiety that is aroused by moving away from the security of the mother-infant bond.

How may this crisis be resolved? Obviously, the most desirable solution will be one that gives some satisfaction to the several conflicting elements. Identification with the caretaking aspect of the mother figure is such a solution. When the child has reached a level of cognitive and fantasy development that permits—that is, when he is in the preoperational or intuitive stage—he can deal with the crisis by pretending to mother himself. He plays a game, imitates maternal gestures, and acts as if he is his mother taking care of himself. In order to perpetuate love and reduce anxiety, the child makes a part of himself like the mother: he identifies with her by incorporating a part of her caretaker role into his own behavior. When he does this repeatedly, the role that the child plays becomes a permanent part of himself. This is an early instance of how self or ego develops by adding roles; it reveals identification as a process in which an emotional relationship between the child and mother becomes an internal relationship in which the child experiences those same emotions toward parts of himself.

Two important emotions provide the motivational power for identification during this period—love and anxiety. The mother's love for her child becomes internalized as his love—what Erikson terms "basic trust"—for himself. Loss of this love arouses anxiety and this component of the external relationship also becomes internalized through identification. What begins as the child's anxiety over separation from his mother becomes a fear of disapproval aroused by those events which symbolize loss of love. This is an early form of social anxiety. As development progresses, social anxiety extends in two directions: outward to the larger group, and inward to a more firmly established conscience. Anxiety over parental disapproval extends to teachers, the peer group, and, eventually in adolescence and adulthood, to those larger social groupings—community, nation, church, ideology—with which adults identify. Inwardly, social anxiety becomes attached to those symbols—the child's own thoughts, acts, and feelings—which signal loss of love. Inner anxiety also undergoes a developmental progression and it is only when higher levels of symbolic thought are reached that this aspect of conscience acquires its full power.

Several points should be noted in summarizing the consideration of identification up to this point. First, we are talking about an ongoing process not a single event. Growth of the self by imitation and modeling, motivated by competence and admiration, occurs more or less continually throughout childhood and later life as well. Although such conflict-free growth is more or less continuous, major restructurings of self are likely to be resisted and will come about only when a crisis forces change. Such crises are more in the nature of "events," but in reality, they too are processes. A crisis builds up, reaches a peak, and then fades into resolution as the child transforms himself by adding a new role. Such resolutions are part of the larger developmental process, and conflicts, such as dependence-independence, will be rearoused and worked through at later stages.

Finally, it is important to note that much of identification is unconscious. The young child does not deliberately set out to make himself like mommy or daddy by imitating their gestures. Imitation, as Piaget has shown so clearly, is one of the earliest modes of intelligent adaption. It appears very early in life and is almost automatic or reflexive. Imitation and early identification precede what we adults are familiar with as consciousness of self (which, in one sense, only becomes established after adolescence). This is one way in which identification lies outside of consciousness. In addition, much of identification is accomplished via play, fantasy, and dreaming and, as we have seen in chapter 6, these modes are "unconscious" in a somewhat different sense. They are experienced as just happening to the person. Finally, those identifications which have their origin in anxiety-arousing conflict situations will become dissociated in the sense described in chapter 7. For all these reasons, then, identification and the resulting internal structures of self are likely to lie outside of consciousness.

Earlier, I described the way the first crisis of dependency leads to the internalization of both a maternal or caring attitude toward oneself and the connection of anxiety with acts and thoughts which signal a loss of love. This is the first occurrence of this major life conflict and the quality of identification is affected by the dominant preoperational or intuitive thought of the period. When the child moves more clearly into the world of school and peers during middle childhood, he must again give up some of the prerogatives of his special place in the family. He becomes one of many children in a larger group. The conflict over dependence-independence is rearoused. Identifications with the group and with other, particularly older, children ease this transition. The identification of this period partakes of the qualities of concrete operational thought. It is more clearly symbolic and, correspondingly, farther removed from the action-dominated and less flexible earlier mode of thought. A later version of the dependence-independence conflict is encountered in adolescence and young adulthood as childhood finally passes and the individual is faced with shaping a life on his own. Identifications with the adolescent peer group and with symbolic figures—heroes and heroines from novels, films, or other sources—point to the wider symbolic sweep of the formal operational thought of this period.

In summary, we see how the stage of thought at each successive encounter with a core conflict influences the form of identification used to resolve the conflict. Without negating the importance of later development, it is probably worth emphasizing the greater importance of identifications from the early years. Certain basic directions of personality development— basic security, sex-role, and the underlying structure of conscience—are heavily influenced by these early identifications. Subsequent events can influence the course of these developments, but what happens later always rests on the foundation laid down earlier.

Aggression, Autonomy, and Control.   Much of what goes on in this area overlaps with what I have just discussed in the preceding section. Autonomy and aggression are similar to independence; both involve an assertion of self that brings the child into conflict with his parents, siblings, and others. It is worth focusing here on the role of anger in interpersonal conflicts and in subsequent internal regulation.

The aggression and anger characteristic of our species is apparent in infancy as the baby reacts to frustrations with screams of rage and diffuse physical activity. Separations arouse anger as well as anxiety. Even in the very early years, wide differences exist among infants in their degree of general activity, aggressiveness, and tolerance to frustrations.

Aggression and anger take a more specific form from about age two onward, leading to the conflicts described in chapter 5. To briefly summarize that period, we saw how the new skills and independence of the young

child led to an overassimilation or overextension of his aggression and
willfulness, causing increasing conflict with parents. This battle of wills,
often fought out around toilet and cleanliness training in our culture, though
certainly not limited to these spheres, is the first major crisis in which the
child's aggression is aroused and frustrated by the restraints imposed by
authority.

The child wishes to gratify his impulses and has an investment in
preserving his newly structured, independent sense of self. He wants what
he wants when he wants it and will lash out at those who anger or frustrate him. At the same time, and for all his exaggerated independence, he
needs the care of his parents and craves their love and approval. His
independence itself is an imitation of their desirable "big" characteristics.
Parental control of impulse is frustrating but also arouses anxiety which is
increasingly connected with the disapproved impulses themselves.

These are the dimensions of the crisis and, once again, identification
provides a solution that gives some satisfaction to the various competing
interests. The identification of this period has been described earlier (chapter 5) as "satellization." Unable to defeat the more competent parents and
unwilling to simply give in, the child does the next best thing: he makes
them and their power a part of himself.

Since he cannot control them, and they are controlling his aggressive
impulses, he can become like them and control the impulses himself. This
he does by incorporating their "impulse-controlling" role into himself as
he did earlier with the "caretaking" role. This can be seen in the young
child who tells himself, with his parents' words, "Don't hit baby sister,
hitting is bad, Mommy won't like you if you do." Key instances of the
incorporation of a parental attitude toward one's own aggression occur
during play. Here, the child can work on the problem by acting out both
sides of the conflict—being the bad child as well as the admonishing and
controlling parent. As he works through such a developmental conflict, the
parental role becomes increasingly ingrained until, eventually, it is an
internalized part of self.

Identification with parental control of aggression points up the role
of *anger* in the motivation of conscience. One of Freud's great insights
stems from his observation that adults with severe "superegos" (persons
who are very self-critical or intolerant of their own moral lapses) were
particularly aggressive and rebellious as children. He explains this with
the model of identification. That is, a particularly strong conflict between
child and parent will, when incorporated via identification, become a
particularly strong conflict between one part of the self and another. This
hypothesis is sometimes described in terms of the superego deriving its
power from anger directed inward. This is a hypothesis with broad implications, for example, in explaining depression, masochism, and self-puni-

tive guilt. It is a general attempt to account for why people are hard on themselves, and why they feel guilty even when outwardly successful.

Freud's notion that conscience derives its power from anger or aggression directed at one's own impulses is a special case of the general model of identification and internalization that we have been examining. As we have seen, the child resolves conflicts by making an external relationship into an internal one. The general model at this stage is: child anxious over parental disapproval of impulse ———→ identification and internalization of parental "impulse-control" role into self ———→ child anxious over own impulses ———→ child strives to control own impulses on the model of the parental control. The theory then applies specifically to anger. Where initially the child is angry at his parents for frustrating his wishes, his incorporation of their role into himself sets the stage for anger directed at a part of himself. Schematically we may say: child is angry at parental control of impulses ———→ parents control and show disapproval of anger ———→ child incorporates parental role into self (identification) ———→ one part of child (conscience) angry at another (anger and other disapproved impulses). Since the internal relation between conscience and impulse is modeled after the external relationship between child and authority, it follows that the specific features of the external relationship—the degree of the child's anger, the severity of parental control, the extent of ambivalence—will shape identification and conscience.

It should be noted that although this account draws on psychoanalytic theory, it differs from it in certain respects. The general model of identification is taken from Freud, as are some of the ideas concerning the early conflict between the child's aggression and parental control. However, in the typical psychoanalytic account the superego is not internalized until after the oedipal stage. This delays the major identification until later in childhood and also restricts its focus to the oedipal conflict which, although it has components of willfulness and anger, is primarily centered around the frustration of romantic longings and sensual pleasure. In its most extreme form, the orthodox psychoanalytic account presents identification as an event which resolves the Oedipal complex and structures conscience once and for all. This restricts the time and scope of moral development and also presents conscience or superego development as separate from the development of the self or ego.[2] Let me briefly sum up the ways in

---

[2] This is one way in which Freud's ideas have been taken, though not the only way, of course. More recent psychoanalytic theorists such as Loevinger (1970) and Klein (in press) interpret psychoanalytic theory in a manner consonant with that presented here.

which the present account differs from the orthodox psychoanalytic one.

First, conscience development is a part of the larger process of self-development. The superego is not a separate agency of the mind which exists alongside of the ego, though many children and some adults experience their moral urgings in this dissociated way. Morality is internalized by the same process of identification which characterizes all self-development. Second, all the major emotions—love, anxiety, anger—motivate identifications, as does the striving for competence and the general need to understand and restructure experience in more differentiated and complete systems. That is, both *emotions* (of the sort stressed by psychoanalysts) and *intellectual motives* (of the sort stressed by Piaget) play important roles in the development of self and morality. Third, the internalization of conscience does not occur at one specific time nor is it restricted to the feelings and conflicts of the oedipal crisis. Identification begins with the simplest imitations of the late sensorimotor and early preoperational periods. It occurs in middle childhood in concrete operational form and later in adolescence when formal operational thinking gives it greater symbolic scope. The core conflicts occur repeatedly throughout life and identification plays an important role in their resolution at successive stages. Indeed, their cyclic recurrence allows the person to transform himself and to rework the inner structuring of conscience at successively more complex levels.

In the examples discussed so far, identifications dominated by preoperational thinking have been explored. The child's early move to independence and his initial experience with control of his own anger and aggression lead to internal structures defined with action-symbols—mental structures not far removed from sensorimotor action. These structures are present-centered almost to the point of obliterating the past. What is more, the child only crudely distinguishes what is inside him (his own thoughts and motives) and what is outside (the thoughts and motives of others). Before the rise of concrete operational thought, morality remains largely a matter of obedience to authority. Even when the young child has internalized an impulse-controlling role he continues to *experience* authority as "out there." He treats his conscience as an alien part of himself. The lack of a clear differentiation between inner and outer, and the tendency to dissociate the painful or unpleasant from oneself, are important features of this preoperational or intuitive conscience. Young children feel pushed around by tyrannical authorities one minute, and the next minute are basking in praise for being "good." They dissociate themselves from responsibility for the former and take credit for the latter, without feeling hypocritical, thanks to the limitations of their intellectual level. Feeling guilty for one's past deeds is hardly possible in early childhood. Development in the following years brings new levels of thought as well as new conflicts between child and society. Particularly important are the conflicts stemming from the child's emerging sex role and the related control of sensual impulses. Let us turn to this issue now.

   The Oedipal Conflict and Renunciation of Desire. The resolutions and accomplishments of the early years lead to a sense of self characterized by greater independence and an internalized desire to be like, and liked by, the parents. The child's physical and cognitive maturation and his social accomplishments—especially the acquisition of sex-role appropriate skills —arouse his hopes and wishes for romantic success within the family. That is, what was earlier a simple desire for physical closeness and love with the parents, now acquires the appropriate male or female romantic direction. Young boys, just discovering the meaning of their maleness, are attracted to their mothers in a new way; the same occurs with young girls and their fathers. On their side, the parents are faced with rejecting, in part, the love that they once encouraged in their children. As agents of society they must transmit the taboo on incest. Some conflict is inevitable as parental rejection and loss of love arouses anxiety, and the frustration of strongly felt desire leads to anger. The intensity of the conflict is a function of the strength of the child's desires and anger and, more importantly, the parents own ambivalence. Serious Oedipal problems arise when seductive or lonely parents overstimulate the child's sensual desires or when a parent with a tenuous hold on his own impulses overcontrols the child in a punitive manner.

   Not all parent-child relations are dominated by intense conflict at this stage, but some ambivalence is the rule. The child cannot "win" in any real sense; his desires within the family always meet with some degree of frustration, leading to the arousal of anxiety and anger. His self-esteem is threatened by his romantic incompetence, his inability to do those mysterious and infinitely desirable things that he imagines happening behind bedroom doors.

   The Oedipal conflict and its resolution exist simultaneously on two levels: the outward level of competition, rivalry, and later compliance with authority, and the inward level in which these some relationships find more vivid expression in fantasy and dreams. The child's sensual desires are more or less directly expressed as sexual curiosity, and the return of baby habits, such as coming into the parents' bed at night. Competitiveness is seen as the child acts difficult or rebellious and, in a variety of ways, attempts to parade his or her newly understood male or femaleness. These outward expressions of desire, competitiveness and jealousy lead, in the later stages of the conflict, to outward compliance and renunciation. The child, when all goes well, solidifies his sex role identity by modeling himself after his rival. Although all this may be observed to some degree in the outward parent-child relations, it is in fantasy that the Oedipal conflict finds its most intense expression.

The more advanced intellectual abilities of the child at this age (approximately five to seven) allow him to construct games, dreams, and fantasies in which his desires, jealousies, and anxieties are experimentally taken to their extremes. The child's rivalrous anger can be symbolized by the murder or ousting of the same-sex parent. Such fantasies also portray the turning of this same anger against himself. Since he wishes and imagines such extreme violence on his rivals, it is only natural that his fantasies should picture the turning of such violence on himself. Fear of "monsters," "robbers," or the sorts of "castration anxiety" that Freud first noted, all are expressions of the typical anxieties of this period. These conflicts and emotions are well illustrated in that classical children's story *Jack and the Beanstalk*. By way of example let us examine this perennially interesting tale.

As you no doubt remember, Jack lives with his mother who lacks both husband and money. The father figure is, thus, already displaced; Jack has his mother to himself. Given a man's job to do—sell the family cow at market—Jack "foolishly" exchanges it for some magic beans. Symbolically, the cow, a source of milk, nurturance, and baby needs, is exchanged for a source of new power, the magic beans. The beans when planted grow into a huge beanstalk, symbolizing the new surge of competence and power felt by the child (and perhaps a boy's newly discovered erection as well). Jack climbs the stalk, encounters a menacing, if somewhat inept, giant at the top who, we may guess, represents father's power. Risking the giant's wrath, even tempting it, Jack steals his source of wealth —the goose that lays the golden egg. He and the giant then face each other in dangerous combat; the giant threatens to devour Jack and Jack eventually escapes, kills the giant by chopping down the beanstalk, and returns to mother, bringing her riches far greater than he could have gotten for the cow at market. Child triumphs over adult, fearful male power is confronted and overcome, the boy is both defiant and rebellious, but ultimately successful and loved by mother.

Schematically the tale represents the young boy's desire to replace his father; to give to his mother a better, "richer" form of love than she has. The presumptuousness of his ambitions and the danger of going too far are clearly portrayed. The rivalry with the father and the fear that his own aggression will be turned against him are symbolized in the figure of the menacing giant who must be killed before he destroys the child. Jack can accomplish all this, of course—he can win mother for himself and provide more for her than the gross, hairy old man—through "magic" as symbolized by the beans and the goose. Magic equals fantasy, that realm of experience in which children can accomplish all those feats that their size and skill prevent in reality.

The tale also clearly shows how the feelings of anger and anxiety find extreme expression in fantasy. Murdering one's father and being terrified that he will do the same or will castrate or eat one up are not necessarily the feelings and conscious preoccupations of the Oedipal-age boy. Many adults view Freud's observation of castration anxiety as a bit far-fetched. But fantasies of the *Jack and the Beanstalk* type are extremely common during this stage. Not many real fathers threaten to eat their sons or cut off their genitals, but many sons imagine doing these things and it is easy for their fantasies to be carried to extremes. Part of the fascination of *Jack and the Beanstalk* lies in the excitement of confronting and overcoming Oedipal anxiety.

As the child develops, the resolution of this conflict proceeds on both levels, fantasy and reality, with a number of important consequences. Identification with the parents plays the central role in the resolution of the Oedipal conflict. At the same time, the specific nature of the desires and conflicts of this period—the fact that the child's heterosexual wishes must be delayed for such a long time, and his ability to operate on two levels, fantasy and reality—all lead to the "repression" of the Oedipal complex. Let me attempt to clarify this idea.

The child wishes to retain the parents' love and respect and to do this he outwardly complies, giving up his competitive sexual ambitions, controlling his anger and jealousy. The model for this is the same as that of the earlier period. The child's anxiety over loss of love becomes attached to those internal symbols—his own feelings of sensual arousal, anger and jealousy—which are connected with parental disapproval. This anxiety, in combination with a wish to be like the loved parents, motivates identification with them. The specific form at this stage is the internalization of what we might call a "renunciation of desire" role. Where the internalization of an "impulse control" role at the preceding stage led to the connection of anxiety with willfulness and self-assertion, at the Oedipal stage, anxiety becomes connected with general sensual feelings, with related pleasures, and with the sexual areas of the body.

We see, at this stage, the origin of a morality of self-denial which finds its extreme expression in Puritanism. The incorporation of a renunciation of desire role, which begins during the oedipal period, finds subsequent support in those cultural institutions and practices which stress the value of hard work, the evils of pleasures too easily gained, codes of modesty, taboos on masturbation or physical affection too openly expressed, and a variety of other beliefs and values. All these teach and reinforce a general belief that virtue is equivalent with self-denial; a belief that makes sense insofar as self-denial is necessary to protect the rights of others but that leads to meaningless and unnecessary frustrations and a destructive "righteous morality" when carried to Puritan extremes. There is much more to morality than self-denial, but reaching a higher understanding requires a more advanced level of thought than that possessed by the Oedipal-age child. Although his thought at this period is much advanced over what it was earlier, transformations crucial to moral reasoning are yet to come.

The greater sophistication of the thought of the Oedipal-age child gives identification a wider scope at this time period. Where earlier, the preoperational child's identifications were closely tied to actions and feelings of the moment, the oedipal-age child, capable of concrete operational thought, applies his newly internalized controls in a more principled manner. The most important consequence of this is seen in the child's reactions to his own thoughts, impulses, and fantasies. The younger child learns to inhibit his anger at his mother, but feels little anxiety in killing the mommy doll in a game. There is an unself-conscious quality made possible by the limitations of his preoperational thinking. The concrete operational child has lost some of this "innocence." *Jack and the Beanstalk* doesn't deal with mommy and daddy; it depicts a boy, his mother, and a giant who lived long ago and far away and, besides, everyone knows that giants aren't real. All of which is to say that the older child has a need to disguise his fantasies or dissociate himself from their direct implications. This is one sense in which the resolution of the Oedipal complex involves repression. As we have seen in the preceding chapter, the dissociation of fantasy and reality, and the related disguise of fantasy itself, are principal ways in which anxiety-related experiences are "repressed"; separated from the conscious experience of self.

The identification and resulting internalizations of the oedipal period lead to a conscience that more closely approximates the conscience of adulthood. Again, this results from the greater breadth of the child's thought. Where earlier internalizations led to signal anxiety, the identifications of this period lead to feelings of *guilt*. The distinction between the earlier signal anxiety and this later guilt is one of degree. Both are unpleasant emotions aroused by those inner cues which signal potential loss of love. The cues for the earlier form of anxiety lie close to action. The very young child does not become anxious about his games and fantasies. The older child constructs wider principles. If it is dangerous to be angry at father then it is also dangerous to harbor direct fantasies of anger. When the child begins to feel anxious about his thoughts and fantasies we call this anxiety *guilt*. It represents a new level of internalization, of decentering from the world of immediate action.

The transition from a lower to a higher level of thought brings with it a transformation of earlier views of oneself and the world. Thus, as the child passes from preoperational to concrete operational thought he becomes increasingly decentered from action and increasingly able to differentiate his own feelings and perceptions from those of others. As we saw in chapter 5, the most important factor in this passage is social interaction in which the child's egocentrism is confronted with the views and wishes of others. The Oedipal complex is one important instance of social conflict, the outcome of which tempers egocentrism and promotes progress to a new level. At the beginning of the Oedipal period, the child still views the world preoperationally or, at most, from the earliest concrete operational perspective. As the Oedipal conflict is worked through and conscience and guilt become more firmly internalized, the child simultaneously moves to a higher level of thought. An important implication of this fact is that earlier conflicts—dependence-independence, aggression and control—and their resolutions are brought under the sweep of the new conscience. That is, as the identifications and internalizations of middle childhood become increasingly well established they encompass earlier moral issues. The new sense of guilt is not restricted to the oedipal issues of its origin; it extends broadly into other conflict and moral areas.

It is worth reiterating that identification is a process in which an outer relationship serves as a model for an inner relationship—a restructuring of self by the internalization of new roles. Freud describes conscience as a superego—an internal agency that stands "over" the ego and judges and admonishes it much as the parent did with the child. This captures the experiential aspect of an internalized parent role. Examples of this are familiar enough, as when we "struggle against" our conscience or are "afraid" of its reproaches or defiantly do something in spite of it. Internalization of the parent-child relationship has its positive side as when one is "pleased with oneself." All of these examples illustrate how the *conflicting, ambivalent relationships with the parents come to be experienced as an ambivalent treatment of one part of oneself by another.*

At first the child is anxious lest his parents see him engaged in wrongdoing. This then becomes "shame," a feeling of discomfort that he will more generally be seen or exposed. The transition from outer to inner control is a gradual one. "Don't look at me!" may mean don't watch me doing something wrong or don't notice my intentions or thoughts. The child's lack of clarity over what is inside and what is outside may lead him to think that his parents can magically divine what is going on in his mind (and, of course, the observant parent can usually make a good guess). *Portnoy's Complaint,* Philip Roth's novel about the tortuous course of guilt and Oedipal concerns, begins with the young boy's description of how he believed his mother magically changed into his teacher and back again each day, thus keeping him under constant surveillance.

Outer watching becomes inner "watching," self-observation, just as criticism by authorities becomes self-criticism. Conscience is frequently experienced as an "inner voice," the internalized version of the spoken commands and admonitions of the parents.

It is worth emphasizing, once again, the role played by ambivalence in the formation of conscience. The fact that the child, during this period, feels both love and hate, anxiety and anger, in his relations with authority, sets the stage for an ambivalent attitude toward his own sensual and aggressive impulses. As Erikson puts it:

> For here the child becomes forever divided in himself. The instinct fragments which before had enhanced the growth of his infantile body and mind now become divided into an infantile set which perpetuates the exuberance of growth potentials, and a parental set which supports and increases self-observation, self-guidance, and self-punishment. (1950, p. 256)

Guilt and inner ambivalence derive their force from the emotions of love, anger, and anxiety involved in the parent-child relations antecedent to identification. This model predicts, in a general way, the effects of early relationships on later conscience. For example, if there is little love and attachment to parents (for whatever reason), there should be little separation anxiety and, subsequently, little signal anxiety and guilt. If this is coupled with harsh, inconsistent, and punitive treatment, the child should grow into someone with a great deal of retributive anger and little guilt or conscience to control it. Studies of delinquent or hyperaggressive children (Redl and Wineman, 1957) and antisocial or psychopathic adults (Mc Cord and McCord, 1956) suggest that this is the case. In general, such individuals have their anger stimulated in a variety of ways, such as by abandonments, brutal or aggressive treatment, and other forms of frustration. Loevinger (1959), in a very insightful article, points out that such children do not develop internalized control of their own aggression because the parents do not control *their* own impulses in dealing with their children. That is, the parents exploit their children in the process of gratifying themselves; they love them when it is convenient to do so (but not when a new adult love becomes available), or vent their anger and frustrations as the mood moves them. The child is thus presented with an adult model who does not control his impulses for the good of others, specifically the child. Such parents act on impulse, not principle, and their children experience the painful results of these impulsive actions as they are alternately loved and abandoned. As the child identifies with such a parent—who is frequently the only model available—he is internalizing a model of impulse-expression rather than impulse-control. Such identification does not lead to any meaningful or stable self-control. The hyperaggressive children described by Redl and Wineman remain victimized by their own impulses just as they were earlier victimized by their parents' impulsive mistreatment.

At the other extreme, one finds persons who suffer from too much conscience or various forms of unresolved inner ambivalence. Excessive guilt and self-punitive fantasies and acts may all result from parent-child struggles characterized by intense anger coupled with a need for parental love and anxiety over its loss. The typical neurotic individual fits such a pattern. That is, an ambivalent—both angry and loving—parent-child interaction becomes internalized, producing an intense ambivalence about one's own impulses. To put this another way, the child comes to treat himself—to feel toward his own impulses and wishes—as the parents treated him. If they aroused intense anger in him, then this can become redirected toward those parts of himself that the parents seemed to disapprove of. His rage toward the parents becomes redirected toward internalized parental roles. A common feature of many neurotic individuals is that they both love and hate those parts of themselves that remind them of their mother or father.

Summary: The Motives for Conscience

In the preceding sections I save attempted to trace the growth of conscience and the transformation of those emotional relationships which give it force. Several points should be emphasized in conclusion.

Identification is central to the process of moral growth as, indeed, it is to the wider growth of self. Identification is frequently misconceived as a process in which the characteristics, standards, or values of the parents are impressed on the child in a direct way—that identification produces consciences which are xerox copies of the parents. Akin to this is the view that identification is an event, for example, something the child does to resolve the Oedipal conflict once and for all. These views are misleading. *Identification is a continuing, creative construction of the child.* From what he is—more or less angry,. demanding, aspiring, loving, anxious; from what the parents do—display certain principles in their own actions (or not), punish, espouse, love or reject; as seen through the framework of a given structure of self and a given intellectual stage; from all these, the child, over a period of years, transforms himself in new directions.

A second caution regards the special emphasis that psychoanalytic accounts give to the Oedipus complex. As should be clear by now, the general model of internalization via identification fits the Oedipal stage but need not be restricted to it. Identification and the internalization of standards occur at stages prior to the Oedipal stage and will continue to occur subsequently. The central theme of the Oedipal crisis is desire and its renunciation. The control of aggression and the move from dependence to independence central to the preceding stages are also worked through again at a level commensurate with the child's more advanced intellectual stage.

Each reworking of these major life conflicts at a particular stage leads to a new transformation of self which, in its turn, leads to new versions of the basic human themes. The passing of the intensity of the Oedipal crisis coincides with the child's entry into the world of peers. In our culture, schooling begins and, over the years to come, more and more of the child's life becomes centered away from home and parents. The peer culture itself becomes a source of new standards and rules for the child to grapple with; to eventually make his own.

Finally, I should add a note concerning the two types of motivation for conscience, that which grows from conflict and that which is relatively conflict-free. Imitation of desirable models, identification based on love, or a desire to please or acquire the status of an admired figure are important sources of motivation in the establishment of conscience. Since these motives are relatively free from conflict and ambivalence on the external level, they lead to relatively unambivalent inner structures—to clear inner ideals and a "loving conscience." Such conflict-free development typically occurs *within* stages of self-development.

Internalization of conflictual relationships more frequently occurs when the person moves from one stage to another. Changing stages is itself an anxiety producing affair because it threatens the security of an established way of being, of a known identity. Such changes are resisted; the child tries to retain the security of the past until he is forced by a crisis to give it up. We have examined these crises and seen that each presents conflicts which the child cannot resolve within the existing structure of self. He must either live with anxiety and impotent rage, suffer a loss of self-esteem, or change himself and advance to a new level. Since changing oneself threatens security, the initial response to conflict is usually an attempt to assimilate it to the existing self and it is only from the failure of assimilation and the continued intensity of threat that accommodation occurs.

The acquisition of conscience and moral standards is, thus, a part of the more general process of self or ego development; a process characterized by the creative, stage-wise, transformation of self through the internalization of new roles. As these roles become a part of the person, the emotions that characterized the original relationships give meaning and feeling to the inner world of dream and fantasy, interpersonal schemas and conscience. A more detailed treatment of stages is found in the work of those authors who focus on the intellectual issues—on moral understanding or the development of moral reasoning. Having completed the review of the motives for conscience, we may now turn our attention in this direction.

MORAL REASONING

The individual's understanding of moral issues undergoes a lengthy development which parallels (or is based on) the more general development of thought. In the realm of intellect, the person progresses from the undifferentiated sensorimotor stage of infancy, to the personalized symbols of the preoperational stage, to the concrete operations of middle childhood, to the attainment of formal operations (the ability to think abstractly) in adolescence and early adulthood. These changes in thought and perception color all of psychological life including the emotional, the interpersonal, and the moral.

The central task in the area of moral reasoning is to explain how the child progresses from a state of pure selfishness to a state in which his actions can be guided by concern for the feelings and rights of others. A parallel with general intellectual development immediately suggests itself, for is not the sensorimotor infant "selfish" or "self-centered"? And, is not concern for others a more abstract, differentiated perspective of the sort made possible by formal operations? That is to say, general intellectual development progresses from the egocentrism of infancy to the attainment of abstract thought which allows one to view the world from more than one perspective. Each stage of intellectual development begins with its own form of egocentrism, defined, in general, as a lack of differentiation between subject and object. Each stage involves a process of *decentering,* of progressing beyond egocentrism to a more differentiated view of oneself and the world.

Egocentrism and decentering are the concepts that form a bridge between the development of moral reasoning and the more general development of intelligence. In this respect, decentering plays an analogous role in the area of moral reasoning to that played by identification in the area of moral motivation. The concepts are, in fact, related. Identification explains how the selfish or asocial infant becomes social; how crucial others are incorporated into the structure of self. Central to this process are conflicts with other selves which lead to crises that motivate identification. Decentering refers to the way in which one's egocentric perspective is forced to change and become more differentiated. Such differentiation takes place on many levels, and, at the level of morality and interpersonal relations, it is conflicts with others that force the child to new levels, illustrating the similarity to identification.

Freud and later psychoanalysts focus on conflicts within the family, primarily between the child and his parents. Piaget lays greater stress on the conflicts among peers that occur in later childhood. We need not adopt either view to the exclusion of the other. In fact, each complements the other, calling our attention to separate, though related, sources of growth-enhancing conflict.

While decentering in the purely physical and intellectual spheres and in the area of morality and human relationships are the same in general form, one would expect the former to take place sooner than the latter.

In other words, the child comes to a differentiated understanding of space, time, causality, and the effects of his actions on the physical world before he has a differentiated view of wishes, feelings, and the interplay of selves. The reason for this is that this latter sphere is less tangible, less tied to the world of action and present-centered experience. As we will see shortly, a truly differentiated moral view is not possible until the attainment of formal operational thinking.

Stages and Decentering

In this section I will trace egocentrism and its vicissitudes (to borrow one of Freud's favorite terms—authors engage in identification also) through the major stages of intellectual growth. This will prepare the way for a more specific review of Piaget's early work on morality and the more recent work of Kohlberg and Loevinger.

Sensorimotor Egocentrism. "I think, therefore I am" said Descartes, stating a view that seems intuitively obvious to adults. Piaget's work on the sensorimotor origin of intelligence shows this belief to be incorrect on two accounts. First, before I can "think," I "act"—sensorimotor action is the necessary precursor to what we are introspectively familiar with as thought. Second, at the beginning of infancy, there is no "I"; a feeling of self must also develop out of action.

At the beginning, all that exists for the infant are shifting, unrelated actions and sensations. He has no sense of himself nor of a world that exists apart from his action on it. Through repeated experience with objects in different modalities (vision, touch, taste, etc.) over the first six months, the infant develops a sensorimotor concept of permanent objects. For example, from experience with a toy rattle as something to see, to touch, and to mouth, all at different times and in slightly different contexts, there develops a motor conception of "toy rattle" as a permanent object apart from the infant's immediate experience with it. A similar development takes place with his own body—the locus of all action. From an initial state in which there is no differentiation between actions and objects acted upon or between body and non-body, the infant comes to distinguish his body as a permanent and distinct object in a world of objects.

This process develops over the first eighteen months of life and involves a gradual decentering, that is, a progression from an undifferentiated (no distinction between self and world or between action and objects) "centered" mode of being to a less egocentric position with an appreciation of rudimentary physical causality, and a sensorimotor conception of space and time. As Piaget puts it:

...The child's initial universe is entirely centered on his own body and action in an ego centrism as total as it is unconscious (for lack of consciousness of self). In the course of the first eighteen months, however, there occurs a kind of Copernican revolution, or, more simply, a kind of general decentering process whereby the child eventually comes to regard himself as an object among others in a universe that is made up of permanent objects (that is, structured in a spatio-temporal manner) and in which there is at work a causality that is both localized in space and objectified in things. (Piaget and Inhelder, 1969, p. 13)

In the social sphere, sensorimotor egocentrism is the infant's symbiotic relation with his mother. Being unable to differentiate between himself as an object and the other objects in the world, including mother, the infant experiences himself and his mother as "one." The sense of himself as a separate entity comes about with the general growth of intelligence and the specific skill of conservation of permanent objects. This process of differentiation is enhanced by those experiences of frustration and separation anxiety which confront the symbiotic oneness of early egocentrism. To put this another way, the infant initially tries to assimilate the world and the failure of the world to cooperate stimulates the accommodation of new schemas. This is true in both the physical and interpersonal areas.

"Physical egocentrism" assumes that "the world is me and I am the world"; social egocentrism assumes that "others exist to satisfy my needs." In both cases it is the confrontation of egocentrism with a reality that does not so readily assimilate, that forces accommodation.

All of this takes place on the level of action and sensation, of course; the infant does not have words or ideas to represent "me" or "mother" or "world." Such mental representations or symbols make their appearance at the next stage.

Preoperational Intelligence: An Egocentrism of Symbols. Action symbols appear toward the end of the sensorimotor stage. For example, in solving a problem which requires the opening of a box, the infant can be observed opening and closing his hand or his mouth as a prelude to the solution. *Imitative gestures,* such as these motor symbols for the concept "open," are the precursors of the internalized symbols that come into wide use in the preoperational stage. Earlier, the infant was confined to actions and crude "action symbols"; the young child now begins to use words, fantasy, play, and related symbolic representations of action, objects, and desires.

The preoperational stage runs from the end of sensorimotor intelligence (approximately eighteen to twenty-four months) to the beginnings of concrete operational thinking (age six or seven years). A tremendous amount of development takes place during this span—language, for example, goes from the simplest object naming to the ability to understand and generate complex sentences—so it is best to think of this as a very active, transitional period. The child's thought is not all the same during this period; the preoperational thought of a two-year-old just emerging from the sensorimotor stage is not the same as the preoperational thought of a five-year-old on the verge of concrete operations.

Egocentrism reemerges in the preoperational stage as the young child pushes his newly developed symbolic capacity to its limits. The preceding stage began with sensorimotor egocentrism, which then underwent a process of decentering. In a related way, this stage begins with an egocentrism of symbols which must run its course of decentering. The earliest symbols of the child are private; having invented a symbol to represent some object or spectacle, the child acts as if the symbol and event were identical. This shows a lack of differentiation between symbol and referent. Young children confuse things and their names. In a similar manner, the young child acts as if everyone else will understand his symbols in the same way he does. For example, if his favorite doll is named Gander he talks to playmates or strangers as if they know who and what Gander is. This shows a lack of differentiation between his own perspective and that of others. The most common example of this failure to differentiate is the equation of fantasy with reality. The young child does not make the same differentiation that adults do between his private world of symbols and the world of socially shared communications.

Language appears during this stage and, since it is such a highly social enterprise, one might think it free of the egocentrism so characteristic of other activities. But this is not the case; the child learns words from others but uses them, at first, as if they were private symbols. The "cute" speech of very young children represents such idiosyncratic usage.

The preceding examples have been drawn primarily from the intellectual sphere. They show how the child is egocentric with respect to his symbols during the preoperational stage, just as he was egocentric with respect to his body and actions during the earlier, sensorimotor stage. Development, again, requires a process of decentering which brings about more differentiated perspectives. A closely related process occurs in the social-emotional area.

The clash between the child's willfulness and parental authority takes place during the early portion of the preoperational stage. This interpersonal crisis is shaped by the egocentrism of symbols and its resolution aids in the decentering process. The two-year-old who says "no" to everyone, sees the world only from the perspective of his own wishes. The confrontation of this wishful-willfulness, leading to satellization, is a decentering in the sphere of human relations that corresponds to the more general intellectual decentering.

Concrete Operations: The Egocentrism of Childhood. As its name implies, the preoperational stage is a preparation for the period of concrete operations which begins around the age of six or seven. The preoperational stage represents progression away from the totally action-centered mode of sensorimotor thought, to the establishment of a truly mental or representational mode. The onset of concrete operational thought represents the end of the second great decentering. The child has first broken free from the totally body- and action-centered mode of sensorimotor intelligence and then recycled through decentering at the first level of symbols and representations. With the completion of these processes he possesses a set of flexible, workable, and reliable mental structures which Piaget calls concrete operations. An examination of the well-known conservation experiment will demonstrate what is meant by "mental structures" and "operations" and also illustrate the difference between preoperational and concrete operational thinking.

The experiment consists of testing the child's understanding of transformations of matter. In one version, the child is shown three glasses: A, B, and C.

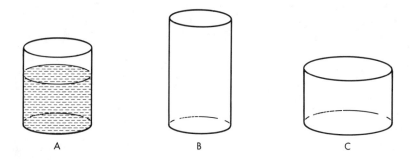

FIGURE 8.1

Glass A contains water and the child is asked what will happen when the water is poured into B or into C. Having obtained a statement of his expectations, the experimenter then pours the water, either confirming or refuting the child's predictions. The child is then asked to explain what has happened; namely, that the water has risen higher in B (the taller but narrower glass) or is lower in C (the shorter but wider glass).

A majority of preoperational children anticipate that the water levels will be the same in all three glasses. They have a somewhat crude concept of a constant quantity of water; they "know" it is the "same" water and expect this "sameness" to appear simply and directly as the same level.

When the water is poured and they see that it is higher in glass B or lower in glass C, and are asked to reconcile this with their stated anticipations, they usually reverse themselves and declare that it is not the same amount of water. Thus, the child at this stage has the ability to symbolize and even a beginning concept of conservation—the idea of "sameness"—but the symbolic capacity is limited; the child is focused on the immediate state of events before his eyes and he lacks a broader representation of a quantity of water whose existence is independent of its immediate state. The reasoning of the preoperational child also illustrates the irreversible or rigid nature of thought at this stage. The child may know what he thinks—that the water is "the same"—but not how he arrived at that knowledge or how it might be modified when confronted with new facts. An increase in "mobility," reversibility, and abstract reasoning, all come into being with the next stage.

The preoperational child who thinks that the water poured from A to B or C increases or decreases in quantity is focused in his thinking on the state of things before his eyes. He is centered on the action—the "pouring"—and does not treat this as a *transformation* in which quantity remains constant while shape changes. With the attainment of concrete operations,

> ...The child says: "It is the same water," "it has only been poured," "nothing has been taken away or added"..."you can put the water in B back into A where it was before" (reversibility by inversion); or, particularly, "the water is higher, but the glass is narrower, so it's the same amount" (compensation or reversibility by reciprocal relationship). The states are henceforth subordinated to the transformations, and these transformations, being decentered from the action of the subject, become reversible and account both for the changes in their compensated variations and for the constant implied by reversibility. (Piaget and Inhelder, 1969, p. 98)

The term *operations* refers to the child's ability to perform more complex mental transformations such as the uniting of classes, the ordering of events or classes, conservation, and the ability to reverse all of these and to apply them to new instances. Such abilities imply organized *systems* of mental structures or schemas and it is the possession of such systems that differentiates concrete from preoperational thought. Thought becomes much less restricted to specific actions on present events. The child, in the years from six to adolescence, can formulate hypotheses and construct explanations, though these tend still to be present-centered and tied to the world of concrete events.

The changes in thought spread into the moral, interpersonal, and emotional areas. The child becomes increasingly able to engage in games and other organized social activities because he can understand rules and is more able to recognize the perspectives of other children. A good illustration of the change in the child's thought can be seen in his perception of his parents.

Very young children tend to view their parents as omniscient and infallible. The discrepancy between parental size, power, and knowledge, and that of the child is so great that the parent easily seems all-knowing. Although the young child is exposed to instances where his parents are wrong or misinformed, such instances do not contradict his perception of their omniscience due to the qualities of preoperational thinking. Just as the child thought the water levels would be the "same" and then switched to thinking that it was "not the same water" in the conservation experiment, so he easily shifts his perception of parental behavior. Since his thinking is relatively unsystematic, he is not bothered by inconsistencies. Daddy can be wrong on some occasion and still remain the omniscient father.

With the onset of concrete operational thought, the parents are in for a fall. The child now thinks more systematically and is concerned with reconciling inconsistencies with his general beliefs. Oedipal rivalry, coincident with the transition from pre- to concrete operational thought, gives added motivation to the dethroning of the parents. From particular experiences in which he sees that his parents make mistakes, or cannot answer his questions, or do not know something that he knows, the child realizes that his earlier view of them was in error.

The fall of the parents may come as a sudden shock—particularly if, like certain authoritarian families, they encouraged the god-like image of the father—or as a gradually dawning awareness. It comes to all children, sooner or later, and in the natural course of events, the child swings over to the opposite extreme. If before the parents were viewed as omniscient, they now are seen as stupid or, at the least, as not very bright in those areas of life so central to children. "Mom, you just don't understand!" Or, "Nevermind!" with an exasperated air of, "these are matters beyond the comprehension of adults."

What happens, of course, is that the concrete operational child over-assimilates; he pushes his newly developed cognitive skill to its limits. Having acquired the ability to deal with assumptions and hypotheses, to detect flaws and errors in adults, he then carries these skills to their extreme. If father is found to be wrong about one thing then, not only is his omniscience disproven, but he is probably wrong about a lot of things. If the child has been clever enough to detect his father's weakness, then he feels smarter and feels able to outwit adults in many areas. As David Elkind points out, the egocentrism of childhood consists of a lack of differentiation between assumption and fact; the child, during these years, does not clearly distinguish between hypotheses and reality; he "treats hypotheses as if they were facts and facts as if they were hypotheses" (Elkind,

1970, p. 55). Elkind calls this "cognitive conceit"; in the present terms this is the form taken by overassimilation during this stage of development. In the example discussed above, the child assumes, on the basis of some parental error, that parents "don't know everything" and then treats this broadened assumption as if it were an established fact.

Another important and closely related discovery plays a crucial role in dethroning parental omniscience and in the initial burst of egocentrism. This is the child's much clearer understanding of the difference between fantasy and reality. The central achievement of preoperational decentering lies in just this; the child comes to clearly understand the difference between symbols and the things symbolized; between his inner world of images, dreams, and fantasies and the outer world of other persons and events. Having made this differentiation, he comes to realize that only he has direct access to his inner world. *His parents cannot read his mind!* If he chooses not to tell them something, they may never know it. He can, in short, have a life of his own that is kept secret from parents and other adults. This discovery plays its part in the fall of parental omniscience which was based on the preoperational child's assumption that his parents could tell what he was thinking or fantasizing. In part, the older child's belief that adults are "stupid" and "don't know everything" refers to this discovery—that they don't know his secret fantasies or the semisecret activities of him and his friends as they skulk around from Secret Hiding Place to Club to Fort. If Huck Finn is the personification of moral innocence encountering the world of adult corruption, then Tom Sawyer is the archetype of the childhood life of secret adventures and intrigues beyond the understanding of adults.

The child's ability to differentiate fantasy from reality helps account for the seeming paradox between the superior attitude toward the parents (cognitive conceit, the dethroning of parental omniscience) and the compliance that is characteristic of postoedipal identification. In an earlier discussion we have seen the child's more or less open conflicts with the parents that occur during the late portion of the preoperational stage. The resolution of these conflicts is accomplished by the child's identifying himself with the parents and incorporating a renunciation of desire role into the structure of self. The outcome of this identification is the period of compliance and calm characteristic of middle childhood (from approximately six to the onset of adolescence). This account stresses the lack of conflict between child and adult during middle childhood. But have I not just described this same period in terms of the egocentrism of the concrete operational stage; of cognitive conceit and the dethroning of parental omniscience? And are these not contradictory? This contradiction is resolved when we recall that his new cognitive skills allow the child to operate on two, semi-independent levels: the level of outward compliance—of socially acceptable acts and manners—and the inward level of fantasy and secret play. Thus, the child can be both compliant, pleasing, a "good" boy or girl *and* feel superior to adults in his play and fatansy life. Most children have a partial awareness of this; they know—and increasingly so as they approach adolescence—that the conceit and superiority are not real.

This life on two levels explains what psychoanalysts mean by the "repression" of the Oedipal complex; it clarifies what is "latent" in the "latency period." For outward compliance coupled with a secret inner life is the essence of dissociation, as we saw in chapter 7. Concrete operational thought allows interpersonal conflicts to go underground. The ability to maintain two separate existences facilitates the moratorium of middle and late childhood. Some typical fantasies will provide further illustrations.

Jack and the Beanstalk has already been noted as a typical Oedipal fantasy in which the boy defeats the menacing father figure and keeps the loving mother for himself. Another aspect of that tale is the contrasting intelligence of child and adult, illustrating the cognitive conceit of concrete operational egocentrism. Jack is seemingly stupid to sell the cow for beans, or to risk the giant's wrath, but events prove him smarter than both his mother and the giant who, for all his size and noise, is easily outwitted.

Peter Pan is another perennially pleasing fantasy without the obvious Oedipal anxieties of *Jack and the Beanstalk* (though there is Captain Hook and that alligator). As Elkind points out, the Peter Pan fantasy depicts the wish to remain a child and the related antipathy toward growing up. Who wants to become one of those hairy, smelly, big people who doesn't really "know anything" important? Better to stay in the land of adventure and magic where children can fly and adults are easily fooled. The literature that most appeals to children during these years—whether it is *Peter Pan* or *Tom Sawyer* or *Alice in Wonderland,* or the many tales of adventure and mystery that reappear in new guises each generation—illustrates the child's fantasied superiority, a superiority based on the overestimation of his new intellectual skills.

One other aspect of the child's skill at separating fantasy and reality should be mentioned here. As we will see shortly, the moral reasoning that is characteristic of this period of childhood is what Kohlberg calls the "good boy orientation." During the earlier stages, morality was based on self-interest and fear of punishment. The intelligence of the concrete operational stage permits the construction of a more complex conscience based on internalized roles. Still, it suffers from the limitations of the egocentrism of this stage—it is a conscience of playing the right or "good boy" role, of pleasing adults and, in turn, of pleasing one's conscience. The lack of differentiation between hypotheses and reality permits a sort of hypocrisy—the child feels good performing the outward role and may be little troubled by the rebellious character of his fantasies. The gradual decentering of the stage brings about a change in moral reasoning. As he moves toward the capacity for abstract thought, a morality of roles becomes less satisfying and there is, once again, a breakdown of egocentrism leading to integration at a more complex level.

Formal Operations and the Egocentrism of Adolescence. Although more systematic, reversible, and flexible than preceding modes of thought, the operations of the period six or seven years to ten or twelve are still "concrete." By this, Piaget means that thought is oriented toward concrete things and events in the immediate present. There may be some simple generalization one step into the future, but the child is still mainly concerned with the *real* rather than the potential. Being able to deal with the hypothetical and potential (as well as the actual and present) is the mark of the final period, that of formal operations. As Flavell puts it:

> The child of 7–11 years acts as though his primary task were to organize and order what is immediately present; the limited extrapolation is something he will do where necessary, but this extrapolation is seen as a special-case activity. What he does not do (and what the adolescent does do) is delineate all possible eventualities at the outset and then try to discover which of these possibilities really do occur in the present data; in this later strategy, the real becomes a special case of the possible, and not the other way around. (1963, pp. 203–4)

Formal operational thought constitutes a final decentering. In the sensorimotor stage thought is tied to action. It progresses through the preoperational stage to concrete operations, where it has become decentered from the child's body and actions but remains tied to the concrete reality of things and events. With the onset of adolescence, the final decentering begins: once possessed of formal operations, the adolescent may contemplate the nonexistent and extrapolate possibilities into the future. In short, he has the capability of becoming a theorist or philosopher; a manipulator of abstractions.

In the next chapter, "Adolescence," I will consider the properties of formal operational thought in greater detail. Let me here describe some of the typical features of this stage very briefly.

Three interrelated processes characterize the new level of thought as the child moves into adolescence: his increased ability to deal with hypotheses and nonexistent possibilities, a shift in time perspective, and the ability to introspect. The concrete operational child can construct hypotheses but only of a limited sort. They are concrete—tied to observations and present events. The adolescent becomes increasingly able to think about the possible as well as the actual; to extrapolate symbols in various hypothetical directions. Second, the adolescent becomes decentered from the present; his time perspective is broadened to include the future. This is seen in his growing preoccupation with future roles; with what his life will be like in the years to come. Finally, formal operations allow the adolescent to introspect, to make his own ideas and hypotheses the objects of thought. All three of these shifts are interrelated and all show the fruits of the decentering from concrete, present-centered reality.

As was true at each preceding stage, the new cognitive skills are at first overdone, leading to the overassimilation characteristic of adolescence. This is seen in the egocentrism of ideals and romanticism common among high school and college age youth. Let me present two examples of this adolescent egocentrism: undifferentiated self-preoccupation and hyper-morality.

Introspection represents a crucial advance over concrete operational thought. The adolescent can think about his own thoughts; he can make the contents of his mind the "object" of contemplation. This new-found ability to introspect permits a kind of self-awareness or self-consciousness that was not possible at earlier stages. As is always the case with a new cognitive skill, this one is overdone; its possibilities are tested by pushing it to its limits. The obvious manifestations of this are seen in the self-consciousness of the teen-age period. This may be a preoccupation with appearance—those long hours in front of the mirror imagining one's horrible or wonderful effect on members of the opposite sex—or the time spent wondering who one is, or letting fantasies spin off into a romantic future. As Elkind points out, adolescents typically construct an "imaginary audience" to whom they direct their fantasies and expectations.

The egocentric aspect of adolescent introspection consists of a failure to differentiate one's own abstract perspective from that of others. The adolescent often acts as if he alone has discovered introspection. He may feel that no one has ever had such a special self-awareness or suffered such acute romantic pain. In a related manner, he may assume that others are as preoccupied with his appearance and thoughts as he is. Real others are not differentiated from the imaginary audience. This accounts for self-consciousness in front of others, for if the adolescent is preoccupied with self-criticism, or is hyperaware of his own appearance, then he assumes that others must also be concerned with the way he looks, or that his failings are as obvious to them as they are to himself. In short, he does not differentiate his perspective from that of others and this constitutes egocentrism as it reappears in the formal operational stage.

Hypermorality is another example of adolescent egocentrism. As we have seen, formal operational thought permits the adolescent to deal in abstractions and future possibilities. In the moral sphere this means he can construct broader moral principles. The adolescent "discovers" ideals and then judges reality in terms of them. Overassimilation produces an egocentrism of ideals—a kind of perfectionistic morality in which the young person "sees through" the world's corruption. This can lead to a second dethroning of the parents. Recall how the rise of concrete operational thought led the child beyond his early view of his parents' omniscience and infallibility. The idealism of adolescence leads to an analogous reevaluation of the parents on a more complex level. As he progresses beyond a "good boy" morality of role playing, he becomes capable of evaluating first his parents and, later, himself, in terms of ideals. He discovers that the world is not what it appears to be in concrete terms, that corruption exists behind various facades, that good boy roles can mask deviousness and dishonesty. Far from being models of goodness, the parents may be seen as models of hypocrisy to be shunned at all costs, as the idealistic adolescent swings to the opposite extreme.

Not all adolescents fit the picture described above, though the general form of egocentrism can be discerned to some degree in most.

It is worth mentioning a few cautions at this point. Adolescence marks the beginning of formal operations and, as these become established, the child has the *potential* to use them. He does not always do so and may frequently rely on concrete operational thought just as the younger child often returns to preoperational or sensorimotor modes. Adolescence does not mark the end of cognitive development either; formal operational thought comes into existence, but its extension into various areas of life takes some time, as our consideration of later moral stages will show. Many people do not progress much beyond a morality of playing "good" roles, and a truly integrated idealism is rare. In general, the progression to new levels of thought and the decline of egocentrism begins in the more tangible, intellectual spheres and occurs later in the areas of morality and interpersonal relations—when it reaches these areas at all.

This concludes the review of the major stages of cognitive development. Before directly taking up the stages of moral development, let me summarize the preceding discussion by pointing up certain features common to all stages.

General Features of Cognitive Development

The ideas I will present here are a selection; they represent those features of cognitive development most pertinent to an understanding of conscience and morality. Three ideas or principles will be considered: progressive decentering; changes in time perspective; and increasing complexity and differentiation with its attendant recycling.

Decentering. All of psychological development may be viewed as a progressive decentering in which the child moves beyond egocentrism with an increasing ability to take wider perspectives. At the beginning of the sensorimotor period all action is centered on the body which is not differentiated from outer reality. The major achievements of this stage are the decline of sensorimotor egocentrism, the attainment of permanent object schemas, and the differentiation of a body and motor "self." The preoperational stage brings with it mental representations, but these are initially marked by egocentrism and the cycle of decentering must be repeated again at this new level.

The preoperational child has great difficulty in conceptualizing how things would look from a perspective other than his own. For example, a four- or five-year-old may be perfectly capable of walking from home to school. He has a motor schema that enables him to negotiate the way. If he is asked to a arrange toy streets, houses, and so forth, in the form of a simple map that represents his route, however, he is incapable of doing so. He cannot take a perspective—the path as viewed from above—other than that connected with his own immediate experience of walking. The concrete operational child can make the map; his thought has become decentered from his actions and he can assume this broader perspective. At the level of formal operations, thought has the capacity to break free from reality; one can take hypothetical perspectives.

These examples have been drawn from the physical world. The same process of decentering is found in the social-affective-interpersonal realm, though it occurs later and with greater difficulty. The child progresses from a stage in which self and others are egocentric motor objects, through a series of decenterings. Eventually, the adult has the potential to imagine what it is like, psychologically, from the viewpoint of another. He is, in other words, capable of empathy. Taking the perspective of another person is a more difficult matter than assuming another perspective in the physical world since it involves less tangible events. For those people who are capable of reaching it, empathy and the higher levels of morality do not develop until the late adolescent and adult years.

Time Perspective. The child's perspective of time evolves through the stages of cognitive development. At the beginning of infancy there are fleeting impressions and the rhythm of sleep and wakefulness. The progress of sensorimotor development locates objects and self in time as well as in space. With the onset of concrete operations, there is a clear sense of time, but the child's conception of reality is dominated by the *present*. For example, young children must often be forced to take medicine or submit to other unpleasant procedures which cause pain. They are not convinced that the future benefits—which are less real to them—are worth the present discomfort. Seeing the value of "homework" is even more difficult, since the rewards are more distant in time and less tangible. Young children are often coerced and bribed (with grades, for example) into doing those unpleasant things now which will be of supposed benefit in the future. The broader moral issue here involves the sacrifice of one's own immediate gains and pleasures for the long range good of others. This is a topic to which we will return when considering the higher levels of morality.

With the attainment of formal operations, the adolescent can operate with an orientation to the future and future possibilities. This change in time perspective makes possible, at a later age, what Erikson calls the stage of "generativity," a stage in which one's life can be oriented toward future generations. Principled moral stages are dependent on a future time perspective as well as the ability to take the perspective of the other person.

Complexity and Differentiation. Each stage of cognitive development is more complex and differentiated than the preceding stage. Each represents a transformation in which the issues of the previous stage are restructured or absorbed within a new framework. The progression moves in one direction only—preoperational thought subsumes sensorimotor (but not the reverse), concrete operations subsume preoperations, and formal operations subsume all the preceding stages. This progression toward greater complexity and differentiation is a general characteristic of all cognitive development. The process of decentering and changes in time perspective, just discussed, are examples of progressive complexity and differentiation.

With the onset ·of each new stage of cognitive development, the characteristic problems and conflicts of the child take on new meaning and may be worked through or recycled in a new way. For example, early in the period of preoperational thought the child asserts his aggressive independence, leading to the battle of wills and satellization. Adolescence also involves an assertion of independence but at this later age the young person possesses formal operational thought (and many other skills and abilities) which casts the struggle in an entirely new dimension. The same emotions are involved in the battle between the two-year-old and his parents over whether he will eat with his fork or stop soiling his pants, and the ideological arguments of a college freshman and his father, but cognitive development casts the latter in a much more complex and differentiated form.

Decentering, an increasing time perspective, and progressive differentiation are characteristic of cognitive growth. The confrontation of egocentrism at each stage, and the attendant decentering, are important parts of the progressive reworking of the core conflicts. These issues bring us to moral development proper. With the general stages and features of cognitive development as a base, let us now turn our attention to this topic.

The Development of Moral Thought

The principal works to be considered are those of Jean Piaget, Lawrence Kohlberg, and Jane Loevinger. These authors have focused their attention on moral judgment and moral reasoning; on the way the person understands and responds to moral issues at various points in development. They have approached these issues by inquiring into children's understanding of rules, "right and wrong," "good and bad"; by obtaining responses to stories that present moral dilemmas; and by examining the responses of adults to incomplete sentences. Based on this work, they describe the progression of moral reasoning through a sequence of stages that parallel, or are based on, the basic stages of cognitive development. For example, Kohlberg traces the progression from a "premoral" egocentric stage, in which morality is a matter of deference to superior power, to a final "principled" stage in which moral judgments rest on universal, shared standards. Let me begin with a brief review of Piaget's early work.

Piaget's Views on Moral Judgment. Piaget's early (1932) work on moral judgment has provided a starting place for a number of subsequent investigators, though Piaget himself has done little with it in more recent years. He studied moral judgment by observing children's responses to stories and by questioning them about good and bad actions, duties, punishments, and their understanding of rules (principally the rules of the game of marbles). On the basis of these observations, Piaget delineated two broad stages of moral judgment to which he gave the names *heteronomous* and *autonomous.*

Heteronomous means subject to the rule or law of another. This is an early form of morality and derives from respect for the parents, the primary rule givers. Initially, the power of such rules is dependent on the physical presence of the parents, but this gradually becomes internalized. Heteronomous morality becomes established during the period of preoperational thought and partakes of the qualities of such thought, particularly the young child's failure to differentiate his subjective experience from reality. This is seen in what Piaget calls "moral realism." The heteronomous, preoperational child attributes a reality—an almost sacred quality—to laws, rules, and orders. He ignores the intentions and motives of the rule breaker or the context in which the action occurred. For example, Piaget presented children with these two stories and asked them which described the naughtier action:

> (A) There was once a little girl who was called Marie. She wanted to give her mother a nice surprise, and cut out a piece of sewing for her. But she

didn't know how to use the scissors properly and cut a big hole in her dress.

(B) A little girl called Margaret went and took her mother's scissors one day that her mother was out. She played with them for a bit. Then as she didn't know how to use them properly she made a little hole in her dress. (1932, p. 122)

The young child says that Marie's action was naughtier because she cut the bigger hole. The relative intentions of Marie and Margaret are ignored. This judgment is similar in *form* to that of the preoperational child in the water-pouring experiment. In both instances, thought is more bound to a literal action in the present, while the more abstract qualities— transformation, intention—are not grasped.

Piaget also discusses the "objective responsibility" characteristic of moral realism. Here, again, an act is evaluated in terms of the degree with which it conforms to rule or law rather than to intention or circumstance. A lie may be judged bad in terms of how "big" it is, as the following example shows. A child is asked which is worse: telling your family you got a good mark in school when you didn't, or telling, after being frightened by a dog, that it was as big as a cow or horse. As Piaget puts it:

...for young preoperational children, the first lie is not "naughty" because (1) it often happens that one gets good marks; and above all (2) "Mama believed it!" The second lie, however, is very naughty, because nobody ever saw a dog that size. (Piaget and Inhelder, 1969, p. 126)

Again, we see that for the heteronomous, preoperational child "badness" is tied to "bigness" in a literal or physical sense.

The early phase of morality is also characterized by obedience to authority for its own sake. Like moral realism, an obedience orientation is based on a literal conception of rules. Rules are thought of as sacred or absolute and punishments as arbitrary and severe rather than involving some form of restitution. Just as the preoperational child does not clearly differentiate the world of private play from the world of social reality, so he tends to equate punishment with the evaluation of an act. If a child is punished then he must have done something "bad," and a big punishment means he did something worse than a little punishment. Young children even expect punishment to be magically visited upon wrongdoers (Piaget calls this "immanent justice"). For example, the child is likely to think that an accidental fall was punishment for telling a lie. Such thinking is closely tied to the view of parents and other authorities as omniscient, an important characteristic of preoperational thought that we examined earlier. Such thinking is not confined to childhood, of course, as the existence of many neurotic and primitive beliefs and rituals attest.

The heteronomous morality of early childhood declines in succeeding years. It is replaced, in Piaget's view, by autonomous morality. Autonomous means subject to one's own rule or law. The rise of autonomous moral reasoning coincides with the rise of concrete operational thought. This stage of cognitive development, as we have seen, is more systematic and differentiated. In the moral sphere, concrete operations lead to the breakdown of moral realism and objective responsibility and to their replacement with a morality based on mutual respect. From the decentered and less action-oriented perspective of the autonomous, concrete operational child, good and bad acts, rules, and punishments begin to be understood in a context of human intentions and motives. Rules, rather than being perceived as God-given, are seen as the result of agreement among contemporaries. It is interesting to note what brings about the shift from heteronomous to autonomous moral reasoning.

In his study of the way children play games with each other, Piaget describes a progression from egocentric to cooperative play. Preoperational four- and five-year-olds play by themselves while playing together. That is, when these younger children play a game such as marbles, each plays according to his own understanding of the rules, which may differ widely from child to child. There is little concern for the correctness of other's play and, in a sense, everyone wins and no one loses. The game is understood as a group of actions and words, loosely fitted together. The play of the seven- or eight-year-old is quite different. A common set of rules is known to the players, mutual surveillance of each other's play is common, attempts are made to enforce honesty ("It doesn't count, you cheated!" "Jimmy went over the line!" "The ball touched you!" "It did not!") and some win while others lose. What was true of Swiss children playing marbles in 1932 is true on American playgrounds today. A large portion of kickball, dodge-ball, and other games of this age are devoted to arguments over cheating and the rules.

Piaget believed that the shift from egocentric to cooperative play is largely a result of arguments and disagreements among peers, a point not completely substantiated by later work. Such conflicts confront the child's egocentrism and force mutual respect and cooperation on him. At the same time, the growth of concrete operational thought allows the child to grasp other points of view and to understand more complex assumptions. The arguments and disagreements among peers which are so central in bringing about the shift from egocentric to cooperative play represent a recycling at a later stage of what the child has earlier undergone with the parents. Both the early battle of wills and the later oedipal conflicts involved a confrontation between parents and childish egocentrism. Cognitively, the child, during these conflicts, was still centered in the family and on himself. The peer conflicts of the later concrete operational period represent a reworking of conflicts between self-interest and the wishes and interests of others; between what the child wants to do—play the game his own way, always win—and the interests and perspectives of other children. This reworking is an important example of how core conflict areas are recycled at new levels of complexity and differentiation.

Piaget's account of the development of moral reasoning from heteronomy to autonomy was a crucial early contribution. It provided both methods and concepts for later workers. At the same time, later work has shown it to be too narrow in scope. Subsequent research (reviewed by Kohlberg, 1963, pp. 315–20) has substantiated only some of Piaget's ideas. The account of early or heteronomous morality, characterized by a failure to differentiate subjective intentions from objective consequences, an orientation to punishment and omniscient authority, and the belief in magical retribution, have all been supported by later research. These are genuine features of the young child's moral reasoning that decline with age and development in various cultures. Research has failed to support Piaget's specific ideas regarding the early rise of autonomous morality, however. Although the sort of peer interaction that Piaget focused on is of undoubted importance in forcing a decline in egocentrism, it does not assume a central role in moral reasoning until the high school and college years. Moral concepts in middle childhood are still largely derived from authorities. While there are clearly differences between the moral reasoning of the pre- and concrete operational child, the more abstract, conscience-like quality of morality that Piaget attributed to middle childhood does not make its appearance until adolescence. Thus, while Piaget accurately delineated the general progression of moral development, his account is too compressed. There are more than two stages and the process extends into later years. In part, the inadequacy of Piaget's account resulted from the sort of games and stories that he used. They did not allow a differentiated assessment of more complex, developmentally advanced levels of moral reasoning. A consideration of Kohlberg's research will take us to these higher levels.

Stages of Moral Reasoning: Kohlberg's Work.   Kohlberg's basic method has been to present children and adults with a series of stories, each of which describes a moral dilemma. The stories have no right or wrong answers—they challenge the subject's reasoning in the moral sphere, and Kohlberg is most interested in the *process* by which the person arrives at his answer. The stories are, thus, a way of obtaining a sample of the person's characteristic moral reasoning or judgment. The following is one of the stories:

> In Europe, a woman was near death from a special kind of cancer. There was one drug that the doctors thought might save her. It was a form of

radium that a druggist in the same town had recently discovered. The drug was expensive to make, but the druggist was charging ten times what the drug cost him to make. He paid $200 for the radium and charged $2,000 for a small dose of the drug. The sick woman's husband, Heinz, went to everyone he knew to borrow the money, but he could only get together about $1,000 which is half of what it cost. He told the druggist that his wife was dying and asked him to sell it cheaper or let him pay later. But the druggist said: "No, I discovered the drug and I'm going to make money from it." So Heinz got desperate and broke into the man's store to steal the drug for his wife. Should the husband have done that? Why?

A young child or person at a very primitive moral level reasons in terms of his own needs; his answer is based on what he thinks he can get away with. Kohlberg calls this Level I morality, a level that is divided into two stages, a "punishment and obedience orientation" (Stage 1) and an "instrumental relativist orientation" (Stage 2). Young children's responses are based on whether they think an adult "will get mad at me" or whether they think they will be caught. This recalls the "objective responsibility" and "moral realism" that Piaget noted in preoperational children. Preconventional reasoning may persist into later years. For example, a seventeen-year-old reform school inmate reasons, "I would eliminate that into whether he wanted to or not. If he wants to marry someone else, someone young and good-looking, he may not want to keep her alive."

The middle level (Level II) is characterized by conformity to conventional rules and roles and is divided into a "good boy orientation" (Stage 3) and an "authority and social order maintaining orientation" (Stage 4). Examples of Level II responses to the story would stress stealing the drug because other people would disapprove of letting one's wife die; or not stealing it because the laws against stealing must be maintained, even at the expense of personal loss. Level III, post-conventional morality, represents principled reasoning. The person's responses are based on values and principles which are his own, as opposed to the group conformity characteristic of Level II. Two stages are distinguished within Level III; a social contract, legalistic orientation (Stage 5) and a universal-ethical-principle orientation (Stage 6). An example of Stage 6 reasoning about the druggist-wife story is as follows: (Should the husband steal the drug to save his wife? How about for someone he just knows?) : "Yes. A human life takes precedence over any other moral or legal value, whoever it is. A human life has inherent value whether or not it is valued. by a particular individual" (from Kohlberg and Kramer, 1969). A more complete description of the six stages is presented here:

> Level I. Value resides in external quasi-physical happenings, in bad acts, or in quasi-physical needs rather than in persons and standards.

Stage 1: *Obedience and punishment orientation.* Egocentric deference to superior power or prestige, or a trouble-avoiding set. Objective responsibility.

Stage 2: *Naively egoistic orientation.* Right action is that of instrumentally satisfying the self's needs and occasionally the needs of others. Awareness of relativism of value to each actor's needs and perspective. Naive egalitarianism and orientation to exchange and reciprocity.

Level II. Moral value resides in performing good or right roles, in maintaining the conventional order and the expectancies of others.

Stage 3: *Good boy orientation.* Orientation to approval and to pleasing and helping others. Conformity to stereotypical images of majority or natural role behavior, and judgment by intentions.

Stage 4: *Authority and social order maintaining orientation.* Orientation to "doing duty" and to showing respect for authority and maintaining the given social order for its own sake. Regard for earned expectations of others.

Level III. Moral value resides in conformity by the self to shared or shareable standards, rights, or duties.

Stage 5: *Contractual legalistic orientation.* Recognition of an arbitrary element or starting point in rules or expectations for the sake of agreement. Duty defined in terms of contract, general avoidance of violation of the will or rights of others, and majority will and welfare.

Stage 6: *Conscience or principle orientation.* Orientation not only to actually ordained social rules but also to principles of choice involving appeal to logical universality and consistency. Orientation to conscience as a directing agent and to mutual respect and trust.[3] (Turiel, 1969, pp. 96–97)

When we contrast the progression of moral development, described by Kohlberg, with Piaget's views, we note both similarities and differences. Like Piaget's general approach to cognitive development, the stages Kohlberg describes represent an invariant progression from a less complex, undifferentiated state, toward greater complexity and differentiation. Each stage is a transformation that encompasses what existed before within a new—cognitive, moral—organization. The progression of stages also represents a gradual decentering. In Level I, morality is egocentric in the sense that the child is only "moral" out of self-interest. He wants to avoid getting caught or punished or, at the least, to win praise. Stages 5 and 6, in contrast, assume a decentering at the level of human relations. Here, the person has the ability to fully take the perspective of another. Finally, like the progression from heteronomous to autonomous morality described by Piaget, progression through Kohlberg's stages is intertwined with general cognitive development. Moral reasoning at the higher stages is dependent on the attainment of the higher levels of formal operational thought.

Kohlberg's account differs from Piaget's in important ways. Where Piaget describes two stages of moral reasoning, Kohlberg describes six. Because his stories pose more complex dilemmas than the "which is naughtier?" choices of Piaget, and because he studies older subjects, Kohlberg traces moral thought further into development. The shift from heteronomous to autonomous morality coincides with the shift from Stage 1 to Stage 2. Stage 3 is probably the most a child can achieve with concrete operational thought, all the higher stages being dependent on the ability to use formal operations. Kohlberg's data (Kohlberg and Kramer, 1969) substantiates this. Stages 1, 2, and 3 are the common forms of reasoning in American ten-year-olds. By age thirteen, Stages 3 and 4 predominate, while by age sixteen, Stages 5, 4, and 3 are the most frequently used, in that order. Stage 6 shows a very gradual increase, for the minority of persons who attain it at all, until age twenty-five. Principled or post-conventional thought (Stages 5 and 6) is born in adolescence and does not become well established until early adulthood. Thus, we see that the development of morality from heteronomy to autonomy is part of a larger process. Kohlberg and Piaget agree that moral reasoning is a construction of the child that is based on the way he cognizes the social world at different points in development, but Kohlberg's sequence is more complex and extends the process into the later years.

An important common feature, stressed in different ways by both authors, is that moral development rests on a decrease in egocentrism and an increasing ability to assume the perspectives and points of view of other selves. This increasing ability to play other roles in a differentiated way—as contrasted with the fantasy role playing of the preoperational child who does not distinguish his own from other viewpoints—comes only with the firm establishment of concrete and formal operations. In addition, such role-taking is dependent on active, social interchange. Thus, although Piaget's hypothesis that autonomous morality derives from peer socialization has not been completely supported, there is support for the general idea that role taking, the decline in egocentrism, and the increasing ability to take another's viewpoint, are all dependent on the interaction of the child—at his particular level of cognitive functioning—and the world of parents, other authorities, siblings, and peers.

I should make it clear that Kohlberg's position on the development of morality, and particularly on the motivation for conscience, does not necessarily coincide with that presented in this chapter. In a comprehensive chapter (*Stage and Sequence: The Cognitive-Developmental Approach to Socialization,* 1969), Kohlberg reviews and criticizes a number of theories and studies. The issues are too many and too complicated to take up at this time, but his position, in brief, is that moral reasoning and the self develop by the addition of new roles. This is an interpretation of identification consonant with that presented here. However, in his account of the motivation for this identification, Kohlberg gives major weight to competence. In his view, the child develops to new levels primarily to acquire the more advanced skills and attributes of parents and older children. In a related vein, Kohlberg sees a kind of innate attractiveness in the higher levels of moral reasoning. He assumes that if a person thinks right he will do right; that is, if he is capable of reasoning at a higher stage, his behavior will be consistent with this reasoning.

Some Vicissitudes in the Development of Morality

Many interesting studies have been carried out by Kohlberg, his students and others using his methods. I will make no attempt to review all this work here, but will note a few points of interest.

As its label implies, *conventional morality* (Level II) is the way the majority of persons reason. In a sample of urban, middle-class males, 64 percent are at the conventional level or lower, with 26 percent reasoning at Stage 5. Only 10 percent reach Stage 6, the conscience or principled orientation (from Kohlberg and Kramer, 1969). Although a minority, one can argue that individuals at the higher levels are the moral leaders of society. The factors facilitating development to these higher levels are thus of special interest.

Kenneth Keniston (1969), after reviewing a variety of studies, concludes that there are three general factors associated with post-conventional moral reasoning: disengagement from adult society, confrontation with alternative moral viewpoints, and the discovery of corruption. Let us examine these in a bit more detail.

The sooner one embarks on an adult career, the more likely one is to remain at a conventional level of moral reasoning. Kohlberg's data has consistently shown that a higher proportion of the members of primitive societies, and lower socioeconomic sectors of advanced societies, reason at conventional levels. Few persons in these groups ever reach the post-conventional level. In such groups, the person is likely to assume adult status and responsibility in early adolescence—take a job, begin a family—making a confrontation with conventional views riskier and less likely. Thus, some form of prolonged disengagement from adult society seems necessary if the individual is to question conventional thought during the late adolescent and early adult years when he is most capable of doing so. This is certainly not the only factor that allows one to step outside and question the moral values of society, but it seems a necessary condition.

Confrontation with alternative viewpoints is the second general factor facilitating development to the post-conventional level. As our earlier discussion of decentering made clear, one abandons an egocentric perspective when clashes with other views force accommodation. Confrontation with alternative viewpoints describes this process at the social level. Whether it is tribesmen coming to the larger village, immigrants to the new world, or adolescents leaving home for college, all are likely to come into contact with beliefs, customs, and value systems that are at variance with their traditional ways of life. Such confrontations challenge conventional moral views and can push the person to new levels of thought.

The final factor discussed by Keniston is the discovery of corruption in the world. This is likely to be especially important if inconsistency, hypocrisy—in short a lack of the highest principles—are discovered in those from whom one originally learned conventional morality. Since this is often the parents, we see here a more complex version of the challenge to parental omniscience that occurred, in simpler form, during the transition from pre- to concrete operational thinking. The discovery of corruption can lead the person to question and reject the conventional morality of his parents and teachers and, again, makes possible—though it does not guarantee—development to the principled level.

The general factors described above can lead to the breakdown of conventional morality, though they obviously do not do so for everyone. Sometimes, this breakdown is associated with "moral regression." The person, having questioned and abandoned the conventional wisdom of parents and established society overassimilates; he pushes this to its limit and questions the necessity for any rules. One sees this in some segments of contemporary youth whose reasoning is essentially at Stage 2: "Everybody do your own thing." Zablocki (1971) describes a similar phenomenon among individuals who "drop out" and form communes. Such persons are disenchanted with the hypocrisy, corruption, and competitive-materialistic values of traditional American society. They return to the land and group living in an attempt to live by new and better principles. In many of the communes studied by Zablocki, there is an initial phase of anarchism— the suspension of all rules of conduct and all attempts to limit or control the lives or actions of others. This is a reaction against conventional morality and rules and represents a temporary regression to the premoral level; everybody attempts to satisfy his own needs in his own way in a fashion somewhat analogous to the way preoperational children play games. The early phase of anarchism meets with characteristic problems and those communes which do not disband develop their own rules and values. (The major portion of Zablocki's book describes the "Bruderhöf," a communal society in its third generation. Whatever else one can say about it, it is certainly not anarchistic; in most ways it is a more structured form of life than the society from which it sprang.) The close life of the commune puts the extremism of the initial break with conventional society to a test and, when the members stay together, forces an accommodation. As best as one can tell from the accounts of commune life, the members resume their moral development where they left off. "Moral regression" is usually a temporary affair and seems necessary for progress to the post-conventional level. This is what Kohlberg finds and what Keniston reports; that progress to the higher levels is often accompanied by a regression—Kohlberg has called it the *Raskolnikoff syndrome*—in which all rules and morality are questioned, but this regression is temporary and can actually facilitate advanced development.

Let me return to the factors which promote development to the post-conventional level. As Keniston points out, all are enhanced by events characteristic of contemporary society. As society and its technology become more complex, the time until one is ready to assume a fully "adult" role becomes greater. More and more young people are spending more years in college and graduate school. In these settings they are disengaged, to a certain extent, from adult society and may question conventional values in relative safety.

College is also a place where one is exposed to alternative points of view, where one is forced to question traditional beliefs. So the delay in assumption of an adult role made necessary by an advanced education also leads to the second factor; the confrontation with alternative moral viewpoints. In the contemporary college setting this may come from fellow students as much as from faculty, but the overall effect is the same. In addition to the college experience, there is a tremendous amount of cross-cultural contact in contemporary society. Much of this is facilitated by the mass media—by television, newspapers, magazines, and other sources. One is more likely to be aware of different customs, views, and ways of life than ever before in history.

Finally, both the spread of higher education and the increase in cross-cultural contact facilitate criticisms of established views and the exposure of hypocrisy. As Keniston points out, we live in an age of cynicism; of heightened awareness of corruption in government; of belief systems (psychoanalysis, Marxism, philosophical analysis) which "see beneath" the surface, which debunk, expose, and criticize.

To sum up: several interrelated forces in the contemporary world challenge conventional moral values. These challenges—experienced most intensely by a minority of persons—lead to the questioning and, in some cases, the abandonment of conventional beliefs. Such questioning is necessary for development to post-conventional levels, but it does not automatically lead to principled thought, much less a principled way of life. What it does produce is an upheaval which can promote creative progress but which also arouses a good deal of anxiety in many persons, particularly those who derive their security from identification with the established order. Change in levels of moral reasoning, like change in general, is likely to arouse anxiety and anger. Let me conclude this section with a few comments on the emotional aspects of moral growth.

As I have hinted earlier, Kohlberg's account of moral development is, in some ways, overly rational. His heavy emphasis on competence motivation and what seems to be his belief that moral thought will take care of moral action, leads to a neglect of those emotions which make a moral life so difficult to achieve. Individuals who remain at a conventional level of moral thought do not experience the conditions—disengagement from an adult role, contact with alternative views, and the discovery of hypocrisy—at a time in their lives when these conditions could promote advanced development. They then become strongly identified with conventional beliefs and values. They derive security from this identification and challenges to this security arouse their fear and antagonism. Such challenge may come from within, in the form of a partial awareness of the inadequacy of their conventional views, or from without in the threatening guise of advantaged youths who flout established manners and social practices. Thus, a number of "middle Americans" attempt to derive security from their identification with country, from their belief in the value of hard work and the control of sensuality. But such security is threatened by an awareness of foreign and domestic corruption and an increasing sense that hard work is not justly rewarded. From without, they see young people—perhaps even their own children—who do not share their patriotism, who question the work ethic and, perhaps most obviously, violate so many of those little rules and codes of dress, grooming, manners, and sexual behavior. While all of this may be a stimulating confrontation with alternative views for the young person who is relatively uncommitted to an adult identity, to the committed older citizen it can pose a tremendous threat. So there are dangers in development beyond conventional levels, particularly when this development is carried into action.

Not all members of conventional society react simply with anxiety and threat to the challenges of a new morality. Some can change their views and learn from new opportunities. And, not all the dangers come from the resistance to change characteristic of those committed to conventional views. Revolutionary zeal can itself lead to the "immoral" uses of morality. As Keniston points out, reasoning from abstract principles does not guarantee compassion and empathy for all those persons who make up the moral universe. One sees this sort of thing most clearly in the anger and lack of sympathy that many revolutionaries, newly arrived at post-conventional levels of thought, have directed toward the establishment of their day. A righteous morality has often served as a vehicle for anger, for getting even or striking back at authority. Historically, this has occurred most often when high moral principles were combined with self-denial and asceticism. It is a hopeful sign that the meaningless self-denial of many earlier moral crusades seems absent in contemporary youth.

These examples, and many more could be cited, show that moral change, even of a complex intellectual variety, is likely to arouse strong emotions which can facilitate development, carry it to unbalanced extremes, or intensify resistance to change. This should not be surprising when we recall that the motives for morality involve those human instinctual systems which give force and direction to our social lives.

Our earlier discussion of the motives for conscience has elaborated the emotional basis for morality. A consideration of Piaget and Kohlberg has shown the levels through which moral reasoning can progress. Moral motivation and moral thought may be separated in books and research studies but in life they coexist. I will conclude this chapter with a discussion of the work of Jane Loevinger who, perhaps more than any other contemporary psychologist, combines both streams in her work.

Stages of Ego Development: The Work of Loevinger

Loevinger's overriding concern has been to accurately describe and measure stages of ego development. The focus is on the growth and transformation of self, within which conscience and moral development play a part. Thus, the ego stages will include the stages of moral reasoning, as described by Kohlberg, but are not so narrowly focused. In fact, Loevinger formulated her early account of stages (1966) by combining the descriptions of Kohlberg and a number of other investigators concerned with related problems. She also draws extensively on a very wide base of theoretical sources—both ancient and modern—ranging across philosophy, psychoanalysis, and psychology (see Loevinger, 1969). What emerges from all this is a view of self as integrator of experience, as a force which gives meaning to experience much in the sense discussed in chapter 7. The course of ego development is concerned with impulse control, character development, interpersonal relations, and self-conception as well as with moral reasoning. Because it combines these various strands, Loevinger's work forms an important bridge between the psychoanalytic theories of motivation for conscience and the work on moral reasoning.

The Loevinger model of ego development was originally constructed from other models and theories, but has been continually modified on the basis of work with a sentence completion measure. Over a period of some years, she and her collaborators have been engaged in a two-way process—modifying their model of ego development as data is gathered with the sentence completion test and, in turn, modifying the way that measure is used to accord with changes in the model. Much of this work is reported in the two volume work, *Measuring Ego Development* (Loevinger and Wessler, 1970).

The sorts of data generated by the sentence completion test are different from those obtained with Piaget's queries or the Kohlberg moral dilemma stories. This, along with the wider theoretical base, accounts for the differences between Loevinger's scheme of ego development and Kohlberg's account of the stages of moral reasoning. Let us examine the sentence-completion test and note some of the differences.

Subjects are presented with the beginnings or "stems" of sentences such as: "Being with other people ..." "When they avoided me ..." "Education..." "My father..." "I feel sorry..." and the like. They are asked to complete each stem in their own words. (Examples will be given shortly.) The method is *projective,* it elicits from the subject a sample of his or her characteristic thinking. Unlike more structured measures, such as multiple choice tests, it reveals the subject's own frame of reference. In this respect, it is similar to the responses to the Kohlberg moral dilemma stories. Both permit a free or relatively unstructured response and both elicit a sample of the person's thought. The sentence completion technique, however, provides a less structured, wider set of stimuli for the person to respond to than the moral dilemma stories. Where the Kohlberg measure samples moral reasoning, Loevinger's sentence completion test taps self-conception, interpersonal relations, views of social roles (male, female, marriage, parenthood), attitudes toward sexuality, and moral values.

The projective nature of the sentence completion test in part accounts for why Loevinger's description of ego stages contain more conflict and emotional material than Kohlberg's description of the stages of moral reasoning. That is, if you present a person with a story, such as the druggist-wife dilemma, and ask him what should be done and why, you will by and large get a *rational explanation,* even though the situation is one likely to arouse conflict and emotion. The form of the test elicits the former and not the latter. There are no rational answers to the sentence completion and, by requesting free responses to stems related to parents, sexuality, the body, and so on, one is more likely to obtain content about conflict and feeling. Now, let us turn to a description of the stages of ego development as constructed from theory and the sentence completion test.

Loevinger describes eight stages, though the first of these is really the stage before the ego comes into being. The entire system and the methods for scoring stages from responses to the sentence completion are somewhat complicated, and I will not attempt to present them here. Let us examine the stages, together with some examples of typical sentence completion responses. Having done this, we can then attempt an integrative comparison of these stages with stages of cognitive development, of moral reasoning, and the earlier account of stages in the evolution of self and conflict.

The eight stages described by Loevinger[4] are: Presocial, Symbiotic, Impulsive, Self-protective, Conformist, Conscientious, Autonomous, and Integrated. Each stage is described in terms of the major conflicts (termed "impulse control and character development"), the "interpersonal style," "conscious preoccupation," and "cognitive style" typical of the period.

The first two stages describe the birth of the ego or self. Interpersonal style is at first totally undifferentiated or presocial and, later, symbiotic. Conscious preoccupation is with differentiating self from the rest of reality. There are no sentence completion responses scored at these levels.

The *impulsive* stage is characterized by self-assertion; for example by early negativism. The person thinks in terms of immediate rewards and punishments.

> Magical ideas probably prevail in place of later conceptions of causation. Punishment seems to be perceived as retaliatory and as immanent in things. Other people are perceived primarily as sources of supply. Good guys give to me, mean ones don't. . . . Good and bad may be equated with clean and dirty.

Examples of sentence completion responses scored at the Impulsive level are:

> A good mother. . .*is nice.*
> A woman should always. . .*keep clean.*
> Usually she felt that sex. . .*is good to me because I get hot.*
> When they avoided me. . .*I cried and ran to mommy.*

The next stage is termed *self-protective.* As the person moves beyond early impulsiveness he begins to acquire concepts of blame and of right and wrong. But these are understood largely in terms of self-advantage. "Persons in this stage understand the concept of blame, but they tend to blame others, or circumstances, or some part of themselves for which they do not feel responsible." Control and being controlled, domination, competition— all in fairly crude form—are the issues of the period.

Examples of sentence completion responses scored at the self-protective level are:

> A good mother. . .*should try to teach her children to obey, and stay out of trouble.*

---

[4] All examples, quotes, and sentence completion responses are taken from J. Loevinger and R. Wessler, *Measuring Ego Development* (San Francisco: Jossey-Bass, Inc., 1970). These and other excerpts from this work are reprinted by permission of the publisher.

Being with other people...*I will watch myself.*
A wife should...*respect her husband and make him feel he is the King of his Castle and she can always have her way.*
My mother and I...*get along when she has money.*
What gets me into trouble is...*running around with the wrong group.*

Next comes the *conformist* stage. This is the most widely recognized stage and represents the major early internalization of moral values. It is also the stage at which most people in most groups are to be found. Children identify with their parents, adults and peers in a stereotyped and simple way. They believe that:

There is a right way and a wrong way, and it is the same for everyone all the time, or for broad classes of people described in terms of demographic traits, most often gender. What is conventional and socially approved is right, particularly the behaviors that define the conventional sex roles.... There is a high value for friendliness and social niceness. Cognitive preoccupations are appearance, material things, reputation and social acceptance and belonging. Inner states are perceived only in their most banal version (sad, happy, glad, angry, loving, and understanding), contrasting with an almost physiological version of inner life at lower levels (sick, upset, mad, excited) and a richly differentiated inner life at higher levels.

Examples of sentence completion responses scored at the conformist level are:

If my mother...*gives me advice, I take it because I know she is always right.*
My father...*is a great guy.*
Being with other people...*is the best thing to do.*
When they avoided me...*I smiled and kept on my way.*
Sometimes she wished that...*she had a million dollars.*

The next stage is the *conscientious* one. It represents progression beyond the relatively simple stereotyped thinking of the earlier stages. There is increasing recognition of inner states, motives, guilt feelings, and the difference between actions and psychological experiences. The conscientious person

...is aware of choices; he strives for goals; he is concerned with living up to ideals and with improving himself. The moral imperative remains, but it is no longer just a matter of doing right and avoiding wrong. There are questions of priorities and appropriateness. Moral issues are separated from conventional rules and from esthetic standards or preferences, this being one aspect of the greater conceptual complexity at this level. Achievement is important, and it is measured by one's own inner standards rather than being primarily a matter of competition or social approval, as it is at lower levels.

The conscientious stage is typical for students early in the college years.

Examples of sentence completion responses at the conscientious level are:

> My father...*is a sweet but unmature man.*
> I am...*eager to be friendly, but shy with new friends.*
> A pregnant woman...*is physically ugly but spiritually beautiful.*
> When I am nervous...*I take it out on my children and husband.*
> My conscience bothers me if...*I don't do what I believe is fair or right.*

If the conscientious stage sees the recognition of psychological experience—of the differentiation of inner states from outer reality—the *autonomous* stage moves on to a recognition of *inner conflict.* Moralism and excessive striving for perfection or achievement become tempered. There is

> ...a feeling for the complexity and multifaceted character of real people and real situations. There is a deepened respect for other people and their need to find their own way and even make their own mistakes. Crucial instances are, of course, one's own children and one's own parents. Striving for achievement is partially supplanted by a seeking of self-fulfillment. In acknowledging inner conflict, the person has come to accept the fact that not all problems are solvable...inner conflict is (not) more characteristic of the autonomous stage than of lower stages. Rather, the autonomous person has the courage to acknowledge and to cope with conflict, rather than blotting it out or projecting it onto the environment.

Examples of sentence completion responses scored at the autonomous level are:

> When they avoided me...*I wondered what the reason was, whether it was something I had done, some unrelated feelings they had, or if it were just by chance.*
> What gets me into trouble is...*first impressions I have of people and cannot change even when they are untrue.*
> A good mother...*tries to understand her children, is honest, and behaves naturally around them.*
> When people are helpless...*it is best to aid them to help themselves than to prolong their helplessness and dependency on others.*

Individual responses to this, and the next stage, perhaps do not give as full a picture as the total protocol. The responses are original and often combine elements found separately at lower levels, illustrating the cognitive complexity of these higher levels.

The final stage is termed *integrated.* Thinking at this stage represents the transcendence of conflict and the reconciliation of polarities. Very few persons reach this stage, perhaps one percent or less in any given social group. Characteristic of the integrated stage is

> ...existential humor and a feeling for paradox, respect for other's autonomy, search for self-fulfillment, value for justice and idealism, opposition to prejudice, coping with inner conflict, reconciliation of role conflicts, appreciation of sex in the context of mutuality, and reconciliation to one's destiny.

Examples of sentence completion responses scored at the integrated level are:

> The worst thing about being a woman... *cannot be generalized, as one woman makes an asset of the same situation decried by another.*
> A good mother... *lets go, loves without demanding conformity to her own ideals and standards—and helps to guide if possible.*
> At times she worried about... *money, health, the state of the world, and whether her son needed new shoes right now.*
> Most men think that women... *are necessary evils when considered collectively, and are wonderful when considered individually (that is to say —wife, mother, sister, lover).*

It should be pointed out that the stages just summarized are based on the responses of women and girls and reflect certain attitudes, values and experiences unique to females. For example, motherhood seems to be one of those highly "moralizing," or development-promoting life experiences involving delay of gratification, taking the role of another, and confrontation with one's own childhood. Some of these experiences are a part of being a father, of course, but in a somewhat different way. Although the original work with the sentence completion is based on female subjects, it is probably true that the general features of the stages apply to males as well as females. Additional work with the sentence completion, and a good deal of evidence from related sources, confirms this expectation.

One other caution: the stages of ego development may be easily misconstrued by persons looking for a simple indicator of adjustment, of a "moral worth," or a "moral IQ." Loevinger cautions against viewing ego development as a straightline from lowest to highest stage. Her statement is worth quoting in full:

> There is a temptation to see the successive stages of ego development as problems to be solved and to assume that the best adjusted people are those at the highest stage. This is a distortion. There are probably well-adjusted people at all stages. Certainly it seems reasonable to assume that there are well-adjusted children at all ages. Probably those who remain below the conformist level beyond childhood can be called maladjusted, and many of them are undoubtedly so, even in their own eyes. Some self-protective, opportunistic persons, on the other hand, become very successful, and it is faintly presump-

tuous of those of us who never quite make it to call them maladjusted. Certainly it is a conformist's world, and many conformists are very happy in it, though they are not all immune to mental illness. Probably to be faithful to the realities of the case one should see the sequence as one of coping with increasingly deeper problems rather than to see it as one of the successful negotiation of solutions.

SUMMARY:
AN INTEGRATION OF MODELS

Let me attempt to tie together the main ideas from the different sections of this chapter. This can be done by showing the interrelations of the general stages of cognitive development (Piaget) with the stages of moral reasoning (Kohlberg) and the stages of ego development (Loevinger). As this is done, I will attempt to note where the emotional conflicts and identifications, described in the earlier section on motives for conscience, fit in. Piaget's specific ideas about moral development will not be discussed since they are subsumed in Kohlberg's model. Similarly, many of the psychoanalytic ideas are incorporated in Loevinger's work.

In Table 1, I have attempted to show the general relations among stages from the three theories.

TABLE 8.1   A Comparison of Cognitive, Moral, and Ego Stages

Cognitive Stage (Piaget)	Stage of Moral Reasoning (Kohlberg)	Stage of Ego Development (Loevinger)
Sensorimotor		Presocial Symbiotic
Preoperational (Intuitive)	Obedience and Punishment Orientation (Stage 1)	Impulsive
	Naively Egoistic Orientation (Stage 2)	Self-Protective
Concrete Operational	Good Boy Orientation (Stage 3)	Conformist
	Authority and Social Order Maintaining (Stage 4)	Conscientious
Formal Operational	Contractual Legalistic Orientation (Stage 5)	Autonomous
	Conscience or Principled Orientation (Stage 6)	Integrated

The earliest stages precede morality and the self. During sensorimotor development, object concepts develop and a body self or ego emerges. Thus, the infant is at first presocial. The central interpersonal issue is attachment and, as this becomes established, the infant develops a symbiotic oneness with the mother figure. The principal emotions are attachment-love, undifferentiated sensuality, anger and rage, and separation anxiety. The major outcome is the delineation of a separate ego or sense of self, preparing the way for the self-assertion of the next stage.

The onset of preoperational thinking makes possible the earliest forms of morality and self-control. Having separated himself from the symbiotic relation with mother, impulse and aggressive assertion are pushed to their limits. This is the stage that Loevinger calls impulsive and that Kohlberg labels the obedience and punishment orientation (Stage 1). There is little internal control of impulse and little recognition of rules. Since early preoperational thought still partakes of sensorimotor qualities, the child easily equates good with immediate pleasure and bad with punishment and pain. There is a preoccupation with the body and body-centered feelings. Punishment may be seen to emanate from things in a magical way since fantasy and reality are still not clearly differentiated.

The clash of wills, typical of this period, leads to early identification (satellization), and the internalization of an impulse-controlling role. Some individuals never progress much beyond impulsiveness or an obedience and punishment orientation in their interpersonal relations or moral life. This is seen, for example, in those persons who view sex as a purely physical act and sexual partners as objects for the gratification of their desires.

When early identification takes root, the person can then progress to the second level characteristic of the preoperational period. This is the stage that Loevinger calls self-protective and Kohlberg calls naively egoistic or instrumental relativist. With a more advanced use of symbols, the person can now comprehend rules, good, bad, blame, and related ideas. But the egocentrism of the period leads him to view all these in terms of self-advantage or harm. The focus is still largely on the immediate present, while the long range consequences of actions tend to be ignored. There is some awareness of the needs of others, but reciprocity is still tempered with self-concern; "I'll scratch your back if you scratch mine," might be the motto of this stage.

Development up to this point may be termed preconventional. In Kohlberg's words, moral values reside in external events, in bad acts, and in quasi-physical needs. Loevinger points out that although there is a concept of blame in the self-protective stage, it is directed outward. The major identifications have included the incorporation of a good or bad, trusting or mistrusting, body-self; the internalization of impulse control, the establishment of sex role identity, and toward the end of the preoperational stage, the incorporation of a renunciation of desire role. With all of this accomplished, and with the rise of concrete operational thought, the way is prepared for conventional morality.

This stage is called conformist by Loevinger and good boy orientation by Kohlberg. There is a clear internalization of rules and good and bad roles, but these are understood in an overly literal way due to the concrete nature of the thought process. Sex roles are clearly internalized and adhered to with a vengeance. While persons at this level are capable of genuine reciprocity, this is typically extended only to a narrow in-group. Hostility is directed at various out-groups who, in a sense, are still conceptualized within the older levels of morality.

The conformity, stereotyped and simplistic understanding of roles (boy-girl and good-bad are the main ones), and banal conception of feeling all stem from the characteristics of concrete operational thought and from the repression or dissociation with which the crises of earlier childhood are resolved. Insofar as the years of middle childhood are a "latency period" —a time without demands for sexual and other forms of adult performance —then repression is a more or less normal phenomenon. A lack of awareness of inner life, feeling, and conflict is characteristic of the large number of persons who never progress beyond this level of development.

Toward the end of this period, concrete operational thinking begins to give way to the greater complexity of formal operational thought. Conventional morality becomes more differentiated, progressing to what Kohlberg terms the "authority and social order maintaining orientation." Conceptual complexity allows the individual to move beyond a stereotyped playing of roles. Morality is still largely tied to the group or the group's rules, however.

With the onset of formal operational thought, post-conventional morality and more complex ego levels become possible though, as has been stressed several times, it does not guarantee development to these levels. Kohlberg distinguishes two stages within the post-conventional level, a "contractual or legalistic orientation" and a "conscience or principle orientation." The first of these corresponds to Loevinger's conscientious stage. The capicity to introspect—for thought to become the "object" of reflection—makes possible a truly internalized morality. There is a marked shift from behavior, rules, and social roles sanctioned by the group to self-evaluation and self-criticism. Formal operational thought brings with it a decentering from the concrete present. The conscientious person is preoccupied with the abstract qualities of himself and others as opposed to material or tangible properties such as size, in-group or out-group membership, and outward signs of status and wealth.

As the individual moves into the post-conventional level there is the usual tendency to overdo things; in establishing a morality that moves beyond the definitions of one's immediate group one easily becomes self-centered again, albeit in an abstract or principled way. An awareness of principle may become the demand for strict adherence to principle. The autonomous and integrated stages, described by Loevinger, refer to a more tempered equilibrium. At the autonomous stage, identifications and principled thought are well-established. Impulse control is no longer a pressing issue; rules and social sanctions are, in one form or another, well internalized. But there is a heightened awareness of conflict, both inner and outer. Preoccupation is with coping with conflicting duties, allegiances, and inner needs. Conflict certainly exists at all earlier stages but, until this level, it tends to be avoided or projected onto others. The intolerance of out-groups, characteristic of the conformist-good boy or conventional levels, and the moral demands and condemnations found at the conscientious and early principled stages, are surpassed. The autonomous person not only shows greater awareness of conflict within himself, within others, and between himself and others, but he becomes more tolerant of such conflicts and differences.

Development to the higher stages requires an openness to experience and change well into the adult years. High levels of anxiety, insecurity, dissociation, and defensiveness all work against such openness and advanced development. Autonomous functioning grows out of such experiences as marriage, parenthood, and the negotiation of adult life's earlier hurdles, such as college, job, and career. It benefits from long moratoria and disengagement from fixed social roles and positions.

The final level described by Loevinger—the integrated stage—has no parallel in Kohlberg's theory. At this level, the individual progresses beyond an awareness of conflict to acceptance; beyond toleration of differences to a deep valuing of views and ways of life other than one's own.

This completes an integrative review of the stages of cognitive, moral and ego development. These stages, together with the earlier account of core conflicts and identification, call our attention to the cyclical nature of conflict and conflict resolution at ever higher levels of differentiation and integration. For example, the child makes an initial resolution of the conflict between aggression and its control during the stage of emerging autonomy and negativism when he is functioning at a beginning level of preoperational thought. This first internalization of an impulse controlling role leads to a morality of obedience and punishment and an opportunistic conception of self and interpersonal relations. The growth of concrete operational thinking—and expanding experience with peers—force a reorganization which, in turn, results in a morality of group conformity and a materialistic, in-group conception of self and interpersonal relations. Adolescence brings with it formal operational thinking and the impending final move toward independence which, in turn, may bring about further reorganizations in the conceptions of self and others, and the move toward principled moral reasoning. Not only aggression, but all the central areas are cyclically reorganized as development makes new experiences, skills, and more complex cognitive modes available.

A cyclically expanding, progressive development is characteristic of all the theories—Piaget's, Kohlberg's, and Loevinger's—that we have been considering. Consideration of the similarities, and one major difference, will bring to a close this summary discussion. First, the similarities.

All these theories are developmental; all describe an inevitable sequence of stages. Each stage is more complex than the previous one, each is a transformation of what existed before in a more complex, differentiated form. A process of decentering and of increasingly broadened perspectives is common to the progression from lower to higher stages in all the theories. One important example is the ability to hold past, present, and future in mind, which is characteristic of the higher stages and contrasts with the moment by moment or present-centered orientation of earlier levels.

When considering cognitive development, we saw how each stage began with egocentrism and how reality confronted the initial over assimilative tendency, forcing accommodation, decentering and an eventual equilibrium at that level. The process is then repeated at the next stage, but in a cognitively more complex, differentiated form. This same progression characterizes development as a whole. The overall movement from lower to higher stages is one from a narrow, egocentric perspective, to an increasingly decentered viewpoint. Cognitive, moral, and ego development all share these developmental characteristics. Moral and ego stages are dependent on cognitive development. Obviously, we have not been examining three separate or distinct forms of development which just happen to go on at the same time. The three are different facets of one general process. If one is interested in intellectual development one focuses attention on problems such as conservation while if one is interested in moral or ego development one studies thinking during dilemmas or conceptions of interpersonal relations. The general features of cognitive development—egocentrism and decentering, assimilation-accommodation, broadening perspectives—underlie all the theories. The differences arise from their special focus.

The major difference can best be stated this way: purely intellectual development occurs faster and the attainment of higher stages is more certain. Moral and ego development lag behind intellectual development and the attainment of higher stages is much less certain. For example, few adults are fixated at preoperational or even concrete operational levels of thought. Barring extreme circumstances such as genetic deficiencies or brain injury, many persons extend their formal operational thinking into the intellectual sphere. Not so with moral reasoning or ego level. Many adults remain at the middle levels and it is only a small minority who attain the principled or integrated stages. What this indicates is that attaining the formal operational level is necessary for the higher moral and ego levels, but it is not sufficient. You cannot reason in a principled manner nor reach an autonomous or integrated ego level without formal operational thought, but having such thought does not guarantee that you will reach these levels.

Two general factors can be noted as the cause of this lag between intellectual and moral-ego development. The first is the greater tangibility of experience in the intellectual area. The data necessary to understand problems such as conservation are physcial objects and substances which can be seen, touched, tasted, listened to, and manipulated. The data in the moral-ego areas are people interacting with each other, one's own ideas and fantasies and the inferences one draws about the ideas and fantasies of other persons. This is much more difficult to put one's finger on—to apprehend in a direct way—because it is, by its very nature, less tangible. Thus, an understanding of physical reality occurs first both in the development of every child, who begins at the sensorimotor level, and in the history of the human race. It is no accident that man's conquest of nature preceded his understanding of himself, that physical science preceded psychology and sociology or that, even today, our technological competence outruns our skill at understanding people and working out harmonious, just, and moral living arrangements.

The second factor accounting for the lag between intellectual and moral-ego development is the greater conflict involved in the latter. Physical reality does not fight back: rocks, water or molecules don't care if we manipulate them nor do they try and maintain their freedom or manipulate us in turn. Our fellow human beings do. The substance of moral development is man's relations with his fellow creatures, the tempering of selfishness, the renunciation of impulse, the control of aggression, and the comprehension of one's place in the wider social community. The human instinctual tendencies of anxiety, aggression, and sensuality make this a process of inevitable conflict and difficulty. And it is the involvement of such instincts and conflicts which makes moral development or the attainment of higher ego levels so much more difficult; which causes development in these areas to lag behind intellectual development, to fixate, and to regress.

chapter nine

Adolescence

The late childhood years are a time of calm stability; of life free from internal conflict. This is especially true for children in stable societies or for those who are not subject to excessive stress. Many Americans can recall a carefree, happy period when they were not exposed to strife and were unaware of the world's evils. Such memories probably overemphasize the happy side of childhood, but nevertheless capture an essential mood of the period.

The child has achieved a state of personal and social equilibrium characterized by well-integrated interpersonal skills, a comfortable morality of in-group conformity, and the relative absence of demands for sexual performance and independence. In a sense, he has mastered a childhood

---

identity; he has become accomplished at being a child. But life is not meant to remain so peaceful.

The calm of late childhood gives way to the upheaval of adolescence just as the earlier security of infancy gave way to the emergence of childhood. This upheaval arises when the equilibrium of late childhood is disrupted by changes in body, mind, and social demands. Like a political revolution, the changes of adolescence are brought on by conditions of great internal necessity. This is a time of intense feeling, sensual arousal, anger, anxiety, and rapidly changing moods. The threat posed to the *status quo* produces change and resistance to change. Conflicts from earlier stages are revived and can be worked through again at new levels. As Bob Dylan's lyrics remind us, the adolescent feels cut off from childhood and home; he is an "unknown" in the sense of having lost the childhood identity he knew well; he is likely to feel adrift "like a rolling stone," searching for a new way of defining himself and his life.

Societies differ widely in the demands they place on children and adolescents. In some preindustrial societies the assumption of an adult role begins in late childhood, with marriage and adult career more or less settled by the mid-teens. Societies such as ours make far fewer adult demands on children, and prolonged schooling often delays the official entry into adulthood until the twenties. Although there are some universal features to adolescence, the opportunities, conflicts, dangers, and levels of thought to be discussed are mainly those typical of modern societies whose advanced technologies and prolonged schooling occasion a relatively long delay between the onset of puberty and the assumption of adult status.

Adolescence begins when the child's body and mind spurt ahead to new levels. The growth and advances, as well as the conflicts and problems, result from rapid change in the physical and cognitive spheres. Bodily changes include the growth to adult size, the emergence of adult sexual characteristics, and the attendant upsurge in aggressive and sexual motivation. Cognitively, the adolescent becomes capable of formal operational thought which enables him to introspect and to encompass the meaning of his emerging adult status. These changes initiate a major—perhaps *the* major—transformation of personality. Beginning at this time and continuing into early adulthood, and sometimes beyond it, the person reworks and reintegrates all that has gone before into a new level of organization. The core areas of conflict are rearoused in new forms commensurate with the new physical and cognitive capacities.

As the person works his way through the opportunities and conflicts of the period he creates an adult identity. Morality develops to new levels and a particular level of ego development is achieved. The adolescent years do not mark the end of these developments; this is the period when they begin and during which the major shape of the processes is set. Later life stages such as marriage, the raising of children, middle and old age, all bring with them characteristic opportunities and conflicts and all affect the course of moral and self-development. But there is a sense in which adolescence represents the last great upheaval. There is nothing in later life to compare with the extensive, almost revolutionary, changes from child to adult body and from concrete to formal operational thinking. It is perhaps more accurate to view later developments as extensions and concluding stages of a process begun during adolescence.

A NEW MIND IN A NEW BODY

Changes in the body are the obvious outward signs of adolescent development and most earlier accounts have placed great stress on such factors as physical growth or the hormonal changes of puberty in accounting for adolescent upheaval. Although such changes are important, their significance can only be understood within the context of cognitive developments which allow the adolescent to conceptualize what happens to his body in new ways. Let us look at these interrelated physical and cognitive developments.

Physical Changes

Adolescence begins with a spurt of physical growth that is more or less rapid in different children. Beginning at approximately the age of twelve, the child gains height and weight and, within a few years, has reached his or her adult size. In addition to sheer growth, hormonal changes bring about adult sexual capacity along with secondary sexual characteristics. Menstruation begins for girls, the hips enlarge, breasts swell, and pubic hair appears. Boys show large increases in physical strength. For example, studies (Dimock, 1953) have shown that boys are twice as strong at sixteen as they were at twelve. Secondary sexual changes in boys also include the appearance of body and pubic hair and beard. For both boys and girls, the hormonal changes and appearance of secondary sexual characteristics are accompanied by a reawakening of sexual feelings and an upsurge in masturbation.

The changes in body size and shape, the onset of menstruation and increase in masturbation mean different things to different children; their impact is filtered through individual meaning systems. Such changes can be pleasurable or threatening depending on the structure of the child's self and the social context. Let me present some examples.

A number of studies have demonstrated wide individual differences in the age of onset and speed with which adult size and sexual capacity is reached. (See, for example, the work on early and late maturing adolescents; Jones, 1957; Jones 1965.) One's own body has, since early infancy, been the locus of self and a source of familiar security. As it changes, one's conception of self or "self-image" must accommodate. Gradual change is often easier to deal with, especially when others in the social world are undergoing the same changes. Thus, normal children gain approximately four to six pounds a year from age two to ten and, with a few exceptions, growth and size differences are not sources of stress during this period. About two years before puberty, girls begin to gain eleven pounds and grow three to four inches a year while boys, who begin later, gain thirteen to fourteen pounds and grow four to five inches during each adolescent year. This big spurt of growth threatens one's self-image by its very rapidity. What is more, differential onset and growth rate is likely to put the adolescent out of phase with his contemporaries. For example, the early-maturing girl may suddenly find herself with a woman's body, menstruating and sexually mature while her friends are still children. Or the late-maturing boy may find himself small and physically inadequate compared to his bigger and stronger male peers. Studies of early-maturing boys, on the other hand, show that they are advantaged in the peer culture and that this advantage carries over into the adult years. Their greater size and strength gives them special status among the other boys. Such dislocations —which lead to feelings of inferiority or superiority, to social backwardness or social accomplishment—are common due to the very rapidity of adolescent development. Let us examine some related examples.

Menstruation is one of those striking physical events that signals a major change in psychological development; in this case the change from girl-child to woman-adult. The way in which the young girl reacts to the onset of menstruation will depend on what this important event means to her as well as the wider meaning of womanhood, sexuality, becoming an adult and a person like her mother. If a girl has repeatedly seen her mother treat menstruation as something unspeakably dirty, or as a painful burden that women must bear, she is likely to react to the onset of her own menstrual period with some foreboding. On the other hand, the girl may look forward to becoming a woman; she may wish to have children and become a mother herself. For a girl such as this, menstruation may be accepted as a normal process which signals her entry into a desirable stage.

Masturbation is extremely common, especially in adolescent boys, and, like menstruation, is reacted to in a variety of ways. The child who has come to associate sensual stimulation with anxiety—who has internalized a severe and rigid renunciation of the desire role—is fated to struggle ambivalently with his emerging sexuality. Masturbation often becomes an important symbol in this struggle with the boy making vows to stop, giving in to his desire for pleasure, and feeling guilty, dirty, and weak afterward. At the other extreme, the child may accept masturbation as a normal form of pleasure during the period prior to heterosexual relations. Social attitudes are extremely important, of course. There are societies which rarely speak openly about the subject and cultures in which children are encouraged to masturbate.

The attainment of adult size and strength brings an upsurge in competence and aggressiveness. The adolescent becomes increasingly able to do the things adults do; to engage in activities long the subject of his envious fantasies. As was the case with emerging sexuality, growing competence and aggressiveness may be more or less caught up in conflict. For the child who views his or her father or mother as a rival, conflict may be intensified to dangerous proportions. If a child has come to feel anxious about his anger (has internalized a severe and rigid "impulse-controlling role") then rivalrous, aggressive, or angry feelings can lead to guilt, inhibition, and self-hatred. On the other hand, many boys are able to throw themselves into aggressive-competitive play with a clear conscience. All of the above examples illustrate the manner in which the growth and changes of adolescence can be understood only within a context of meaning and cognition, of past history and current social reality.

The physical changes of adolescence refocus concern on the body as the center of identity. During infancy, thought and action are centered on the body; sensorimotor egocentrism makes the first sense of self a body-self. With advances in development, additions are made to this core of identity. Cognitive skills, social roles, and internalized values are all acquired. Throughout development, however, the body remains central to identity. An important implication of this fact is that major changes in one's body—whether these are caused by injuries, disfigurements, or spurts of growth—threaten the security of a known self. Anxiety is aroused by any change in identity whether this is a change in cognitive skill or social role. In adolescence, all these areas (cognitive, social, and physical) undergo change. The adolescent may spend a good deal of time looking in the mirror, attempting to create an attractive figure or a muscular physique. Clothes, dress, make-up, affected sloppiness, and the like all attest to this concern with the outward manifestations of self.

Along with this focus, cognitive changes begin which, eventually, will enable the adolescent to transcend the equation of self with body and outward appearance. The disequilibrium of adolescent change creates its own motivation; it impels the person to strive toward a new state of equilibrium in which the various aspects of body and mind are reorganized into a new whole; in which a new, adult identity is created. Let us turn, now, to a consideration of the changes in thought which make this possible.

Cognitive Changes

The major contribution to our understanding of the cognitive changes of adolescence comes from Piaget; especially from his concluding chapter in *The Growth of Logical Thinking from Childhood to Adolescence*. Earlier accounts of adolescence stress physical and sexual changes as the prime sources of stress and upheaval. Some earlier psychologists sensed that adolescence was not simply a matter of physical-sexual change, but had difficulty articulating what they observed, lacking a coherent theory to describe the different stages of thought. I will draw heavily on Piaget's work in what follows, focusing on those aspects of formal operational thinking most pertinent to adolescent personality development.

Formal Operations. A brief description of formal operational thought has been given in the preceding chapter and needs, here, to be somewhat expanded. Formal operations differ from the concrete operational thought of the preceding period in three major ways. The child, thinking within the concrete operational mode, is tied to concrete reality, oriented to the present and essentially incapable of thinking about his own thought. The adolescent, operating within the formal operational mode, can think abstractly, concerns himself with past and future as well as the present, and is capable of making his own thought the object of reflection.

The child is centered on reality as he knows it. He can think about those things he has had experience with but has little ability to construct imaginary possibilities. Children can deal with hypotheses, indeed they often push hypotheses, such as the belief that their parents "don't know everything," to extremes. But hypotheses tend to be treated in a literal or concrete way rather than as creations of the mind which are arbitrary and subject to modification. In addition to this literalness, the child has trouble dealing with more than two classes, relations, or dimensions at one time. When he organizes a problem or does create a hypothesis, he is likely to accept it as true, rather than recognize it as a possibility whose truth must be validated against reality. Where the child organizes and deals with the reality present before him, the adolescent deals with possibilities and then tests these out against reality to establish their validity.

Piaget and Inhelder describe a series of experiments which demonstrate the differences between concrete and formal operational thinking. This work is a bit complicated and I will just present one brief example here. In this experiment, children and adolescents are presented with a group of rods that vary in length and are made of different kinds of metal. Their task is to determine the effects of length and type of metal on the flexibility of the rods. This problem requires that hypotheses about two qualities or dimensions be entertained at the same time. In addition, in order to arrive at an adequate solution, the individual must deal with imaginary possibilities; he must extrapolate from the rods available to him in various hypothetical directions.

Problems such as this are extremely difficult for the child who is confined to concrete operational thought since the rods before him are all metal and all of some real length—he has difficulty thinking about them in any other way. With formal operations, however, the adolescent is capable of considering all the varying possibilities of length and metal. He can then test his hypotheses by comparing the flexibility of rods of the same length, by varying metals, in order to study the effect of type of metal, or by varying lengths, with metal constant, to study the effects of length. He can, in other words, manipulate his hypotheses and compare them with reality.

By observing children at different ages with a variety of problems such as these, Piaget and Inhelder have shown the consistent differences between concrete and formal operational thinking. Most of these examples come from the area of logical problem solving; the children are presented with tasks, such as the rod-flexibility problem, which lend themselves to a kind of scientific hypothesis testing. The abstract quality of formal operational thought is not confined to such examples, however; once established, it permeates the adolescent's personal and emotional life as well. As an example, consider the concept of parents.

To the concrete operational child the concept is dominated by his experiences with his own parents. To be sure, he possesses a broader concept that includes the parents of other children; but most important for him are his parents as he knows them—whether he experiences them as loving or rejecting, nice or mean, better or worse than the parents of a friend. With the onset of formal operations, the adolescent can envision the wider possibilities of parenthood. He constructs ideal categories of parents as they should be, or might be and then evaluates his real parents against these ideals. This may, and often does, lead to profound disappointment with his only too real parents, or to attempts to reform their far from ideal characteristics. His ability to deal with ideals and possibilities illustrates the abstract nature of adolescent thought.

An orientation to the future, the second major difference between concrete and formal operations, is closely related to the abstract quality of adolescent thought. The contemplation of possibilities, of ideals, of how things might be, all involve a suspension of present reality. Although the child can project into the future to a certain extent, for the most part his thought is centered on the present. The adolescent breaks free from this constriction and can imagine future possibilities which then influence his present thought and action. The logical problem solving that Inhelder and Piaget describe involves such manipulation of future possibilities. But, of greater importance, is the effect of a future orientation on the adolescent's social role taking. For Piaget, the major defining features of adolescence are formal operational thought and the taking of adult roles. The adolescent projects himself into the future as professional, mother, power seeker, artist, husband, and so on. These projections then play a central part in shaping his adult identity.

Breaking free from a present-centered orientation has other effects as well. Changes in moral reasoning and ego level, described in the preceding chapter, involve progression to a wider time perspective. The principled thought that becomes possible in adolescence requires a contemplation of the long-range effects of one's actions. Both the ability to think abstractly and a wider time sweep broaden the adolescent's perspective. He can see the world and himself in more ways, with more possibilities through time.

The final difference between concrete and formal operations involves a kind of second order thinking; Piaget terms it second-degree operations or operations to the second power. This is *introspection,* the ability to think about one's own thoughts; to mentally manipulate one's own ideas and hypotheses. This is what the adolescent is doing when he juggles hypothetical possibilities in solving problems such as the rod-flexibility task. Thought itself becomes the object of further thought. Introspection opens a whole new mental world to the adolescent. A heightened awareness or consciousness, both about self and the world, arises from this new introspective ability. The adolescent's preoccupations, his grand plans, his brooding around like a Dostoyevsky character, his attempts to define the meaning of life, all these, and more, result from thought turned in on itself.

To sum up: the onset of abstract, future-oriented, introspective thinking constitutes a "new mind" which, like the adolescent's "new body", destroys the stable equilibrium of childhood and sets the stage for a transformation within the new structure of formal operations. Having outlined the changes in body and mind that bring about the upheaval of adolescence, let us now look at some of the central issues of the period in greater detail.

Feelings and Ideas

It is worth stressing that physical, sexual, cognitive, and emotional aspects of adolescence all develop simultaneously and influence each other. Many previous accounts have emphasized one to the neglect of the others. For example, the dominant place of feeling, emotion or affect has led some writers to underemphasize the cognitive developments discussed in the preceding section. A common reaction to Piaget's account of the role of formal operations might be something like, "that's all very interesting, and it helps in understanding such matters as the solving of logical problems, but what is really important in adolescence are the intense emotions and drives. Don't talk to us about the adolescent's intellect—tell us about his sexual drives, his anxieties, his feelings!" Another version of this stance is found in those psychoanalytic writers who attempt to explain the major features of the period in terms of the increase in sex drive occasioned by puberty. These views are not wrong; rather, they are based on an incomplete understanding of the interrelations of emotion, thought, and body. As the earlier model of instinct indicated, there is no way that emotion or drive can manifest itself except through existing mental structures, just as there are no feelings or ideas floating around unattached to bodies. For the sensorimotor infant, emotion is entwined with actions and body in a relatively simple way. For the concrete operational child, emotion is centered in his child's body and is involved with action in the present. For the adolescent, emotion—sometimes of the most intense sort—is aroused by rapid physical changes which are perceived within the structure of formal operational thought. The adolescent has intense feelings about his new body *and* about his ideals, grand plans, and future roles. Formal operations makes this possible since it allows the adolescent to think about his own thoughts. Some examples will illustrate the interaction of body, thought, and feeling.

Love. Sexual and bodily changes certainly have a good deal to do with the reawakening of romantic desires during adolescence. Along with these, one finds a new way of conceptualizing love and sexuality.

Adolescents are frequently in love with love; they spend a good deal of time immersed in romantic fantasies. As Piaget notes,

> ...what distinguishes an adolescent in love from a child in love is that the former complicates his feelings by constructing a romance or by referring to social or even literary ideals of all sorts. This reflects...the general tendency of adolescents to construct theories and make use of the ideologies that surround them. (Inhelder and Piaget, 1958, p. 336)

For the sensorimotor infant, love is attachment, holding, looking, and cuddling; for the child it is the concrete literalism—the affections and jealousies —of his newly grasped sex role; and for the adolescent, love becomes a romance in which a hypothetical, idealized, future relationship is constructed. Needless to say, all of these "loves" have common features— sensorimotor love and concrete jealousies persist into adulthood—and sensual pleasure is a component of all forms. Similarly, specific conflicts and anxieties may continue throughout development. But the love of formal operational thought is initially taken by the adolescent as something wonderfully new and he spends much time experimenting with it. Adolescent love exemplifies the confluence of body and sexual changes, social opportunities for a new kind of relationship with the opposite sex, and a new mode of conceptualization which brings together all of these factors.

Independence. As Piaget repeatedly stresses, adolescence is a time when the possibility of assuming adult roles is central. With the attainment of physical maturity and formal operations, the adolescent views himself as an equal with adults. His ability to project into the future enables him to act as if he had already achieved the independence he envisions. Along with this goes a new, abstract version of the perennial war of the generations. The two-year-old exaggerates his independence by saying "no" to everything, the child by disavowing babyish habits. For the adolescent, the struggle is the same, but it is phrased in a more abstract language.

Independence necessitates breaking free from the remnants of childhood and this many adolescents attempt to do with a vengeance. "The trouble with our parents," one adolescent remarked, "is that they knew us as children." What the parents knew—their expectations and all that is embodied in the old, dependent relationship—must be fought and resisted. The adolescent may resent complying with his parents' smallest request, not because he is lazy, but because compliance symbolizes their control over him and he must fight against such symbols of a past he is trying to escape. In some extreme instances, the young person may feel that the only way he can define his independence is by hating his parents or by disavowing all that they believe in.

What is true in the areas of love and independence holds for other areas as well. Old relationships and conflicts are reworked within the new, abstract, future-oriented, introspective framework. The exaggerated way in which this is sometimes done brings us to our next topic.

An Egocentrism of Ideas. As the adolescent acquires his new skills he pushes them to their limits. The ability to think abstractly is pushed to an uncompromising idealism; independence from parents becomes so exaggerated that the adolescent may not wish to associate with them at all; future plans become grandiose schemes for new religions, scientific discoveries, or works of art. In short, the adolescent takes each newly discovered skill, which seems unique (and it is *to him*) and pushes it to its limits. In Piaget's terms this is an "overassimilation" of the world to oneself without due regard for reality and without the balance of accommodation. The overassimilation of adolescence leads to an egocentrism of ideas just as corresponding overassimilations during earlier periods led to earlier forms of egocentrism. This tendency is so pervasive throughout personality development, and so important, that it deserves further comment here.

The egocentrism of ideas involves an inflation of the adolescent's sense of self. He acts as if—or, more accurately, *thinks*—he has discovered the world of abstract thought for the first time. His schemes for reforming his life and the world, for doing away with what seem to him the senseless customs that encumber his parents, for living his life in a new way, are new ideas to him and are taken as unique, if not to himself, then at least to the small group in which such ideas are shared. The reason why these ideas seem unique lies in their contrast with the concrete operational thought of the preceding period.

For the concrete operational child, the world is as it is. His concrete schemes lead him to see things in a literal, present-oriented fashion. As a part of this concrete structuring of the world he tends to view other people as either like himself, on the one hand, or as members of an out-group on the other. Since he does not engage in introspection and has little awareness of his own thought processes, he quite naturally doesn't attribute such awareness to others. Recall that the moral reasoning of this period is characterized by conformity to external rules and a materialistic, in-group definition of good and bad and of right and wrong. Goodness or power are easy for the child to determine, he merely sees if the other person is rewarded by in-group approval or is big, or attractive, or wealthy, or successful. Questions about inner happiness or peace of mind do not exist at this level of thought. As formal operational thinking begins to take root, it initially develops in relation to the more obvious aspects of external reality. The adolescent moves onto the plane of abstract thinking, but only gradually extends such thinking to human relationships and moral issues. As Kohlberg's evidence shows, the higher levels of moral thought do not develop until late adolescence or early adulthood. What this means is that the young adolescent develops a set of inner structures for viewing the world abstractly, but he still perceives others, especially adults, as members of an out-group. This contributes to his sense that the ideals and other products of his introspection are uniquely his. The gradual discovery that others, perhaps even his own parents, have had similar ideals is a bit of hard reality that he will encounter later.

In sum, formal operational thought with its introspection and strongly felt ideas, provides a contrasting perspective with concrete operational thought, and this contrast contributes to the adolescent's egocentric over-assimilation of the world to his new point of view. At each new stage, egocentrism reemerges. The cycle of overassimilation ———→ confrontation with reality ———→ accommodation ———→ equilibrium, must be repeated once again.

As a final point, we should note that "reality" changes as development progresses. The sensorimotor egocentrism of the infant is confronted by the world of physical objects. The overassimilation of early and middle childhood is confronted by other people with their size, power, and contrary actions. The egocentrism of ideas characteristic of early adolescence is destined to confront the ideas of others. It is only a confrontation of this final sort that can lead to the higher levels of morality characterized by the ability to take the point of view of another person.

The tendency to overassimilate—the reemergence of egocentrism at each new developmental level—has its advantages as well as its dangers. Pushing a new skill or perspective to its limit is the person's way of seeing how far a new way of thinking, a new form of independence, or a new sex role will take him. Needless to say, such explorations involve the emotions connected with aggressive-dominance, sensual pleasure seeking, striving for competence, and the like. The full exploration of intuitive thought or of one's newly discovered masculinity or femininity, or of abstract idealism, is facilitated by a temporary abandonment of the constraints of reality. This is like the creative phase of any endeavor in which one ignores practicalities, criticism, or social constraints in order to give full reign to new ideas, creative approaches and innovations. And, just as the products of the creative phase must subsequently be honed by a critical reworking, so the initial overassimilation of each developmental phase must accommodate to reality. For example, it is common for adolescents to formulate life plans of a grandiose sort, though they typically do not communicate these to adults, confining them to private fantasies, diaries, or shared confidences with like-minded friends. Inhelder and Piaget report a study of the evening reveries of adolescents which showed that "...the most normal students—the most retiring, the most amiable—calmly confessed to fantasies and fabulations which several years later would have appeared in their own eyes as signs of pathological megalomania (1958, p. 344)." These included a novel written in secret, plans to revolutionize the theatre, and an attempt to reconcile science and religion. Such grandiose life plans show the adolescent pushing his new abstract thought to its limits. Wishes to reform the world typically place the adolescent reformer right in the center, reaping the glory of his efforts. Such grand life schemes play an important role in the eventual direction taken by the person, but to do so they must accommodate with reality. That is, the initial overassimilation of adolescent idealism allows a creative exploration of possible adult roles, careers, accomplishments, and life plans. In order for such creative ideas to be more than idle fantasies, the adolescent must attempt to carry them out in the social world. As he does so, he finds that the world does not so easily assimilate to his wishes. Actual accomplishment requires both assimilation *and* accommodation.

Overassimilation at the onset of a developmental period allows the person to explore his new skills to their fullest. An inability to do this is one of the dangers—overconstriction—that interferes with the full development of new potentialities. On the other side are the dangers of extremisim and of too little contact with reality. Let us turn now to a consideration of these dangers and their affects on adolescent development.

SOME DANGERS
IN ADOLESCENT DEVELOPMENT

The dangers and difficulties in adolescent development can take many forms though the underlying villains are usually the same: anxiety and the related forces which lead to dissociation. Taking advantage of the new opportunities of mind and body necessitates giving up old roles, old ways of relating or thinking; in short, giving up one's childhood identity. The experimental overassimilation of early adolescence involves trying on new roles, pushing romantic or aggressive or competence related fantasies to their extremes. All of this, of course, threatens security; not only the security derived from the position of child-in-the-family but the security derived from an established identity. The reawakening of aggressive independence or sensual desire may rearouse whatever anxiety and conflicts were associated with these areas during earlier periods. New adult roles will rearouse the ambivalence of identifications with parents.

Change and anxiety make adolescence a time when certain dangers manifest themselves. Drawing on Anna Freud's (1958) insightful analysis, let me discuss three of these dangers: extremism, overconstriction, and escape from reality.

Extremism

As the previous discussion has shown, a certain amount of extremism is natural in adolescence. The testing of new roles and new ways of thought is a healthy and necessary form of experimentation. But the breakdown of childhood identity may arouse excessive anxiety in certain young persons; anxiety which can motivate a flight to a premature, extremist identity. Independence-dependence, sensuality-renunciation, aggression-submission, any or all of these may be caught up in extremist solutions.

Conflict over dependency sometimes leads to an exaggerated assertion of independence. The adolescent may literally flee from his family, completely breaking off the relationship. This is most likely to occur when anger and disappointment are prominent and closeness or affection lacking. More common is a turning away from the parents to other models, such as revolutionary heroes, who seem to possess all those virtues that the parents lack. Or the adolescent, resenting his dependency, but too insecure to leave, may remain at home as an "inconsiderate boarder." Others can only express hatred and contempt for their parents; as if there is a danger in admitting to even a little love or dependent need.

Underlying these exaggerated forms of independence one finds anxiety stemming from earlier parent-child interactions. The young person may be so afraid of *not* achieving independence, or so insecure about separating himself, that even a hint of dependency signals the danger of being drawn back to a childish position. He may thus overcontrol his dependency, protesting excessively that he is *not* a child and does not need his parents in any way.

A different form of extremism is seen in certain adolescents whose major conflicts and anxieties are aroused by the budding sexuality of the period. Ascetic solutions are often sought when conflicts are aroused in this area. Here we find the young person who denies himself pleasures, fights battles against his urge to masturbate, and evolves religious and life plans based on puritanical ideals. The underlying danger is one of giving in too readily to emerging sensual impulses. It is typically the case that earlier experiences have led to the connection of anxiety with sensual pleasure. The rearousal of sensuality in adolescence arouses this anxiety and the extremes of asceticism represent attempts to control giving in to feared pleasures.

The arousal of sensuality can lead to hedonistic as well as ascetic extremes. Late adolescence often sees a questioning of seemingly senseless moral rules, along with experiments at living one's life free from the constrictions of such rules. Sexual experimentation, the use of drugs which promote various feelings, an abandonment of the work ethic, of career and middle-class goals, all may be part of a hedonistic extremism. One sees a related version of this pattern in the Raskolnikov syndrome, mentioned in the last chapter. Here, an awareness of the arbitrary nature of moral values, along with a heightened sensitivity to corruption, produces "moral regression"—an abandonment of conventional morality in favor of hedonistic gratification or "doing your own thing."

In Erikson's terms, the danger in this stage of the life cycle is one of "role confusion," of not knowing who one is. The young person is often impelled to rebel against parents and other symbols of authority, yet, paradoxically, he craves some authoritative model to identify with who will give a clear definition to his role in life. In part this model is supplied by the peer group which typically exaggerates those small ways—speech mannerisms, dress—in which *their* generation differs from the older members of society. But peers all suffer from the same insecurity and, although impelled to differentiate themselves from established authority, they also seek heroes and movements to identify with. As Erikson (1968) notes, these forces make adolescents, and adults who are still at an adolescent level of development, open to the lure of revolutionary movements. Such movements may be a very healthy way for the young person to engage his sympathies for the downtrodden, or they may produce a rigid adherence to an ideology that provides a ready-made identity, a secure new role that alleviates the anxiety of role confusion. The fixed beliefs and practices of certain movements, whether Fascist, Marxist, or, in an earlier time, Christian, define secure new ways of life; they provide ready-made identities for the person who seeks to abandon his childhood but cannot tolerate the insecurity of open experimentation with different roles. The revolutionary leader may become a substitute for the parents or other authorities the adolescent seeks to disavow, while revolution itself can become the vehicle for the war of generations—for expressing an exaggerated and aggressive independence.

Again, I must point out that breaking with parents, experimenting with new ideologies, new values, and new modes of life, are not pathological. On the contrary, they are important sources of innovation without which any society or person becomes stagnant. What is pathological is the extremity to which such tendencies may be carried in an attempt to disavow or disown dependent, sensual, or other anxiety-laden components of the personality. The adolescent who experiments with the different sides of his personality, being now an ascetic hermit, next a dependent child, and still later a father and husband—and who is free to carry each of these tendencies to their fantasied extremes—can eventually evolve a stable adult identity from these various experiments. On the other hand, the adolescent who must exaggerate independence to control a feared dependence, who must make a revolutionary break with parents because he fears becoming like them, or who flees into asceticism out of a fear of sex, is moving in potentially pathological directions that will prevent the exposure of anxiety-laden portions of himself to the accommodating forces of reality. What begins as extremism in the attempt to achieve a temporary security can become a permanent and one-sided identity. Out of such premature extremes are born perennial malcontents, self-denying neurotics, and those who seek the solutions of internal conflict solely in external causes.

Whether experimentation with extremes takes a healthy or pathological turn is strongly influenced by the social response it meets. This important topic will be reserved for a later section since I wish here to consider another danger from the adolescent years.

Overconstriction

A very different pattern is exhibited by those adolescents whose anxiety leads them to a premature stability. Where the extremist creates stability out of his rebellious independence—thus attempting to avoid the anxiety of an uncertain identity—the overconstricted adolescent creates stability by conforming too soon to what he assumes are socially acceptable adult roles. In the recurring conflict between freedom and authority, such persons have typically given in, or been crushed by, too much authority, internalized too early. For example, in the study cited earlier of the grandiose life plans of a class of early adolescents, Inhelder and Piaget report:

> There were only two members of the class who did not reveal any astounding life plans. Both were more or less crushed under strong "superegos" of parental origin, and we do not know what their secret daydreams might have been. (1958, p. 344)

Behind the overconstricted reaction one typically finds a good deal of anxiety over asserting oneself in any way that might mean standing up to, or defying, authority. Along with this, of course, may go the usual anxieties associated with adolescent disorganization.

The great danger of overconstriction is that it interferes with free experimentation. The person forces himself to fit some role; he tries to be what he assumes others want him to be. This blocks the experimentation with various roles of his own choosing which is necessary to the creation of an identity that combines both his own potentialities and the expectations of others. The overconstricted person too often submerges his own desires, and particularly angry or rebellious feelings, to the realm of secret dreams where they are not exposed to the accommodating effects of social interchange. As Anna Freud stresses; turmoil and conflict, wide swings of mood from depression to elation, shifting back and forth between rebelliousness and conformity, are all normal in adolescence. Their absence is pathological. Too much stability indicates a premature solidification of identity.

Escape from Reality

Many adolescents are uncomfortable in the social world; they feel clumsy with their new bodies, ashamed of their sexuality, and preoccupied with their introspections. Because of these factors, a number may shun social exchange; they escape from reality into fantasies of romantic, athletic, or social success. Like extremism and the search for stability, escape from reality is a normal aspect of adolescence. And, like these other tendencies, it may take on pathological proportions.

Escape from reality can become the most severe of all the dangers inherent in adolescent development. Although it is a normal aspect in the development of many young persons, those with the most intense social anxiety—those who are most conflicted and insecure over their emerging emotions and role possibilities—will be prone to escape into a world of dreams and fantasies. By doing so, they hope to escape the anxiety, fear, and pain that they expect will come from contact with other persons. But, all too often, such escape creates more problems than it solves.

Late childhood is a time when it is relatively easy to affect a normal exterior. The lack of demands for sexual performance or for intimacy, and the acceptability of a kind of crude conformity, all make it easy to control anxiety behind a mask of superficial social relations. Playing at social roles is the characteristic morality of the period and the child may be outwardly "good"—that is, he may make little trouble for parents and teachers—while in reality he is excessively passive and withdrawn from emotional relations. Other children, lacking sensitivity to inner states, may simply not notice those peers who live this way.

With the breakdown of childhood stability, the rearousal of sexual and aggressive feelings, the demands for independence, and the possibility and need for intimacy, anxiety returns. When its proportions become intense, and when the person has a history of dealing with anxiety and conflict by withdrawal into fantasy he turns, once again, to this pattern. In its most extreme form, withdrawal from reality may herald the onset of a schizoid way of life.

The skills of formal operational thinking are important in the elaboration of fantasy "solutions" to adolescent stress. The ability to deal in abstractions and future possibilities and, of course, the ability to treat one's own ideas as objects, all add significant new dimensions to what was, in earlier years, a simpler, preoperational version of fantasy. The adolescent can, in effect, take all of the external relationships that he is too fearful to face and enact them on an internal stage. Fantasies of grandeur unchecked by reality, masochistic suffering, hypochondriacal body symptoms, and other aspects of the private world all represent attempts to work out the problems of the period completely within oneself.

The use of drugs such as marijuana and LSD by young persons who are attempting to come to grips with the anxieties and conflicts of adolescence can be harmful precisely because these drugs facilitate an escape from social reality. I do not wish to enter the complex controversy over drug use; the evidence clearly shows that marijuana is not the evil substance that many thought it was, and it also seems clear that repressive legislation creates problems rather than solves them. I wish simply to stress that escape from the reality of other persons is a dangerous direction in adolescent development and that drugs which intensify fantasy states may all too easily facilitate this sort of escape. "Getting high" in a group may create an illusion of social interchange while, in fact, the participants are each turned in on their own fantasies.

Escape from reality may take many forms. There is the normal withdrawal that many adolescents engage in; temporary flights or "breaks" with reality; the escape of the drug culture; and, most extreme, the beginnings of a schizoid identity. In all these forms, an assimilation of reality to one's fantasied self outweighs accommodation of self to others. In cases where anxiety is intense, withdrawal can increasingly become a permanent way of life. As this happens, every approach to real others intensifies anxiety. What is more, such a pattern gives little real satisfaction—either sensual, loving, or that which comes from actual accomplishments. Escape from reality leads to a profound loneliness. The person sacrifices all in order to avoid the anxiety associated with interpersonal exchange, while it is only through such exchange that he can arrive at a satisfying adult identity.

Summary: Dangers of Adolescence

Extremism, overconstriction, and escape from reality have certain features in common. All arise when anxiety is unusually intense. All are attempts to seek an immediate respite from this anxiety and, because of the pressure for immediate or rapid solution, all prevent the person from facing uncertainty, exploring various role possibilities, and allowing initial overassimilations to be tempered by contact with others.

In the previous chapter, we saw a related process in the development of morality. Keniston has pointed out how development to post-conventional moral levels is facilitated by a prolonged delay in the assumption of adult roles. Conversely, individuals who assume responsibilities early have more invested in their new adult identities and are less likely to continue their development to advanced levels. Questioning of conventional values is a threat to their identity and such persons are resistant to development; they become stuck or fixated. The danger in extremism, overconstriction, or escape from reality does not inhere in these patterns themselves; in one form or another they may be found in all adolescents. The danger arises when such patterns solidify into an identity—when instead of experimentation they come to define what the young person *is*.

Each pattern, in its own way, leads the individual to dissociate certain aspects of himself. In extremism, the person may dissociate dependent and tender feelings behind an overstated, revolutionary independence. Or a sense that one is too much like a parent may lead to the playing out of its opposite side—for example, the minister's son who becomes an alcoholic or the professor's son who flunks out of college—in order to dissociate an inner likeness. In overconstriction, one dissociates the urge to break away; to be different, to explore new possibilities, to rebel. One closes off such dangerous possibilities behind a premature, caricatured version of adulthood. Flight from reality is, of course, the ultimate dissociation. In its most extreme form, schizophrenia, the person dissociates himself from the world of reality.

As Laing (1960) points out, the schizoid person constructs a world in which he (or more accurately his fantasy "self") is experienced as real while his body becomes just a "thing," moving zombie-like through a world of dimly perceived others.

Dissociation in all these forms leads to developmental arrest; to unresolved conflicts which persist into later life. The full development of self necessitates exposure to social exchange. In order for the person to reach an equilibrium based on realistic accommodation, the anxiety associated with conflicted areas must be faced and dissociated feelings, ideas and identifications brought back within the compass of an active self. It is only in this way that development can proceed to new levels. When dissociation persists, the person develops unevenly; conflicts remain separated from the sense of self, making their presence known by the periodic appearance of anxiety or through symptom and defense.

Much of the preceding discussion is a bit abstract. Let me give a concrete example of a young man who, although neither real nor typical, exemplifies many of the features of adolescence we have been examining.

HOLDEN CAULFIELD

Studies of adolescence (Douvan and Adelson, 1966; A. Freud, 1958) show that adults can usually recall the events from this time of life. There is nothing comparable to the "amnesia" of early childhood; what is lost is the emotional intensity. We remember what we did as adolescents but not how ecstatic or awful we felt. One of the many excellent qualities of J. D. Salinger's novel *The Catcher in the Rye* is the way it captures the intensity of adolescent feeling. Thanks to Salinger's genius, we enter the world of Holden Caulfield, the novel's 16-year-old hero; we think and feel with him, perceiving people and the world through his eyes. If you haven't read *The Catcher in the Rye*—or reread it lately—do so before proceeding. The intensity of Holden's life will, of necessity, be lost in the following analysis.

Here is a bare outline of the major events in the novel: Holden, an extremely sensitive 16-year-old, is unable or unwilling to engage his intelligence in conventional ways and the novel begins with his flunking out of prep school for the third time. It is the day of the big football game, but Holden does not attend. What is more, he has just ruined a trip by the fencing team, for which he is manager, by losing the team's equipment.

He pays a goodbye visit to an old history professor who seems interested in him and concerned with his failure to apply himself. But, when the professor begins lecturing him, Holden becomes uncomfortable and withdraws behind a facade of shooting the bull. That is, he presents the professor with some platitudes and leaves at the earliest opportunity.

He returns to his dormitory room and finds that Stradlater, his handsome and athletic roommate, has a date with Jane, a girl Holden spent time
with during a previous summer. Holden remembers Jane as the child of an
unhappy homelife; in her innocence she would keep all the kings in the
back row during their checker games. Despite cause for jealousy, Holden
agrees to write an English paper for Stradlater. He writes about his dead
brother Allie's baseball mitt which had poems written on it. Allie, like the
Jane of Holden's memory, is a child-innocent. Thinking about him gives
Holden a few moments of pleasure. When Stradlater returns from the date
with Jane, however, Holden becomes increasingly agitated by his speculations about the sexual activity that may have occurred between them. He
attacks Stradlater and gets his nose bloodied in return.

Feeling terribly lonely and alienated from the school, the teachers,
and his peers, Holden leaves, late at night, for New York City. There follows a series of events during a period of approximately two days and nights
in the city. Though his parents live there Holden does not contact them,
fearing their reaction to his failure at still another school. He decides, instead, to stay in a hotel. He is continually preoccupied with girls and sex,
thinks of calling various ones on the phone, and even makes some calls, but
nothing much comes of this. At the same time, he is critical of his own
emerging sexual desires and questions the place of sex in male-female relations. He cannot reach any resolution on this point. For example, he arranges for a prostitute in his hotel, but when she appears he finds her more
depressing than sexy, gives her money and one of his typical lies (he has
had an operation and cannot have sex) and sends her away. She returns
with her pimp and asks for more money, which Holden refuses to pay.
They take the money and he provokes the pimp into hitting him.

The next day he arranges a date with Sally, who, of the different
women in the novel, is closest to a conventional girlfriend. He alternately
pets with her and tries to speak openly, revealing his dissatisfaction with
school and conventional adult life. As he does so, he becomes carried away
and proposes that they run off together. She reacts conservatively, recognizing the unrealistic nature of his plans; he becomes angered, precipitates a
quarrel by calling her "a pain in the ass" and leaves.

His feelings of depression and agitation intensify—he gets drunk that
night and begins to vacillate more wildly from one mood to another. He
seeks out his younger sister Phoebe who he feels capable of relating to in an
honest fashion.

After talking with her, he goes to the apartment of Mr. Antolini,
a former teacher. There follows an important incident. Mr. Antolini is one
of the few sympathetic adults in Holden's life. He is intelligent, interested in
Holden, and he attempts to speak seriously with him about life and Holden's
inability to engage himself. Following their conversation, Holden is finally

calm enough to go to sleep, but he awakes in a panic to find Mr. Antolini patting his head. Holden interprets this as a homosexual advance and flees the apartment.

He seeks out Phoebe again to tell her he is running away. During this period his depression becomes worse, he is particularly upset at seeing "fuck you" written on walls where Phoebe or other young children might notice it. Phoebe attempts to join him in his flight, but he decides to return home; and does so in a state of near-collapse. He is subsequently sent to a psychiatric institution of some sort from where the novel is related in retrospect.

So much for the events. Through all of this, Holden's mood swings from childlike and elated spoofing, to boredom, to nervous agitation, to depression. Wide swings of mood and feeling are, of course, typical in adolescence. In this, and other ways, Holden displays some of the representative features of the period. There is the preoccupation with sex and the difficulty reconciling physical sexual desire with the need for personal intimacy of a nonexploitive kind. There is the "new" adult body: Holden informs us that he has grown over six inches and has a patch of gray in his hair. There is the experimentation with new roles; he repeatedly plays at being an adult. And, his abstract cognitive skill is revealed as he judges people in terms of newly created ideals. Indeed, the clash between his ideals —his model of how the world *should be*—and his too accurate perception of the failure of real people to live up to these ideals, is a cause of much unhappiness. Let us look at this last point in more detail.

Phoniness and Adolescent Idealism

Holden is obsessed with phoniness. He sees little but pretense in the adults around him, in his roommates and acquaintances at school, in his admired older brother who has compromised himself by going to work for the movies, in almost everyone. In one respect, this shows the application of formal operational thought and a new moral level. Where the child sees people as they appear to be, the adolescent can judge them in terms of how they should be; he is sensitive to discrepancies between the ideal and the actual. When Holden ridicules the prep school and its teachers because the actuality of school life, as he experiences it, is discrepant from its advertised image, he is making the kind of moral judgment that is common when abstract thinking is pushed to its limits. Holden lives ·in a world of ideas and introspections; of sensitivity to the newly discovered meaning and nuances of human behavior. But his ideals and introspections are over-extended and unbalanced; they betray the egocentrism common to adolescence.

The list of the ways in which Holden's problems are typical would not be complete without mentioning his pervasive difficulty in moving toward an adult identity. His obsession with phoniness—for it does take on obsessive proportions—greatly complicates his search for an acceptable adult role. Holden rules out almost all of the adults in his life as models. His father is either absent or is a vague presence who will be angry at his failure at yet another school. The headmaster at the prep school and his colleagues and counterparts, are seen as phonies who play up to the rich parents. Mr. Antolini is "perverted." Holden's older brother D.B. is a writer who comes close to being an acceptable model, and English is the one subject Holden allows himself to pass. But even here, D.B. is judged to have sold out in terms of Holden's critical standards.

If Holden suffers from the typical problems of adolescence, he seems to have a specially serious case. Many persons his age are cynical in their judgment of the world, but Holden can find *no* acceptable adult model. Difficulty engaging oneself in active pursuits is common, but Holden does not let himself become involved in anything: he does not work at school, cannot sustain social or sexual relations with girls, is not athletic or musical, or involved in other nonacademic affairs, and even lacks those peer relationships that are often so helpful in getting through these difficult years. The specialness of his case requires a special explanation.

Alienation and Role Playing

Holden's feelings about others and himself are intensely *ambivalent.* He is both a cynical observer of the faults, foibles, and phoniness of the world, and a sympathetic fellow-sufferer. He cannot be with anyone, peer or adult, without noticing their phoniness. Stradlater is in love with his own good looks and, besides, keeps a dirty shaving kit, revealing that he is only clean and presentable on the surface. Sally seems to like Holden and is attractive, but, at the same time, he can't help noticing her affectations and wish to be noticed by prestigious others. The boys at the prep school have secret cliques; they discriminate against those of their fellows with poor complexions or whose personalities do not fit a narrow mold. Mr. Antolini, one of the few adults that Holden trusts, reveals (or so Holden thinks) perverted or homosexual tendencies. Holden notices the most minute actions with his cynical eye—how the old history professor picks his nose while pretending to rub it, or the way in which Mr. Antolini's intellectual wit is a trifle overdone.

His cynical perception is applied to himself; at least part of the time. He dislikes himself for joining the boyish discrimination of the prep school. If he is critical of Stradlater for sexually exploiting girls, he is continually at war with his own sexual thoughts and wishes. And if the world is filled with phonies there is a sense, as we shall see in a moment, in which Holden is the biggest phony of all.

There is another, positive side, to his feelings about others. When he is not with them, Holden can be quite sympathetic. The history professor and Mr. Antolini have their good qualities when Holden thinks about them from a distance. They are, after all, concerned for him out of genuine affection. The book ends with Holden's confession that he misses everybody—even Stradlater and the pimp who slugged him. He is torn between his need for closeness with others and his cynical judgments which continually block or interfere with the satisfaction of this need. Unable to resolve this conflict, unable to either attempt relationships or to isolate himself, he vacillates back and forth feeling terribly alienated all the while.

Holden is constantly playing roles, concealing his thoughts and feelings behind a mask of pretending, "shooting the old bull," and "fooling around." While some of this is common in adolescence, Holden is compelled to pretend in excessive ways. Other young persons in the novel play at being older than they are—Stradlater presents the image of big-man-on-campus and Sally affects a hypersophisticated manner—but their role playing is a part of their developing identities. One can see the nascent form of their adult selves in these adolescent experiments. Not so with Holden. His role playing has a much more *dissociative* quality to it; it is more like child's play; like pretense and outright lying. Consider some examples.

Throughout the novel Holden wears a red hunting cap, usually with the peak turned to the back, reminiscent of a child playing dress-up in his parent's clothing. He is constantly trying out bits and scraps of identity in a playful manner. He describes himself, jokingly, as a great liar and plays out scenes from movies, at one point pretending to be blind and, later, when the pimp has hit him in the stomach, going into a gangster routine in which he imagines himself shot and about to take revenge.

These small bits of role playing—of obvious pretending—are part of a much larger and less well-controlled pretense. When he meets adults he is compelled to go into an act. He lies to the old history professor, to a classmate's mother that he meets on the train, to the prostitute, to some young women he meets in a bar, and to others. With his new body and intelligence he has certain of the outward signs of adulthood, but becoming an adult in any real sense is something he cannot allow himself to do. For if the world is filled with phonies, Holden himself is the biggest phony. He is incapable of acting his age—of assuming an adult identity—except by the grossest sort of play-acting.

As he moves through the school and the city, he is faced with various paths to an adult identity; the paths of academic competence, of sexual relations, or of aggressive self-assertion. But he does not follow any of these.

He flunks out of school despite his intelligence because he cannot bring himself to do the required work. His several attempts at sexual relations are clearly unsuccessful. He cannot allow himself to engage in this very real form of adult action. In other ways he betrays the same pull toward failure in the adult world. He is unable to accept the interest or affection of those adults—the old history professor, Mr. Antolini—who wish to help him. So, along with Holden's exaggerated role playing and pretense goes a persistent self-defeating pattern, a self-inflicted form of failure and suffering. Such a pattern usually indicates a strong sense of guilt and, in a moment, we will consider some hypotheses about this.

Why is it so difficult for Holden to follow any of the paths leading to an adult identity? Why is he compelled to pretend and dissemble? Why must he fail and bring defeat on himself? The answers to these questions can best be approached by examining his view of childhood.

Children and Adults

What does Holden want to be? He clearly does *not* want to be another of the phony adults that he sees around him. What he *does* want to be is a "catcher in the rye," a goal whose importance Salinger asserts by making it the title of the book. Holden misremembers the line from the Robert Burns poem "if a body *meet* a body coming through the rye" as, "if a body *catch* a body." He describes a fantasy in which many little children are playing in a field of rye, with no adults present. Holden stands on the edge of a cliff and his job is to catch any of the children and prevent them from falling over. As he describes this he notes that it is "crazy," but he still feels it is the only job—the only adult identity—that appeals to him.

A most interesting and revealing life plan: he will become an adult in a world with no other adults. He is amongst children, yet not a child; but neither must he assume a responsible adult role. He need not discipline the children, nor teach them, nor act in any way like parent or model or authority. He is just a vague caretaker who protects but does not interfere with their innocent games.

The way Holden misremembers the line from Burns shows a related pull toward childhood—in this instance toward a concrete operational mode of thought. He distorts the line in the direction of concrete literalness —"if a body meet a body" becomes Holden "catching" bodies. And, of course, where the original suggests a romantic encounter between male and female, Holden distorts it to place himself in the asexual world of children.

Holden himself notes that this is an unrealistic life plan, even as an adolescent fantasy. The reason for its specialness and for Holden's despair must be sought in his dissociated view of childhood innocence.

If the world of adults makes Holden depressed, children and things childish give him his few moments of good feeling. Especially his younger sister and the memories of Allie, his dead younger brother. For example, when he sets out to write Stradlater's composition the usual topics do not interest him. Then he hits on the idea of Allie's baseball mitt which was covered with poems that Allie had put there to read while standing in the field. Holden gets a big kick thinking about Allie and his mitt and has no trouble writing the essay. Almost everything about his little sister Phoebe makes him feel good. When he does return home it is to talk with her, not his parents. He buys her a children's record and the mere thought of giving it to her fills him with joy. He meets a little girl in the park when he is looking for Phoebe and tightens her roller skate. Again he gets great pleasure from the interaction with her and, especially, from the direct, childish comments she makes. The little girl's comments "kill him" as does Phoebe with her diary and other childish fantasies. In fact, almost everything about Phoebe "kills him," a slang expression he uses to mean enjoyment but that also expresses the sense in which his ability to enjoy only those things associated with children is "killing him"—is a part of his self-destructive pattern.

There is, for Holden, a continuous contrast between the world of children—innocent, filled with good feeling, fun, and honest relationships —and the world of adults, which he sees as corrupt and phony. Children make him feel good, adults drive him to despair. This same equation applies to himself. His childish qualities—his fooling around and pretending, his red hat with the peak turned around, his memories of the innocent checker games with Jane—all these make him feel good. On the other hand, his emerging adult qualities—his sexual desires, his competitive anger, his new size and intellect—all these cause problems and bring forth unpleasant, agitated or depressed feelings. Perhaps the clearest example of this contrast is seen in his relations with girls and women.

There are several examples in the novel of relations with females in which Holden is quite comfortable, in which he feels good. There is, of course, Phoebe who is not only his sister (and hence ruled out as a romantic or sexual partner) but, more importantly, a child. There is a schoolmate's mother who sits next to Holden on the train. He finds her physically attractive though her age makes her somewhat unavailable. Holden is compelled to go into one of his lying acts with her, however, and enjoys the interchange. He meets a nun whom he finds quite sympathetic, not a phony, and so on. Being a nun, she is in a safe category; she is, like Holden, a drop-out from the conventional world of adult sexuality and competition.

Contrasting with these ineligible females are those who make Holden depressed. Sally is both eligible and available. Despite her obvious interest in him—or rather *because* of it—Holden must pick her character apart and eventually is compelled to insult her. The prostitute and some women he meets at a bar also draw forth his ambivalence. So we see, in all these examples, that Holden is relatively comfortable with women as long as they are not potential sexual partners; as long as their status does not demand an adult response from him. Women such as Sally or the prostitute, on the other hand, are a threat and he either runs from them, goes into an act, or drives them away. His thoughts and feelings about Jane provide the clearest illustration of this ambivalence.

Holden finds the memory of his relationship with Jane quite comforting. They would play tennis, hold hands, and play those famous checker games where "old Jane" wouldn't even move her kings from the back row. In other words, Holden remembers her as an innocent child, reluctant, like him, to enter into sexual or competitive action. This image is threatened by Stradlater's date with her. For Holden knows only too well that Stradlater is not interested in childish play. They have gone on double dates and Holden is aware that Stradlater, unlike many of the other school boys, doesn't just talk about sexual exploits, he really has sexual intercourse with girls!

The thought of Stradlater's sexual relations with Jane shatters Holden's image of her childlike innocence. For sexual intercourse is one of those undeniably *real* adult acts. (It is, in many cultures, a symbol of the passage from child to adult status.) Throughout his wanderings Holden keeps thinking of calling Jane on the telephone. But he never does, perhaps because, since her date with Stradlater, he fears that the real Jane will not match his image of the innocent-child, kings-in-the-back-row, Jane.

His attack on Stradlater is the external manifestation of an anger that he directs at himself. For if Stradlater is a symbol of the boy who has turned into a big, sexual male, these same changes are occurring within Holden. He is no longer a child like Phoebe, if indeed he ever was. He is big, preoccupied with sex, a phony with his lies, and even, on occasion, violent. But whenever these internal aspects remind him of the very real ways in which he is becoming a "corrupt" adult—of the distance between his adult qualities and his image of childish innocence—he is compelled to bring failure or punishment down on his head. He hates this side of himself, and must attack it just as he hates and is saddened by those external reminders of adult corruption. He longs to be an innocent—a catcher in the rye—but senses the impossibility of this goal.

Phoebe is pretty and bright; his older brother is a successful writer, and Allie, the brother who died, is remembered as almost saintly. In contrast, Holden sees himself as the dumb one; as a failure, a source of disappointment to his parents and, perhaps, even as a "crazy" one. He is not dumb, of course, due to lack of intelligence; his failures are an unrecognized rebelliousness that blocks growing up or success.

If Holden's sexual impulses are apparent, his aggression is somewhat less so. But we must remember that he is, in his way, a rebel—someone who will not comply with the rules or demands of others. This is seen in his persistent failure at school and in such unconscious acts as losing the fencing team's equipment. And he is a constant put-on; his lies and pretending are very hostile ways of treating others, though, of course, he is not aware of this.

The Myth of Childhood Innocence

Holden's view of childhood innocence is so compelling that we must step back from the impact of the novel to remember that children are not really as he pictures them, that his view is a myth in which selfishness, anger, and other undesirable qualities are dissociated. What real brothers and sisters display the sort of relationships that Holden describes? Was there never any rivalry and anger between Holden and Allie, two years younger? Did he never find Phoebe a pain-in-the-neck little sister intruding on his life? Was he never resentful of their success, angry at being "the dumb one"? Rivalry, fighting, and resentments are as much a part of any real family as love and companionship. They are conspicuous by their absence in Holden's feelings toward his brothers and sister. What this means is that his view of them—and the wider view of childhood innocence—is a myth that Holden has created. The myth is a way of dissociating these undesirable qualities from himself. It states, in effect, "children are innocent; they have no real anger, resentments, rivalries, phoniness; all these come from the corrupt world of adults." As long as Holden is a child—or living in a child-fantasy like "the catcher in the rye"—these threatening qualities can be dissociated from his view of himself. *The myth of childhood innocence is his way of attempting to dissociate his own anger and sexuality by identifying himself with a mythical, innocent childhood.*

As he becomes an adult he must go to increasing extremes to uphold this myth. As his sexual feelings grow and his frustrations and anger increase, the pressure to dissociate these feelings from his self-view increases.

So much seems clear from the material presented in the novel. Why growing up involves these uniquely intense conflicts for Holden is not as clear. There are, however, a few bits of evidence from which to speculate. The earliest self-destructive act that Holden describes occurred following Allie's death. Certainly the death of a close family member is a normal cause for despair. But the self-destructive side of Holden's reaction was excessive; he seriously injured himself by smashing his hand through a number of windows. Did Allie's death touch off his dissociated anger and arouse a strong sense of guilt, leading to self-punishment? This idea, while speculative, is consistent with the later pattern of dissociation and self-destruction that we have just examined.[2]

Allie's death seems to be a continuing source of anxiety that Holden controls by reaffirming the myth of Allie's goodness. His memory of the good Allie becomes, in a way, a symbol for his own lost innocence. Late in the novel there is a crucial passage that illustrates Holden's underlying anxiety and his use of Allie as a supportive myth. Holden is wandering the streets in a state of despair and, as he gets to the end of each block he becomes terrified that he will not be able to reach the other side. He sweats with panic at the idea he might just disappear. To combat this terrible feeling, he begins to talk to Allie, pleading that Allie prevent him from disappearing and, then, thanking him when he reaches the other side of the street. What Holden experiences is the breakthrough of intense anxiety associated with the loss of self; with the loss of the security that comes from a defined identity. He carries the myth of his good relationship with Allie in his mind and tries to sustain himself with it in this moment of crisis. But, as we have seen, many forces within Holden and his world are making it increasingly difficult to maintain his identity as innocent-child, hence the frightening feeling of disappearing—of becoming nothing—of being a person with no identity.

The underlying ambivalence toward Allie, and the related guilt following his death, seems one important source of Holden's conflict over becoming an adult. If he can stave off being an adult, he can magically do away with all the unpleasant feelings and motives that he projects onto adults. He keeps trying to fit himself into this mythical child identity, denying that bad adult qualities reside within him. When he lies to people or plays roles it is done within the context of childhood innocence; it is "just horsing around," or the bragging, but harmless, "I'm the biggest liar you ever saw." Like all dissociative myths, this one cannot survive exposure to reality, the reality of his emerging adult qualities.

In sum, the nature of Holden's dissociations make the transition to adulthood a particularly difficult one for him. Since he deals with the unacceptable parts of himself by projecting them onto the world of adults, he cannot be an adult without hating himself. But he is, inescapably, becoming an adult and is forced to face his adult qualities with the result that his self-hatred is intensified. Throughout his wanderings he makes approaches toward some expression of adulthood, yet each time he is impelled to defeat himself. His form of adolescent conflict causes him to try and be an adult and flee from being one at almost the same time. He is psychologically torn

[2] As an interesting aside, the death of a virtuous, talented, almost saintly brother and its guilt-inducing effects on the remaining siblings is a recurring theme in Salinger's work.

apart and has no clear way of putting himself together; no way of constructing a viable new identity.

Holden exemplifies the manner in which an intense, underlying conflict—an anxiety related, dissociation—can make the transition from childhood to adulthood extremely difficult. Let us now examine the relationship of dissociation and reality in more general terms.

DISSOCIATION AND REALITY

The contrast between dissociation and accommodation with reality has been noted at various points in the preceding discussion of the dangers of adolescence, as well as in the presentation of Holden Caulfield's particular conflicts. Extremism, overconstriction, and escape from reality all involve a dissociation of some part of the personality. Holden reveals a complex pattern in which he attempts to dissociate those not-so-innocent parts of himself by projecting them onto a world of corrupt adults. In all these forms, some side of the person—his dependency, his angry rebelliousness, his sexual desires, his lack of innocence—is disguised, submerged, or actively disowned. The person becomes committed to a prematurely rigid identity or is caught up in playing a role that has no place for his dissociated side. In more traditional terms, one speaks of repression, defense, or relegation to the unconscious.

Exaggerated role playing or keeping up a front—whether it be a front of toughness, helplessness, or innocence—may fall within the normal limits of adolescent experimentation and overassimilation. But such dissociated postures can become so pervasive that the disowned portion of self is never exposed to social interchange. This is where the real danger of dissociation lies; for development of self depends on such interchange. When anxiety and dissociation prevail, social interaction is blocked and only an incomplete accommodation to reality is possible.

The tempering effects of social exchange have been noted by many theorists. Psychoanalytic writers speak of "reality testing." In their terms, anxiety and defense seal portions of the self or ego off from reality. Anger, sexuality and so forth remain in the "unconscious"; an unconscious which is "timeless," which does not change or accommodate. In the discussion of psychoanalytic therapy in chapter 7, we saw that "making the unconscious conscious" was a process in which private dissociations are undone through public exchange, and in which a particular form of communication between therapist and patient reintegrates anxiety laden conflicts into an active or accommodating self.

Piaget's account of reality testing traces the cycle of over-assimilation ———→ contact with reality ———→ accommodation ———→ equilibrium through progressive levels of development. At these different levels the nature of "reality" keeps changing, a point that is not clearly made in the psychoanalytic account. For example, the school age child accommodates to the behavior and wishes of other children, his parents, and other adults. This is an accommodation to social reality as seen from the perspective of concrete operational thought. Consideration of its form will take us closer to the problem faced by the adolescent.

In his account of the development of early morality, Piaget (1932) gives a clear description of accommodation at the level of concrete operations. For example, when the young child attempts to play games with other children he initially does so to satisfy his own desires. In his egocentric state he tries to win by any means and will attempt to adjust the rules of the game to suit himself. But the other children have the same intentions, resulting in discussions, fights, and arguments. This process constitutes an encounter with social reality and with the contrary intentions and wishes of others who can be just as egocentric as he is. Such encounters, if sustained, force the child to accommodate. What is true of games is true in a number of other life areas. Through active social encounters with other children and adults, accommodation occurs and eventually a state of relative equilibrium is reached. This constitutes the stability of late childhood.

With the onset of adolescence, the whole process must be repeated at the level of formal operations. The adolescent overassimilates; he pushes his ability to think abstractly, his orientation toward the future and assumption of adult roles, and his introspective idealism to their limits. This results in the grandiosity of early adolescence as typified by exaggerated attempts at independence, overly ambitious life plans, and unrealistic idealism. All of these manifestations of the egocentrism of ideas can best be tempered through accommodative interchange with other people. This usually takes the form of discussions with peers. Adolescence is a great time for intimate peer relationships; for the sharing of secrets with one's best friend; for the interminable bull session. The peer group society—whether it be the gang, a small group of friends, roommates at college, or members of a club—becomes the social reality against which the individual tests himself and his ideas. The peer group is a natural situation, of course, because it allows him to feel an equal, something of extreme importance to his new self-conception as adult. With his parents or other adults, he still feels a child; but with like-minded friends he can, with increasing confidence as the years progress, share his plans, aspirations, and fantasies.

The thrust of adolescent social interchange is a new version of decentering. The adolescent progresses from the egocentric position where he feels that *his* ideals, *his* life plans, *his* cynical perception of corruption are unique, to a realization that these views are shared by others. A large part of Holden's difficulty, and especially his alienation and loneliness, stems from a lack of shared experience with peers. Let me illustrate dissociation and reality with a further example.

The War of the Sexes

The segregation of the sexes, long a part of American school life, is one of many harmful legacies of our puritan heritage. It must have been assumed that if boys and girls were allowed to mix freely, especially as they got older, sexual licentiousness would run rampant. So the same beliefs and values that led mothers to tie their infant's sleeves down to prevent thumb sucking and masturbation, led adults to introduce a number of obstacles and artificial constraints that have served to make accommodation and understanding between the sexes more difficult than it need be. (There are signs of a healthy change—of a breakdown of sexual segregation at the high school and college levels—so the following remarks apply to a situation that may be changing.)

During the years of late childhood, boys and girls tend naturally to segregate themselves. The in-group conformity of this period is in large measure a conformity to stereotyped sex roles. Girls in the typical American elementary school emphasize their "goodness," their skill at pleasing teachers and controlling their aggression. Boys play out exaggerated versions of our culture's concept of masculinity, emphasizing toughness and athletic skill. And for both girls and boys, members of the other sex are seen through prejudicial stereotypes. All of this may be harmless enough in late childhood —though our society no doubt overdoes it—but its perpetuation into adolescence causes real problems.

Adolescents, as we have seen, become aware of romantic longings and strong sexual desires. These longings and desires necessitate an abandonment of the sexual segregation of late childhood. Boys and girls are now ready to resume relations or, more accurately, to begin relating in new ways. This is difficult, however, because the initial form of male-female relations is still colored by the views and values of childhood. They may wish to relate and not know how and fumble their way through the early versions as girls try to join in athletic contests or boys attempt, awkwardly, to dance.

Such fumbling beginnings are relatively harmless; what creates more serious obstacles is the difficulty appreciating the psychological perspective held by members of the opposite sex. That is, as the boy or girl moves into adolescence, he or she becomes aware of a complexity of feelings and ideas within himself. These are felt to be unique at first, and this initial egocentrism is gradually tempered through contact with members of one's own group. In our society, one's own group has meant members of one's own sex. Douvan and Adelson (1966) report that, for adolescent girls, an intimate female friend is a widespread and important source of support during these years. The same is true, on a less intense scale, for boys. Through such intimate social exchange, one comes to see that someone else feels the same frustrations and fears, the same embarrassments and desires. But members of the opposite sex are still outside the scope of this broadening perspective.

From the perspective of the adolescent American male, girls may be largely tantalizing sexual "bodies"—budding breasts and swaying buttocks that are the subject of his masturbatory fantasies or of crude jokes among his friends. If the girl is unavailable then she is seen as a source of frustration; if she is available, she is likely to be categorized as a "whore," a "slut," or a "piece of ass." That is, from the boy's perspective, the girl is viewed as a *sexual object* rather than a person subject to longings, frustrations, and confusions similar to his own.

From the girl's side, there is another version of sexual stereotyping. Although she may desire attention and closeness with boys, the girl feels she must guard against being "used" by males who are "just out for sex," interested in her body but not in her as a person. Or she may construct a romantic ideal of her "true love," her knight in shining armor. These views of males as either pure exploitation or pure romance are as unbalanced as the adolescent boy's perception of girls as sex objects. There is, in other words, a good deal of egocentric distortion on both sides.

The social stereotyping and segregation of the sexes has, in traditional American society, served to perpetuate these distortions. For example, one finds the most blatant versions of sexual stereotypes in monosexual groups. All-male fraternities, clubs, bars, and the like are places where men can continue the grown-up versions of early adolescent dirty talk. Such groups give support to the view of women as sexual objects. In a general way, segregation of the sexes has contributed to the lack of shared viewpoints— to a failure to perceive common qualities—just as racial segregation or national isolation has contributed to similar narrowness of views.

Within recent years a breakdown of our traditional sexual attitudes has been in progress. One beneficial effect of this change is an increase in the sort of *shared experience,* on both the physical and intellectual levels, that can correct egocentric distortions. If a boy who views girls primarily as sexual objects has the opportunity for sustained conversation, he may realize that they have thoughts, uncertainties, plans, and fears much like his own. Or, if a girl who categorizes boys into those who are "nice"— meaning safe as friends because they are nonsexual—and "dirty"—meaning unsuitable as friends because they are "only interested in sex"—has the opportunity for sustained interaction, she may find that "nice" boys have sexual needs and "dirty" boys are capable of personal friendships.

What is necessary, then, is a kind of shared social experience in which both male and female perceptions confront one another and are forced to accommodate. Neither intellectual nor sexual relations will be sufficient in themselves, since the first will leave feelings and sensations connected with the bodily aspects of love in a state of dissociation, while the second leaves ideals and misconceptions unexplored.

The breakdown of the dating system and the trend for college age men and women to share living arrangements provide increasing opportunity for the kind of sustained personal contact that leads to less stereotyped views of members of the opposite sex. For example, Joseph Katz (1968) and his associates report findings from a four year study of college students that shows that intimacy between men and women is facilitated by shared common tasks and informal contacts. Students who live in coeducational dormatories, or who attend an overseas campus together, are able to develop relationships that go beyond what occurs within the traditional dating system with its emphasis on sexuality in the narrower sense.

The foregoing discussion points up a major social difficulty in adolescent sexual relations. Obviously, not all American males treated women as sex objects, even in the heyday of such thinking. Nor did all women wait for knights in armor, even when it was fashionable to affect such a romantic pose. Any social custom or view gives support to trends in the individual, and there is always latitude in the use or misuse of social beliefs and practices. Those persons with intense anxiety concerning sexuality will make use of beliefs that stress the purity of abstinence or the sinfulness of premarital relations. The tragedy of paths chosen out of anxiety is that they lead to stasis; they prevent future accommodations because they do not permit those sustained, intimate relationships that can put to rest old fears, stereotypes, and misconceptions.

Summary: Emerging Identity and Society

Social views and values interact with the developed tendencies of the individual. Narrow, rigid, or stereotyped social practices bring out the worst in people. Those adolescents with excessive anxiety; those most in need of support and tolerance, of time and flexibility to find their way to a balanced identity, are most likely to be damaged by social practice that labels them "slut" on the basis of sexual experimentation, or "delinquent" because of rebellious acts, or "schizophrenic" or "mental patient" because of a temporary withdrawal from reality. Such enforced identities and labels, often eagerly grasped by the anxious young person, may foreclose future growth.

To sum up, we have seen how a variety of forces in both society and the individual can lend their weight to dissociation or to an honest facing of conflicts within and among persons. As adolescence progresses into adulthood, the young person tries out various roles, dissociates or faces up to conflict, affiliates with groups or withdraws into isolation, makes and breaks friendships, experiments with sexuality, and much more. Out of all these experiences, identity is shaped and, as the years progress, becomes increasingly stabilized. Choices persistently chosen, roles persistently played, actions persistently taken all add up to what the person is. "We are what we pretend to be," Kurt Vonnegut reminds us, to which must be added Allen Wheelis's (1969) "we are what we do. . . . Identity is the integration of behavior."

The capacity for abstract thought that begins in adolescence makes the very concept of identity, in its wider meaning, possible. Adolescence is a time of transformation—an opportunity to redo, remake, rethink all that has gone before and orient one's life to future possibilities. These possibilities are then given reality by life as one lives it.

chapter ten

Identity

*For neurosis is after all only a sign that the ego has not
succeeded in making a synthesis, that in attempting to do
so it has forfeited its unity.* — Sigmund Freud

Psychological development does not end with adolescence. The ingredients
of personality, the particular appearance, talents, interests, fears, conflicts,
and memories are all assembled like blueprints and building materials
awaiting their final construction. It remains for the person to put these
together into a viable whole, to construct an adult identity that brings
together past experiences, present views, and the opportunities offered by
a society at a particular point in history.

What, then, is identity? Is it the same as "self" or "ego," concepts
that we have encountered throughout the previous chapters? Erikson, who
has contributed a great deal to our understanding of these issues, uses
identity in preference to self or ego since these give too exclusive an emphasis to the individual or internal side of personality. Identity is a way of
expanding the concept of self to include social factors. Erikson's best known
work, *Childhood and Society,* shows how the identity of particular individuals—be they Americans from different social strata, Sioux or Yurok

Indians, Germans, or Russians—is woven together from individual history and social possibilities. The closely related concept of identification also bridges the gap between the individual self and the society of other selves, for identification describes the process whereby the social gets inside the individual as the self develops by adding roles modeled on others.

Thus one meaning of identity is the self, comprised of the various identifications of development. Consistent with this meaning we may think of the many selves of development: the body-centered self of infancy, the self as male or female, the good boy or girl of middle childhood, the idealistic self of adolescence, the self of dreams, fantasy, and play, as well as the self of public action. But identity has another meaning. The dictionary defines it as: "Sameness of essential character...self-sameness, oneness. Unity and persistence of personality; individuality." The word also relates to "identical," to be the same or exactly equal to something else and, as we have seen, to "identification."

These definitions call our attention to two contrasting aspects of identity. Identity as a sum of roles and identifications suggests many selves, while oneness, unity, and individuality suggest a single, whole, or integrated self. Adopting a developmental perspective should clarify the apparent contradiction between these two meanings of identity. During the early years, the child has different selves and is not bothered by inconsistencies between them, by his lack of unity or wholeness. He may be one person with his parents, another with his friends, and still another in his dreams. The limitations of intuitive and concrete operational thought permit such shifting about and contradictions. There are several reasons for this. Children engage in a great deal of unconscious role playing. In a sense, much of the valuable experimental play of childhood is dissociative or unconscious in nature—the child pretends, fantasies, dreams, and plays himself into all sorts of roles and situations that are not "him," as the discussion and examples in chapter 6 attempted to show. What is more, moratoria of various kinds are a necessary and regular part of development. So, in this sense also, the years of childhood lack wholeness. Finally, the nature of childhood thought precludes wholeness or unity in the most complete meaning of these terms. Before adolescence, the concrete operational nature of the child's thought limits his ability to conceive of complex abstractions. He is present-centered and has difficulty holding several hypothetical possibilities in mind simultaneously. Since the very idea of identity is a complex abstraction with past, present, and future time dimensions, the child cannot really conceive of it. That is, the idea of a unitary or whole self in which past memories of who one was, present experience of who one is, and future expectations of who one will be, is the sort of abstraction that the child simply does not think about. Thinking about one's self—introspecting—is also something that the child does not do. So the concrete operational child is not concerned with his identity or with the integration of self because of the limitations of his intellectual level.

With the emergence of formal operations in adolescence, wholeness, unity, and integration become introspectively real problems. Central to the idealism of adolescence is concern with an ideal self. Holden Caulfield's preoccupation with phoniness is a striking example of this concern. He, and many young persons like him, become critical of those who only play at roles, who are one moment this and another moment that. This critical stance is taken toward themselves as well. Wholeness is, thus, an *ideal* conceived in late adolescence; a goal which may be pursued threafter. This goal, made possible by the advanced intellectual capacity of the young person, will be achieved to varying degrees depending on social opportunity and, crucially, on predispositions toward dissociation. For adolescence, as we have seen in chapter 9, is a time for the reopening of moratoria; a time when old issues, conflicts, identifications, and fragments of the self will continue to be dissociated or can be faced anew and integrated into a cohesive identity. And it is during this process of integration that identifications with strong components of anxiety present obstacles to the attainment of a unified self.

As adolescence progresses toward adulthood, the young person is concerned with integrating the identity fragments of his childhood, his present sense of self, and his expectations for the future, and with relating all these to the role or career possibilities offered by his society. The task of creating a unified identity may be more or less difficult depending on two factors: those predispositions toward anxiety and dissociation that remain from childhood; and the opportunities for a meaningful, integrated, adult life offered by one's society. In the next section I wish to examine the factors within the person which bear on the unity or fragmentation of the self; then we may turn our attention to the role of society.

THE DIALECTICS OF DEVELOPMENT

Development through the life cycle is characterized by the pull of two opposing forces. For purposes of discussion I will call these *anxiety* and *competence*—concepts closely related to the *anxiety-dissociation* versus *integration* dimension presented in chapter 7.

The self, once structured even to a limited degree, tends to perpetuate itself. Departure from a known or secure self at any particular point in time has the potential to arouse anxiety. In the early years, this anxiety arises directly from separation; separation anxiety is the prototype for many later threats to the security of a known or established self. As development proceeds, the components of identity become progressively *internalized*. The child derives security from his identification with father, mother, siblings, and peers; with the male or female role; and, later in adolescence, with more broadly defined groups and ideals. The internal structures that result from these identifications—the new roles incorporated into the self—become the internal sources of security, and departures from these roles arouse anxiety. Once the child knows he is a boy (or she is a girl) the sex role will be strongly adhered to. Traits, feelings, or actions associated with the opposite sex are experienced as threatening and are frequently dissociated.[1] Later in adolescence, as the young person comes to an introspective awareness of himself, the lack of a definite identity can arouse anxiety and motivate a sometimes frantic search for a set of beliefs to cling to. Erikson (see especially 1959) terms the great danger of this period "identity diffusion," an anxious state in which the lack of a secure identity leads the adolescent to grasp at something—anything—to believe in; he may seek membership in groups or identify with exaggerated roles or strong leaders because these give a secure structure to his diffuse feelings about himself.

Opposed to anxiety and the search for security is that force which motivates growth, change, and the seeking of higher levels of integration— a force that I will term *competence*. The infant seeks the security of his mother but is also a curious and interested explorer of the world around him. His explorations take him farther and farther afield and, in the process, he is impelled to grow by incorporating new knowledge into the structure of his self. In previous chapters we have examined Piaget's description of intellectual growth, motivated by a need to function (the mind's need for new intellectual challenges) and regulated by the principles of assimilation and accommodation. This account gives a clear picture of the forces behind change and growth. Of particular importance is the tendency to seek higher levels of integration and understanding. The child is not content once he has reached a stable equilibrium with the world, be it sensorimotor, pre- or concrete operational. Prodded by the growth of body and mind and lured by new social opportunities, he strives to expand his competence and, in the process, he reaches new levels of integration which incorporate material from earlier stages in more comprehensive forms. This striving for competence and integration need not stop when adult status is achieved; it can continue throughout life.

The drive toward higher levels of integration is not restricted to the realm of intellect. Moral and ego development are motivated by this same

---

1 In our society this is especially true for boys who exaggerate their maleness and are often threatened by so-called feminine traits, or even by associating with girls. This no doubt stems from the lower status accorded to women, as well as from the boy's need to separate himself from the earlier dependent relationship with his mother.

force. The person has a need to make sense of himself, his relations with others, and his place in society and the world. As his intellect grows he becomes dissatisfied with earlier roles and stereotypes. Adolescents often attempt to dispense with earlier conceptions of self, to break with their place in the family, and to achieve a new identity that integrates the self in a more broadly conceived social group. There are also new expectations imposed from without; as he nears adulthood, the adolescent is pushed toward self-support, career, marriage, and childrearing.

In sum, the two poles of anxiety-security, on the one hand, and competence-growth-change, on the other, represent the basic dialectic of psychological development. As the person passes through the various ages, stages, and crises, first one pole predominates and then the other. The security-seeking infant becomes the independent-minded two-year-old, concerned to "do it myself." The school age child derives security from playing "good" roles at home, in school, and with the peer group. He has internalized, within the limits of concrete operational thought, certain roles and identifications, and feels secure within these. Adolescence, with its great changes in body and intellect, sees a swing over to the change-growth side of the dialectic. The breakdown of the secure self of childhood requires growth and integration at a higher level. Development is dialectical in the sense that Hegel originally used that term. Each stage partially opposes, partially incorporates, and eventually reintegrates the stage before it. In Piaget's terms, the initial assimilation is countered by accommodation leading to equilibrium at a particular stage and then the repetition of the whole process at the next level. In addition to the dialectical nature of development, we have noted the way in which identity becomes progressively internalized. Let us now examine this process in more detail.

An Identity from Identifications

The self develops by modeling, imitating, and eventually internalizing —making a part of itself—persons of emotional significance. Identification is the general term for this process and, as he develops, the child makes many such identifications: he plays many roles or has many selves. He may be, at one time or another, a loving or demanding baby; a cute or annoying young child; a competent "big" boy or girl, or one who is "too big" for his or her age; an adolescent on the verge of assuming desired adult roles, or one frightened that he is turning into something he hates. Each of these selves is given shape by the way in which social expectations interact with the particular child, though it is worth stressing that each identification is a creative construction of the child. Family, peers, the school, and society present him with actions, models, rules, opportunities, frustrations, rewards, and punishments. But it is always he who pays attention or ignores, imitates, and models (or chooses not to), is attracted or unimpressed, and, eventually, who identifies.

As adolescence moves toward adulthood the person strives to create a consistent identity from the identifications of his past. The general motives that I am referring to as *competence* promote the creation of an integrated, whole, or unified identity. And those summarized with the term *anxiety* interfere with or block integration; they foster the continuation of dissociations. How does this operate? We have seen that identification consists of the internalization of emotionally charged relationships. Now if we look at *what* emotions are involved in the various identifications of development, we find that they may be grouped into two broad categories that correspond to the two motives—anxiety and competence—which block or promote change. The child identifies with those he loves and admires; he models himself after older siblings or more competent friends, parents, heroes, and the like. Such identifications are relatively easily incorporated into an expanding self. The internalized version of these relationships are unambivalent; are easy to accept, to live with, to *be*. Contrasting with these positive or competence-related identifications, are those based on fear, anxiety, frustration, and rage. Such emotions, which are present in different degrees in every child's life, also motivate identifications; internalized versions in which the child inwardly struggles with ambivalent relationships. These anxiety-laden identifications are, like anxiety in all its other forms, the enemies of wholeness and integration. Let me try and explain this last point a bit further.

In chapter 7, two processes characteristic of development were outlined: dissociation and integration. Identifications imbued with ambivalence and anxiety persist within the person but tend to be dissociated from the sense of self. The person deals with such "traumatic" relations by relegating them to spheres such as fantasy where they are experienced as "happening to" someone who is not quite he; where they are *passively suffered*. The contents of this dissociated realm—this set of anxiety-tinged, dissociated identifications—make up a large part of what Freud called the unconscious. Identifications of this sort are "set aside" as they occur during childhood, though their presence continues to be felt, especially in dreams. Dissociated identifications are not the only material set aside during the childhood years, of course. The fact that particular roles, relationships, or conflicts are subject to moratoria may simply be due to the child's lack of size, intellect, or skill. Anxiety-laden, dissociated identifications are a special class of experiences subject to moratoria during the years of development—a class with untoward implications for the later achievement of unity.

A crucial distinction between dissociated and integrated identifications is that the first are experienced passively and the second actively. The passive-active dimension (discussed at greater length in chapter 7) is central both in the initial formation of dissociated versus integrated identifications and in the later reopening of moratoria based on these two sorts of initial conditions. Relationships leading to dissociations are those that the child cannot affect with his own actions, either because of the loss or absence of important identification figures, or their insensitive, ambivalent, or double-binding treatment of him. The most striking evidence comes from studies of families with schizophrenic children (see chapter 7). The parents in such families, dissociated from their own emotions and conflicts and desperately playing out a caricatured version of normality, act in such a way that the child cannot affect them with his emotional communications. His loneliness or need for love are overlooked or mislabeled, his anger both stimulated and denied. He eventually comes to feel that he cannot affect those closest to him in any active or meaningful way and retreats to a position of passivity and dissociation.

Integrated development, by contrast, grows from relationships in which the child *actively encounters* others, in which his actions and emotional communications have meaningful and predictable effects on the important persons in his life. Experiences of this kind lead to identifications that can be integrated into an expanding self. Some of these identifications are also set aside, but without the charge of anxiety that accompanies dissociated identifications. Integration does not mean that every aspect of a person's experience, every identification, is incorporated into a unified whole. Some traits may remain peripheral without seriously impairing the individual's unity. It is the identifications that develop from the core life areas—what I have earlier called the core conflicts—that must be integrated if the person is to achieve a unified self. The sense of maleness or femaleness, independence with a clear conscience, the ability to accept and deal with one's anger and sensual impulses, and to establish closeness and intimacy with others, these are the core areas. When identifications in these areas are heavily laden with anxiety, serious dissociations occur which make the creation of an integrated self difficult.

To sum up: identifications through the years of development are of two general sorts: those which predispose the person toward a fragmented, split, or dissociated identity, and those which predispose him toward unity, wholeness, and integration. I use the term predispose because at the time identifications are made, during the years of childhood, wholeness or integration is not the issue it will become later. The drives toward competence and integration lead the late adolescent and young adult to construct an identity which encompasses the core aspects of self and experience—sexual and aggressive ideas and feelings, masculine and feminine traits, active and passive tendencies, dependent and independent wishes (as well as memories, events, and issues peculiar to the individual) —into a unified whole, an integrated identity which can receive support and a place within society. Dissociated identifications—internalized experiences charged with anxiety—make this task difficult. To the degree that the individual's earlier life has left a residue of dissociations, these make the reopening of issues fraught with anxious apprehension; an apprehension which provokes continued dissociations.

At points in the discussion so far, reference has been made to society's role in facilitating an integrated identity or in perpetuating dissociations. It is now time to consider this issue directly.

IDENTITY AND SOCIETY

Every society defines the inevitable roles of infant, child, adult, mother, and father, as well as the many possible careers open to its members, in its own way. In addition, each society must come to grips with the instinctual heritage of the human species; each has its own manner of channeling man's sensual appetites, his propensity toward anger and aggression toward fellow group members, his need for closeness and contact with these same persons, his restless curiosity and need to understand and integrate experience. Identity, as Erikson has shown so well, results from the intersection of the individual with these differing societal definitions, taboos, and possiblities. The history of an individual may predispose him toward dissociation or integration and, in a related way societies may be ordered on the dissociation to integration continuum. There are those which foster integration, whose members, to a large degree, can achieve a meaningful wholeness within the role and career possibilities offered to them. And, at the other extreme, there are societies whose practices seem to produce a great deal of anxiety and dissociation among their members.

Society and Alienation

When speaking of anxiety and dissociation at the social level, the term "alienation" is often employed. An alienated person is one who is dissociated from social values and beliefs or from the other persons in his society. Alienating societies are those which foster anxiety and dissociation in their members and, conversely, which make the achievement of integration difficult. To put this another way, we can say that a feeling of oneness with the social group corresponds to the security of individual attachment, while alienation from the group is the social manifestation of separation anxiety.

As we have seen, the prototype of anxiety is the state of helplessness arising from separation. Attachment expands from mother to family to society and separation acquires broader symbolic connotations; meanings which make it possible for the adolescent and adult to feel "separated" from his family or society because he holds different ideals. Thus, the anxiety which is aroused early in life by loss of sensorimotor contact can be aroused later by a variety of complex conditions which produce a feeling of separation or alienation from social institutions, practices, values, and from other persons. Identification with society—as seen, for example, in the assumption of an identity that fits with an accepted role—leads to a feeling of oneness; to a more complex version of attachment-security. Failure to achieve such an identity leads to alienation, a complex social version of separation anxiety. The term alienation captures the feeling quite well; it connotes estrangement, the sense of being an alien or a foreigner in one's native land.

In what follows I will examine some of the conditions in contemporary American society that lead to anxiety and dissociation on the individual level, and to alienation on the social level. For purposes of discussion I will present this in the form of a comparison between contemporary society and the hunting and gathering cultures described in chapter 3.

Karl Marx argued that the alienation of man in industrial societies resulted from the exploitation of one class by another. Workers were separated from the results of their work, they were not treated as human beings but as "labor" to be utilized in the interest of profits. Contemporary theorists who draw on Marx's ideas have carried this analysis forward. For example, Erich Fromm (1947) notes how the dominant values of our society produce what he terms a "marketing personality," an individual who conceives of himself as a "product" to be packaged and "sold" on the market place. Such a self-view neglects or distorts basic human needs for love, community, and relationships of a nonexploitive kind and, hence, leads to feelings of isolation and alienation from one's own actions and feelings, as well as from one's fellow citizens. A more recent critique of this same sort can be found in Philip Slater's *The Pursuit of Loneliness.*

I believe that the general criticisms of industrial society put forth by the above authors can be pushed back in time. The origins of alienation lie not with the industrial revolution and the rise of capitalism—though these have their special alienating effects—but with the invention of agriculture, several thousand years earlier, which brought an end to the hunting and gathering way of life. (The following analysis may sound a bit oversimple —like a glorification of the noble savage—but my intention is to highlight present problems by contrasting modern life with societies that were radically different. Some cautions about such a comparison will follow.)

Hunting and gathering culture, as we saw in chapter 3, represented a stable equilibrium: a way of life in which human instincts could find expression; in which children were raised in a manner that well-prepared them for the assumption of adult roles; and in which man lived in a closer, more harmonious relationship with nature. Persons in these cultures lacked almost all the benefits of technology: they had few possessions and were prey to disease, to extremes of temperature, and to scarcities of food. They hunted animals with spears, harpoons, and bows and arrows rather than with guns; they were dependent on wild game and vegetation rather than on domesticated animals and cultivated crops; they traveled on foot rather than on horse or camel, train, car, or plane; and they had little knowledge of the world beyond the small area within which they lived. On the other hand, they seemed better able to accept illness and death than we; were physically healthy and well-fed, and seemed unconcerned with scarcity of food, or of much else for that matter. While lacking guns to hunt with, they also lacked them (or their big brothers with nuclear war-heads) to wage our wars of rampant destruction. If they lacked rapid means of transportation, more sophisticated dwellings, and industrialization, they also lacked traffic congestion, automobile accidents and plane crashes, overcrowded cities filled with polluted air, high rates of crime, violence, divorce, and mental breakdown.

The relationship between man and work in the two cultures further highlights the hunter's integration and our alienation. Hunting and gathering are simple activities with a direct relationship to life. There is no money, no organization or bureaucracy between the work itself and the goal of such work; that is, the obtaining of food. In a related way, the hunter's relationship to his technology and implements was much more direct and meaningful than that of many modern men and women. While he may have worked slowly to make a clay pot, a spear, or a flint tool, the completed product was recognizably his own and its function clearly understandable in the scheme of his life. Contrast this with the output of a worker on an assembly line who has little feeling for, or identification with, his rapidly produced, standardized product. In sum: while lacking the benefits of technology, many of the most alienating, anxiety-producing aspects of our way of life were also missing from these early human societies.

Before proceeding, let me voice some cautions. It is easy to idealize cultures which existed long ago and which we know from incomplete evidence. When the many problems of modern life are a part of our everyday experience, and no ready solutions seem forthcoming, it is tempting to engage in escapist fantasies which overestimate the positive side of earlier cultures and underestimate the advantages of progress and technology. Although I feel that the evidence justifies, in a general way, the picture I am drawing, it is worth keeping in mind that it is a simplified sketch that leaves out much about both sides. There were, no doubt, anxious and alienated hunters just as there are modern men who find contentment and a meaningful life in the midst of the largest cities. It is a question of relative balance. Hunting and gathering societies made it possible for a very large proportion of their members to become unified persons whose lives were integrated with their fellows in mutually comprehended, meaningful experiences. It seems very difficult to achieve such an existence in contemporary society. Few persons do and large numbers feel anxious and alienated, their lives unstable and fraught with uncertainty.

The comparison also leaves out the many societies in between the earliest known human cultures and the modern world. Early agricultural societies, the civilizations of ancient Egypt, Greece, Rome, China, India, Mexico, or Peru, peasant and feudal cultures, the city life of the Renaissance, and many others, represent adaptations of more or less stability, of greater or lesser alienation and integration. All this is skipped in this simplified account.

As a final caution, I should stress that time cannot be reversed; we can never go back to earlier ways of life, no matter how much we might admire them. Like Adam having partaken of the fruit of knowledge, we are both blessed and condemned by our sophistication. The lessons to be learned from an examination of early societies must be creatively shaped to our own existence if we are to gain anything from them.

Human Instincts.   Here let me note the ways in which human instincts are recognized, gratified, channeled, and frustrated in the two kinds of societies. Perhaps most central is the way in which earlier cultures are based on a deep recognition of the intensely *social* nature of the human species. Hunter-gatherer societies, as we saw in chapter 3, are organized along familial lines. Everybody is related to everyone else as parent-child, husband-wife, grandparent-grandchild, uncle, aunt, nephew, niece, cousin, or thinks of himself as related in these ways. The comfortable oneness that modern man feels within his family—when he feels it there—is experienced by the hunter-gatherer within his total social group. Bands are small, of course, making such an integration based on personal experience and prolonged contact possible. Contrast this with the huge size of modern cities which fosters impersonality and makes it literally impossible to know more than a small fraction of one's own group.

Members of early societies are in constant contact with each other. The expression of social instincts is accomplished not only through kinship relations and language; members of the typical band are rarely out of sight of other group members and there is a great deal of physical contact. The sorts of touching and stimulation that we restrict to relations between parents and young children, or to private love making, are much more prevalent and public among these groups. The members of these societies *know* each other's bodies, habits, gestures, talents, weaknesses, and idiosyncrasies through long and continuous contact on many levels.

Such continuous contact makes for security but can also lead to boredom. Much of the movement, travel, and change of modern life is, after all, motivated by interest, curiosity, and a wish to get away from that which is *too* familiar. Hunter-gatherers no doubt felt the same emotion. Boredom was countered in at least two ways. First, their dependence on game and wild vegetation kept them moving about in pursuit of ripening fruit, the migration of animals, the shifting availability of water, and related conditions. They lived within a fixed territory and became familiar enough with it to feel secure, but also moved enough within it to sustain interest and excitement. Second, the well-established custom of visiting with nearby bands provided variety in human contact. Bored with the same territory and the sight of the same people day after day the hunter could easily pack up and visit a neighboring group, exchange gossip and thus combat his boredom. The custom of visiting also played a useful role in the handling of aggression. As we saw in chapter 3, when anger reached dangerous proportions within the band it was easy for one party to a dispute to simply leave for another band, a move prepared for in advance by the custom of visiting.

Hunter-gatherers were not free from anxiety. Many aspects of their lives no doubt aroused this painful emotion—the sudden death of babies or loved ones that they were powerless to prevent, for example. But, in contrast to modern man, one feels certain that they did not experience anxiety or alienation in relation to the members of their bands. A secure oneness with the primary group is a striking feature of all these early cultures, as it was of the nonhuman primates who preceded man in evolution.

Man and Environment.   The relation between the members of hunter-gatherer societies and the natural environment within which they live is characterized by similar feelings of security and oneness—by a lack of alienation—that contrasts strongly with our relationship to nature. In general, hunter-gatherers view themselves as a part of nature. Marshall's sensitive film of a Bushmen hunt (*The Hunters,* 1956), Turnbull's (1961) account of the Pygmies of the Congo, or the many descriptions of Eskimo life all convey the oneness that these people feel with the land, trees, animals, snow, and other features of their habitat. This integrated feeling is expressed in language which gives familiar or human names to important parts of the environment.

Early man treats his environment as if it were human. His religion and myths explain the origins of stars, sun, moon, sky, earth, trees, and animals as due to the actions of human-like spirits and gods or to supernatural animals endowed with human qualities. (Such explanations persist in contemporary religions, of course, but are not taken literally; they seem to mean less as education and sophistication increase.) This anthropomorphic view of his environment reflects the primitive oneness that the hunter felt with his surroundings. It was as if the environment was part of the human family and could be influenced in similar ways: by supplication and pleading (prayer), by bribery and gifts, or by forceful action. Although such customs appear inadequate and unscientific in our eyes, leaving early man less protected from nature's ravages, from his point of view they are part of the secure oneness that he feels in his natural world.

We have ceased to view our habitat anthropomorphically. We objectify nature, dissect it, control it, wage war on it and, in many areas have succeeded in conquering it. Our conquest has freed us from many kinds of disease, increased our ability to produce food, vastly multiplied our technology, in short, given us the capability of erecting whole new artificial environments—cities—within which to live. The benefits of such technological advances are well known. We view as foolish, attempts to influence the weather with a rain dance, or to placate the spirits of the animals we kill and eat. And who would not rather treat his sick child with the wonders of modern medicine than with primitive rituals and magic?

Yet our very triumph over nature has been accompanied by an alienation, a sense of separation, from the world within which we live. Our successful war against the elements, other animals and microorganisms has played its part in this alienation. That is to say, central to the attitude which fosters technological progress and the conquest of nature is a removal of oneself from intimate identification with the objects of such conquest. This ranges from the objectivity of the scientist, to the impersonality of the slaughterhouse worker. Unlike his hunter-ancestors, the butcher does not feel a brother to the steers and hogs that he kills. Such dehumanization, in quite a literal sense, of the animals and environment has been a necessary part of modern man's exploitation of them as resources. But this dehumanization also involves a separation—an alienation—from nature. The progress of culture has had unexpected drawbacks along with its obvious advantages.

We now find ourselves alienated in two ways; from our fellow men and from our very surroundings. The extreme example is the city dweller, living in a residence he did not build, dependent on sources of power and transportation he poorly understands and cannot easily influence, and surrounded by people he does not know.

Many other examples of the alienation of modern life could be cited but let me, rather, focus on a characteristically American phenomenon: our emphasis on individualism and self-reliance. What could be farther from the constant social contact, stimulation, and intercourse of early culture than our ideal of the self-reliant man? The frontiersman ideal, that cowboy figure who is capable of existing "on his own," is seen in many guises in our society, from the "frontier spirit," to the taboo on the public display of affection and other kinds of physical contact, to various attempts to deny dependency, the need for love, or the admission of "weakness." Such exaggerated self-reliance is a dangerous myth, it is based on a negation of one of man's most powerful instincts, his need for sustained physical, verbal, and symbolic contact with others. We are capable of muting or transforming this instinct, but individuals who do so pay a great price in anxiety, frustration, and rage. And, societies, to the extent that they move away from the expression and gratification of the need for social contact, are characterized by alienation.

The myth of self-reliance is often a way of denying dependence; it is an exaggeration of the independence side of the dependence-independence dimension which, when carried to extremes, blocks the recognition of man's need for others. The hunter goes relatively easily from being his mother's baby to his family's child to his society's member. For us the move from child in the family to member of society is often difficult; one must often struggle to overcome the earlier dependency. The gap between one's role in the family and in society produces feelings of anxiety and alienation and the further struggle with these feelings can lead to an exaggerated independence or self-reliance, with its concommitant dissociated dependence. This inner dissociation only compounds the alienation. One finds himself, at the end of this process, neither secure within a network of family relations, nor part of a wider community that takes the place of the family (think of the typical job in a large bureaucracy or factory). To compound the problem, one even loses touch with one's feelings of dependent need. Alienating societies are thus populated with dissociated individuals.

The discovery of agriculture was the beginning of the shift from a hunting and gathering way of life to one based increasingly on technology. Although the life of a peasant farmer is more like that of a Bushman than that of a contemporary American, the underlying changes in custom and value were set in motion by this first great technological advance. Among its many effects were the substitution of a fixed living area for the earlier nomadic existence; the beginning of an emphasis on individual possessions and private property, with a concommitant breakdown in the ethic of sharing; and the increase in group size made possible by a more stable and controllable supply of food. This last change meant that the basic social group became less and less familiar as it grew in size. Along with these changes went a number of others which did not assume importance until after the industrial revolution. Specialization of labor, for example, which finds its ultimate expression in the assembly line where the worker repetitively performs one or a few small tasks, is foreshadowed by the early growth of technology, but it did not have much effect during the many years of a predominantly agricultural economy. Simple farming can be performed by everyone in much the same way as hunting or gathering and the farmer is not alienated from the results of his labor as many modern workers are.

The breakdown of band-familial society disrupted the stable expression and gratification of the need for social contact. In addition, ownership of land and other possessions interfered with the ethic of sharing central to the control of greed in hunter-gatherer groups. From a society based on bands where everything was owned in common and in which everyone had a right to use the small number of tools, weapons, and vessels, culture began evolving toward our present state in which individuals possess land, technological implements, and wealth, and typically do not share these with others. Where the hunter-gatherer's identity is tied to this group, a part of our identities has become entwined with our possessions—our land, houses, cars, and money. To a certain extent, we seek our missing social gratifications in these possessions which, being things rather than human beings, cannot provide emotional reciprocation. However much you may love your car or money, they cannot love you back.

Essentially the same point may be made about social position, class, caste, or status. Hunter-gatherer society is classless. There is no chief; leadership is shifted about depending on whose talents are most appropriate to the job at hand. This does not mean that all group members are equal in some homogenized way that destroys individuality. Some are brighter, stronger, more energetic, better mothers, hunters, dreamers, dancers, or more attractive, and these various talents are expressed and rewarded. The difference is that the individual has less of his identity tied up in such roles. He has less need to because he feels secure as a member of a group and is not driven to shore up an insecure identity with status and position. Many of us, on the other hand, search for status and position, just as we covet wealth and possessions, to help define an identity that is not well anchored in group life.

Much more could be said about the ways in which human instincts are handled in these two contrasting cultures. For example, the breakdown of the ethic of sharing and the growth of group size have had profound effects on the management of aggression. We are potentially no more or less aggressive than our hunting and gathering ancestors but we do a much poorer job in managing this instinct. Although we are less open and direct in the expression of anger, we have become much more lethal killers of other human beings. We are separated, protected—in short, alienated—both from our feelings of anger and from the long range effects of our aggressive acts.

A similar indirectness characterizes our handling of sensuality. Hunter-gatherer society is not free from taboos and sexual inhibitions, but it is more open with regard to permissible sensual gratifications. In general, modern society is more concerned with hiding the body; we are characterized by more stringent inhibitions, by an increase in all that is conveyed by the phrase "puritanical morality."

Technological Extremism. I should add a final word about the instinctual basis of our technological progress. Many theorists have pointed to the disruptive effects of human aggression and anxiety but few have singled out our instinctual drive toward competence—our curiosity, need to explore and to expand our understanding and mastery of the world—as a cause of alienation. Indeed, many analyses of the difficulties of modern life call for greater understanding, for a more thorough-going application of intelligence, a view that is hard to dispute. And yet, the previous analysis suggests that our very urge to understand has played its part in disrupting the stability of a well-adapted way of life and, by so doing, has contributed to our alienation from nature and from our fellow man.

Sometimes competence motivation has been mixed with aggression—the early domestication of animals involved skill and thought but was also a variant of the custom of hunting which is, in part, motivated by aggression. Similarly, many early tools were invented for use as weapons suggesting, again, a blending of competence and aggressive instincts. But many other technological advances were preceded by experimentation and play for their own sake; by a pure curiosity and desire to know. The domestication of plants and the many uses to which they have been put was probably motivated more by interest in the early phase than by hunger. The purification and utilization of metals, the discoveries of early astronomy, geology, biology, and physiology—all these were primarily motivated by interest and the desire to expand understanding.

You will recall, from earlier discussion of this instinctual system, that interest is aroused by phenomena that are new and different (but not too different) from what the person is familiar with. Thus, the system has a built-in pacing quality such that knowledge will keep expanding to new levels. That is what seems to have happened in many scientific fields. How, then, has this instinctual system played a causal role in our present state of alienation? It has done so, in my view, by being carried to an extreme. Given man's need to continually expand his understanding and competence, it is inevitable that he will be attracted to new, more complex, interesting, and "better" ways of doing things. What hunter, who has experienced the dangers and hardship of killing large animals with a spear, would not prefer a gun? And who would not be attracted by the value of growing your own plants as opposed to trekking for miles in search of wild vegetation? Such advances are as inevitable as the young child's acquisition of language or his exploration of the space and objects around him, activities to which they are related, of course. Just as the child pushes his new skills to their limits at each stage of development, so modern man has become an inventive extremist. Competence, like other human capacities, causes trouble when carried to unbalanced levels. It is not our greater knowledge and technology itself that alienates us from nature—indeed, scientific understanding can make one feel an integral part of the larger universe—but our overreliance on it at the expense of other needs, particularly the needs for love, intimate social contact, and integration into human groups. Just as the extremism of each developmental stage of childhood must eventually be tempered toward greater balance or equilibrium, so modern man's competence and technological brilliance is in need of balance.

Childhood and Society

Society's impact on human instincts is mediated through its attitude toward, and treatment of, children and childhood. While a great deal has already been said on this topic, let me elaborate a few points on the contrasting treatment of children at the two extremes of cultural development.

As I have attempted to make clear in earlier chapters, the interactions surrounding the care and treatment of children are influenced by the strongest of instincts. If we examine societies through history, we see that each has its distinctive way of raising chlidren; each has its customs and practices that prepare the child to be a future member of his social group. While the range of permissible practices is wide, there are boundaries which cannot be overstepped without creating serious difficulties. When these boundaries are passed, a foundation of anxiety and dissociation is laid, in contrast to practices within the permissible range which lay down predispositions for an integrated existence.

Child rearing in hunter-gatherer groups produces adults who are, by and large, prepared for easy integration into the adult life of their societies. Many of the practices of rearing children in contemporary society, on the other hand, have moved beyond the range permitted by human instincts and, because of this, predispose modern man to personal dissociation and social alienation. Like so much else, this is a complex issue and I will only touch briefly on some selected differences between child rearing in early and modern cultures.

Perhaps the central thing to note is that child rearing itself in early cultures is a shared, communal enterprise. The individual relationship between mother and child remains, but the mother-child pair live in a more open social setting which provides support and guidance for child care. In America, by contrast, children are the property of their families. The anthropologist Jules Henry, in his provocative book *Culture Against Man,* points out the striking way infant care in contemporary America contrasts with that in almost all previous cultures. As he puts it:

> In our culture babies are a private enterprise—everybody is in the baby business as soon as he gets married. He produces his own babies; they are his, only he has the right to a say-so in their management; they cannot be taken from him without due process of law; he has the sole responsibility for their maintenance and protection. He has the right to expand production of babies indefinitely and curtail it whenever he wishes. As long as he takes care of his young children the outside world has no right to cross his threshold, to say "No" or "Yes" about anything he does with his children.

This contrasts with child care in earlier societies,

> ...where many relatives are around to take an active interest in one's baby, where life is open, or in large households, where many people can see what a mother is doing and where deviations from traditional practice quickly offend the eye and loosen critical, interested tongues, it is impossible for a parent to do as he or she pleases with his children. (1963, pp. 331–32)

Henry's remarks are particularly cogent since they are based on his experience studying families with psychotic children. He shows, as have others, the ways in which the isolation of families permits the psychological destruction of infants. To take a related example, an all too frequent recent phenomenon is the "battered child"—infants and young children who are physically beaten by their parents. Study of such cases often reveals an insecure young mother with little knowledge or experience in the care of children who, trying to raise her baby by herself, becomes frustrated and turns her anger on the child. This would not happen in earlier cultures because, first, both men and women have much more experience caring for infants and children through the years of development and, second, because mothers and their babies are almost never isolated.

Changes in society since its early days have made possible a wider range of techiqnues of infant care. Specialization of labor, the evolution of a class of leaders, and the accumulation of wealth and power have broken down the stable ethics of child care. Emperors and kings had slaves raise their babies. Black families in America were literally torn apart during the years of slavery. And today, middle-class citizens may have much less sensorimotor contact with their infants due to separate rooms, bottles, playpens, nursemaids, and public institutions. I do not mean to suggest that every mother must constantly hold her infant and that every separation is potentially traumatic for the child. Young children are quite adaptable and will develop normally with a range of practices. The major point is that the conditions of modern life often make it difficult for persons to stay within the range; to fulfill adequate parental roles.

In addition to the lack of experience and the isolation of the individual family, mentioned above, other sources of stress are important. Poverty or divorce may force a woman to work; discrimination or ghetto life may prove so stressful and depressing that parents do not have enough time or interest to do a good job; or passing fads and ill-considered "expert advice" may cause a parent to engage in practices that go against his or her own nature. For although components of parent-child relations are instinctually bounded, the specific acts of child care, as well as the general role-identities of mother and father, are acquired within a culture.

In early cultures, contact between adults and children of all ages is open and continuous, while modern societies are characterized by separations, isolation, and the fragmentation of social roles. The effects here are to make the child's identification, not only as a parent, but as a total adult, a much more complex and difficult task. Consider some examples.

A young girl in a hunting and gathering society knows from an early age what older girls and women do. She is constantly with her sisters, cousins, aunts, and mother as they perform their functions of food gathering, child care, and social intercourse. There are no other roles available; she cannot consider, for example, becoming a nurse, a teacher, a scientist, or a movie star; the limitations of opportunity make identification as a woman much easier. She will become—like her grandmother and mother and sisters before her—what all women have become. *Her personal identity, her social role, and her total conception of womanhood are all the same thing.* Similarly for the boy growing up in such a culture. He knows from first-hand experience the things that his father and other men do. As a young boy, he plays at hunting and many persons and social practices prepare him for, and support him in, his growth toward an adult identity. Like his female counterpart, his personal identity as father-hunter-male is so inextricably bound to his social role and total understanding of maleness that they are identical.

The contrast of this continuous, integrated development from child to adult with development in societies such as ours is almost too obvious to mention. It is quite possible for girls to grow to adulthood without even having seen a baby being cared for. Boys may have little direct contact with their fathers and what contact there is—usually outside of working hours —comes at a time when the father is not directly performing his social role. The boy's conception of what his father does "in the office" or "at work" is necessarily much less direct and more fragmented than is that of the young hunter. Added to this lack of direct experience are the problems introduced by the great number of *possible* roles open to the young person.

The examples so far have been simple and almost stereotyped but actual experience shows that the possibilities of maleness and femaleness, of fatherhood and motherhood, in a society such as ours, are extremely complex. This complexity is heightened by the rapid change in career possibilities and values from one generation to the next. It is also compounded by the competitive spirit of American life, for in a competitive society like ours, with its constant push for upward mobility, the young person may feel he is failing if he does not become something *more* than his mother or father; whether this *more* means amassing more money or reaching a higher status, having more education, becoming a "better" parent, or even attaining greater peace of mind.

All these factors make the development of an integrated adult identity very difficult. Identity as child-in-the-family, as girl or boy-in-school, as child-among-peers, or the way one measures up to social and personal ideals, all these can pull in different directions.

The difficulties of achieving an integrated identity in modern society often lead to attempts to dissociate the very existence of infancy and childhood. Insofar as one felt powerless and unable to influence the world as an infant, or felt caught as a child between conflicting roles that could not be easily integrated into what one wishes to be as an adult, the temptation to dissociate the whole set of experiences becomes strong. A society such as ours which values success, power, and other aggressive virtues has an additional stake in the dissociation of infancy and childhood; for these are years when one was more openly frightened and anxious, lacked adult power and competence, craved (more openly and directly) love and support. We see, again, how the exaggeration of one side of a dimension leads to a dissociation of the other, an imbalance in which the attempt is made to banish powerful instinctual tendencies. Erik Erikson, in the concluding chapter of *Childhood and Society,* presents an insightful discussion of this issue:

> ...man continues to identify himself with abstractions of himself, but refuses to see how he became what he really is and how, as an emotional and political being, he undoes with infantile compulsions and impulsions what his thought has invented and what his hands have built. All of this has its psychological basis—namely, the individual's unconscious determination never to meet his childhood anxiety face to face again, and his superstitious apprehension lest a glance at the infantile origins of his thoughts and schemes may destroy his single-minded stamina. He therefore prefers enlightenment away from himself; which is why the best minds have often been least aware of themselves.
>
> But may it not be mainly superstition that makes man turn away from his latent anxiety as if from the head of a Medusa? May it not be that man, at this stage of the game, must and can expand his tolerant awareness to his latent anxieties and to the infantile origins of his preconceptions and apprehensions?
>
> Every adult, whether he is a follower or a leader, a member of a mass or

of an elite, was once a child. He was once small. A sense of smallness forms a substratum in his mind, ineradicably. His triumphs will be measured against this smallness, his defeats will substantiate it. The questions as to who is bigger and who can do or not do this or that, and to whom—these questions fill the adult's inner life far beyond the necessities and the desirabilities which he understands and for which he plans. (1950, p. 404)

IDENTITY AS MORALITY

If the general comparison that I have been sketching between early cultures and our own is a valid one, we can say that the task of identity construction—the path to an integrated adult self within the structures of one's society—was once relatively simple and that it has become progressively more difficult with the evolution of more complex cultures. There has been an accelerating growth in our understanding of the world outside ourselves and a corresponding growth in our skill at the control and use of minerals, plants, animals, and, sad to say, other men. While this great movement of culture has enabled us literally to transform our habitat, it has, step for step, complicated our lives and made the attainment of secure, integrated identities increasingly difficult. It is thus no accident that the greatest social alienation—the extremes of personal fragmentation, anxiety and dissociation—are found in the centers of large cities in the most technologically advanced nations.

Man has lost the oneness he once felt in the world and cannot recapture it. We cannot go back to the simple lives of early societies, anymore than we can become children again. The question remains: is it possible to work toward integrated identities of a new sort, identities based on social values and ways of living compatible with the realities of life in modern technological societies? I have no answer to this question; indeed, it would be presumptuous to attempt one. Rather, I will conclude with some brief remarks on the necessity of pushing self-development to higher levels.

Hunting and gathering man lived an integrated, nonalienated life on what we can call, following the schemes of Kohlberg and Loevinger (chapter 8), relatively low levels of moral and ego development. The oneness he felt with his fellows was within the bounds of a conventional morality. Technical skill was simple and easy to learn, and social values, rituals, taboos, and customs within everyone's range of understanding. As we saw in chapter 3, the hunting and gathering way of life required little long-range planning, as contrasted with the life of even the simplest agriculturalist who must cultivate and plant with an eye to the future. Not needing a future orientation, the hunter had less need for a sense of responsibility or to delay gratification; in short, he had less need for the sort of conscience and morality that arouses feelings of guilt in modern man. The large majority of persons in these societies attained a conventional level of moral development and remained there, a fact confirmed by anthropological description and suggested by research with Kohlberg's measures (Kohlberg and Kramer, 1969).

Conventional levels of development—what Kohlberg calls the good boy orientation and Loevinger the conformist stage of ego development—permitted a relatively easy integration between man and his society. Paradoxically, it is the persistence of these moral-ego levels into the contemporary world that contributes to alienation.

The solidarity and in-group feeling that is characteristic of man is early cultures is faciliated by several features of conventional thinking. There is, first, an unquestioning acceptance of cultural standards and values. The world is as it is; the sort of changes and possibilities for the future that we take for granted are largely outside the experience of hunter-gatherers. Further, although many of the actual social practices of these societies—such as the communal way of life, the ethic of child care and of sharing—can be seen to reflect high levels of morality, they are not arrived at by a process of introspection. Members of these cultures would have difficulty articulating them; they are, in a sense, almost reflexive or, more accurately, accepted in the same way the concrete operational child accepts his social world. The analogy does not hold in all respects, yet persons in early societies are like children who have still to go through the questioning, introspective throes of adolescence.

A final feature which exemplifies the conformist level of development is the ease with which hatreds, fears, anxiety, and other troublesome emotions and conflicts are projected into foreigners, gods, spirits, witches, and devils. This is, again, similar to the in-group morality of late childhood in which a comfortable integration into the local group is accompanied by prejudice toward outsiders, on the one hand, and intolerance and ostracism of group members who deviate from conventionally defined ways of life, on the other. We saw in chapter 3 how this projection serves a useful function, particularly in the channeling and control of aggression. The close living arrangements of early societies no doubt stimulated the anger and aggression so characteristic of the human species. The ability to control this aggression in satisfactory ways was a major factor in the long-term stability of these societies. Central to this control was the projection of anger and malevolent intentions onto external sources and the direction of aggression toward these sources. Projection of anger and aggression outward has been, and continues to be, a widespread, strongly approved means of controlling this destructive instinctual system. By directing anger and aggression outward, man preserves peace and harmony within his own group. But, it is important to note, the price of such harmony is ethnocentrism, prejudice toward outsiders and intolerance of human differences.

The ease with which anger and conflict could be handled by externalization and projection gave little impetus to attempts to understand the inner sources of anger, anxiety, and conflict. Reports of hunter-gatherer groups convey a picture of naive innocence. Again, there is a similarity to late childhood with its unquestioning, nonintrospective acceptance of conformist morality. What worked in these early cultures works no longer. If introspection, self-scrutiny, and self-understanding were unnecessary for the naive harmonious life in early social groups, they become increasingly necessary now. What was a relatively harmless projection of aggression and conflict outward has taken on increasingly destructive proportions due to the growth of technology. The hunter-gatherer whose hatred was directed at foreigners had few ways of affecting those foreigners. With each step of technological progress, mobility and the power of weapons grew and, increasingly, destructive fantasies have been carried out on real people. To put this another way, the tremendous growth in scientific understanding which has given us the capacity to wield power—to control and manipulate nature—has not been accompanied by a corresponding growth in morality or self-understanding. Man, with his burgeoning technology, has most often behaved like a child who suddenly finds himself in possession of a real gun or bomb with which to play out his fantasies and games. The history of civilization since its early stages has been a history of the unthinking exploitation of nature, of wars on neighboring groups, of the widespread practice of slavery, and of intolerance and discrimination. Even today, the most technologically advanced nations wage wars which are explained in the same old ways: we see our own worst qualities in "the enemy" who we then set out to control and destroy. The old externalizations serve, as they have for thousands of years, as rationalizations for discrimination and violence perpetuated on others. Man as warrior or slaveholder fails to take the perspective of his victim or slave, just as children typically do not take the perspective of those outside their group who they reject or ridicule.

The limitations and dangers of a conformist level of development are thus apparent. While such a moral outlook may have enhanced the security of man in early society, its continuation today produces victims, on the one hand, and conquerors who must dissociate themselves from the consequences of their aggression, least they feel an intolerable guilt, on the other.

There are some hopeful signs that conformist morality is being questioned; that the old stable ways of viewing self and the world are changing. If there is any validity to the analogy between cultural evolution and self-development, what is needed now is an increase in insight, a better understanding of the emotions and conflicts that have been dealt with up to now by externalization. The grounds for new, integrated identities will be prepared by a more comprehensive view of ourselves; a view that contains a first-hand apprecation of human instincts, emotions, and conflicts. Man's cultural development began with an external orientation and the focus of our energies has largely been on objects and events outside ourselves. This has led to the growth of science and technology and the conquest, and all too often the destruction, of nature and of other ways of life. All this was accomplished within a limited moral perspective; a perspective that did not require inward understanding nor the extension of love and empathy beyond a narrow group.

If the anxiety, dissociation, and alienation that characterize so much of modern life are to be overcome, we must push the possibilities for self- and moral development to higher levels. By turning inward and recognizing the childish fears and rages, the conflicts and identifications, the tabooed impulses, that we all harbor, the cycle of projection-destruction may hopefully be ended. This is no easy task, for in focusing on inner conflict one must experience the pain and anxiety that originally caused us to flee from it. The world has reached a point, however, where it is no longer safe to *not* face what is within us.

An integrated identity is one based on equilibrium and unification; one which has a place for the outer person of accomplishment and power and the inner person of fantasy and feeling; for the private individual and the social person. Since the boundaries of the human group are now world-wide, integration cannot be accomplished by social values which define persons too exclusively in terms of local custom, ritual, or appearance. Perhaps an introspective awareness of our common human heritage can become the basis for an identification with all mankind.

Postscript

...and so there ain't nothing more to write about, and I am rotten glad of it, because if I'd a knowed what a trouble it was to make a book I wouldn't a tackled it, and ain't a-going to no more.

HUCK FINN

References*

AINSWORTH, M. D. S. *Infancy in Uganda: Infant care and the growth of love.* Baltimore: Johns Hopkins Press, 1967.

AINSWORTH, M. D. S. and S. M. BELL. Attachment, exploration and separation: A discussion illustrated by the behavior of one year olds in a strange situation. Paper presented at Meetings of American Psychological Association, San Francisco, 1968.

ALTMANN, S. A. (ed.). *Social communication among primates.* Chicago: University of Chicago Press, 1967.

ANSBACHER, H. L. and R. R. ANSBACHER. *The individual psychology of Alfred Adler.* New York: Basic Books, 1956.

ARIES, P. *Centuries of childhood: A social history of family life.* New York: Knopf, 1962.

AUSUBEL, D. P. Negativism as a phase of ego development. *The American Journal of Orthopsychiatry,* 1950, *20,* 796–805.

AVERILL, J. GRIEF: Its nature and significance. *Psychological Bulletin,* 1968, *70,* 721–28.

BANDURA, A. and R. H. WALTERS. *Social learning and personality development.* New York: Holt, Rinehart & Winston, 1963.

* In cases where there are two dates for a reference, that of the original publication is given after the title, in parentheses.

BATESON, G., D. D. JACKSON, J. HALEY, and J. WEAKLAND. Toward a theory of schizophrenia. *Behavioral Science,* 1956, *1,* 251.

BETTELHEIM, B. Individual and mass behavior in extreme situations. *Journal of Abnormal and Social Psychology,* 1943 *38,* 417–52.

BIEBER, I. Clinical aspects of male homosexuality. In J. Marmor (ed.), *Sexual inversion.* New York: Basic Books, 1965, 248–67.

BIRCH, H. G. The relation of previous experience to insightful problem-solving. *Journal of Comparative and Physiological Psychology,* 1945, *38,* 367–83.

BOWLBY, J. Separation anxiety. *International Journal of Psychoanalysis,* 1960, *41,* 89–113.

————. Processes of mourning. *International Journal of Psychoanalysis,* 1961, *42,* 317–34.

————. *Attachment and Loss, Vol. I. Attachment.* New York: Basic Books, 1969.

BREGER, L. Function of dreams. *Journal of Abnormal Psychology Monograph,* 1967, *72,* 1–28.

————. Motivation, energy, and cognitive structure in psychoanalytic theory. In J. Marmor (ed.) *Modern psychoanalysis: New directions and perspectives.* New York: Basic Books, 1968, pp. 44–65.

———— (ed.). *Clinical-cognitive psychology: Models and integrations.* Englewood Cliffs, N.J.: Prentice-Hall, 1969a.

————. Children's dreams and personality development. In J. Fisher and L. Breger (eds.), The meaning of dreams: Recent insights from the laboratory. *California Mental Health Research Symposium,* 1969b, No. 3, 64–100.

————, I. HUNTER, and R. W. LANE. The effect of stress on dreams. *Psychological Issues,* Vol. VII, No. 3, Monograph 27, 1971.

BRONOWSKI, J. and U. BELLUGI. Language, name and concept. *Science,* 1970, *167,* 669–73.

BROWN, C. *Manchild in the promised land.* New York: Macmillan, 1965.

CARPENTER, C. R. The howlers of Barro Colorado Island. In I. De Vore (ed.), *Primate behavior: Field studies of monkeys and apes.* New York: Holt, Rinehart & Winston, 1965, pp. 250–91.

CHODOFF, P. A critique of Freud's theory of infantile sexuality. *International Journal of Psychiatry,* 1967, *4,* 35–64.

CHOMSKY, N. *Aspects of the theory of syntax.* Cambridge, Mass.: M.I.T. Press, 1965.

————. *Language and mind.* New York: Harcourt Brace Jovanovich, 1972.

COLES, R. *Children of crisis.* New York: Little, Brown, 1964.

COWAN, P. *Piaget and Knowledge.* Berkeley, Calif. (in preparation).

DARWIN, C. *Origin of species* (1859). New York: Crowell Collier and Macmillan, 1961.

————. *The descent of man* (1871). London: Watts and Co., 1946.

————. *The expression of the emotions in man and animals* (1872). Chicago: Phoenix Books, 1965.

DEVORE, I. (ed.), *Primate behavior: Field studies of monkeys and apes.* New York: Holt, Rinehart & Winston, 1965.

DIMOCK, H. S. Research in adolescence. I. Pubescence and physical growth. *Child development,* 1953, *6.*

DOLLARD, J. and N. E. MILLER. *Personality and psychotherapy.* New York: McGraw-Hill, 1950.

DOUVAN, E. and J. ADELSON. *The adolescent experience.* New York: John Wiley, 1966.

DURBIN, E. F. M. and J. BOWLBY. Personal aggressiveness and war. In E. F. M. Durbin and G. Catlin (eds.), *War and democracy: Essays on the causes and prevention of war.* London: Kegan Paul, 1938.

ELKIND, D. *Children and adolescents: Interpretive essays on Jean Piaget.* New York: Oxford University Press, 1970.

ELLEFSON, J. O. Territorial behavior in the common white-handed gibbon, *Hylobates lar Linn.* In P. Jay (ed.), *Primates: Studies in adaptation and variability.* New York: Holt, Rinehart & Winston, 1968, pp. 180–99.

ENGEL, G. L. Is grief disease? *Psychosomatic Medicine,* 1961, *23,* 18–22.

ERIKSON, E. H. *Childhood and society.* New York: Norton, 1950.

———. Identity and the life cycle. *Psychological Issues,* 1959, *1,* No. 1, (Monograph No. 1).

———. *Identity, youth and crisis.* New York: Norton, 1968.

FANTZ, R. L. Pattern vision in young infants. *The Psychological Record,* 1958, pp. 43–47. Reprinted in Y. Brackbill and G. G. Thompson (eds.), *Behavior in infancy and early childhood.* New York: Free Press, 1967, pp. 189–94.

FENICHEL, O. *The psychoanalytic theory of neurosis.* New York: Norton, 1945.

FINGARETTE, H. *The self in transformation.* New York: Harper & Row, 1963.

FLAVELL, J. H. *The developmental psychology of Jean Piaget.* New York: Van Nostrand Reinhold, 1963.

FLETCHER, R. *Instinct in man.* New York: International Universities Press, 1957.

FOULKES, D. *The psychology of sleep.* New York: Scribner's, 1966.

———. Dreams of the male child: Four case studies. *Journal of Child Psychology and Psychiatry,* 1967, *8,* 81–97.

———, T. PIVIK, H. S. STEADMAN, P. S. SPEAR, and J. D. SYMONDS. Dreams of the male child: An EEG study. *Journal of Abnormal Psychology,* 1967, *72,* 457–67.

———, E. M. SWANSON, and J. D. LARSON. Dreams of the preschool child: An EEG study. Paper read at meetings of the Association for the Psychophysiological Study of Sleep, Denver, 1968.

FREEMAN, D. Human aggression in anthropological perspective. In J. D. Carthy and F. J. Ebling (eds.), *The natural history of aggression.* New York: Academic, 1964, 109–19.

FREUD, A. *The ego and the mechanisms of defense* (1936). New York: International Universities Press, 1946.

———. Adolescence. In *The psychoanalytic study of the child, Vol.* 13, pp. 255–78. New York: International Universities Press, 1958.

FREUD, S. *The origin and development of psychoanalysis* (1910). Henry Regnery Gateway Editions, 1965.

———. Beyond the pleasure principle (1920). In J. Strachey (ed.), *Standard edition of the complete psychological works of Sigmund Freud.* London: Hogarth Press, 18, 1955, 1–64.

———. Inhibitions, symptoms and anxiety (1926). In J. Strachey (ed.), *Standard edition of the complete psychological works of Sigmund Freud*. London: Hogarth Press, 20, 1959, 87–174.

―――. Dostoevsky and parricide (1928). In J. Strachey (ed.), *Standard edition of the complete psychological works of Sigmund Freud*. London: Hogarth Press, 21, 1961, 177–94.

―――. Civilization and its discontents (1930). In J. Strachey (ed.), *Standard edition of the complete psychological works of Sigmund Freud*. London: Hogarth Press, 21, 1961, 64–145.

―――. Introductory lectures on psychoanalysis (1916–1917). In J. Strachey (ed.), *Standard edition of the complete psychological works of Sigmund Freud*. London: Hogarth Press, vols. 15 and 16; 1963.

FROMM, E. *Man for himself: An inquiry into the psychology of ethics*. New York: Holt, Rinehart & Winston, 1947.

FROMM-REICHMAN, F. Psychoanalytic and general dynamic conceptions of theory and of therapy. *Journal of the American Psychoanalytic Association*, 1954, *2*, 718.

GARDNER, A. R. and B. T. GARDNER. Teaching sign language to a chimpanzee. *Science*, 1969, *165*, 664–72.

GESELL, A. and F. L. ILG. *Infant and child in the culture of today*. New York: Harper & Row, 1943.

GESELL, A. and H. THOMPSON. *The psychology of early growth*. New York: Macmillan, 1938.

GOFFMAN, E. *Behavior in public places*. New York: Free Press, 1963.

GREENBERG, R. *Dreaming and memory*. In E. HARTMAN (ed.), *International psychiatry clinics*. Vol. 7 (2) Sleeping and dreaming. Boston: Little, Brown, 1970.

―――, C. PEARLMAN, F. FINGAR, J. KARTROWITZ, and S. KAWLICH. The effects of dream deprivation: Implications for a theory of the psychological function of dreaming. *British Journal of Medical Psychology*, 1970, *43*, 1–11.

GRIFFITHS, R. *A study of imagination in early childhood* (1935). London: Kegan Paul, 1945.

HALL, K. R. L. Aggression in monkey and ape societies. In P. Jay (ed.), *Primates: Studies in adaptation and variability*. New York: Holt, Rinehart & Winston, 1968, pp. 149–61.

――― and I. DeVore Baboon social behavior. In I. DeVore (ed.), *Primate behavior: Field studies of monkeys and apes*. New York: Holt, Rinehart & Winston, 1965, pp. 53–110.

HAMBURG, D. A. Emotions in the perspective of human evolution. In P. H. Knapp (ed.), *Expression of the emotions in man*. New York: International Universities Press, 1963, pp. 300–317.

―――. Evolution of emotional responses: Evidence from recent research on non-human primates. In J. MASSERMAN (ed.), *Science and psychoanalysis, vol. 12*. New York: Grune & Stratton, 1971, pp. 39–51.

HARLOW, H. F. The nature of love. *American Psychologist*, 1958, 13, 673–85.

―――. *Learning to love*. San Francisco: Albion Press, 1971.

HARTSOEKER, N. *Essay de dioptrique*. Paris: 1694 (From Needham, 1959.)

HAYES, C. *The ape in our house*. New York: Harper & Row, 1951.

HEBB, D. O. and W. R. THOMPSON. The social significance of animal studies. In G. Lindzey (ed.), *Handbook of social psychology,* Vol. I. Reading, Mass.: Addison-Wesley, 1954.

HENRY, J. *Culture against man.* New York: Random House, 1963.

——. *Pathways to madness.* New York: Random House, 1971.

HESS, E. Ethology: An approach toward the complete analysis of behavior. In *New directions in psychology.* New York: Holt, Rinehart & Winston, 1962, pp. 157–266.

HOLT, R. R. A review of some of Freud's biological assumptions and their influence on his theories. In N. S. GREENFIELD and W. C. LEWIS (eds.), *Psychoanalysis and current biological thought.* Madison: University of Wisconsin Press, 1965, pp. 93–124.

—— (ed.). Motives and thought, psychoanalytic essays in memory of David Rapaport. *Psychological Issues,* 1967, *5,* No. 2–3, (Monograph No. 18–19).

INHELDER, B. and J. PIAGET. *The growth of logical thinking from childhood to adolescence.* New York: Basic Books, 1958.

JANIS, I. L., G. F. MAHL, J. KAGAN, and R. R. HOLT. *Personality: Dynamics development and assessment.* New York: Harcourt Brace Jovanovich, 1969.

JAY, P. (ed.), *Primates: Studies in adaptation and variability.* New York: Holt, Rinehart & Winston, 1968.

JONES, M. C. The later careers of boys who were early- or late-maturing. *Child development,* 1957, *28,* 113–28.

——. Psychological correlates of somatic developments. *Child development,* 1965, *36,* 899–911.

JONES, R. M. *The new psychology of dreaming.* New York: Grune & Stratton, 1970.

KATZ, J. Four years of growth, conflict and compliance. In J. Katz and associates, *No time for youth.* San Francisco: Jossey-Bass, 1968, pp. 3–73.

KAUFMANN, I. C. and L. A. ROSENBLUM. Depression in infant monkeys separated from their mothers. *Science,* 1967, *155,* 1030–31.

KENISTON, K. Moral development, youthful activism and modern society. *Youth and society,* 1969, pp. 110–27.

KESSEN, W. and G. MANDLER. Anxiety, pain and the inhibition of distress. *Psychological Review,* 1961, *68,* 396–404.

KLEIN, G. S. On hearing one's own voice: An aspect of cognitive control in spoken thought. In N. S. Greenfield and W. C. Lewis (eds.), *Psychoanalysis and current biological thought.* Madison: University of Wisconsin Press, 1965, pp. 245–74.

——. Freud's two theories of sexuality. In L. Breger (ed.), *Clinical-cognitive psychology.* Englewood Cliffs, N.J.: Prentice-Hall, 1969, pp. 136–81.

——. *Psychoanalytic theory: An exploration of essentials.* (In press.)

KOHLBERG, L. Moral development and identification. In H. STEVENSON (ed.), Child psychology. *62nd yearbook of the National Society for the Study of Education.* Chicago: University of Chicago Press, 1963, pp. 277–332.

——. Stage and sequence: The cognitive-development approach to socialization. In D. A. Goslin (ed.), *Handbook of socialization theory and research.* Skokie, Ill.: Rand McNally, 1969, 347–480.

—— and R. Kramer. Continuities and discontinuities in childhood and adult moral development. *Human Development,* 1969, *12,* 93–120.

Köhler, W. *The mentality of apes.* New York: Harcourt Brace Jovanovich, 1925.

La Crosse, R. E., F. Litman, D. M. Ogilvie, and B. L. White. The preschool project: Experience and the development of human competence in the first six years of life. *Monograph No. 9,* Harvard University Publications Office.

Laing, R. D. *The divided self.* Baltimore: Penguin, 1960.

—— and A. Esterson. *Sanity, madness and the family.* New York: Basic Books, 1964.

Lancaster, J. B. Primate communication systems and the emergence of human language. In P. Jay (ed.), *Primates: Studies in adaptation and variability.* New York: Holt, Rinehart & Winston, 1968, pp. 439–57.

Lawick-Goodall, J. van. Chimpanzees of the Gombe Stream Reserve. In I. DeVore (ed.), *Primate Behavior: Field studies of monkeys and apes.* New York: Holt, Rinehart & Winston, 1965, pp. 425–73.

——. Mother-offspring relationships in free-ranging chimpanzees. In D. Morris (ed.), *Primate ethology.* Chicago: Aldine-Atherton, 1967, pp. 287–346.

——. The behavior of free-living chimpanzees in the Gombe Stream Reserve. *Animal Behavior Monographs,* 1968a, 1 (3), 165–311.

——. A preliminary report on expressive movements and communication in the Gombe Stream chimpanzees. In P. Jay (ed.), *Primates: Studies in adaptation and variability.* New York: Holt, Rinehart & Winston, 1968b, pp. 313–74.

——. *In the shadow of man.* Boston: Houghton Mifflin, 1971.

Lee, R. B. What hunters do for a living, or, how to make out on scarce resources. In R. B. Lee and I. DeVore (eds.), *Man the hunter.* Chicago: Aldine-Atherton, 1968, pp. 30–48.

—— and I. DeVore (eds.), *Man the hunter.* Chicago: Aldine-Atherton, 1968a.

——. Problems in the study of hunters and gatherers In R. B. Lee and I. DeVore (eds.), *Man the hunter.* Chicago: Aldine-Atherton, 1968b, 3–12.

Lenneberg, E. H. (ed.). *New directions in the study of language.* Cambridge, Mass.: M. I. T. Press, 1964.

——. *The biological foundations of language.* New York: John Wiley, 1966a.

——. The natural history of language. In F. Smith and G. A. Miller (eds.), *The genesis of language: A psycholinguistic approach.* Cambridge, Mass.: M.I.T. Press, 1966b, pp. 219–52.

Levi-Strauss, C. *The savage mind* (1962). Chicago: University of Chicago Press, 1966.

Lewis, O. *Five families: Mexican case studies in the culture of poverty.* New York: Basic Books, 1959.

——. *The children of Sanchez.* New York: Random House, 1961.

Lidz, T., A. Cornelison, D. Terry, and S. Fleck. Intrafamilial environment of the schizophrenic patient. VI. The transmission of irrationality. *AMA Archives of Neurology and Psychiatry,* 1958, *79,* 305–16.

Lindemann, E. Symptomatology and management of acute grief. *American Journal of Psychiatry,* 1944, *101,* 141–48.

Lindzey, G. Some remarks concerning incest, the incest taboo, and psychoanalytic theory. *American Psychologist,* 1967, *22,* 1051–59.

LOEVINGER, J. Patterns of parenthood as theories of learning. *Journal of Abnormal and Social Psychology*, 1959, *59*, 148–50.

———. The meaning and measurement of ego development. *American Psychologist*, 1966a, *21*, 195–206.

———. Three principles for a psychoanalytic psychology. *Journal of Abnormal Psychology*, 1966b, *71*, 432–43.

———. Theories of ego development. In L. Breger (ed.), *Clinical-cognitive psychology*. Englewood Cliffs, N.J.: Prentice-Hall, 1969, pp. 83–135.

——— and R. WESSLER. *Measuring ego development*. San Francisco: Jossey-Bass, 1970.

LOIZOS, C. Play behavior in higher primates: A review. In D. Morris (ed.), *Primate ethology*. Chicago: Aldine-Atherton, 1967, 176–218.

LORENZ, K. *On aggression*. New York: Harcourt Brace Jovanovich, 1966.

MALCOLM X. *The autobiography of Malcolm X* (as told to A. Haley). New York: Grove Press, 1964.

MARSHALL, J. *The hunters* (16mm film). Cambridge, Mass.: Film Study Center of the Peabody Museum, Harvard University, 1956.

MAY, R. *The meaning of anxiety*. Ronald Press, 1950.

McCORD, W. and J. McCORD. *Psychopathy and delinquency*. New York: Grune & Stratton, 1956.

MEAD, G. H. *Mind, self and society: From the standpoint of a social behaviorist*, ed. C. W. Morris. Chicago: University of Chicago Press, 1934.

MORRIS, D. The response of animals to a restricted environment. *Symposium of the Zoological Society of London*, 1964, *13*, 99–118.

———. (ed.), *Primate ethology*. Chicago: Aldine-Atherton, 1967.

NEEDHAM, J. *A history of embryology*. New York: Abelard-Schuman, 1959.

PIAGET, J. *The moral judgment of the child* (1932). New York: Free Press, 1948.

———. *Play, dreams and imitation in childhood*. (1951) New York: Norton, 1962.

——— and B. INHELDER. *The Psychology of the Child*. New York: Basic Books, 1969.

PROVENCE, S. and R. LIPTON. *Infants in institutions*. New York: International Universities Press, 1962.

RABIN, A. I. Behavior research in collective settlements in Israel: Infants and children under conditions of "intermittent" mothering in the Kibbutz. *American Journal of Orthopsychiatry*, 1958, *28*, 577–86.

RABKIN, L. and K. RABKIN. Kibbutz children. *Psychology Today*, 1969.

RADCLIFFE-BROWN, A. R. Social organization of Australian tribes. *Oceania Monographs*, 1., 1931.

REDL, F. and D. WINEMAN, *The aggressive child*. Glencoe, Ill.: Free Press, 1957.

REYNOLDS, V. *Budongo: A forest and its chimpanzees*. London: Methuen, 1965.

RHEINGOLD, H. L. Controlling the infant's exploratory behavior. In B. M. Foss (ed.), *Determinants of infant behavior*, Vol. 2. New York: John Wiley, 1963.

———. The social and socializing infant. In D. A. Goslin and D. C. Glass (eds.), *Handbook of Socialization Theory and Research*. Skokie, Ill.: Rand McNally, 1969.

RICHARDSON, L. F. *Statistics of deadly quarrels*. London: Stevens and Sons, 1960.

ROBSON, K. S. The role of eye-to-eye contact in maternal-infant attachment. *Journal of Child Psychology and Psychiatry and Allied Disciplines,* 1967, *8,* 13–25.

ROFFWARG, H. P., J. N. MUZIO, and W. C. DEMENT. Ontogenetic development of the human sleep-dream cycle. *Science,* 1966, *152,* 604–19

ROGLER, L. H. and A. B. HOLLINGSHEAD. *Trapped: Families and schizophrenia.* New York: John Wiley, 1965.

ROSENBERG, B. G. and B. SUTTON-SMITH. *Sex and identity.* New York: Holt, Rinehart & Winston, 1972.

ROTH, P. *Portnoy's complaint.* New York: Random House, 1969.

SACKETT, G. P. Unlearned responses, differential rearing experiences, and the development of social attachments by rhesus monkeys. In *Primate behavior: Developments in field and laboratory research,* Vol. 1. New York: Academic, 1970, pp. 111–40.

SADE, D. S. Inhibition of son-mother mating among free-ranging rhesus monkeys. *Science and psychoanalysis,* J. Masserman (ed.), 1967, *12,* 18–38.

SAHLINS, M. D. Notes on the original affluent society. In R. B. LEE and I. DEVORE (eds.), *Man the hunter.* Chicago: Aldine-Atherton, 1968, 85–89.

SALINGER, J. D. *The catcher in the rye.* Boston: Little, Brown, 1951.

SARTRE, J. P. *Nausea.* Norfolk, Conn.: New Directions, 1938.

———. *The words.* New York: George Braziller, 1964.

SCHACHTER, S. *Emotion, obesity and crime.* New York: Academic, 1971.

SCHAFFER, H. R. The onset of fear of strangers and the incongruity hypothesis. *Journal of Child Psychology and Psychiatry,* 1966, *7,* 95–106.

——— and P. E. EMERSON. The development of social attachments in infancy. *Monographs in Social Research in Child Development,* 1964a, *29,* No. 3.

———. Patterns of response to physical contact in early human development. *Journal of Child Psychology and Psychiatry,* 1964b, *5,* 1–13.

SCHALLER, G. B. *The mountain gorilla: Ecology and behavior.* Chicago: University of Chicago Press, 1963.

———. The behavior of the mountain gorilla. In I. DeVore (ed.), *Primate behavior: Field studies of monkeys and apes.* New York: Holt, Rinehart & Winston, 1965, pp. 324–67.

SERVICE, E. R. *Primitive social organization: An evolutionary perspective.* New York: Random House, 1962.

———. *The hunters.* Englewood Cliffs, N.J.: Prentice-Hall, 1966.

SLATER, P. *The pursuit of loneliness: American culture at the breaking point.* Boston: Beacon Press, 1970.

SLOBIN, D. I. *Psycholinguistics.* Glenview, Ill.: Scott Foresman, 1971.

SPITZ, R. A. Anxiety in infancy: A study of its manifestation in the first year of life. *International Journal of Psychoanalysis,* 1950, *31,* 138–43.

SULLIVAN, H. S. *The interpersonal theory of psychiatry.* New York: Norton, 1953.

SZASZ, T. *The myth of mental illness.* New York: Hoeber-Harper, 1961.

TOKUDA, K. A study on the sexual behavior in the Japanese monkey troop. *Primates,* 1961–62, *3,* 1–40.

TURIEL, E. Developmental processes in the child's moral thinking. In P. MUSSEN, J. Langer, and M. Covington (eds.), *New directions in developmental Psychology.* New York: Holt, Rinehart & Winston, 1969.

TURNBULL, C. M. *The forest people.* New York: Doubleday, 1961.

———. The importance of flux in two hunting societies. In R. B. LEE and I. DE-VORE (eds.), *Man the hunter.* Chicago: Aldine-Atherton, 1968, pp. 132–37.

TWAIN, M. (CLEMENS, S. L.). *Huckleberry Finn.* New York: Harper & Row, 1884.

VONNEGUT, K., JR. *Mother night.* New York: Harper & Row, 1961.

WASHBURN, S. L. Speculations on the inter-relations of the history of tools and biological evolution. In J. N. Spuhler (ed.), *The evolution of man's capacity for culture.* Detroit: Wayne State University Press, 1959.

——— and I. DEVORE. Social behavior of baboons and early man. In S. L. Washburn (ed.), *Social life of early man.* Chicago: Aldine-Atherton, 1961, pp. 91–105.

WASHBURN, S. L. and D. A. HAMBURG. The implications of primate research. In I. DeVore (ed.), *Primate behavior: Field studies of monkeys and apes.* New York: Holt, Rinehart & Winston, 1965, pp. 607–22.

———. Aggressive behavior in old world monkeys and apes. In P. Jay (ed.), *Primates: Studies in adaptation and variability.* New York: Holt, Rinehart & Winston, 1968, pp. 458–78.

WEIR, R. H. *Language in the crib.* The Hague: Mouton, 1962.

WHEELIS, A. How people change. *Commentary,* May 1969, 56–66.

WHITE, R. W. Competence and the psychosexual stages of development. In M. R. Jones (ed.), *Nebraska symposium on motivation,* 1960. Lincoln: University of Nebraska Press.

———. Ego and reality in psychoanalytic theory, *Psychological Issues,* 1963, *3,* No. 3 (Monograph No. 11).

———. *Lives in progress,* 2nd ed. New York: Holt, Rinehart & Winston, 1966.

WOLFENSTEIN, M. Trends in infant care. *American Journal of Orthopsychiatry,* 1953, *23,* 120–30.

WOLFF, P. H. Observations on the early development of smiling. In B. M. Foss (ed.), *Determinants of infant behavior,* vol. 2. New York: John Wiley, 1963.

———. The causes, controls and organization of behavior in the neonate. *Psychological Issues,* 1966, *5,* No. 1 (Monograph No. 17).

WYNNE, L. C., J. M. RYCKOFF, J. DAY, and S. S. HIRSCH. Pseudo-mutuality in the family relations of schizophrenics. *Psychiatry,* 1958, *21,* 205–20.

ZABLOCKI, B. *The joyful community.* Baltimore: Penguin, 1971.

ZUCKERMAN, S. *The social life of monkeys and apes.* London: Routledge and Kegan Paul, 1932.

Index